PETERSON'S
#1 IN COLLEGE PREP

ACT
SUCCESS

MATHEMATICS, MARK WEINFELD • ENGLISH, ELAINE BENDER
READING, ALISON CRAIG • SCIENCE REASONING, BERYL J. PACKER

Peterson's

Princeton, New Jersey

Visit Peterson's Education Center on the Internet (World Wide Web) at
www.petersons.com

Library of Congress Cataloging-in-Publication Data

ACT success / Mark Weinfeld . . . [et al.].
    p.   cm.
  ISBN 0-7689-0013-1 (book and CD).
   1. ACT Assessment—Study guides. I. Weinfeld, Mark.
LB2353.48.A295 1996
378.1'662—dc20   96-24931
                                            CIP

Printed in the United States of America

10 9 8 7 6 5 4 3 2

C O N T E N T S

ACT Study Plan 1

Red Alert: Introduction to the ACT 5

Pretest 11
> Part 1: English Test / Part 2: Mathematics Test / Part 3: Reading Test / Part 4: Science Reasoning Test / Explanatory Answers to the Pretest

Red Alert: Strategies for Taking the English Test 77

Unit 1: English Grammar Review 85

Red Alert: Strategies for Taking the Mathematics Test 111

Unit 2: Mathematics Review 121
> Arithmetic / Coordinate Geometry / Trigonometry

Red Alert: Strategies for Taking the Reading Comprehension Test 189

Unit 3: Reading Review 201

Red Alert: Strategies for Taking the Science Reasoning Test 211

Unit 4: Science Review 221

Practice Test 1 262
> English Test / Mathematics Test / Reading Test / Science Reasoning Test

Quick-Score Answers to Pracatice Test 1 304

Explanatory Answers to Practice Test 1 305
> Part 1: English / Part 2: Mathematics / Part 3: Reading / Part 4: Science

Practice Test 2 324
> English Test / Mathematics Test / Reading Test / Science Reasoning Test

Quick-Score Answers to Practice Test 2 367

Explanatory Answers to Practice Test 2 368
> Part 1: English / Part 2: Mathematics / Part 3: Reading / Part 4: Science

ACKNOWLEDGMENTS

The authors wish to thank the following contributing editors and reviewers for their assistance: Paul Boyer, Ph.D., Fairleigh Dickenson University; Christopher Cramer, Ph.D., University of Minnesota; Gloria Dyer, Ph.D., Fairleigh Dickenson University; Richard A. Hart, Ph.D., Northwest Missouri State University; Tony Julianelle, Ph.D., University of Vermont; Sandra LaPeter, Ph.D.

ACT Study Plan

You can prepare for the ACT in several ways. We offer you three basic study plans to help maximize your time and studying. The first is the **8-Week Plan**, which involves concentrated studying and a focus on the sample-test results. The second is the **16-Week Plan**, or **Semester Plan**, favored by schools; and finally, the **Panic Plan**, for those of you who only have a few weeks to prepare. Obviously, the more time you have to prepare, the easier it will be to review all of the material and find yourself somewhat more relaxed when taking the actual exam.

These plans are not set in stone—feel free to modify them to suit your needs and your own study habits. But start immediately. The more you study, the better will be your results.

THE 8-WEEK PLAN—2 LESSONS PER WEEK

Week 1

Lesson 1: Diagnostic Test. Take parts one and two (English Usage and Mathematics) of the diagnostic ACT Pretest, pages 11–33, and check the answers carefully.

Lesson 2: Diagnostic Test. First: Take parts three and four (Reading Comprehension and Science) of the diagnostic ACT Pretest, pages 35–53, and check the answers carefully.

Second: Amend this entire plan to take into account your strengths and weaknesses. It makes sense to focus upon those areas that need more work, and you will be able to determine this from the diagnostic test.

Week 2

Lesson 1: English Grammar. Begin with the chapter "Strategies for Taking the English Test." Read through it carefully, and answer the questions at the end of the chapter. Again, check your answers carefully, and if you don't understand something, go back and reread the answers.

Lesson 2: Math. Read the Red Alert *"Strategies for Taking the Mathematics Test"* and Unit 3 *Mathematics Review* pp. 111–187. If you encountered any specific difficult areas, find those topics in the balance of this chapter.

Week 3

Lesson 1: More Math. Go back to the diagnostic pretest and check your mathematics answers. You should now have a better understanding of this material. Now review pages 121–144, *Arithmetic* through *Algebra*. This is basic mathematics, and represents almost 25 percent of the mathematics test.

Lesson 2: Reading. Review the Red Alert entitled, *Strategies for Taking the Reading Comprehension Test*, pages 189–200. This section will give you a good overview of how to approach these types of questions.

Week 4

Lesson 1: More Math. It's important to keep on top of this, for most people the most difficult subject. Review pages 144–160, from *Algebra* through *Coordinate Geometry*, and answer the practice questions throughout.

Lesson 2: Science. Now review the Red Alert on *Science Reasoning: Strategies*. We've saved this for last, because in some ways, these questions also require reading comprehension skills, which you have already been reviewing in Week 3. Answer one-half of the review questions, and check your answers carefully.

Week 5

Lesson 1: Science. Complete the balance of *Science Reasoning* questions and check your answers. If you've had difficulty with any of the three types of questions (Data Interpretation, Research Summaries, or Conflicting Viewpoints), reread the strategies again until you feel comfortable with these types of questions.

Lesson 2: More Math. *Coordinate Geometry* and *Plane Geometry* represent almost 40 percent of the mathematics portion of the test. Take the time now to review these sections, pages 161–178, and answer the practice questions.

Week 6

Lesson 1: First—Math—The End. Finish your mathematics review of *Trigonometry*, pages 184–187. It's a very short section, so you may want to go back to the geometry sections and review them again.

Second: Review the *English Grammar* section. There are questions and answers throughout to give you examples of the types of questions you will encounter on the test. Answer them, review the samples, and make sure you're comfortable with the basics of grammar.

Lesson 2: Science Review. Although you won't be required to have a knowledge of science in order to answer the questions in the Science Reasoning portion of the ACT, the *Science Review* (pp. 221–246) is designed to provide you with a passing familiarity with basic scientific concepts. Thus, when you take the test, the words, phrases, and scientific ideas won't seem like a foreign language to you, and may help you understand what you are reading, a little better than if you had no concept at all of these terms. Skim this section, jot down unfamiliar terms, reread where necessary.

Week 7

Lesson 1: Practice Test #1. Take the entire test in a quiet room, and time yourself.

Lesson 2: Practice Test #1. Check your answers, and review any questions that gave you trouble.

Week 8

Lesson 1: Practice Test #2. Take the entire test in a quiet room, and time yourself.

Lesson 2: Practice Test #2. Check your answers, and review any questions that gave you trouble.

THE 16-WEEK PLAN—1 LESSON PER WEEK

In the 16-Week Plan, you obviously will have more time to study. You can spread out your plan into one lesson a week. This plan is ideal because you are not under any pressure, and you can take more time to read through the review sections. You will also have the time to go back and repeat a section of the test that might have given you a problem. After all, the basis for all test success is practice, practice, practice.

THE PANIC PLAN

Whoops! Suddenly the ACT is upon you, and you haven't had any time to study. Perhaps you were busy with school work, or you were also preparing for the SATs. What can you do. While this is not an ideal way to prepare for this, or any test, here are some pointers.

1. Read through the test booklet or this *ACT Success* book and *memorize* the directions. This may sound strange to you, but if you don't have to read them when you take the actual exam, you will save yourself valuable time.

2. Read the first Red Alert in this book, *Introduction to the ACT*. This will help you be prepared for the different types of questions that you will encounter. The chapter makes an important point about how much time you will have for each question, depending upon which test you are taking. Learn to pace yourself.

3. Take the diagnostic ACT pretest, as well as the two practice ACT tests. You'll learn a lot by checking your answers. You will also become familiar, very quickly, with the different types of questions that will be on the actual exam.

4. Focus whatever time you have left on those areas of the test that gave you the most difficulty when you took the full-length tests in this book. If you have the time, read the review sections, and answer the questions in those chapters.

5. Practice filling in the blanks when you take the practice tests. Nothing will hurt you more than skipping a question to come back to later on, and then filling in the wrong blanks on your answer sheet.

6. Remember that you are not penalized for wrong answers, so answer every question!

The ACT Assessment is a multiple-choice test that is required for admission by many colleges throughout the United States and Canada. Taking this test can be an anxious time for many students, but by its very nature of being a multiple-choice test, you can prepare for this examination by learning some of the tricks and approaches to answering this type of question format.

The ACT Assessment tests are offered five times during the school year: October, December, February, April, and June. Check your state's schedules, however, since the test may not be offered in your state during a particular month. If you are planning to take the test, you can obtain a registration packet from your school, or contact ACT at:

> ACT
> PO Box 168
> Iowa City, Iowa 52243
> 319-337-1000
> http://www.act.org

This book has been written for you—the student—to help you prepare for the examination. It will give you an understanding of the overall test, and guide you, step by step, through each of the four areas covered on the exam. There is a logical approach to this process, exemplified by the content and format of this book. Let's take a moment to look at what you will find in this book.

Introduction: This section of the book presents an overview of the exam. It is designed to help you understand the nature of the test, what you have to know, and how to go about preparing for it.

Part I — Diagnostic Pretest: In order to help you focus on your studying, the Diagnostic Pretest is a full-length ACT Assessment examination, similar in content to the one you will eventually take. The purpose of this test is to help you diagnose your strengths and weaknesses. After you have taken the test and marked your scores, you will quickly be able to zero in on those specific subjects or question types that give you trouble. Armed with this knowledge, you can then focus only on those areas that need additional work. After all, why spend weeks reviewing material that you already know? Make sure, however, that you read the analysis of each answer. This will help you understand more fully what will be required of you on the actual examination.

Part II — Review Section: The ACT Assessment consists of four subject areas: English, Mathematics, Reading, and Science Reasoning. This section contains review material and practice questions for each of these subjects. Once you have taken the diagnostic pretest and have determined what areas require further study, you can go right to the specific section in Part II to concentrate your time and energy on reviewing the appropriate material.

Part III — Evaluation Tests: Once you have studied and reviewed the necessary subject areas or question types, it's time to evaluate your progress. Part III contains two full-length ACT Assessment exams to afford you further practice and determine if there are any additional areas that need to be studied. Take the first exam, grade yourself, and read through the explanations of the answers. Go back and review anything that requires further studying. Then take the second examination. The more you practice, the more you increase your chances for a higher score on the actual examination.

THE EXAM

The actual examination is composed of four sections:

English Test	75 questions	45 minutes
Math Test	60 questions	60 minutes
Reading Test	40 questions	35 minutes
Science Reasoning Test	40 questions	35 minutes

ENGLISH TEST

This portion of the examination will test your understanding of the basics of standard written English. It will cover punctuation, grammar and usage, and sentence structure. In addition, you will be tested on rhetorical skills—strategy, organization, and style. You will not be tested on things like spelling or vocabulary, nor do you have to worry about spitting back rules of grammar.

The test will present 5 prose passages accompanied by about 15 multiple-choice questions. These questions will test your basic understanding of writing and rhetorical skills.

This chart will give you a good idea of the actual types of questions you will encounter:

Content/Skills	Number of Items	Percentage of English Test
Usage/Mechanics	**40**	
Punctuation	10	13%
Grammar and Usage	12	16%
Sentence Structure	18	24%
Rhetorical Skills	**35**	
Strategy	12	16%
Organization	11	15%
Style	12	16%

Although the question content will be fairly evenly presented on the English test, you can see that the greatest number of questions will focus on Sentence Structure. It becomes obvious, then, to concentrate a little more of your studying on those types of questions.

MATHEMATICS TEST

The mathematics you will be tested upon is material that you have probably already learned and covers the content of mathematics courses given from the 9th through 11th grades. The test includes Pre-Algebra, Elementary Algebra, Intermediate Algebra, Coordinate Geometry, Plane Geometry, and some Trigonometry.

Following is a chart that gives the breakdown of the Mathematics Test:

Content	Number of Items	Percentage of Mathematics Test
Pre-Algebra	14	23%
Elementary Algebra	10	17%
Intermediate Algebra	9	15%
Coordinate Geometry	9	15%
Plane Geometry	14	23%
Trigonometry	4	7%

This chart should give you a good idea on where to focus your study efforts. Pre-Algebra and Trigonometry will require the most effort.

READING TEST

The subjects covered in this portion of the test include topics that usually appear in books and magazines read by high school seniors and college freshmen, and cover the following areas: social studies, prose fiction, humanities, and natural science. Rather than test specific facts or your vocabulary knowledge, the test focuses on your skills in "referring" and "reasoning." This means that you will be required to derive meaning from the passages by referring to what is specifically stated in them and to draw conclusions and other meanings based on reasoning.

Following is a table of the different types of questions you will encounter on the Reading Test. There will normally be one passage covering each of the four content areas, and each passage will contain 10 questions. Although there are four different content areas, there is really only one skill that is being tested—reading comprehension.

Reading Content	Number of Items	Percentage of Reading Test
Social Studies	10	25%
Natural Science	10	25%
Prose Fiction	10	25%
Humanities	10	25%

SCIENCE REASONING TEST

The Science Reasoning test will present seven sets of scientific information covering four major areas of study—Biology, Chemistry, Physical Science, and Earth and Space Science. It is primarily a test of reasoning and problem-solving skills. The information is presented in three different forms of questions:

Data Representation (graphs, charts, tables, illustrations, etc.)

Research Summaries (one or more related experiments)

Conflicting Viewpoints (two or more hypotheses or views, inconsistent with one another)

This test will require some science background in the different topics, but more than likely you will have learned much of this material in a general-level science course. This knowledge will give you an edge in answering questions since you will have some understanding of what the material is about.

This test contains 40 questions, usually spread out over seven sets of scientific information or passages. The following chart will give you an idea of the types of questions (format) that you can expect.

Format	Number of Items	Percentage of Science Test
Data Representation	15	38%
Research Summaries	18	45%
Conflicting Viewpoints	7	17%

These four subject areas will be covered and explained in greater detail later on in this book in each of the specific chapters in Part II.

SCORING

It is probably not that important to understand the scoring procedure. What is obvious is that the better you do on the examination, the higher your score. The higher your score, the better chance you have of being accepted to the school of your choice. The ACT Assessment bulletin will give you the tables and charts to help you understand *how* your score is computed, if you are really interested. You would probably be better served by spending your time studying for the test.

STRATEGIES

1. Know How Much Time You Have

From the preceding information, you can quickly determine how much time you will be allocated to answer each question and know why you will have to be familiar with the material on the test.

English Test	About 1/2 minute per question
Math Test	1 minute per question
Reading Test	Less than 1 minute per question
Science Reasoning Test	Less than 1 minute per question

This shouldn't intimidate you at all. Instead, it should give you a goal toward which to aim. The more you practice, the faster you will become, until you are able to breeze through the material that you know even faster than the allotted time and give yourself a few extra minutes to concentrate on the material you don't know.

2. Understand the Directions

By understanding the directions for each examination, you will save time on the actual ACT Assessment test. Since you have only a limited amount of time for each section and each question, don't waste time reading and rereading directions when you can learn them here and now, commit them to memory, and never have to look at them again. Each section in Part II will give you the directions. Memorize them!

3. Understand the Question Formats

Each section of the exam presents the material in different formats. However, there will be no surprises. Learn the different formats for each of the four sections. If you are comfortable with that knowledge, it will eliminate some test anxiety.

The good news, however, is that all of the questions in all of the areas are multiple-choice. This gives you an advantage when you have to guess (See number 7, page 9). Later on in this book you will encounter strategies for answering multiple-choice questions.

4. Fill in the Blanks Carefully

Nothing would be worse than getting to the end of almost three hours of testing to find that you have run out of little answer ovals because you skipped one. Make sure you are careful about filling in the blanks, especially if you decide to skip some questions so you can come back to them after you have answered the easier questions. Check the blanks every few questions on the Mathematics Test, or every time you begin a new passage in English, Reading, or Science.

5. Erase Completely

If you have skipped an oval and need to go back, or you have answered a question incorrectly, make sure you erase the incorrect answer *completely*. If you don't, there is a good possibility that the machine reading your answer page may mark it incorrectly.

6. Start with the Easy Questions, Then Try the Harder Ones

As with most tests, it makes sense to answer the easiest questions first. These should take less time to answer, thus giving you some extra time for those that are more difficult. This is especially important for any test that is timed. If there is actually time left over when you have filled in all of the blanks, try to review your work.

7. ANSWER EVERY QUESTION

This topic is highlighted because it is vitally important. Your ACT score is based on the number of questions you have answered correctly, and you are not penalized for wrong answers. Therefore, it is worth your while to guess. One technique that is recommended is as follows:

    a. Answer the easy questions first.
    b. Check your time.
    c. Then try the more difficult ones.
    d. Check your time.
    e. Try those questions that are most difficult.
    f. Fill in the remaining blanks.
    g. Check your time again and review if you can.

Some test experts recommend a different approach. They suggest filling in all of the answers consecutively, just in case you run out of time. If you are not confident that you will be able to get through the easier questions quickly and have enough time left over to go back, fill in the answers as you come to them. Also, if you are concerned that by skipping some of the answers you may forget to leave the appropriate questions blank, then it is also better to work consecutively. Practicing with the three full-length tests in this book will help you decide which technique is best for you.

8. Practice Under Simulated Situations

As you practice with the tests in this book, time yourself. Make believe you are in the room where you are actually taking the test. Use a stopwatch if you can to time each section. Since you are only *practicing* for the test, it is probably more realistic to take one section at a time, and take them on separate days. It is often difficult to set aside three full hours during a school week, or even on a busy weekend, to take the entire test. After all, the purpose of practicing with this book is to improve your speed on each test. Obviously, as you improve the timing of each test, your total time will also decrease.

9. Prepare Yourself for the Actual Test

There are some specific pointers that the ACT advises. They include: getting plenty of rest before the test; arriving at the test site promptly; bringing your admission ticket, acceptable identification, a watch, and *at least* three sharpened, soft-lead (no. 2) pencils with erasers. The ACT Registration Packet will give you some additional specifics. Be sure to read through that material.

Now, it's time to get to work! Begin by taking the Diagnostic ACT Assessment Exam that follows this section. You may approach it in two ways. First, you can take the exam as if you were in actual testing conditions, which means timing yourself. Second, you can take each section of the test at different times, merely to get an idea of how well you can answer these different types of questions.

In either case, check your answers carefully. Pay attention to those questions you answered incorrectly and read the explanations. These will give you a clue as to what types of questions you will need to study further. Remember that most of the material on the ACT Assessment requires some type of answering technique. And this book will help you develop the techniques for *ACT Success.*

Pretest — Part 1

In the five passages that follow, certain words and phrases are underlined and numbered. At the end of the passage, you will find alternatives for each underlined part. You are to choose the one that best expresses the idea, makes the statement appropriate for standard written English, or is worded most consistently with the style and tone of the passage as a whole. If you think the original version is best, choose "NO CHANGE."

You will also find questions about a section of the passage, or about the passage as a whole. These questions do not refer to an underlined portion of the passage, but rather are identified by a number or numbers in a box.

For each question, choose the alternative you consider best and fill in the corresponding oval on your answer document. Read the passage through once before you begin to answer the questions that accompany it. You cannot determine most answers without reading several sentences beyond the question. Be sure that you have read far enough ahead each time you choose an alternative.

Passage I

[1]

Hamlet is a household word associated by most people with someone who talks to Yorick's skull. Somehow Hamlet's image lingers, even though fewer and fewer high school students ever read Shakespeare's play. If every age <u>had made</u> Hamlet into
                         1
<u>their</u> own image and has found relevance in
  2
his story, so should we; like most of us, he struggles to keep his identity and his honesty in an increasingly meaningless and violent world. <u>Flung abruptly</u> into a society
                        3
intent on power and indulgence, and it is not long before he learns <u>how to accept</u>
                                      4
<u>death, his own included.</u>
            4

[2]

Hamlet's emotional and moral honesty is first revealed <u>in how he cannot dismiss</u>
                              5
the death of his father, the King, and his mother's hasty remarriage to his uncle, Claudius. Hamlet feels that only superficial people or schemers could accept these events as natural or morally correct. Claudius is both, and, as the ghost tells Hamlet, has

actually murdered Hamlet's father. Unsure of the ghost's story, Hamlet sets out to test Claudius <u>and presents</u> a play patterned after
6
the actual murder. <u>With Claudius revealing</u>
7
his guilt, Hamlet kills Polonius <u>while he is</u>
8
<u>visiting his mother.</u>
8

[3]

Intent on the necessity for emotional honesty, he berates his mother for her weakness and her love for Claudius. But he has lost control of his actions by killing Polonius, and the King sends him off to England and arranges for his murder en route. <u>In Hamlet's absence,</u> the work of the
9
court deteriorates; Ophelia goes mad and kills herself; Laertes leads a small rebellion against the King; <u>Claudius himself has to</u>
10
<u>hang on</u> by scheming.
10

[4]

<u>When we see Hamlet again,</u> having
11
foiled the King's attempt to have him killed, <u>you sense that</u> his honesty has turned
12
inward and he has learned something about death. He is resigned to human mortality, speaks sadly of kings and clowns, and

professes undying love for both Laertes and the dead Ophelia. In a short speech to his friend Horatio, Hamlet reveals the essence of his new attitude, <u>by his saying that</u> "Readi-
13
ness is all."

[5]

Earlier, in the "To be or not to be" speech, he had noted that revenge might lead to his own death, and <u>retreats</u> from the
14
prospect, but he is now ready to die if that is to be his fate. He accepts a dueling match with Laertes, arranged by Claudius, whom he knows may be planning his death.

[6]

<u>The evil Claudius and the innocent</u>
15
<u>connivers, his mother and Laertes, die with</u> <u>him. Learning how to die a philosopher's</u> <u>death, he remains true to his emotional and</u> <u>moral ideas.</u>

1. A. NO CHANGE
   B. has made
   C. has been making
   D. was making

2. F. NO CHANGE
   G. there
   H. its
   J. his

3. A. NO CHANGE
B. Having been flung
C. Although he is flung
D. He is flung

4. F. NO CHANGE
G. how to accept death, not only his own.
H. how to accept death, even his own.
J. to accept the idea of death.

5. A. NO CHANGE
B. not being able to accept
C. in that he did not dismiss
D. by his anguish over

6. F. NO CHANGE
G. and he
H. because he
J. by presenting

7. A. NO CHANGE
B. When Claudius reveals
C. After Claudius has revealed
D. Having revealed

8. F. NO CHANGE
G. while Hamlet is visiting his mother.
H. in the queen's chambers.
J. visiting his mother.

9. A. NO CHANGE
B. Being absent,
C. While being absent,
D. Having been absent,

10. F. NO CHANGE
G. Claudius himself hanging on
H. and Claudius hangs on
J. Claudius being even more of a hanger-on

11. A. NO CHANGE
B. (Begin a new paragraph) When Hamlet reappears
C. (Do not begin a new paragraph) When Hamlet appears
D. (Begin a new paragraph) When we see Hamlet appear

12. F. NO CHANGE
G. it appears that
H. we sense that
J. OMIT

13. A. NO CHANGE
B. phrasing it thus:
C. in the phrase,
D. saying, ''Readiness

14. F. NO CHANGE
G. had therefore retreated
H. was retreating
J. had thereby retreated

15. Which would be a good introductory sentence for this paragraph?

A. Hamlet betrays his ideals.
B. Hamlet dies fully aware of the treachery of the world.
C. T. S. Eliot thought Hamlet's madness was unmotivated.
D. Hamlet compromises his ideals here and elsewhere in the play.

Passage II

[1]

The cathedral of Chartres in France, rebuilt in the Gothic style after the fire of 1195 A.D., is one of the most admired and photographed structures in the world. Its harmonies do not derive so much from the symmetrical designs of one guiding architect

as the lucky collaboration of many hands of
16
many periods. They are not simple, but
17
complex; not easily achieved, but built on

the sweat and suffering of many people.

[2]
The western facade, however, was built
18
over a span of four centuries. The portals and

lancet windows date from around 1145 (the

Romanesque period), the arrangement of the
19
towers, the rose window, and the south tower

date from the Gothic rebuilding after

1195, being that the north tower is built in the
20
Renaissance (1507–13) or very late Gothic style,

which is charactered by a spidery complexity
21
quite different from the other styles on the
22
facade. Exact measurements showing the
23
portals a little off-center, and likewise the rose
23
window — discrepancies that do not detract
23
from the vital unit found from the fact that all of
24
the elements work together.
24

[3]
After 1195, the church was rebuilt in

the Gothic style with a remarkable degree of
25
wall space filled with stained glass. This

achievement attests to the expertise of the

local glassmakers, to the skill of the archi-

tects, and to the power of the School of

Chartres, whose emphasis on light symbol-

ism influenced the others. If the sun is the

symbol of the good and the beautiful, and

therefore a symbol of God, a church should

let as much light in as possible, preferably
26
through stained glass depicting the lives of

saints, of apostles, and of Christ himself.

[4]
The glassmakers could not put their
27
glass in place unless the architects released
28
large portions of the wall from bearing the

weight of the roof. The weight was directed

along graceful ribs in the vault down slender
29
columns in each bay, and then outside,

down flying buttresses.

[5]
So complex is the effect of the nave,

with its stained glass, it slim pillars, its regular

bays, and its soaring vaults, and so subtle are

the proportions between gallery, triforium,

and clerestory elements. The eye is directed
30
quickly upward, toward the front of the

cathedral, and then down toward the altar.

[6]

Thus, despite the interaction of many minds and hands over a long period of time, the Chartres cathedral is a remarkably effective and cohesive work, both outside and in.

16. F. NO CHANGE
    G. as from
    H. as they derive from
    J. but are derived from

17. A. NO CHANGE
    B. These hands
    C. These periods
    D. These harmonies

18. F. NO CHANGE
    G. nevertheless
    H. for example
    J. happily

19. A. NO CHANGE
    B. , but the
    C. ; nevertheless, the
    D. ; the

20. F. NO CHANGE
    G. ; and the
    H. . The
    J. ; but the

21. A. NO CHANGE
    B. is characterized by
    C. is typical of
    D. is devoted to

22. F. NO CHANGE
    G. different than
    H. unsimilar to
    J. opposing to

23. A. NO CHANGE
    B. show the portals and the rose window a little off-center
    C. shows the portals and the rose window likewise off-center
    D. was showing the rose window and the portals a little off-center

24. F. NO CHANGE
    G. when all the elements work together.
    H. in all the elements working to-gether.
    J. if all the elements work together.

25. A. NO CHANGE
    B. amount
    C. expanse
    D. length

26. F. NO CHANGE
    G. let in as much light as possible
    H. let as much light as possible in
    J. be as light-filled as possible

27. A. NO CHANGE
    B. could not be putting
    C. could not have put
    D. did not put

28. F. NO CHANGE
    G. was to release
    H. had released
    J. would have released

29. A. NO CHANGE
    B. vault; then down
    C. vault. Then down
    D. vault, down

30. F. NO CHANGE
    G. elements; finally, the
    H. elements that the
    J. elements inasmuch as the

Passage III

[1]

The Parthenon, a Doric temple finished in 432 B.C. and still standing on the Acropolis of Athens, balances two strains of ancient Greek culture — the militant, rational Doric; and the artistic, emotional Ionic. This seems
<u>31</u>
to have been one of the aims of the Golden Age of Pericles, as much of the surviving sculpture, building, and writing <u>attest</u>. The
<u>32</u>
Parthenon embodies this whole culture in its sculpture, its subtle architectural blends, and <u>how technology was used.</u>
33

[2]

The sculptured scenes depicted on the metope, frieze, and pediment represent balance and self-control. The large sculptures of the east pediment (the birth of Athena) and the west pediment (the triumph of Athena's cult over <u>Poseidon</u>) can be inter-
34
preted as mind (Athena) controlling the body (Poseidon). The power of Athena's presence in the center of both sculptures flows out naturally through the groups of gods and goddesses <u>who are arranged on</u>
35

either side. The metope sculptures under
35
the eaves involve four mythological episodes in which mind and reason balance out chaos: the Gods are shown defeating giants, the Greeks <u>in their fight with</u> the Amazons,
36
and the Lapiths defeating the centaurs.

<u>Finally, the frieze sculpture,</u> high around the
37
outside of the cella (inner building), depicts a procession with worshippers bringing a new robe for Athena. As they worship, the figures demonstrate the balance and control shown by Athena in the other sculpture. The circuit of the goddess, from her birth through her heroic action to her <u>Athenian worshippers is complete.</u>
38

[3]

The balancing of Doric and Ionic architectural styles is also successfully achieved. The temple is conceived in the Doric order refined by the Ionic. The columns are more slender and closer together than the typical Doric temple at Olympia, finished twenty years before the Parthenon. The Parthenon's columns are 5.48 times higher than their diameter,

whereas Olympia's columns are 4.7 times
                    39
their diameter. This difference means that
                    40
the Parthenon would seem taller and lighter
                    40
than the temple at Olympia when they were
                                    41
placed side by side. Another Ionic motif,
        41   42
which would have been readily apparent to

an ancient Athenian, are the freize sculpture

on the cella and the six porch columns

behind the peristyle at each end. The

architects took steps to balance the good

qualities of both orders, like Mnesicles
                            43
would later do when he placed both Doric

and Ionic columns in the Propylaea, or

entrance temple to the Acropolis.

[4]

Furthermore, the architects made slight

corrections to enhance the sense of balance

and tension. The ends and sides of the

columns swell slightly upward in the

middle; they lean inward, are closer together

near the corners of the building, and

each column swelling to its greatest
                    44
circumference about two-thirds of the way
        44
up. These adjustments give the building a

lightness and a sense of physical tension.

[5]

Even in its ruined state, the Parthenon

retains a sense of balanced aesthetic forces

that are no longer seen in Greek culture.
                    45
The Parthenon's greatest enemy now is the

final development of the technology that

once built it — the modern polluted air is

slowly destroying the ancient marble.

31. A. NO CHANGE
    B. This difference
    C. This balance
    D. This merging

32. F. NO CHANGE
    G. attests
    H. informs
    J. attempts

33. A. NO CHANGE
    B. its use of technology
    C. technological adjustments
    D. its careful sight adjustments

34. F. NO CHANGE
    G. Poseidon's one
    H. Poseidon's
    J. that belonging to Poseidon

35. A. NO CHANGE
    B. which are arranged on either side
    C. on either side
    D. that are arranged on either side

36. F. NO CHANGE
    G. when they fought
    H. fought
    J. defeating

37. A. NO CHANGE
    B. (Begin new paragraph)
    C. (Begin new paragraph) The frieze sculpture, finally,
    D. (Do not begin new paragraph) The frieze sculpture, however,

38. F. NO CHANGE
    G. Athenian worshippers is thereby
    H. Athenian worshippers is terrifyingly complete
    J. Athenian worshippers, is thereby complete

39. A. NO CHANGE
    B. those in Olympia are
    C. the columns in the Doric order are
    D. the Doric columns are

40. F. NO CHANGE
    G. , making the Parthenon seem
    H. , rendering the Parthenon
    J. ; this means

41. A. NO CHANGE
    B. were they placed
    C. were they to be placed
    D. had they ever been placed

42. F. NO CHANGE
    G. Another Ionic motifs
    H. Other Ionic motifs
    J. Other Greek motifs

43. A. NO CHANGE
    B. as
    C. and
    D. but

44. F. NO CHANGE
    G. swell to their greatest circumference
    H. each column swells to its great circumference
    J. the circumference of each column is greatest in the middle

45. A. NO CHANGE
    B. long since vanished from
    C. now not in the
    D. that is absent from today's modern

Passage IV

[1]

In the early days of the American space program, watching the splashdowns were scary. For Mercury, the capsule,
46   47
plucked from the water with a crane, could
47
drop. Apollo was even scarier. After the
47
parachuting capsule hit the water, the crew blew open the hatch with explosive bolts. What if sea water swamped the capsule before the scuba divers in their raft could reach it? By comparison, watching the landing of the space shuttle is tame. When seen on television, its not much different
48
from watching any large airplane land. However, being at Edwards Air Force Base and watching the shuttle land is thrilling. But there isn't much to see, the spectators
49
feel as if they themselves had flown in the
50
hostile environment of space.

[2]

[1] Huddled in the grandstand, a sense
51
of community develops. [2] Like the
51

18

astronauts, they will not leave until their mission is completed. [3] The spectators feel it is their shuttle, their mission, their landing. [4] This is the one they have come to see and be part of, in spite of the traffic jams while driving to the base, the chilly air, and the dusty desert landscape.

[3]

The sense of adventure and excitement becomes stronger as the time for landing
_____
53
approaches. Over the P.A. system, the capsule communicator is heard. "STS 42 is now over Brandenburg, making its turn toward the coast. Then it will again turn inland." Where is it? When a woman stands and turns to look above the grandstand rail
_____
54
everyone stands and turns.

[4]

[1] No one sees the craft until after the
_____
55
sonic boom is heard. [2] The sound shakes the stands and reverberates in the quiet desert air, and then the straining to sight the craft becomes intense.

[5]

"There it is"! First merely a wobbling,
_____
56
swaying black dot, the craft takes shape, looking like a silhouette of a toy airplane. As it nears, the chatter intensifies. "How the heck can it come down so steep?
_____
57
Look at that angle!"
_____
57

[6]

After the rear wheels touch down, the
_____
58
drag chute deploys, and the final puff of dust indicating nose is down, after the P.A. blares "The Stars and Stripes Forever," some applaud, while others are teary-eyed with emotion. The shuttle taxis down the desert strip and out of sight. The spectators look at one another, smile, shake hands. Mission
_____
59
accomplished.
_____
59

46. F. NO CHANGE
   G. was scary
   H. become scary
   J. has been scary

47. A. NO CHANGE
   B. the capsule, plucked from the water, with a crane, could drop.
   C. the capsule plucked from the water with a crane could drop.
   D. the capsule plucked from the water with a crane, could drop

48. F. NO CHANGE
    G. television its
    H. television it's
    J. television, it's

49. A. NO CHANGE
    B. Because
    C. Although
    D. However

50. F. NO CHANGE
    G. themselves
    H. they
    J. by themselves they

51. A. NO CHANGE
    B. a developing sense of community occurs.
    C. the community develops a sense of spectators.
    D. the spectators develop a sense of community.

52. Which of the following sequence of sentences will make Paragraph 2 most coherent?

    F. NO CHANGE
    G. 2, 1, 3, 4
    H. 3, 4, 2, 1
    J. 1, 3, 4, 2

53. A. NO CHANGE
    B. become stronger
    C. strengthening
    D. have strength

54. F. NO CHANGE
    G. grandstand, rail
    H. grandstand rail,
    J. grandstand rail

55. The writer is considering adding these two sentences to Paragraph 3 instead of having them as a separate paragraph. The best reason to do so is because:

    A. Paragraph 4 is too short.
    B. The paragraph is about the sound of the landing, as well as about sighting the craft.
    C. The paragraph continues the idea that the spectators are looking for the craft.
    D. The last sentence of the paragraph ends on a note of suspense.

56. F. NO CHANGE
    G. "There it is".
    H. "There it is!"
    J. "There it is."

57. The writer is considering changing the wording of these sentences. Which would fit best with the tone and context of these sentences?

    A. NO CHANGE
    B. "It is impossible to believe that an aircraft could come down at such a steep angle."
    C. "Wow! Look at that! Can you believe it?"
    D. "I ain't never seen any plane do nothing like that one!"

58. F. NO CHANGE
    G. After the rear wheels touch down, after the drag chute deploys, after the final puff of dust indicates the nose is down, after the P.A. blares "The Stars and Stripes Forever,"
    H. The rear wheels touch down, the drag chute deploys, the final puff of dust indicates the nose is down, the P.A. blares "The Stars and Stripes Forever,"

J. The rear wheels are touching down, the drag chute is deploying, the final puff of dust is indicating the nose is down, and the P.A. blares ''The Stars and Stripes Forever,''

59. The writer is thinking of changing the last sentence. Which would be most appropriate?

   A. NO CHANGE
   B. All's well that ends well.
   C. Happy landings!
   D. They got what they came for.

60. The writer wishes to add the following sentence to the essay: ''As it nears, the shuttle resolves itself into three dimensional reality. It is merely a large, sophisticated, specialized airplane.'' The most logical place for this sentence is

   F. at the end of Paragraph 1
   G. at the end of Paragraph 3
   H. at the end of Paragraph 4
   J. at the end of Paragraph 5

Passage IV

[1]

On Saturday, I get in my car and go to the mall. The athletic shoes I need are on sale. As usual when I'm at the mall, I'm into an experience that provides a
                    61
special pleasure. When I'm at the mall, I know I will be treated well. I'm a customer, I'm in control, and the mall's purpose is to
            62
provide service to me.

[2]

As I wander past the music store and look into the window, each of the store's personnel smile invitingly. Maybe the smiles
                    63
mean ''I need commission,'' but yet they
                                   64
create an atmosphere that makes me think I may stop in after I do my errand and pick
                              65
up the new CD by my favorite rap group.

[3]

When I pass the candy store, someone outside offers me a free sample taste of peanut brittle. It's so delicious I can't resist going in to buy some. The sales clerk couldn't be more friendlier, and since there
                    66
is a special on peanut brittle (buy a pound
                               67
and receive a free bag of jelly beans), I buy
                    67
the pound instead of the half pound I thought I would buy.

[4]

When I enter the large department store, playing pleasant contemporary music,
                              69
I am greeted by the sound of the pianist. At the perfume counters, rows of testers allow
                                              70
me to spray a little of each new scent on to my wrist to see if I like it. With all the different ones I try, I leave smelling

wonderful. The makeup consultant offers a
                71
free makeover, and I'm not required to buy

any of her company's products. But I look

so good when she is finished that I buy the

products so I can re-create the new look at

home. Which doesn't happen.
          72

[5]

[1] In the relaxed and friendly atmo-

sphere created by the mall's controlled

climate, entertainment, and pleasant people,
                    73
I'm in a special world where I am treated

like royalty. [2] How can I not take advan-

tage of the wonderful opportunities offered

to me? [3] Everyone in the mall is there to

serve me; when I'm at the mall, I'm the one

who controls my world. [4] I don't get the
74   74
athletic shoes, but I do return to the music

store for the CD.

61. A. NO CHANGE
  B. there is an experience
  C. I'm provided with an experience
  D. I have an experience

62. F. NO CHANGE
  G. control and
  H. control and,
  J. control: and

63. A. NO CHANGE
  B. smiles
  C. smiled
  D. have smiled

64. F. NO CHANGE
  G. thus
  H. so then
  J. but

65. A. NO CHANGE
  B. eat my lunch
  C. finish shopping
  D. buy the shoes

66. F. NO CHANGE
  G. friendlier
  H. most friendly
  J. most friendliest

67. A. NO CHANGE
  B. brittle (buy a pound and receive a
     free bag of jelly beans)
  C. brittle, (buy a pound and receive a
     free bag of jelly beans),
  D. brittle, (buy a pound and receive a
     free bag of jelly beans)

68. The author wishes to add a sentence to
  paragraph 3: "Another candy I enjoy is
  licorice."

  F. The author should not add the
     sentence because it makes the
     paragraph too long.
  G. The author should not add the
     sentence because it disrupts the
     paragraph's unity.
  H. The author should add the
     sentence because it is interesting
     information.
  J. The author should add the
     sentence because it increases the
     paragraph's coherence.

69. A. NO CHANGE
    B. Move the underlined phrase to the beginning of the sentence.
    C. Move the underlined phrase to after the word "sound."
    D. Move the underlined phrase to after the word "pianist."

70. F. NO CHANGE
    G. permit
    H. invite
    J. ask

71. A. NO CHANGE
    B. wonderfully
    C. more wonderful
    D. wonderfuller

72. F. NO CHANGE
    G. home, which doesn't happen.
    H. home; which doesn't happen.
    J. home. It doesn't happen.

73. A. NO CHANGE
    B. climate, entertainment and pleasant people,
    C. climate entertainment and pleasant people,
    D. climate, entertainment, and pleasant people

74. The writer is thinking of omitting these clauses. The best reason not to do so is:

    F. They state the main idea the speaker in the essay wants to convey about the mall.
    G. Without them, the paragraph would be incomplete.
    H. The "I" in this essay doesn't realize that the essay's content makes them ironic.
    J. The "I" in this essay is a sophisticated shopper who knows what she wants.

75. The best order for the sentences in paragraph 5 is:

    A. NO CHANGE
    B. 3, 1, 4, 2
    C. 3, 4, 2, 1
    D. 4, 1, 2, 3

Pretest — Part 2

Solve each problem, choose the correct answer, and then fill in the corresponding oval on your answer document.

Do not linger over problems that take too much time. Solve as many as you can; then return to the others in the time you have left for this test.

You are permitted to use a calculator.

Note: Unless otherwise stated, all of the following should be assumed:

1. Illustrative figures are NOT necessarily drawn to scale.
2. Geometric figures lie in a plane.
3. The word *line* indicates a straight line.
4. The word *average* indicates arithmetic mean.

1. Which fraction has the greatest value?

   A. $\dfrac{4}{13}$

   B. $\dfrac{5}{12}$

   C. $\dfrac{3}{11}$

   D. $\dfrac{4}{11}$

   E. $\dfrac{5}{13}$

2. The area of the circle is 16π. Find the length of the diameter of the circle.

   F. 4
   G. 2
   H. 16
   J. 32
   K. 8

3. Tom's bowling scores were 175, 155, and 210. What is his average?

   A. 540
   B. 270
   C. 180
   D. 135
   E. 210

4. The difference between the measures of two complementary angles is $50°$. Find in degrees the measure of the smaller angle.

   F. 40
   G. 50
   H. 70
   J. 20
   K. 10

5. The expression $\dfrac{-40D^2E^5}{-5DE^2}$ is equivalent to:

   A. $\dfrac{-8D}{E^3}$

   B. $\dfrac{-8}{DE^7}$

   C. $8DE^3$

   D. $\dfrac{8D}{E^3}$

   E. $\dfrac{-8D^3}{E^7}$

25

6. Rounded to the nearest tenth, 46.97 would equal

    F. 46.0
    G. 46.9
    H. 46.10
    J. 47.0
    K. 50

7. Marilyn invested $6,000 at a simple interest rate of 4¾%. What is the total value of her investment after one year?

    A. $240
    B. $285
    C. $6,240
    D. $6,285
    E. $6,260.40

8. Solve for d.

$$\frac{d-4}{d} = \frac{5}{6}$$

    F. 24
    G. 20
    H. −20
    J. 5
    K. 4

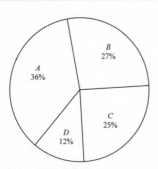

9. Student Ages at Notkcots College
    Enrollment = 4,200

    A. 16–20 years
    B. 21–25 years
    C. 26–30 years
    D. over 30 years

How many students are over 25 years old?

    A. 2,206
    B. 1,554
    C. 1,050
    D. 155
    E. 504

10. Two consecutive angles of a parallelogram contain $x°$ and $(x + 20)°$.

Find the value of x.

    F. 100°
    G. 180°
    H. 360°
    J. 80°
    K. 40°

11. A salesman earns a commission of 6 percent of his total sales. How much must he sell to yield a commission of $135?

    A. $8,100
    B. $2,250
    C. $810
    D. $8.10
    E. $2,700

12. If $2a + 2b = c$, then $a =$

    F. $\dfrac{c-2}{b}$

    G. $\dfrac{c+2}{b}$

    H. $\dfrac{c-2b}{2}$

    J. $\dfrac{c+2b}{b}$

    K. $\dfrac{c+2b}{2}$

13. Suppose there are seven roads between Troy and Utica, New York. In how many different ways can Mr. Smythe travel from Troy to Utica and return by a different route?

    A. 36
    B. 49
    C. 35
    D. 42
    E. 54

14. $18 \div .04 =$

    F. 4.5
    G. 45
    H. 450
    J. 4,500
    K. 45,000

15. $(-4)^2 - 3(-4) =$

    A. -4
    B. 52
    C. -52
    D. 192
    E. 28

16. If the hypotenuse of a right triangle is 6, and one of the legs is 5, the length of the other leg is

    F. 1
    G. 11
    H. $\sqrt{11}$
    J. 30
    K. $\sqrt{61}$

17. Find three consecutive odd integers whose sum is -45.

    A. 13, 15, 17
    B. 14, 15, 16
    C. $-14, -15, -16$
    D. $-22, -23, -24$
    E. $-13, -15, -17$

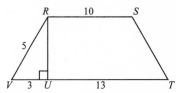

18. Find the area of trapezoid *RSTV*.

    F. 32
    G. 65
    H. 52
    J. 24
    K. 38

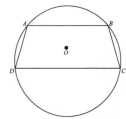

19. Trapezoid *ABCD*, with bases *AB* and *CD*, is inscribed in circle *O*. Arc *AB* = 60° and arc *CD* = 160°. Find arc *AD*.

    A. 220°
    B. 140°
    C. 70°
    D. 360°
    E. 60°

20. What is .1 percent expressed as a decimal?

    F. .001
    G. .01
    H. .1
    J. 1
    K. 10.0

21. $(4z + 3)(z - 6) =$

- A. $4z^2 + 21z - 18$
- B. $4z^2 - 21z - 18$
- C. $4z^2 + 21z + 18$
- D. $4z^2 - 21z + 18$
- E. $4z^2 - 27z - 18$

22. Evaluate $3a^2 - 2b$, if $a = -3$, and $b = -1$.

- F. -29
- G. 29
- H. -25
- J. 25
- K. 83

23. If $|2t + 3| - 4 = 3$, then $t =$

- A. -5
- B. -2
- C. 2
- D. -5 or 2
- E. -2 or 5

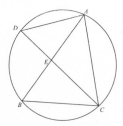

24. In the circle above, $\triangle ABC \sim \triangle ADE$. If $AE = 8$, $EB = 7$, and $AC = 12$, find AD.

- F. 20
- G. 19
- H. 15
- J. 12
- K. 10

25. What is the equation of the circle with center $(-2, 4)$ and radius 3?

- A. $(x - 2)^2 + (y + 4)^2 = 9$
- B. $(x + 2)^2 + (y - 4)^2 = 3$
- C. $(x - 4)^2 + (y + 2)^2 = 9$
- D. $(x - 2)^2 + (y + 4)^2 = 3$
- E. $(x + 2)^2 + (y - 4)^2 = 9$

26. What is the slope of the line described by the equation $3y + 5x = 8$?

- F. $-\dfrac{5}{3}$
- G. $-\dfrac{8}{3}$
- H. $\dfrac{3}{5}$
- J. $-\dfrac{3}{5}$
- K. $\dfrac{3}{8}$

27. What is the distance between the points $(2, 3)$ and $(5, 7)$?

- A. 5
- B. 10
- C. 15
- D. 20
- E. 25

28. A coat is on sale for $120 after a discount of 20 percent. Find the original price.

- F. $96
- G. $144
- H. $150
- J. $180
- K. $140

29. If one angle of a parallelogram has $68°$, then the angle adjacent to it has:

- A. $22°$
- B. $32°$
- C. $42°$
- D. $52°$
- E. $112°$

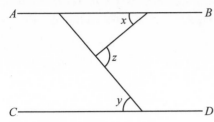

30. Line *AB* is parallel to *CD*.

$$x = 40°$$
$$y = 80°$$

Find the measurement of *z*.

F.   60°
G.   40°
H.   80°
J.   120°
K.   160°

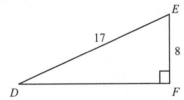

31. In right triangle *DEF* above, what is the value of cot *D*?

A. $\dfrac{8}{17}$

B. $\dfrac{8}{15}$

C. $\dfrac{15}{8}$

D. $\dfrac{17}{15}$

E. $\dfrac{15}{17}$

32. Find the perimeter of a rectangle whose length is 7 centimeters and whose width is 5 centimeters.

F.   35 centimeters
G.   70 centimeters
H.   12 centimeters
J.   24 centimeters
K.   48 centimeters

33. There are 240 seats in the balcony of a theater. The number of seats in each row is 14 more than the number of rows. Find the number of rows.

A.   3
B.   6
C.   8
D.   10
E.   24

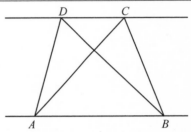

34. *AB* ∥ *CD*. What is the ratio of the area of △*ABD* to the area of △*ACB*?

F.   1:4
G.   4:1
H.   2:3
J.   3:2
K.   1:1

35. Which of the following can be the lengths of the sides of a triangle?

A.   7, 7, 16
B.   5, 7, 12
C.   4, 8, 13
D.   5, 6, 10
E.   5, 5, 10

36. Which of the following is true for two perpendicular lines?

F.   Their slopes are the same.
G.   Their slopes are both 0.
H.   Their slopes are both undefined.
J.   Their slopes are the reciprocals of each other.
K.   Their slopes are the negative reciprocals of each other.

37. When $(12x^4 - 3x^3 + 6x^2) \div 3x^2$, the quotient is

A. $9x^2 - 3$
B. $5x^2$
C. $4x^2 - 3x + 2$
D. $4x^2 - x + 2$
E. $6x$

38. Triangle ABC has vertices A $(-6, -4)$, B $(4, 2)$, and C $(0, 4)$. Find the area of triangle ABC.

F. 24
G. 22
H. 8
J. 30
K. 4

39. The expression $2(a + 1) - (1 + 2a)$ is equivalent to

A. 1
B. -1
C. 0
D. $4a$
E. 2

40. $\sqrt{30}$ is closest to

F. 5
G. 5.4
H. 5.5
J. 5.6
K. 5.7

41. Jill jogged ½ of a mile, rested, then jogged ⅓ of a mile. What fractional part of a mile must she jog to complete 1 mile?

A. $\dfrac{2}{5}$
B. $\dfrac{3}{5}$
C. $\dfrac{1}{6}$
D. $\dfrac{5}{6}$
E.. $\dfrac{1}{12}$

42. Bill's weekly salary increased from $175 to $201.25. Find the percent of increase.

F. 1.15 percent
G. 1.5 percent
H. 8.7 percent
J. 87 percent
K. 15 percent

43. What are the values of x that satisfy the equation $5x^2 - 2 = 3x^2 - x + 4$?

A. -2 and $\dfrac{3}{2}$
B. $-\dfrac{3}{2}$ and 2
C. -2 and $-\dfrac{3}{2}$
D. $\dfrac{3}{2}$ and 2
E.. -2 and $\dfrac{2}{3}$

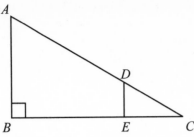

44. In the accompanying figure, triangle *ABC* is a right triangle and $\overline{DE}$ is perpendicular to leg $\overline{BC}$.

If *AB* = 12, *DE* = 4, and *EC* = 6, find *BE*.

F. 12
G. 18
H. 9
J. 14
K. 24

45. A boy takes 3 minutes to read a story of 315 words. How many minutes will it take him to read a story of 945 words at the same rate?

A. 2
B. 8
C. 6
D. 3
E. 9

46. Find *S*, using the formula $S = \dfrac{a(1-r^n)}{1-r}$, if *a* = −1, *r* = 3, *n* = 2.

F. 4
G. −4
H. 2
J. −2
K. 8

Population in Thousands

47. The drawing shown here is part of a bar graph showing population trends in a village. How many people lived in the village in 1920?

A. 2.5
B. 25
C. 250
D. 2,500
E. 25,000

48. If *a* does not equal 0, then $\dfrac{(3a^2)^4(2a)^2}{(-2a^3)^5}$ simplifies to

F. $-\dfrac{9}{4a^4}$

G. $\dfrac{81}{8a^5}$

H. $-\dfrac{81}{8a^5}$

J. $\dfrac{81}{8a^4}$

K. $-\dfrac{9}{8a^5}$

49. Solve for y:

$$\frac{y}{8} - \frac{y}{10} = 3$$

A. 50
B. 40
C. 6
D. 120
E. 5

50. Two calculators and three pens cost $19. Three calculators and two pens cost $21. Find the cost of one pen.

    F. $3
    G. $4
    H. $5
    J. $6
    K. $7

51. Which is a rational number?

    A. $\sqrt{2}$
    B. $\sqrt{3}$
    C. $\sqrt{9}$
    D. $\sqrt{5}$
    E. $\sqrt{11}$

52. $(-4r^3s)(-2rst^3)$ is equivalent to

    F. $-8r^4s^2t^3$
    G. $8r^4st^3$
    H. $-8r^3s^2t^3$
    J. $-8r^4st^3$
    K. $8r^4s^2t^3$

53. If $f(x) = 3x - 5$, what is the value of $f(-2)$?

    A. -21
    B. -11
    C. -7
    D. 1
    E. 11

54. Which of the following is equivalent to $\sin^2\alpha + \cos^2\alpha + \tan^2\alpha$?

    F. $\sin^2\alpha$
    G. $\cos^2\alpha$
    H. $\tan^2\alpha$
    J. $\sec^2\alpha$
    K. $\csc^2\alpha$

55. The solution set of $3x - 3 > 2x + 1$ is

    A. $\{x \mid x < 4\}$
    B. $\{x \mid x > -2\}$
    C. $\{x \mid x > 4\}$
    D. $\{x \mid x > -4\}$
    E. $\{x \mid x < -2\}$

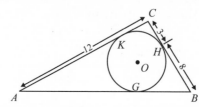

56. *AB*, *AC*, and *BC* are tangents drawn to circle *O*. Find the length of *AB*.

    F. 19
    G. 17
    H. 14
    J. 6
    K. 3

57. Solve for *x* and *y*:

$$x + 4y = 6$$
$$9x - 4y = 14$$

    A. (1, 2)
    B. (2, 1)
    C. (−1, 2)
    D. (−2, 1)
    E. (−2, −1)

58. If $\sec A = 8$, what is the value of $\tan A$?

    F. $3\sqrt{7}$
    G. $\dfrac{1}{8}$
    H. $\dfrac{3\sqrt{7}}{8}$
    J. $\dfrac{\sqrt{7}}{21}$
    K. $24\sqrt{7}$

59. Which of the following correctly describes the solutions of the equation $x^3 - 2x^2 + x = 0$?

   A. no real solutions
   B. three rational solutions
   C. one irrational solution
   D. one rational solution and two solutions that are not real
   E. three irrational solutions

60. A support cable to a radio antenna is 19 meters long. The angle that the support cable forms with the ground is 57°. What is the distance, in meters, from the point where the cable touches the ground to the base of the antenna?

   F. $19 \sin 57°$
   G. $\dfrac{19}{\sin 57°}$
   H. $19 \cos 57°$
   J. $\dfrac{19}{\cos 57°}$
   K. $19 \tan 57°$

Pretest — Part 3

There are four passages in this test. Each passage is followed by several questions. After reading a passage, choose the best answer to each question and fill in the corresponding oval on your answer document. You may refer to the passages as often as necessary.

Passage I

Line   Mr. Garth was not at the office, and Fred rode on to his house, which was a little way outside the town—a homely place with an orchard in front of it, a rambling,

5   old-fashioned, half-timbered building, which, before the town had spread, had been a farmhouse, but was now surrounded with the private gardens of the townsmen. We get the fonder of our houses if they

10   have a physiognomy of their own, as our friends have. The Garth family, which was rather a large one, for Mary had four brothers and one sister, were very fond of their old house, from which all the best

15   furniture had long been sold. Fred liked it, too, knowing it by heart even to the attic which smelt deliciously of apples and quinces, and until today he had never come to it without pleasant expectation; but his

20   heart beat uneasily now with the sense that he should probably have to make his confession before Mrs. Garth, of whom he was rather more in awe than of her husband. Not that she was inclined to

25   sarcasm and to impulsive sallies, as Mary was. In her present matronly age, at least, Mrs. Garth never committed herself by over-hasty speech; having as she said, borne the yoke in her youth, and learned self-

30   control. She had that rare sense which discerns what is inalterable, and submits to it without murmuring. Adoring her husband's virtues, she had very early made up her mind to his incapacity of minding his

35   own interests, and had met the consequences cheerfully. She had been magnanimous enough to renounce all pride in teapots or children's frilling, and had never poured any pathetic confidences into the

40   ears of her feminine neighbors concerning Mr. Garth's want of prudence and the sums he might have had if he had been like other men. Hence these fair neighbors thought her either proud or eccentric, and some-

45   times spoke of her to their husbands as "your fine Mrs. Garth." She was not without her criticism of them in return, being more accurately instructed than most matrons in Middlemarch, and – "where is

50   the blameless woman?"— apt to be a little severe toward her own sex, which in her opinion was framed to be entirely subordinate. On the other hand, she was disproportionately indulgent toward the failings of

55   men, and was often heard to say that these were natural.

    Also, it must be admitted that Mrs. Garth was a trifle too emphatic in her resistance to what she held to be follies:

60   The passage from governess into housewife had wrought itself a little too strongly into her consciousness, and she rarely forgot that while her grammar and accent were above the town standard, she wore a plain

65   cap, cooked the family dinner, and darned all the stockings. She had sometimes taken pupils in a peripatetic fashion, making them follow her about in the kitchen with their book or slate. She thought it good for them

70   to see that she could make an excellent lather while she corrected their blunders "without looking"—that a woman with her

sleeves tucked up above her elbows might
know all about the Subjunctive Mood or
75 the Torrid Zone—that, in short, she might
possess "education" and other good things
ending in "tion," and worthy to be
pronounced emphatically, without being a
useless doll. When she made remarks to
80 this edifying effect, she had a firm little
frown on her brow, which yet did not
hinder her face from looking benevolent,
and her words, which came forth like a
procession were uttered in a fervid
85 agreeable contralto. Certainly, the exem-
plary Mrs. Garth had her droll aspects, but
her character sustained her oddities, as a
very fine wine sustains a flavor of skin.
Toward Fred Vincy she had a moth-
90 erly feeling, and had always been disposed
to excuse his errors, though she would
probably not have excused Mary for
engaging herself to him, her daughter being
included in that more rigorous judgment
95 which she applied to her own sex. But this
very fact of her exceptional indulgence
toward him made it the harder to Fred that
he must now inevitably sink in her opinion.
And the circumstances of his visit turned
100 out to be still more unpleasant than he had
expected; for Caleb Garth had gone out
early to look at some repairs not far off.

1. Mrs. Garth takes pride in her

A. education and practical usefulness
B. home and self-control
C. droll humor
D. business sense

2. Fred apparently

I. is engaged to Mary.
II. dreads this visit to the Garths.
III. fears and respects Mrs. Garth more
than he does Mr. Garth.

F. I and II
G. II and III
H. I, II, and III
J. I and III

3. The purpose of the first paragraph of
this passage is best described as

A. detailing the nature of Fred's visit
B. allowing the reader a glimpse of
the family
C. portraying Mrs. Garth's views on
education
D. establishing the character of Mrs.
Garth

4. The author states that Mrs. Garth's
character "sustained her oddities, as a
very fine wine sustains a flavor of
skin." This comparison tells the reader
that

F. Mrs. Garth's character was marred
by her eccentricities
G. oddities improve both wine and
people
H. Mrs. Garth's oddities were perceptible but not overpowering
J. nothing is perfect

5. The word *peripatetic*, as used in the
passage, means

A. housewifely; domestic
B. dictatorial
C. presenting a good example
D. instructing while walking about

6. Mrs. Garth would agree that her
attitude toward her husband was

F. confident
G. realistic
H. impulsive
J. pathetic

7. Which of the following does not
describe Mrs. Garth?

A. self-controlled
B. indulgent toward men
C. critical of women
D. frivolous

8. The passage suggests that Mr. Garth is

    F.   unwise in business dealings

    G.   more stern than Mrs. Garth

    H.   lacking virtue

    J.   critical of his neighbors

9. Fred preferred to "confess" to Mr. Garth rather than Mrs. Garth because

    A.   Mrs. Garth, a gossip, would tell Mary

    B.   Mr. Garth was not intelligent enough to understand Fred's offense

    C.   Fred didn't want Mrs. Garth to think less of him

    D.   Mr. Garth could not mind his own interests

10. The passage states that "all the best furniture had long been sold." The reader can infer that this was done

    F.   to assist Mrs. Garth in redecorating

    G.   to clear out space in the attic

    H.   to keep the neighbors from realizing the extent of the Garths' wealth

    J.   to supplement the family's income

Passage II

Line By the 1890s Cuba and the nearby island of Puerto Rico comprised nearly all that remained of Spain's once vast empire in the New World. Several times Cuban insurgents
5 had rebelled against Spanish rule, but they had failed to free their country. As discontent with Spanish rule heightened, in late February 1895 revolt again broke out.

    Cuban insurgents established a junta
10 in New York City to raise money, purchase weapons, and wage a propaganda war to sway American public opinion. Conditions in Cuba were grim. The insurgents engaged in a hit-and-run, scorched-earth policy to
15 force the Spanish to leave while the Spanish commander tried to corner the rebels in the eastern end of the island and destroy them.

    After initial failures, Spain in January
20 1896 sent General Weyler to Cuba. Relentless and brutal, Weyler gave the rebels ten days to lay down their arms. He then put into effect a "reconcentration" policy designed to move the native
25 population into camps and liquidate the rebels' popular base. Herded into fortified areas, Cubans died by the thousands— victims of unsanitary conditions, over-crowding, and disease.
30   There was a wave of compassion for the insurgents stimulated by the American newspapers. The so-called yellow press printed lurid stories of Spanish atrocities. But yellow journalism did not cause the
35 war. It stemmed from larger conflicts in policies and perceptions between Spain and the United States. Throughout his presidency, Grover Cleveland counseled neutrality, and initially President McKinley,
40 who came into office in March 1897, did the same. But McKinley tilted more toward the insurgents. Before the end of 1897, the new president was criticizing Spain's "uncivilized and inhuman" conduct. The
45 United States, he made clear, did not contest Spain's right to fight the rebellion but insisted it be done within humane limits.

    Late in 1897 a change in government
50 in Madrid brought a temporary lull in the crisis. The new government recalled Weyler and agreed to offer the Cubans some form of autonomy. The new initiatives pleased McKinley, though he again warned Spain
55 that it must find a humane end to the rebellion. Then in January 1898 Spanish army officers led riots in Havana against the new autonomy policy and shook the president's confidence in Madrid's control
60 over conditions in Cuba.

    McKinley ordered the battleship *Maine* to Havana to "show the flag" and to evacuate American citizens if necessary. On February 9, 1898, the *New York Journal*
65 published a private letter stolen from de Lome, the Spanish ambassador in Washington. McKinley was worried about sections

of the letter, which revealed Spanish insincerity in the negotiations. De Lome
70 immediately resigned and went home, but the damage was done.

A few days later, on February 15, when an explosion tore through the hull of the *Maine,* sinking the ship and killing 266
75 sailors, Americans suspected that Spain was responsible. McKinley cautioned patience, but Americans cried for war.

In early March 1898, McKinley asked Congress for $50 million in emergency
80 defense appropriations, a request Congress promptly approved. On March 27 McKinley cabled Spain his final terms. He asked Spain to declare an armistice, end the reconcentration policy, and—implicitly—move
85 toward Cuban independence. The Spanish answer conceded some things, but not, in McKinley's judgment, the important ones. It made no mention of a true armistice, McKinley's offer to mediate, or Cuba's
90 independence.

Reluctantly McKinley prepared his war message, which Congress heard on April 11, 1898. On April 19 Congress passed a joint resolution declaring Cuba
95 independent and authorizing the president to use the army and navy to expel the Spanish from Cuba. An amendment . . . pledged that the United States had no intention of annexing the island. On April
100 25 Congress passed a declaration of war, and late that afternoon McKinley signed it.

Some historians have suggested that McKinley was weak and indecisive in confronting the war hysteria in the country;
105 others have called him a wily manipulator for war and imperial gains. In truth he was neither. Throughout the Spanish crisis McKinley pursued a moderate middle course that sought to protect American
110 interests, promote Cuba's independence, and allow Spain time to adjust to the loss of the remnant of empire.

11. The word *insurgents*, as used in the passage, means

  A. natives
  B. rebels
  C. militia
  D. reconcentrationists

12. The insurgents opposed the

  F. junta
  G. United States
  H. Cubans
  J. Spanish

13. The primary purpose of reconcentration as described in paragraph 3 was

  A. to reduce the size of rebel forces
  B. to relocate the native Cubans
  C. to cause disease among the rebels
  D. to carry out the scorched earth policy

14. Yellow journalism refers to the newspapers'

  F. cowardliness
  G. causing conflicts in policies
  H. compassion
  J. use of sensationalism

15. Events discussed in the selection include evidence of which of the following?

  I. dishonesty
  II. assumption
  III. diplomacy

  A. I and II
  B. II and III
  C. I and III
  D. I, II, and III

16. The passage states that "in January 1898 Spanish army officers led riots in Havana against the new autonomy policy and shook the president's confidence in Madrid's control over conditions in Cuba." Which one of the following statements, according to the quotation, is correct?

   F. The Spanish president lost confidence in autonomy in Cuba.

   G. The American president doubted Spain's control of Cuba.

   H. Spanish army officers lost confidence in conditions in Cuba.

   J. The autonomy policy was not worthy of confidence.

17. Which of the following events is *not* an example of an underlying conflict that eventually led to war?

   A. McKinley's confidence in the 1897 Madrid government slipped.

   B. McKinley made certain requests of Spain on March 27, 1898.

   C. McKinley learned of Spanish duplicity in negotiations.

   D. The new government recalled Weyler.

18. The author believes that the war resulted primarily because

   F. McKinley was weak and indecisive

   G. McKinley manipulated for war

   H. Spanish and American national interests conflicted

   J. yellow journalism caused larger conflicts

19. It can be inferred that at the time of events described, the feelings of the United States government toward Cuba were

   A. protective

   B. imperialistic

   C. laissez-faire

   D. suspicious

20. The purpose of the passage as a whole is to

   F. exonerate McKinley

   G. analyze United States public opinion

   H. establish blame for the war

   J. present circumstances that led to war

Passage III

Line The early Greek philosophers were very interested in the nature of the universe. In particular, they were interested in the source from which all things come. Thales

5 of Miletus posed the first solution in about 600 B.C. The transformation of water from ice to water to steam convinced him that the original "stuff" was water. He proposed everything from rocks to air originated as

10 and returned to water. Anaximander then suggested that a space filling living mass rather than water was the original "stuff." Anaximander referred to the mass as the "infinite" and taught that it was whole

15 rather than broken into pieces. Thales of Miletus proposed that this matter contained motion, which caused it to begin to move in all directions. Slowly pieces were broken off, due to the motion; subsequently, all

20 things in the universe were formed by the broken-off pieces. Anaximander believed that all the pieces would eventually be reunited, thus re-forming the infinite.

     The explanations of these two

25 thinkers did not satisfy Anaximines, who suggested that everything in the universe was made up of air. He observed that humans and animals needed to breathe in

order to live. He postulated that the air was
30 turned into flesh, blood, and bone. He
concluded that air could also become wind,
water, earth, and stone.

After these philosophers tried to
discover what the "stuff" was that made up
35 the universe, a group of philosophers
known as Pythagoreans raised the question
of how the many things in the universe
were related. The Pythagoreans were led by
Pythagoras and were impressed by the fact
40 that many things in the universe were
related in ways that could be stated by
numbers. The Pythagoreans, therefore,
reasoned that the "stuff" which the earlier
philosophers were looking for was in fact
45 numbers. The Pythagoreans taught that the
whole universe was built on numbers and
developed a complex system explaining
how everything was made of numbers.

Heraclitus did not believe Pythagoras's
50 explanation; he believed that fire was the
original "stuff." He based this belief on his
theory that fire, like everything else in the
universe, was constantly changing. Not all
of his contemporaries believed that the
55 world was constantly changing. Xenophanes believed that the universe was a
solid mass which was forever unchange-
able. He believed that although parts might
change, the whole could never change. In
60 an attempt to reconcile these different
philosophies, Empedocles proposed a
compromise. Empedocles admitted that in
the strict sense there could be no change—
that is, nothing could be created or
65 destroyed. He also believed that there was
mingling and separation. He proposed that
the universe was composed of four
elements: earth, air, fire, and water.
Empedocles went on to propose that there
70 were millions and millions of tiny particles
of each element that combined in various
ways to form everything in the universe.
These elements might combine to form
new things or separate to change as when
75 things decayed. The elements were
permanent and never changed but they
mingled and separated to give the appearance of change.

21. Which of the following titles best
describes the content of the passage?

A. "The Development of Scientific
Thought in Early Greece"
B. "Greek Thought from Thales of
Miletus to Empedocles"
C. "Early Greek Thought on the
Meaning of the Universe"
D. "The 'Stuff' the Universe Is Made
Of"

22. Thales of Miletus taught that everything
came from

F. water
G. ice
H. steam
J. fire

23. Anaximander disagreed with Thales of
Miletus in that he taught

A. everything came from fire not
water
B. numbers had no meaning
C. the "infinite" was a whole rather
than consisting of pieces
D. ice was different from water

24. Anaximines's explanation of the nature
of the universe was most closely related
to that of

F. Anaximander
G. Thales of Miletus
H. Pythagoras
J. Xenophanes

25. The Pythagoreans

A. were contemporaries of Thales of
Miletus
B. came after Heraclitus
C. came after Anaximander
D. preceded Thales of Miletus

26. Pythagoreans differed from their predecessors in that they

   F. were concerned with how things were related

   G. wanted to understand the nature of the universe

   H. thought the universe was made of many elements

   J. thought everything was made of air

27. The definition of *xenophobia* is fear and hatred of strangers or foreigners; it probably had its origin in Xenophanes's belief that

   A. everything came from water

   B. everything came from air

   C. numbers explained how things were related

   D. change was impossible

28. Empedocles may be said to have contributed

   F. bringing compromise to philosophy

   G. the concept of elements

   H. the idea that change is impossible

   J. the concept of mingling

29. In developing an understanding of the meaning of the universe, the early Greek philosophers' most fundamental disagreement was about

   A. what the original ''stuff'' was

   B. the meaning of numbers

   C. the importance of motion

   D. whether change was possible

30. Which pair of philosophers had the most contradictory teachings?

   F. Thales of Miletus and Xenophanes

   G. Thales of Miletus and Anaximines

   H. Heraclitus and Thales of Miletus

   J. Pythagoras and Thales of Miletus

Passage IV

Line

I was with my wife, Wendy, on a visit to seven of Costa Rica's national parks and nature reserves. This was our first stop, Monteverde Cloud Forest Reserve, and
5 already we had learned an important lesson. To see something interesting in this naturalist's paradise of a country, all we had to do was sit down and wait. Something was sure to come by, and it was likely to
10 be something new and wonderful. Names tell the story: quetzals, iguanas, and howler monkeys; sloths, scarlet macaws, and green parrots; yellow toucans, anteaters, roseate spoonbills, giant turtles, and more. End-
15 lessly more.

    A country slightly smaller than West Virginia, Costa Rica is blessed with political stability and natural beauty. It lacks an army, but claims more than 830 species of
20 birds living in a wide range of habitats— from volcanic summit to white-sand beach, from coral reef to rain forest. A large portion of its land, an amazing 25 percent, has been set aside in one of the world's
25 best systems of reserves and national parks, some thirty-five in all. And because the country averages only 150 miles across and 200 miles long, it's easy to get from one place to another.

30   For example, Monteverde is less than 100 miles from Costa Rica's capital, San José. We drove there—through the temperate central valley down into hot, dry country along the Pacific coast, and then
35 up to misty forest—in one morning.

    Monteverde (Spanish for ''green mountain'') was set aside by a group of United States Quakers who, attracted by Costa Rica's nonmilitary convictions, settled
40 there in the early 1950s. They cleared some of the native forest for pastures in order to establish a dairy cooperative, an act that they balanced by designating 1,200 acres as a reserve. The reserve has grown to more
45 than 22,000 acres, encompassing some 500 species of trees, 200 kinds of ferns, 300 different orchids, and a wealth of other living things. It is a prime sample of tropical cloud forest, named for its ability
50 to derive moisture not only from rain but

also from the misty touch of clouds, which almost always blanket the area. Administered by a private Cost Rican organization, the Tropical Science Center, Monteverde is
55 world-famous and well served by informal lodges and pensions along its border. Biologists come here to study, and people like us come to walk the trails and learn what we can of the forest. On our first
60 morning, Wendy and I took a walk with an American biology student, Linda Lehman, who, in return for room and board at the reserve's field station, was volunteering as a naturalist.

65   Entering the trees felt like going underwater, sinking beneath the shimmering surface into a new and alien world. Trails bored like tunnels through an apparently undecipherable tumult of
70 vegetation. But gradually, with Linda's help, we began to see a sort of order—an order defined by the need for sunlight. Great trees had muscled their way skyward, blocking the sun from the forest floor. In
75 their shade, ground-level plants had survived by growing huge leaves, often several feet in diameter, to collect what light they could. We came to a single tree with a cluster of substantial trunks: a
80 strangler fig. Starting as a seedling in the canopy, the fig had dropped shoots that took root in the forest floor and then gradually enveloped and choked their host. The original tree, having served as a ladder
85 to the soil, had long since disappeared.

    The relationships of plants and animals weave into the complex fabric of the forest like the vines. Start with any fact, follow any thread of knowledge, and
90 eventually it will take you through every niche of the forest. Why do trees grow buttresses? Perhaps for structural support in the thin soil. Why is the soil thin? Most likely because it has been leached by
95 millennia of rains. Nutrients are taken up so quickly by living things that a fallen leaf can be recycled in a week. I began to think of the forest as an organism itself, growing at a fantastic pace.

31. When, in paragraph 1, the author states that "names tell the story," he means that

A. names of Monteverde's animals are unusual
B. there are more giant turtles than other animals in Monteverde
C. Monteverde is a cloud forest
D. Monteverde has many kinds of animals

32. The main idea of paragraph 2 can be best stated as

F. Costa Rica offers several advantages to naturalists
G. Political stability increases Costa Rica's desirability to naturalists
H. Costa Rica, though small, has great biological diversity
J. The proximity of preserve areas to one another makes Costa Rica an ideal study area to naturalists

33. The author's purpose in paragraph 3 is

A. to establish the fact that the capital is close to Monteverde
B. to provide examples of climate differences in Costa Rica
C. to provide an example supporting ease of getting from place to place
D. to support the author's statement that there is a wide range of habitats

34. It can be inferred that

   F. Monteverde is currently a dairy cooperative

   G. United States Quakers helped establish Costa Rica's nonmilitary convictions

   H. the establishment of a dairy cooperative was not environmentally motivated

   J. the reserve has grown in size since its establishment

35. What is the author's attitude toward Costa Rica's preserves?

   A. strongly favorable

   B. favorable, with reservations

   C. neutral

   D. unimpressed

36. The author is probably a

   F. Quaker living in Costa Rica

   G. visitor to Costa Rica

   H. biologist working in Costa Rica

   J. climatologist

37. The author states that one sort of order in the Monteverde Cloud Forest occurs because of a need for

   A. sunlight

   B. niches

   C. tumult

   D. recycling

38. A strangler fig apparently

   I. originates in the canopy.

   II. supports its own weight when the host tree disappears.

   III. is a parasitic plant.

   F. I only

   G. II and III

   H. I and II

   J. I, II, and III

39. Which statement is not true of the strangler fig?

   A. It uses the host tree to reach the ground.

   B. It is a ladder to the soil.

   C. It has a cluster of trunks.

   D. It sends out shoots.

40. The best title for the selection as a whole is

   F. "Costa Rica, a Biologist's Paradise"

   G. "Biological Diversity in Monteverde"

   H. "Monteverde Cloud Forest"

   J. "A Visit to Costa Rica"

Pretest — Part 4

There are seven passages in this test. Each passage is followed by several questions. After reading a passage, choose the best answer to each question and fill in the corresponding oval on your answer document. You may refer to the passages as often as necessary.

Passage I

An experiment is performed in which the Pressure (P), Volume (V), and Temperature (T) of a gas are measured. All measurements are taken on the same gas sample. The results are summarized in Table I, Table II, and Table III, below.

Table I

P in N/m^2	V in m^3	T in °K
10.0	20.0	300
20.0	10.0	300
40.0	5.0	300
80.0	2.5	300

Table II

P in N/m^2	V in m^3	T in °K
50.0	1.0	75
50.0	2.0	150
50.0	4.0	300
50.0	6.0	450

Table III

P in N/m^2	V in m^3	T in °K
100.0	1.0	150
200.0	1.0	300
300.0	1.0	450
400.0	1.0	600

1. Based on the information in Table I, one could conclude that the pressure of a gas whose volume is 40.0 m^3 and temperature is 300°K would be

   A. 5.0 N/m^2
   B. 10.0 N/m^2
   C. 30.0 N/m^2
   D. 100.0 N/m^2

2. According to the data presented in Tables I, II, and III, what can be concluded concerning the relationship among the pressure, volume, and temperature of this gas?

   F. At constant temperature, the pressure and volume are directly proportional.
   G. At constant pressure, the volume and temperature are directly proportional.
   H. At constant volume, the pressure and temperature are inversely proportional.
   J. At constant pressure, the volume and temperature are inversely proportional.

3. According to the tables, which values of pressure and volume would result in this gas having the lowest temperature?

   A. P = 20 N/m^2 V= 10.0 m^3
   B. P = 40 N/m^2 V= 5.0 m^3
   C. P = 50 N/m^2 V= 3.0 m^3
   D. P = 200 N/m^2 V= 1.0 m^3

4. From the information provided, one can conclude that as the temperature of this gas increases, then

  F. the volume of the gas must increase
  G. the pressure of the gas must increase
  H. the pressure times the volume must increase
  J. the pressure increases while the volume decreases

5. An investigation concludes that the pressure, volume, and temperature of this gas may be expressed in a single equation. Which equation is best justified by the information provided?

  A. PVT = constant
  B. VT/P = constant
  C. PV/T = constant
  D. PT/V = constant

6. Which graph best illustrates the relationship between pressure and volume at constant temperature?

  F.
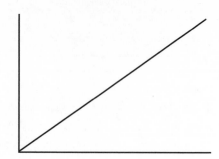

  G.
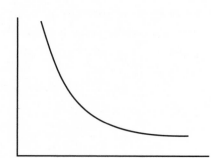

  H.
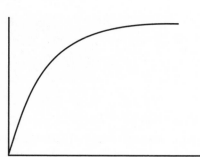

  J.
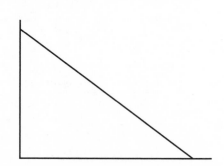

Passage II

Below is a discharge hydrograph for the Red Cedar River at East Lansing, Michigan, for the April 1975 flood. The stage of a river is the depth of the water in the river channel.

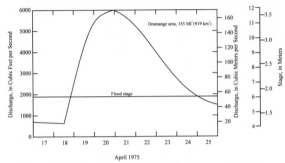

Discharge hydrograph for the Red Cedar River at East Lansing for the April 1975 flood.

Below is the flood frequency graph for the Red Cedar River at East Lansing, Michigan. The frequency of a flood may be expressed in terms of recurrence interval or probability of occurrence. Recurrence interval is the average interval of time within which a flood of a given magnitude will be equaled or exceeded once. Probability of occurrence is the inverse of recurrence interval.

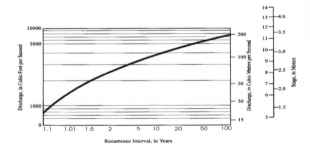

7. What is the peak discharge for the Red Cedar River during the April 1975 flood?

    A.   700 cubic feet per second
    B.   1,900 cubic feet per second
    C.   5,000 cubic feet per second
    D.   5,900 cubic feet per second

8. How many feet above flood stage was the Red Cedar River at the point of maximum discharge?

    F.   5 feet
    G.   7 feet
    H.   10 feet
    J.   12 feet

9. On what day did the Red Cedar River reach its maximum discharge?

    A.   April 18
    B.   April 19
    C.   April 20
    D.   April 24

10. Approximately how many days was the Red Cedar River above flood stage?

    F.   1 day
    G.   2 days
    H.   6 days
    J.   9 days

11. What is the recurrence interval for the April 1975 flood on the Red Cedar River at East Lansing, Michigan?

    A.   10 years
    B.   20 years
    C.   40 years
    D.   70 years

12. What would be the peak discharge in cubic feet per second for a flood with a recurrence interval of 100 years?

    F.   700 cubic feet per second
    G.   4,000 cubic feet per second
    H.   6,000 cubic feet per second
    J.   7,800 cubic feet per second

Passage III

In a chemistry experiment, 0.1 M NaOH was titrated against 25.0 mL of hydrochloric acid. The pH was recorded after each 5 mL portion of the base was added.

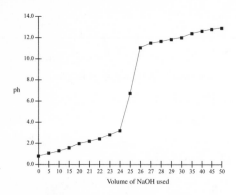

Volume of NaOH used

Volume of NaOH added	pH
0	1.00
5	1.18
10	1.37
15	1.60
20	1.95
21	2.06
22	2.20
23	2.38
24	2.69
25	7.00
26	11.29
27	11.59
28	11.75
29	11.87
30	11.96
35	12.22
40	12.36
45	12.46
50	12.52

13. What is the concentration of the acid initially?

   A. 1.0 M
   B. 0.5 M
   C. 0.1 M
   D. 0.75 M

14. How many mL of NaOH were required to neutralize the acid?

   F. 10 mL
   G. 24 mL
   H. 25 mL
   J. 26 mL

15. The graph takes a sharp upward turn when between 24 and 26 mL of NaOH are added because

   A. the solution is almost saturated with OH^-
   B. the solution is almost saturated with H_3O^+
   C. $[H_3O^+]$ and $[OH^-]$ are almost equal
   D. $[H_3O^+]$ is in excess

16. As the number of OH^- ions increases,

   F. the H_3O^+ ion concentration increases because no new H_3O^+ ions are being introduced
   G. the H_3O^+ ion concentration increases to match the OH^- ion concentration
   H. the H_3O^+ ion concentration decreases because it is being neutralized by the OH^- ions
   J. the H_3O^+ ion concentration decreases because the pH decreases.

17. When neutralization occurs,

   A. the pH equals 7
   B. the pH equals 2.69
   C. the pH equals 11.29
   D. the pH equals 1.00

18. When 24 mL of NaOH are added,

   F. the solution is neutral
   G. the solution is acidic
   H. the solution is slightly basic
   J. the solution is extremely basic

Passage IV

Table I Average Concentration of Metabolites in Blood, Kidney Filtrate, and Urine of Healthy Individuals

Material	Blood Concentration (mM/l)	Filtrate Concentration (mM/l)	Urine Concentration (mM/l)
Urea	25	25	1805
Glucose	Varies with diet	Varies with diet	0
K+	6	6	62
Na+	144	144	126
Cl–	101	101	132

19. According to Table I, which substance is more highly concentrated in the blood than in the urine?

    A. K+
    B. Cl–
    C. Urea
    D. Na+

20. A scientist wants to examine the effects of exercise on blood and urine glucose levels in diabetics. Which of the following experiments might give her a valid comparison of specimens taken from diabetics who engage daily in treadmill exercise?

    F. Compare specimens from diabetics and nondiabetics who exercise routinely.
    G. Compare specimens from men and women of varying ages.
    H. Compare specimens from diabetics with a variety of other disease states.
    J. Compare specimens from the same individuals when they are exercising routinely with specimens collected when they are not exercising.

21. According to Table I, which substance(s) is (are) more highly concentrated in the urine than in the blood and filtrate?

    A. Glucose
    B. Urea
    C. Na+
    D. Glucose and Na+

22. Which of the following is a valid conclusion based on the data in Table I?

    F. The composition of filtrate differs from that of blood.
    G. Excess glucose is transferred to urine for excretion.
    H. Excess urea is excreted in urine.
    J. The body retains more K+ than it excretes in urine.

23. As fluid passes from the blood into the kidneys, it is called filtrate. As filtrate passes through capillaries into nephrons of the kidneys, some molecules are filtered out and returned to the blood, while others are deposited in urine for excretion. Which of the following hypotheses is supported by the data in Table I?

    A. A body in homeostasis will have equal concentrations of urea in the blood, the filtrate, and the urine.
    B. An imbalance in metabolism results in more urea in the urine than in the blood or filtrate.
    C. Excretion of wastes (urea) and excess ions (K+, Cl-) in urine help the body maintain homeostasis.
    D. Failure to excrete glucose in urine indicates advanced diabetes and a need for insulin treatment.

24. Assume the data in Table I were collected from individuals of the same age, sex, weight range, and health status. Additional data from hundreds of individuals of widely varying age, both sexes, and differing weights gave essentially the same results. It is reasonable to conclude that:

F. the first study was flawed in experimental design because it excluded men

G. age was a major factor in the outcome of test results

H. individuals in homeostasis exhibit similar levels of these materials in blood, filtrate, and urine without regard to age, sex, or weight

J. age, sex, and weight clearly need to be evaluated separately in this study

Passage V

A scientist was investigating factors contributing to the color of scales on dragons from The Lost Planet. All of these dragons have either pink or blue scales. The scientist bred pure lines of pink-scaled or blue-scaled dragons for the experiments. The results of the dragon-breeding experiments were as follows:

Experiment 1:

Dens were stocked with "Breath of Fire" mints, which were conducive to the growth and reproduction of the dragons. Two hundred pink-scaled dragons and 200 blue-scaled dragons were lured into the dens. Three out of four first-generation dragons had pink scales. The rest had blue scales. The proportion remained constant over ten generations.

Experiment 2:

Additional dens were stocked with "Breath of Fire" mints to promote dragon growth and reproduction. Pink-scaled males and blue-scaled females were lured to the dens. The first generation of dragons all had pink scales. After fifteen generations, about 25 percent of the dragons had blue scales. A single albino dragon was produced in the tenth generation.

Experiment 3:

Dens were stocked with "Breath of Fire" mints to promote dragon growth and reproduction. Only blue-scaled dragons were lured to the dens. After eight generations, only blue-scaled dragons were observed.

25. Which experiment controlled for the purity of the strain of dragon?

A. Experiment 1

B. Experiment 2

C. Experiment 3

D. There was no control.

26. How could you explain the appearance of an albino dragon in Experiment 2?

F. Pink-scaled male and and blue-scaled female dragons produce albino offspring.

G. Blue-scaled male and pink-scaled female dragons produce albino offspring.

H. The white-scaled dragon was a mutation.

J. All of the dragons carried a recessive gene for albinism.

27. Which of the following is a good control for purity of strain?

    A. pink-scaled male dragons
    B. blue-scaled female dragons
    C. blue-scaled male and female dragons
    D. blue-scaled female and pink-scaled male dragons

28. Experiment 3 alone best supports which of the following conclusions?

    F. Blue-scaled dragons are sterile.
    G. Blue-scaled dragons frequently mutate.
    H. Blue scales are dominant over pink.
    J. Pure strains of blue-scaled dragons produce blue-scaled offspring.

29. Based on these experiments, which of the following is a valid conclusion?

    A. All blue-scaled dragons are heterozygous.
    B. All pink-scaled dragons are female.
    C. Pink scales are dominant among dragons from The Lost Planet.
    D. Blue scales are dominant among dragons from The Lost Planet.

30. If, in a new experiment, blue-scaled males and pink-scaled females were paired, how would the results differ from Experiment 2?

    F. There would be no difference.
    G. There would be more mutations.
    H. All offspring would have pink scales.
    J. The proportion of pink and blue scales would be reversed.

Passage VI

Studies were conducted to determine the effects of dosage and length of time of administration of a new drug (Z10) on the development of carcinoma, cancer of the epithelial cells, in mice. The drug was administered daily for the length of time shown in Table 1.

Table I. Development of Carcinoma in Mice Treated with Drug Z10

Group	Dose Z10 (mg)	Length of Time	# Mice w/Tumors
A	0	3 mos.	0/15
A	0	6 mos.	0/15
A	0	9 mos.	0/15
B	20	3 mos.	2/15
B	20	6 mos.	5/15
B	20	9 mos.	7/15
C	40	3 mos.	3/15
C	40	6 mos.	5/15
C	40	9 mos.	8/15
D	60	3 mos.	6/15
D	60	6 mos.	12/15
D	60	9 mos.	15/15

31. According to Table I, which group served as the control group?

    A. Group A
    B. Group B
    C. Group C
    D. Group D

32. According to Table I, which groups responded essentially the same way?

    F. Groups C and D
    G. Groups B and C
    H. Groups B, C, and D
    J. Groups B and D

33. Which of the following is a valid conclusion based on the data in Table I?

   A. Drug dosage had no effect on tumor development.

   B. The number of mice developing tumors increased as the drug dosage decreased.

   C. Regardless of dosage, tumor development increased as the length of time of drug administration increased.

   D. Tumor development occurred even in the absence of Z10.

34. Assume that the data in Table I showed that the same number of mice in each group developed tumors at each of the three time points, with the number of total tumors increasing at 3, 6, and 9 months, respectively. What would be a valid conclusion based upon these results?

   F. The number of mice developing tumors increased as the drug dosage increased.

   G. The drug was not the cause of tumor development, because all of the control groups responded the same way.

   H. The number of mice developing tumors decreased as the drug dosage increased.

   J. The drug caused tumors, and regardless of dosage, the number of tumors increased with increasing time of administration.

35. Based on the data in Table I, which of the following would be a valid conclusion about the effect of length of time of drug administration on tumor development?

   A. Tumor development will occur in more mice as the length of time of drug administration increases.

   B. Tumor development will occur in fewer mice as the length of time of drug administration increases.

   C. Tumor development will occur in the same number of mice regardless of the length of time of drug administration.

   D. Length of time of drug administration has no effect on tumor development.

36. Assume that the mice in Group A developed the same number of tumors as those in Group B. Which of the following would then be a valid conclusion?

   F. Group D is the control group.

   G. Some factor other than drug dosage causes tumor development.

   H. All mice develop tumors as they age.

   J. Length of time of drug administration has no effect on tumor development.

Passage VII

Le Châtelier's Principles

In 1888, Henry Louis Le Châtelier formulated a principle governing chemical equilibrium. His principle states that if a system at equilibrium is subject to a change in conditions (concentration, temperature, or pressure), the system will change in a direction that will tend to restore a new set of equilibrium conditions. Examine the following equations, which represent a chemical reaction (at equilibrium, in a closed container). The symbol ⇔ in the equations listed below represents equilibrium (or a reversible reaction).

A. $4 HCl_{(g)} + O_{2(g)} \Leftrightarrow 2 Cl_{2(g)} + 2 H_2O_{(g)}$

B. $CO_{(g)} + H_2O_{(g)} \Leftrightarrow CO_{2(g)} + H_{2(g)}$

C. $798.2 \ kcal + 4 Al_{(s)} + 3 O_{2(g)} 2 \Leftrightarrow Al_2O_{3(g)}$

D. $N_{2(g)} + 3 H_{2(g)} \Leftrightarrow 2 NH_{3(g)} + 92.2 \ kJ$

37. In equation A above, increasing the pressure on the system will have what effect on equilibrium?

A. no effect
B. The equilibrium concentrations of both oxygen and chlorine will increase.
C. The equilibrium concentrations of both chlorine and water will increase.
D. The equilibrium concentrations of both hydrogen chloride and oxygen will increase.

38. In equation A, adding some more chlorine to the system will have what effect on equilibrium?

F. The equilibrium concentration of water will decrease and there will be no effect on either hydrogen chloride or oxygen.
G. The equilibrium concentrations of both hydrogen chloride and oxygen will increase.
H. The equilibrium concentration of hydrogen chloride will increase and the equilibrium concentration of oxygen will decrease.
J. no effect

39. In equation B, doubling the pressure will have what effect on the equilibrium concentration of carbon monoxide?

A. no effect
B. It will double.
C. It will be reduced by 50 percent.
D. It will increase.

40. In equation B, adding more carbon dioxide to the system will have what effect on equilibrium?

F. The concentrations of the other three chemicals in the reaction will increase.
G. The concentrations of both carbon monoxide and water will increase.
H. The concentration of hydrogen will increase.
J. The concentration of carbon monoxide will increase, but the concentration of water will decrease.

QUICK-SCORE ANSWERS

ANSWERS TO PRETEST

English		Mathematics		Reading		Science	
1. B	39. A	1. B	31. C	1. A	21. C	1. A	21. B
2. H	40. F	2. K	32. J	2. H	22. F	2. G	22. H
3. D	41. D	3. C	33. D	3. D	23. C	3. C	23. C
4. J	42. H	4. J	34. K	4. H	24. G	4. H	24. H
5. D	43. B	5. C	35. D	5. D	25. C	5. C	25. C
6. J	44. G	6. J	36. K	6. G	26. F	6. H	26. H
7. C	45. B	7. D	37. D	7. D	27. D	7. D	27. C
8. H	46. G	8. F	38. G	8. F	28. G	8. F	28. J
9. A	47. A	9. B	39. A	9. C	29. D	9. C	29. C
10. H	48. J	10. J	40. H	10. J	30. F	10. H	30. F
11. B	49. C	11. B	41. C	11. B	31. D	11. C	31. A
12. J	50. H	12. H	42. K	12. J	32. F	12. J	32. G
13. D	51. D	13. D	43. A	13. A	33. C	13. C	33. C
14. G	52. J	14. H	44. F	14. J	34. H	14. H	34. J
15. B	53. A	15. E	45. E	15. D	35. A	15. C	35. A
16. G	54. H	16. H	46. G	16. G	36. G	16. H	36. G
17. D	55. C	17. E	47. D	17. D	37. A	17. A	37. C
18. H	56. H	18. H	48. H	18. H	38. H	18. G	38. G
19. D	57. A	19. C	49. D	19. A	39. B	19. D	39. A
20. G	58. G	20. F	50. F	20. J	40. H	20. J	40. G
21. B	59. A	21. B	51. C				
22. F	60. J	22. G	52. K				
23. B	61. D	23. D	53. B				
24. H	62. F	24. K	54. J				
25. C	63. B	25. E	55. C				
26. G	64. J	26. F	56. G				
27. C	65. D	27. A	57. B				
28. H	66. G	28. H	58. F				
29. D	67. A	29. E	59. B				
30. H	68. G	30. J	60. F				
31. C	69. D						
32. G	70. H						
33. B	71. A						
34. H	72. G						
35. C	73. A						
36. J	74. H						
37. A	75. A						
38. J							

EXPLANATORY ANSWERS TO THE PRETEST

PART 1   ENGLISH

1. **B**   The past perfect requires the idea of action completed in the past. This action occurred in the past and continues to occur in our own time, and so requires the present perfect tense. "Has made" parallels "has found" later in the sentence.

2. **H**   "Every" is a singular concept and the antecedent is "age"; therefore, "its" is appropriate.

3. **D**   This corrects the dangling participle. There was nothing for "Flung" to modify.

4. **J**   "Accept" is a mental and emotional verb and, therefore, "the idea of death" is appropriate. It also avoids a certain redundancy found in the other answers.

5. **D**   This makes the impossibly awkward constructions of the other alternatives clearer with fewer words.

6. **J**   This makes the connection between the two ideas even clearer.

7. **C**   The present perfect here puts Polonius's death clearly after the other event. Answer (D) turns it into a dangling participle.

8. **H**   This avoids the possibility of confusing "his" with Polonius. The next sentence makes it clear that Queen Gertrude is Hamlet's mother.

9. **A**   The alternatives create dangling participles.

10. **H**   The three absolute clauses ("Ophelia goes mad," "Laertes leads a small rebellion," and "Claudius himself has to hang on") constitute a series; therefore, "and" is needed before the last clause.

11. **B**   This avoids the wordy shift in point of view, "we see" and starts a new section of the argument.

12. **J**   This eliminates wordiness and the unnecessary use of "you."

13. **D**   This is more natural; the others are inaccurate or awkward.

14. **G**   In this complex sentence it is important to clarify the relation of the verbs to each other and to their subjects. Answer (G) accomplishes both of these tasks.

15. **B**   This is the only answer that makes sense in the context of the paragraph.

16. **G**   This keeps the extended parallelism clear. Parallelism refers to similarity of structure.

17. **D**   It is better to make sure the reference is clear.

18. **H**   The context suggests that this sentence contains an example of the "collaboration of many hands and periods" mentioned in the first paragraph.

19. **D**   This is an elaborate series with each major part separated by a semicolon. The second and third items have self-contained commas and require semicolons to distinguish them.

20. G This continues the punctuation of the series.

21. B This is idiomatic, which means peculiar to the language or dialect. "A spidery complexity" is typical of that period, but the terms can't be reversed.

22. F "Different than" is used very rarely, the others not at all.

23. B This avoids the fragment and the wordiness of the original. "Likewise" is not needed, and "was showing" makes no sense. A sentence fragment lacks a complete subject or predicate.

24. H All the elements work together at all times, not "when" and "if" they work together.

25. C This is an exact word to describe space that is not merely length, but length, height, and width combined.

26. G It is better to have "in" follow "let" because it is part of the verb.

27. C It is clear from the context that the glassmakers did this, and (C) tells us they inserted the windows only after the architect had finished.

28. H This past perfect tense tells us that the architect achieved his aims before the glassmakers inserted the glass. None of the other alternatives indicates that the architect succeeded.

29. D This is the proper punctuation in a series—a comma between the first and second items.

30. H This completes the construction started by "So complex."

31. C "This" is a vague reference referring to any number of items in the previous sentence. "Balance" is the specific word needed.

32. G "Much" is a singular idea ("a large part") requiring a singular verb. "Attests" is the right verb, often used in archaeology.

33. B The original breaks the parallelism of nouns. This alternative is as specific as the others and is the subject of a whole subsequent paragraph.

34. H A cult does not triumph over another god, but over another god's cult.

35. C This eliminates wordiness and makes good sense.

36. J This brings it into line with the other participles in this parallel construction.

37. A The topic sentence of this paragraph indicated that the freize sculpture would be included; therefore, no new paragraph should begin here.

38. J A word that draws all the ideas of the long paragraph together into this concluding sentence is needed. Answer (J) is simplest and easiest. A comma after "worshippers" closes out the parenthetical material.

39. A "Olympia's" is the equivalent of "Parthenon's." The rest are inaccurate or wordy.

40. F The other choices create problems with sentence structure.

41. D This is a present perfect subjunctive in the passive voice. The subjunctive indicates contrary to fact (the two temples never stood side by side) and with "ever," indicates a kind of condition. The present perfect indicates that sometime during the past they might have placed the two temples together.

42. **H** The sentence subsequently mentions two different motifs.

43. **B** "As" introduces clauses; "like" introduces prepositional phrases.

44. **G** This maintains the parallelism started with "lean" and "are." The subject of the clause need not be repeated.

45. **B** This best expresses the conclusive tone of the selection.

46. **G** The subject of the verb is "watching," which requires the singular "was."

47. **A** "Plucked from the water with a crane" is a participal phrase, so it is set off by commas.

48. **J** A dependent clause is followed by a comma; it's means "it is."

49. **C** "Although" is the most logical connective for this sentence.

50. **H** The other choices are redundant or ungrammatical.

51. **D** All the other choices provide no logical word for "Huddled in the grandstand" to modify.

52. **J** Sentence 2 is the most logical concluding sentence for the paragraph; it sums up the other sentences.

53. **A** "Sense" is the subject, so a singular verb is needed.

54. **H** A dependent clause that begins a sentence is followed by a comma.

55. **C** All sentences in support of one idea should be in the same paragraph.

56. **H** When quoting speech, terminal punctuation always goes inside the quotation marks.

57. **A** The spectators are being quoted; their speech would be informal and colloquial.

58. **G** Maintain parallelism of similar grammatical elements.

59. **A** The other choices are inappropriate clichés.

60. **J** That is the point when the spectators can see the shuttle.

61. **D** This is the most direct and least redundant choice.

62. **F** Clauses in a series may be separated by commas.

63. **B** "Each" is the subject of the verb. It is an indefinite pronoun that requires a singular verb.

64. **J** The other choices are redundant or illogical.

65. **D** This phrase is the most specific, and it unifies this paragraph and paragraph 1.

66. **G** This is the correct comparative form of "friendly."

67. **A** Do not use a comma before parentheses. A comma is required after the parentheses in this sentence because it concludes a dependent clause.

68. **G** The author should not add the sentence because it disrupts the paragraph's unity. It is not relevant.

69. **D** The other choices result in a dangling or misplaced modifier.

70. **H** This word has the most appropriate connotations for the context.

71. **A** In this sentence, "smell" is a linking verb, so it is followed by an adjective.

72. G This response best corrects the sentence fragment error.

73. A Items in a series are joined by commas. The comma is needed after the series because it is the conclusion of an introductory prepositional phrase.

74. H The "I" in this essay doesn't realize that the essay's content makes them ironic.

75. A Putting sentence 4 last unifies the introduction and conclusion, and it stresses the irony in the previous sentence.

PART 2   MATHEMATICS

---

1. B When comparing fractions, use two rules: If fractions have the same numerator, the fraction with the smallest denominator is the larger number. If fractions have the same denominator, the fraction with the largest numerator is the larger number.

$$\frac{3}{11} < \frac{4}{11} \qquad \frac{4}{11} > \frac{4}{13} \qquad \frac{5}{12} > \frac{5}{13}$$

Now compare $\frac{4}{11}$ and $\frac{5}{12}$. Find the common denominator = 132.

$$\frac{(4)(12)}{(11)(12)} \qquad \frac{(5)(11)}{(12)(11)}$$

$$\frac{48}{132} < \frac{55}{132}$$

2. K $A = \pi r^2$

$$16\pi = \pi r^2$$
$$16 = r^2$$
$$4 = r$$

$$D = 2r$$
$$= (2)(4)$$
$$= 8$$

3. C 180

To find an average of a set of scores, add the scores and divide the sum by the number of scores.

$$\begin{array}{r} 175 \\ 155 \\ \underline{210} \\ 540 \end{array}$$

$$\begin{array}{r} 180 \\ 3\overline{)540} \end{array}$$

4. J Let

$$x = \text{first angle}$$
$$90 - x = \text{complement of first angle}$$

Difference:

$$x - (90 - x) = 50$$
$$x - 90 + x = 50$$
$$2x - 90 = 50$$
$$2x = 140$$
$$x = 70 \text{ first angle}$$
$$90 - x = 20 \text{ complement}$$

5. C $\dfrac{-40D^2E^5}{-5DE^2}$

$= \left(\dfrac{-40}{-5}\right)\left(\dfrac{D^2}{D}\right)\left(\dfrac{E^5}{E^2}\right) = 8DE^3$

Note: $D = D^1$ (subtract exponents in denominator from exponents in numerator)

6. J   1. Write down as many digits of the given decimal as required and drop the other digits.

2. Starting from the left and going to the right, if the first digit dropped is 4 or less, the number obtained in the first step is correct. If the first digit dropped is 5 or more, increase by one the last digit in the number obtained in step one.

46.97
46.9 to nearest tenth, 7 was dropped > 5; increase by 1.

46.9 +.1

46.9
+ .1
47.0

7. D $6,285
First find the amount of interest.

$I = P \cdot R \cdot T$
$ = \$6,000 \times .0475 \times 1 = \$285$

Then add the amount of interest to the original investment.

$\$6,000 + \$285 = \$6,285$

8. F   The product of the means equals the product of the extremes.

$$\dfrac{d-4}{d} = \dfrac{5}{6}$$

$6(d - 4) = 5d$
$6d - 24 = 5d$
$\underline{-5d + 24 = -5d + 24}$ (additive
$d = 24 $ inverse)

9. B   1,554

The students over 25 would include those in categories C and D.

25% + 12% = 37%

Then find 37% of 4,200.

$4,200 × .37 = 1,554

10. J   Consecutive angles of a parallelogram are supplementary. Hence

$x + x + 20 = 180$
$2x + 20 = 180$
$2x = 160$
$x = 80$

11. B $2,250

Here again, we must find the base.

$B = \dfrac{P}{R}$

$ = \dfrac{135}{.06} = \$2,250$

12. H $\dfrac{c-2b}{2}$

To solve literal equations, use the usual equation-solving techniques.

$2a + 2b = c$
$ -2b = -2b$
$\dfrac{2a}{2} = \dfrac{c-2b}{2}$

$a = \dfrac{c-2b}{2}$

13. D Mr. Smythe can go in any of seven ways, but once a road is chosen there are only 6 roads to return by.

$6 \cdot 7 = 42$

14. H 450

When dividing decimals, be careful of the decimal points.

$$
\begin{array}{r}
450. \\
.04\overline{)18.00.} \\
\underline{16} \\
20 \\
\underline{20} \\
0
\end{array}
$$

15. E 28

Follow the correct order of operations.

$(-4)^2 - 3(-4)$
$= 16 - (-12)$
$= 28$

16. H In a right triangle, the sum of the squares of the legs equals the square of the hypotenuse:

$a^2 + 5^2 = 6^2$
$a^2 + 25 = 36$
$a^2 = 11$

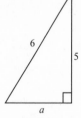

Take the square root of
$a^2 \rightarrow a = \sqrt{11} \leftarrow$ square root of 11

17. E First find variable expressions to represent the three consecutive odd integers. Let n be the first odd integer. Then $n + 2$ is the second integer, and $n + 4$ is the third.

Now translate ". . . whose sum is −45" into an equation.

$n + (n + 2) + (n + 4) = -45$

Then solve the equation.

$$
\begin{array}{rl}
3n + 6 &= -45 \\
-6 &= -6 \\
\hline
\dfrac{3}{3}n &= -\dfrac{51}{3} \\
n &= -17
\end{array}
$$

Finally, find the other two odd integers and check.

$n + 2 = (-17) + 2 = -15$
$n + 4 = (-17) + 4 = -13$

Check:

$(-17) + (-15) + (-13) = -45$

It would have been easier to answer this question by eliminating the solutions given. Answers (B), (C), and (D) could have been eliminated since none of these answers is three consecutive odd integers. Then by adding the integers in Answer (A), we can eliminate this possibility. This procedure of eliminating impossible solutions is an extremely important test-taking skill.

18. H By the Pythagorean theorem, $a^2 + b^2 = c^2$.

To find $RU \rightarrow (RU)^2 + (3)^2 = 5^2$

$a^2 + 9 = 25$
$a^2 = 16$
$a = 4$
$RU = 4$

The area of the trapezoid is:

$A = \dfrac{1}{2}h(b_1 + b_2)$

$= \dfrac{1}{2}(4)(10 + 16)$

$= \dfrac{1}{2}(4)(26)$

$= 52$

19. C A trapezoid has two parallel sides. Hence $AB \parallel CD$. If $AB \parallel CD$, then $AD = BC$ because parallel lines intercept equal arcs on a circle. The circumference of a circle $= 360°$. Thus,

$$AB + BC + CD + AD = 360$$
$$60 + x + 160 + x = 360$$
$$2x + 220 = 360$$
$$2x = 140$$
$$x = 70$$

Hence $AB = 70$.

20. F To convert percents to decimals, multiply the percent by $\dfrac{1}{100}$

$$.1 \times \dfrac{1}{100} = \dfrac{.1}{100} = .001$$

21. B $4z^2 - 21z - 18$

To multiply two polynomials, multiply each term of one by each term of the other. Then combine like terms.

$$(4z + 3)(z - 6)$$
$$= 4z(z - 6) + 3(z - 6)$$
$$= 4z^2 - 24z + 3z - 18$$
$$= 4z^2 - 21z - 18$$

22. G 29

To evaluate, substitute the numerical values and compute.

$$3a^2 - 2b$$
$$= 3(-3)^2 - 2(-1)$$
$$= 3(9) - (-2)$$
$$= 27 + (+2) = 29$$

23. D $|2t + 3| - 4 = 3$

$$2t + 3 - 4 = 3$$
$$2t = 4$$
$$t = 2$$
$$-2t - 3 - 4 = 3$$
$$-2t = 10$$
$$t = -5$$

Therefore $t = -5$ or 2

24. K

$\triangle ABC \sim \triangle ADE$

$$\dfrac{AB}{AC} = \dfrac{AD}{AE} \qquad AB = AE + EB$$
$$\dfrac{15}{x} = \dfrac{12}{8} \qquad = 8 + 7$$
$$12x = (15)(8) \qquad = 15$$
$$= 120$$
$$x = 10 = AD$$

25. E The general form for the equation of a circle is $(x - b)^2 + (y - k)^2 = r^2$, where (b,k) is the center of the circle and r is the radius. The equation of the circle with center $(-2,4)$ and radius 3 is thus,

$$(x-(-2))^2 + (y-4)^2 = 3^2, \quad \text{or}$$
$$(x+2)^2 + (y-4)^2 = 9$$

26. F $3y + 5x = 8$

This question can be answered by putting the equation in slope intercept form.

$$3y = -5x + 8$$
$$y = -\dfrac{5}{3}x + \dfrac{8}{3}$$

The slope of the line is the coefficient of x, which is $-\dfrac{5}{3}$.

27. A Using the distance formula,

$$D = \sqrt{(2-5)^2+(3-7)^2}$$
$$= \sqrt{(-3)^2+(-4)^2} = \sqrt{9+16} =$$
$$\sqrt{25} = 5$$

28. H $150

Since the sale price is 80% of the original price.

$$B = \frac{P}{R}$$
$$= \frac{\$120}{.8} = \$150$$

29. E Adjacent angles of a parallelogram are supplementary.

$$180° − 68° = 112°$$

30. J Extend the line to CD. $AB \parallel CD$, alternate interior angles $= x = 1$. Sum of angles in $\Delta = 180$.

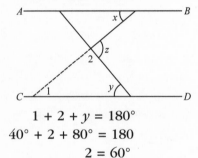

$$1 + 2 + y = 180°$$
$$40° + 2 + 80° = 180$$
$$2 = 60°$$

2 and z are supplementary

$$2 + z = 180°$$
$$60° + z = 180°$$
$$z = 120°$$

31. C Using the Pythagorean theorem, the length of the side of the triangle adjacent to angle D can be determined to be 15.

Then $\cot D = \dfrac{\text{Adjacent}}{\text{Opposite}} = \dfrac{15}{8}$

32. J 24 centimeters

To find perimeter, use the formula

$$P = 2l + 2w$$
$$= 2(7) + 2(5)$$
$$= 14 + 10$$
$$= 24 \text{ cm}$$

33. D Let

x = number of rows

$x + 14$ = number of seats

$$x(x + 14) = 240$$
$$x^2 + 14x = 240$$
$$x^2 + 14x − 240 = 0$$

Factor: $(x +24)(x − 10) = 0$

Set each factor equal to 0:

$$x + 24 = 0 \quad x − 10 = 0$$

Solve for x: $x = −24 \quad x = 10$

Discard negative number for objects—hence:

$x = 10$ = rows
$x + 14 = 24$ = seats

34. K Draw the altitudes. The area of

$\Delta = \dfrac{1}{2}bh$.

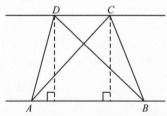

Each triangle has the same base, AB. If the two lines are perpendicular to the parallel lines, the perpendicular segments are of equal measure. Hence the altitudes are equal. Therefore the area of ΔADB = area of ΔACB. The ratio is 1:1.

35. D In any triangle, the sum of any two sides must be greater than the third side. Only example D is true: 5 + 6 > 10.

36. K The slopes of the perpendicular lines are negative reciprocals of each other.

37. D $(12x^4 - 3x^3 + 6x^2) \div 3x^2$

$= \dfrac{12x^4}{3x^2} - \dfrac{3x^3}{3x^2} + \dfrac{6x^2}{3x^2}$

Divide numbers and subtract exponents:

$4x^2 - x + 2$

38. G Draw a triangle on the coordinate axes.

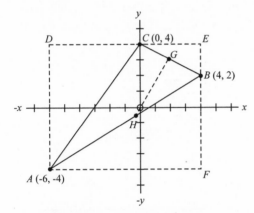

Draw the rectangle *DEFA*.

$DE = AF = 10$
$DA = EF = 8$

area of $DEFA$ = A = (10)(8)
     = 80

To find the area of $\triangle ABC$:

1. Find the area of $\triangle ADC$, $\triangle CEB$, $\triangle BFA$.
2. Subtract the result from the area of rectangle *DEFA*.

area of $\triangle ADC = \dfrac{1}{2}(8 \times 6)$

$= \dfrac{1}{2}(48)$

$= 24$

area of $\triangle CEB = \dfrac{1}{2}(4 \times 2)$

$= \dfrac{1}{2}(8)$

$= 4$

area of $\triangle BFA = \dfrac{1}{2}(10 \times 6)$

$= \dfrac{1}{2}(60)$

$= 30$

area of $\triangle ABC = 80 - (24 + 4 + 30)$
     $= 80 - 58$
     $= 22$

39. A $2(a + 1) - (1 + 2a)$
$2(a + 1) = 2a + 2$ distributive property
$-(1 + 2a) = -1 - 2a$ subtraction property

Rewrite: $2a + 2$
$\underline{\quad -2a - 1}$
Add: +1

40. H 5.5

To approximate square roots, estimate and multiply.

5.5	5.4
×5.5	×5.4
275	216
275	270
30.25	29.16

Since 30.25 is closer to 30, 5.5 is the answer.

41. C $\dfrac{1}{6}$

In this problem, we must first find out how far Jill has jogged.

$$\dfrac{1}{2} = \dfrac{3}{6}$$
$$+\dfrac{1}{3} = \dfrac{2}{6}$$
$$\overline{\dfrac{5}{6}}$$

Then subtract from 1 mile.

$$1 = \dfrac{6}{6}$$
$$-\dfrac{5}{6}$$
$$\overline{\dfrac{1}{6}}$$

42. K 15%

To find the percent of increase, divide the amount of increase by the original amount.

$\$201.25$
-175.00
$\overline{\ \$26.25}$

$$\dfrac{\$26.25}{\$175} = .15 = 15\%$$

43. A $5x^2 - 2 = 3x^2 - x + 4$
$$2x^2 + x - 6 = 0$$
$$(2x - 3)(x + 2) = 0$$
$$x = +\dfrac{3}{2}, -2$$

44. F Two right triangles are similar if two angles of one triangle are equal to two angles of the other triangle.

$\triangle ABC \sim \triangle DEC$

$$\dfrac{EC}{BC} = \dfrac{DE}{AB}$$

$BC = BE + EC$
$ = x + 6$

$$\dfrac{6}{x+6} = \dfrac{4}{12}$$

$$4(x + 6) = (6)(12)$$
$$4x + 24 = 72$$
$$4x = 48$$
$$x = 12 = BE$$

45. E Let x = number of minutes. The product of the means equals the product of the extremes.

$$\dfrac{3 \text{ minutes}}{x \text{ minutes}} = \dfrac{315 \text{ words}}{945 \text{ words}}$$

$315x = (3)(945)$
$315x = 2835$ (Divide by 315)
$x = 9$ minutes

46. G -4
Again, substitute and compute.

$$S = \dfrac{a(1-r^n)}{1-r}$$
$$= \dfrac{(-1)[1-(3)^2]}{1-(3)}$$
$$= \dfrac{(-1)(1-9)}{1-3}$$
$$= \dfrac{(-1)(-8)}{-2}$$
$$= \dfrac{8}{-2}$$
$$= -4$$

47. D Multiply 2.5 x 1000 = 2500.

48. H $\dfrac{(3a^2)^4(2a)^2}{(-2a^3)^5} = \dfrac{(3^4a^8)(2^2a^2)}{(-2^5a^{15})} = \dfrac{3^4a^{10}}{-2^3a^{15}}$

$= \dfrac{81}{-8a^5}$

49. D Multiply by L.C.M.:

$40\left(\dfrac{y}{8} - \dfrac{y}{10} = 3\right)$

$5y - 4y = 120$

$y = 120$

50. F $3

This problem can be solved by setting up two equations.
Let a calculator cost $c and a pen cost $p. Now multiply the first equation by 3 and the second equation by –2.

$3 (2c + 3p = 19)$
$-2 (3c + 2p = 21)$

Then add

$6c + 9p = 57$
$+ \ -6c - 4p = -42$
$\overline{5p = 15}$
$p = \$3$

51. C A rational number is a quotient of two integers x and y; $y \neq 0$. $\sqrt{2}, \sqrt{3}, \sqrt{5}$, and $\sqrt{11}$ are all irrational numbers; not expressed as rationals. $\sqrt{9}=3$, which can be expressed as $\dfrac{3}{1}$ (rational number)

52. K $(-4r^3s)(-2rst^3) = (-4)(-2)(r^4)(s^2)(t^3)$
$= 8r^4s^2t^3$

53. B If $f(x) = 3x-5$, $f(-2) = 3(-2)-5$
$= -6-5 = -11$

54. J In order to simplify the expression, use the identities

$\sin^2\alpha + \cos^2\alpha = 1$ and $1 + \tan^2\alpha = \sec^2\alpha$
$\sin^2\alpha + \cos^2\alpha + \tan^2\alpha = 1 + \tan^2\alpha = \sec^2\alpha$

55. C $3x - 3 > 2x + 1$
$\dfrac{-2x + 3 \quad -2x + 3}{x > 4}$ (additive inverse)

56. G Tangents equal in length: $BG = BH = 8$; $CH = CK = 3$; $AG = AK$. Since $AC = AK + CK$

$2 = AK + 3$
$9 = AK = AG$

then

$AB = BG + AG$
$= 8 + 9$
$= 17$

57. B Add the two equations:

$x + 4y = 6$
$9x - 4y = 14$
$10x = 20$

Divide by 10: $x = 2$

Substitute in the first equation to find y:

$2 + 4y = 6$
$4y = 4$

Divide by 4: $y = 1$
$\{2, 1\}$

58. F Using the identity $\tan^2A+1 = \sec^2A$, we obtain

$\tan^2A+1 = 8^2$
$\tan^2A = 63$
$\tan A = \sqrt{63} = 3\sqrt{7}$

59. B $x^3 - 2x^2 + x = 0$

$$x(x^2 - 2x + 1) = 0$$
$$x(x - 1)(x - 1) = 0$$
$$x = 0, -1, -1$$

The equation has three rational solutions.

60. H

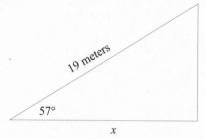

Let x = the distance from where the cable touches the ground to the base of the antenna.

$$\cos 57° = \frac{x}{19} \text{ or}$$

$$x = 19 \cos 57°$$

PART 3   READING

1. The correct answer is A. Mrs. Garth felt it good for people to see that one might possess an education without being a useless doll. She cooked the family dinner and darned all the stockings. Answer B is incorrect because nothing suggests pride in her home itself although she does see herself as having self-control regarding acceptance of her husband's shortcomings. An answer, however, is not correct unless ALL parts of it are correct. Answer C is incorrect; it is the author (not Mrs. Garth) who mentions Mrs. Garth's droll aspects. Choice D is incorrect since all references to business pertain to Mr. Garth.

2. The correct answer is H; all answers apply to Fred. The passage states that Mrs. Garth probably would not have excused Mary for engaging herself to Fred; statement I is supported. Statement II is supported by information in the passage that Fred's heart beat uneasily with the sense he would have to ''confess'' before Mrs. Garth and that the actual circumstances proved ''more unpleasant'' than expected. Since the passage states that Fred was more ''in awe'' of Mrs. Garth than of her husband, statement III is supported.

3. The correct answer is D. The paragraph deals with Mrs. Garth, her views on a variety of subjects (men, education, her husband), her feelings, and her attitudes. Choice A is unsupported by the text. The reader does not learn at this time why Fred has come to see Mr. Garth. Choice B is incorrect because the reader does not meet the Garth family, but only Mrs. Garth. Choice C is tempting since the passage does discuss Mrs. Garth's views about education, but that discussion is but a part of the passage and is too narrow for a correct answer.

4. The correct answer is H; the wine remains "a very fine wine" even though the flavor of skin is perceptible. Choice F is incorrect because neither Mrs. Garth nor the wine is "marred" by the oddities. Choice G is incorrect since nothing suggests that Mrs. Garth or wine is improved by oddities. Choice J is a generalization that extends beyond Mrs. Garth and wine.

5. The correct answer is D, as the remainder of the sentence that contains the word *peripatetic* suggests. Mrs. Garth had the students follow her as she moved around the kitchen. All other choices are also possible, but are not supported in the context given, while choice D is directly indicated in the text: "making them follow her about. . . ."

6. The correct answer is G. Mrs. Garth could discern what is inalterable, but did not complain. In her view, Mr. Garth was not much of a businessman (he had an "incapacity of minding his own interests") and might have had more money. She adored her husband's virtues. Choice F would not describe a woman who sees her husband as a business failure. Mrs. Garth herself was not impulsive, and nothing suggests that her attitude toward her husband was impulsive; choice H is not correct. The word *pathetic*, as used in this passage, describes *confidences*, not Mrs. Garth's attitude toward Mr. Garth.

7. The correct answer is D. *Frivolous* suggests excesses and extravagances, neither in keeping with Mrs. Garth's lifestyle. She cooks her family's food, does the sewing, keeps the house, instructs students in her home, and does not care about "teapots or children's frilling." Mrs. Garth is self-controlled (choice A). She is not overhasty in speech, having learned self-control in her youth. Choice B is supported by the direct statement that Mrs. Garth was "disproportionately indulgent toward the failings of men," as well as by the statement that Mrs. Garth had a tendency to excuse Fred's errors while applying more rigorous standards to her daughter, Mary. Choice C, critical of women, describes Mrs. Garth, who included her daughter in "that more rigorous judgment that she applied to her own sex."

8. The correct answer is F. The passage refers to Mr. Garth's want of prudence and the sums (of money) he might have had. Choice G can be eliminated on the basis of Fred's preference of confessing to Mr. Garth. Choice H is incorrect; Mrs. Garth adored her husband's virtues. No information is available to provide information about Mr. Garth's feelings toward the neighbors.

9. The correct answer is C. The passage states that Fred did not want to sink in Mrs. Garth's opinion. Choice A is false. The passage tells us that Mrs. Garth did not share personal information with her neighbors. Choice B is incorrect; no statements or implications about Mr. Garth's intelligence are available in the passage. Choice D, a statement from the passage, is information unrelated to Fred's feelings, and, therefore, an incorrect choice.

10. The correct answer is J. The passage states that Mr. Garth had an "incapacity of minding his own interests" and mentions the sums he might have had if he had been like other men. Mrs. Garth has simple tastes and instructs pupils in her home. These details suggest a lack of affluence. Choice F is incorrect, because no mention is made of redecorating. Choice G is incorrect; the attic is mentioned only to show how familiar Fred was with the family. Nothing in the passage supports the notion of wealth among the Garths. Mrs. Garth does her own housework and cooking, as well as teaching pupils in her home. Mr. Garth is portrayed as second-rate in providing for his family. For these reasons, choice H is incorrect.

11. The correct answer is B; the insurgents had rebelled against Spanish rule and established a junta in New York City. The Spanish commander tried to corner "the rebels" and destroy them. Choice A would include the insurgents, but also many other Cuban natives not involved in rebellion. Choice C, militia, suggests a fighting force. Insurgents based in New York, for example, were not directly involved in fighting. Choice D, reconcentrationists, is a word that relates to reconcentration, which was a Spanish policy. Such a word would not describe the Cubans rebelling against Spanish rule.

12. The correct answer is J, the Spanish. The passage explains that Cuba was still part of Spain's empire, that insurgents had rebelled against Spanish rule and rebelled again in 1895. Choice F is incorrect. The insurgents *established* a junta. Choice G is faulty because the United States had no political power over native Cubans. Choice H is incorrect because the insurgents *were* native Cubans.

13. The correct answer is A. The passage states that the policy was "designed to move the native population into camps and liquidate the rebels' popular base," that is, to remove the source of additional rebel troops, the common people. Native Cubans were relocated in camps, making choice B seem promising; however, the primary *purpose* of reconcentration was military in nature, not just relocation. Disease (choice C) was a result of reconcentration, but not a purpose. Choice D refers to insurgent activity mentioned in paragraph 2, not the relocation carried out by the Spanish.

14. The correct answer is J. The answer is supported by the statement that the press printed "lurid" stories of Spanish atrocities. Although "yellow" may mean cowardly in some settings, choice F is incorrect in this particular context. Choice G is a paraphrase from this sentence: "It stemmed from larger conflicts in policies. . . ." The pronoun *it* refers to the war, not to yellow journalism. The compassion referred to in choice H was the compassion of the American public.

15. The correct answer is D; evidence in the passage suggests I, II, and III. Dishonesty (statement I) was evidenced by the fact that de Lome's letter was stolen, as well as by the fact that the Spanish were insincere, according to the letter, in negotiation. When the *Maine* was sunk, Americans assumed that the Spanish were responsible, lending support for statement II. Statement III, diplomacy, is also indicated throughout the passage, particularly in the communication and negotiation between Spain and the United States.

16. The correct answer is G. Understanding the quoted sentence is a matter of unraveling the key sentence parts. The Spanish army officers led riots in Havana and shook the (American) president's confidence. The riots were against Cuban self-rule, or autonomy. The confidence was confidence in Madrid's (Spain's) control. Choice J is an opinion that has no basis whatsoever in the article or in the quoted sentence. Choices F and H are both incorrect since the question is about the president's confidence being shaken, not the lack of confidence of the Spanish or army officers.

17. The correct answer is D. When Madrid recalled Weyler and agreed to offer the Cubans autonomy, the United States was pleased and there was a "lull" in the crisis. Other choices all contributed directly or indirectly to growing mistrust, misunderstanding and, eventually, war. Choice A indicates that what had been a "lull" in the crisis ended when Spanish army officers led riots in Havana. Choice B relates that McKinley sent an ultimatum to Spain, which maintained political control in Cuba; the United States had no political jurisdiction in Cuba. Events of choice C added to mistrust. McKinley learned that there was a lack of honesty in Spanish negotiations.

18. The correct answer is H, as directly stated: "Yellow journalism did not cause the war. It stemmed from larger conflicts in policies and perceptions between Spain and the United States." Choices F and G are both incorrect since the passage states in the last paragraph that "in truth he was neither" weak and indecisive *nor* a wily manipulator. Choice J can be eliminated on the basis of the direct statement that "yellow journalism did not cause the war."

19. The correct answer is A, protective. Although the United States had no jurisdiction in Cuba, there was interest in humanitarian and political issues affecting Cuba. Choice B can be eliminated because the joint resolution of Congress included an amendment that pledged that the United States would not annex Cuba. Choice C can be eliminated because the United States was not satisfied with current conditions in Cuba and was not willing to accept them as they were. Choice D describes the attitude of the United States toward Spain, not Cuba.

20. The correct answer is J. The selection provides an overview of the political climate prior to the war and presents specific incidents that contributed to it. Choice F is incorrect since the entire passage is not devoted to freeing McKinley of blame. Choice G is vague, not mentioning *what* the public opinion might be *about*. In addition, public opinion is mentioned only in connection with the sinking of the *Maine*. Choice H is incorrect since it suggests that there is a party to be "blamed." The passage states that the war resulted from conflicting national interests of involved parties.

21. The correct answer is C. A is incorrect; the emphasis was not on scientific thought. B is incorrect as the emphasis is on the philosopher's teachings about the meaning of the universe rather than about their thoughts, in general. D is incorrect, as this is only what some of the philosophers discussed.

22. The correct answer is F, as stated in paragraph 1. Thales of Miletus taught that everything came from water.

23. The correct answer is C, as stated in paragraph 1.

24. The correct answer is G; both philosophers believed the world consisted of the original "stuff." Anaximenes believed the "stuff" was air. Thales of Miletus believed the "stuff" was water.

25. The correct answer is C. A, B, and D contradict the reading and, therefore, are incorrect. Pythagoras came after the early one (A); Heraclitus did not believe in Pythagoras (B); and Thales of Miletus was mentioned as one of the early ones (D).

26. The correct answer is F, as stated in paragraph 3. While others proposed one element, as suggested in choice H, all wanted to understand the nature of the universe (choice G); only Anaximenes's proposed that everything was made of air.

27. The correct answer is D. A was Thales of Miletus's belief and is, therefore, incorrect. B was Anaximenes's belief and is, therefore, incorrect. C was Pythagoras's, belief and is, therefore, incorrect. Thus, D is the correct answer as stated in paragraph 4.

28. The correct answer is G. F is incorrect; although he did invoke compromise, it is hardly plausible that other philosophers were unaware of the concept. G is correct, since Empedocles was the first to suggest things were made up of combinations of elements. H and J are incorrect; these concepts had been introduced prior to Empedocles.

29. The correct answer is D. A, B, and C are incorrect, since each of these topics was addressed by different groups of philosophers, but these were not subjects of the most fundamental disagreement. B is incorrect because only the Pythagoreans were concerned with numbers. They were not mentioned by the others. C is incorrect since Heraclitus stressed change, Miletus stressed motion, and Anaximander believed in pieces united through movement. Therefore, many did agree with the idea of change and motion. D is the correct answer; many philosophers' teachings were dependent on their answers to this question.

30. The correct answer is F, as they were in complete contradiction; Thales of Miletus taught that change was constant and Xenophanes taught that change was impossible. Heraclitus, Thales of Miletus, and Anaximines all believed the universe was made up of original "stuff," so G and H are incorrect. Pythagoras and Thales of Miletus both believed in "stuff"—it was just their concept of what "stuff" was that was different; J is therefore incorrect.

31. The correct answer is D. The author states that "something was sure to come by." He also ends the paragraph by referring to endlessly more (wildlife). Choice A is incorrect because the "story" is the story of the animals, not of their *names*. Choice B is incorrect; there are not more turtles, but more animals. Choice C, a true statement, is unrelated to the names of the animals.

32. The correct answer is F. The paragraph lists factors that make Costa Rica a naturalist's paradise: political stability, natural beauty, large numbers of species, wide range of habitats, the relative proportion of forest preserve land, and the size of the country. No one factor would be more important than others. The main idea statement must be a generalization from all details given. Other answer choices each mention just one advantage.

33. The correct answer is C. The words "for example" send the reader to the previous sentence. The trip from Monteverde to San José, a trip that takes just one morning, is an example of how easy it is to get from one place to another. Choice A could not be correct. The words "for example" always refer the reader to previous text. Choice B is incorrect because placement of the climate information (between dashes) tells the reader that this is information intended to be supplementary to the main part of the sentence (we drove there in just one morning.) Choice D is not intended as the primary message of the paragraph. Although the paragraph mentions several climate words, these are placed within dashes, subordinating them to the remainder of the sentence.

34. The correct answer is H. Since Quakers *balanced* creation of a dairy cooperative with creating a reserve, the two activities present a contrast of ideas. Choice F is incorrect since no information is stated or implied that would support this assumption. Choice G is not correct because the nonmilitary convictions of Costa Rica existed *before* the Quakers arrived and attracted the Quakers. Choice J is a true statement, but *not* an *inference*.

35. The correct answer is A. Words such as *blessed, naturalist's paradise,* and *one of the world's best systems of reserves* underscore this point. The author's positive comments and the absence of any negative comments make all other choices inappropriate.

36. The correct answer is G. This conclusion is supported by the author's mention of "our first stop," which suggests that there will be other stops. The author also states that "people like us come to walk the trails and learn what we can of the forest." Nothing stated or implied in the paragraph indicates that the author is a Quaker, making choice F inappropriate. Since the author states that "biologists come here to study, and people like us come . . ." the author is clearly *not* a biologist; choice H is incorrect. Since climate is not emphasized throughout the article, choice J is not indicated.

37. The correct answer is A. The author states that the order is "defined by the need for sunlight." Choice B is incorrect; although the author mentions niches, there is no stated relationship between niches and order or need. Choice C, tumult, means confusion. Choice D, recycling, is addressed, but not in a context of order.

38. The correct answer is H. Choice I is true, as the second sentence of the paragraph states. Choice II is true; the paragraph states that the original tree has disappeared. The paragraph also mentions the "substantial trunks" of the strangler fig. Choice III is not true; even though the word *host* is used, the strangler fig does not obtain nourishment from the tree, as it would in a parasitic relationship.

39. The correct answer is B; the *original tree* was the ladder *for* the strangler fig. Choice A is true; the original tree disappears after having served as a ladder to the soil. Choice C is true; the strangler fig is a single tree with a cluster of substantial trunks. Choice D is true; the strangler fig dropped shoots that took root in the forest floor.

40. The correct answer is H because the author discusses the origin and size of Monteverde, as well as his personal observations. Answer F is too general; the focus of this selection is Monteverde. Since only *one* aspect of Monteverde is discussed, answer G is too narrow in scope to be a general title. Answer J is too general; the focus of this article is Monteverde.

PART 4   SCIENCE REASONING

1. The correct answer is A. According to Table I, when the temperature is constant, the pressure is inversely proportional to the volume. One sees that $P \times V = 200$ for all values of P and V. If $V = 40$, then $P = 5$.

2. The correct answer is G. Directly proportional means that V/T = constant. As one quantity increases, then the other must increase by a proportional amount. In Table II, as the volume doubles, the temperature also doubles.

3. The correct Answer is C. From the tables one sees that the $P \times V$ is related to the temperature of this gas. For answers A, B, and C, $P \times V = 200$. For C, $P \times V = 150$.

4. The correct answer is H. In all cases, as the temperature of this gas increases, then $P \times V$ also increases proportionally. Answers F and G are not necessarily correct, as shown in Tables II and III, wherein the pressure and the volume remained constant, respectively, even though the temperature changed.

5. The correct answer is C. For all values in the tables we see that $PV/T = 2/3$. Testing answers A, B, and D, different values are obtained when substituting into these equations.

6. The correct answer is H. At constant temperature according to Table I, $P \times V$ = constant. As P increases, V decreases, which describes a hyperbola.

7. The correct answer is D. 5900 cfs was the maximum discharge from the discharge hydrograph.

8. The correct answer is F. The maximum stage was 12 feet. Flood stage for the Red Cedar is 7 feet. 12 feet − 7 feet = 5 feet.

9. The correct answer is C. Peak discharge was reached on April 20 very late in the day.

10. The correct answer is H. The Red Cedar flooded on April 19 and receded below flood stage on April 24 for six days of flooding.

11. The correct answer is C. Peak discharge was 5900 cfs. From the flood frequency graph, 5900 cfs intersects the curve at forty years.

12. The correct answer is J. A flood with the recurrence interval of 100 years would have a discharge of 7800 cfs.

13. The correct answer is C. The pH is 1.0 when no NaOH is added. $[H_3O^+]$ = antilog -pH. Antilog of -1.0 = 0.1.

14. The correct answer is H. The graph shows that the pH is 7.0 when 25 mL of NaOH has been added.

15. The correct answer is C. When the hydronium ion and hydroxide concentrations are almost equal, it takes only one excess ion of either type to influence the pH.

16. The correct answer is H. The objective of a titration experiment is to have the hydronium ion and hydroxide ion neutralize each other. Each time a hydroxide ion is introduced, one of the hydronium ions will be neutralized. This causes the reduction of the hydronium ion concentration.

17. The correct answer is A. A solution that has a pH of 7 is neutral. It contains the same number of hydronium and hydroxide ions.

18. The correct answer is G. When 24 mL of the base is added to the 25 mL of acid, there is still acid in excess. The pH will be below 7 when the solution is acidic.

19. The answer is D. The values for Na+ are the only ones shown that are higher in blood than in urine.

20. The answer is J. It would be ideal to have the same test subjects evaluated so that exercise would be the only test variable.

21. The answer is B. The only possibilities are urea and K+ and Cl-, and of these, urea is the only available choice.

22. The answer is H. Since these are healthy individuals in homeostasis, one should realize that the high levels of urea in urine must be part of normal metabolism, and since urine is ex-creted, this must be a normal mecha-nism for getting rid of excess urea.

23. The answer is C. The data are for healthy individuals, which indicates that they are in homeostasis. Again, this answer is similar to that in question 4.

24. The answer is H. These results would indicate that age, sex, and weight are not causing variability in the results.

25. The correct answer is C. Using only blue scales enables one to see if any pink-scaled dragons are produced as a recessive trait. None was. The strain is pure (homozygous).

26. The correct answer is H. If this were a recessive gene, there would probably have been a higher and more predictable incidence of albinism.

27. The correct answer is C. The same color scales for both sexes is a reasonable control for purity. Either color would be acceptable.

28. The correct answer is J. The pure strain breeds true, producing only offspring identical to the parents. In this case, it was blue-scaled offspring from blue-scaled parents.

29. The correct answer is C. The dominant trait is determined in Experiment 1. Pink scales are dominant by a ratio of 3:1 in a classic hybrid cross (2 strains).

30. The correct answer is F. Reversing the color of males and females makes no difference with non-sex-linked traits. Dominance is a gene trait, regardless of the sex of the carrier in this case.

31. The answer is A. Group A was treated the same as the other groups, except that it was not given the drug.

32. The answer is G. A difference of just one animal in two of the groups is not likely to be significant.

33. The answer is C. It is the only answer consistent with the data presented.

34. The answer is J. If the same number of mice developed tumors at the different dosages at the same point in time, then dosage was not a factor. Length of time of drug administration would account for the differences observed.

35. The answer is A. Table I shows that both time and dosage of drug contribute to tumor development. However, time is the only option in the possible answers.

36. The answer is G. Some other factor must be causing the tumors to develop. Time alone cannot account for the results because Group D is quite different from the other groups.

37. The answer is C. In equilibrium problems dealing with changing pressures, count the total number of "compressible moles" (moles of gases) on both the reactant side and then on the product side. In this reaction, there are 5 moles of gas on the reactant side (4 moles of hydrogen chloride and 1 mole of oxygen), compared to 4 moles of gas on the product side (2 moles each of chlorine and water). Increasing the pressure will shift equilibrium to the "smaller side"; therefore, the concentrations of both chlorine and water will increase!

38. The answer is G. Adding additional chlorine will cause the following sequence of events to happen: With more chlorine in the reaction chamber, there will be additional molecules to react with the available water molecules, which will then force the reaction to "reverse," producing more hydrogen chloride and oxygen, until a new set of equilibrium conditions is met. If more reactants are added, more products will be produced. In reversible reactions, adding more product will produce more reactants (such is the case here).

39. The correct response is A. See the explanation for question 37. Counting the moles of gas of both the reactants and the products in the equation gives an equal number of gas moles on either side. Therefore, increasing the pressure will favor neither side. No effect.

40. The correct response is G. The same "logic" is applied here as in answer 38. Adding more products to this reaction will shift equilibrium to the reactant side, thus increasing the concentrations of both carbon monoxide and water.

The English portion of the ACT measures skills you presumably have acquired during the course of your education. Your performance on the exam can be improved significantly by careful review of the grammar and rhetorical overviews in this section. The test consists of several prose passages. Each passage is accompanied by a series of multiple-choice questions. Often, the questions refer to an underlined word or phrase in the passage. Sometimes, the questions involve more general concepts (what is the main idea of the passage?). Spelling, vocabulary, and rote recall of grammatical rules are *not* tested.

The ACT tests your knowledge of standard written English (grammar and usage, sentence structure, and punctuation) and of rhetorical skills (style, organization, and strategy). Here is a brief description of the two basic categories of questions:

(1) USAGE/MECHANICS

Sentence Structure (24%) These questions test your understanding of sentence construction, placement of modifiers, and the function and placement of clauses and phrases.

Basic Grammar and Usage (16%) These questions test your knowledge of verb formation, pronoun case, parts of speech, subject-verb agreement, noun-pronoun agreement, use of idioms, and use of modifiers. All this is covered in the grammar overview.

Punctuation (13%) These questions test your knowledge of internal and end-of-sentence punctuation.

Sentence structure, grammar, and punctuation are all covered in the grammar overview.

(2) RHETORICAL SKILLS

Style (16%) These questions test your ability to choose appropriate words and phrases, as well as avoid wordiness, redundancy, clichés, and ambiguous references.

Organization (15%) These questions test your ability to organize ideas and make decisions about order, coherence, and unity. Here are some typical questions you may encounter on the ACT testing of rhetorical skills:

Which sentence does not belong in the above paragraph?

Which is the best topic sentence for the paragraph?

Unscramble the above paragraph and choose the correct sequence of sentences from the following choices:

Strategy (16%) These questions test your ability to choose effective transitional words and phrases, effective opening and closing sentences, shifts in ideas that denote the start of a new paragraph, and words and expressions appropriate to the essay's purpose and audience. Here are some typical questions you may encounter:

Which of these statements best expresses the author's intentions?

The main point the author is concerned with is . . . .

Which of the following titles would be appropriate for the preceding passage?

Style, organization, and strategy are all covered in the rhetorical overview.

TIPS ON APPROACHING THE QUESTIONS

1. Pace yourself carefully.

The ACT English exam contains 75 questions that must be answered in 45 minutes. That leaves you about half a minute per question. If you're not sure of a correct answer, go on to the next question; then return to the ones you are unsure of later.

2. Examine the underlined portion of the passage in relation to the questions.

Study the answer choices carefully. If you examine the answer choices, it will be clear what you are being tested for (grammar, punctuation, word choice, wordiness).
Here are some examples:

Ralph Waldo Emerson had <u>Socrates</u> example in mind when he . . .

A. NO CHANGE
B. Socrates's
C. Socrate's
D. Socrateses'

Obviously, you are being asked to identify the proper possessive form for Socrates. The answer is B.

<u>To succeed,</u> one must learn to conform to the wishes of a larger group to be successful.

A. NO CHANGE
B. Succeeding
C. In order to succeed
D. OMIT

The correct answer is D. You are being given several examples that are redundant. Since "successful" is mentioned at the end of the sentence, it is not necessary at the beginning.

3. Choose the best answer.

Sometimes more than one answer may be correct or possible, particularly if you are being tested for rhetoric rather than usage. Choose the answer you think is best.

<u>Due to the fact that production costs are so high,</u> most commercial plays have difficulty today recouping their investment.

A. NO CHANGE
B. Because of the fact that production costs are so high
C. In light of the fact that production costs are so high,
D. Since production costs are so high,

The correct answer is D. You are being tested for wordiness. Although A, B, and C are not grammatically incorrect, D is less wordy, more economical, and the best choice.

Notice answer choice B. There is no comma after "high." Here you are being asked to deal with more than one element of writing—the proper use of the comma *as well as* wordiness.

4. Always reread the sentence and substitute your selected answer for the underlined portion. Check your work.

5. Be aware of the style of the passage.

Each of the passages covers a different topic. Take the style of each paragraph into consideration when you answer the questions. If you're being tested for correct word choice or for a rhetorical skill, read the whole paragraph carefully before answering the question.

Often, questions that test your rhetorical skills will not refer to an underlined word or phrase, but will refer to the passage or paragraph as a whole. Here are some examples of typical questions.

The main point of the paragraph is. . . .

Which of the following is an appropriate title for the passage?

Which sentence does not belong in the above passage?

In the review section that follows, there is a series of short passages followed by several questions. Answer the questions and then check your answers with the answer key. If you have trouble with a question, read the explanation offered in the answer key. The explanation will help you understand the material more fully.

Practice Questions

Passage 1

Poets have always sung of the richness and power of early fall. <u>For example,</u> the
₁
beauty of John Keats's "To Autumn," in which the season is portrayed as an extension and fulfillment of late summer, a defense and rebellion against death. <u>Another example,</u> the power that Shelley
₂
feels in the west wind that brings the autumn, with its promise of storms, of revolutions, and <u>the death will spread new</u>
₃
<u>rebirth in the spring.</u> Keats's poem is slow
₃
and meditative, full of peacefully vivid sounds, textures, and sights, <u>as opposing Shelley's,</u> which is full of
₄
forceful, stormy images.

Late autumn, however, after the leaves <u>are falling</u> has its beauty, too. Distant hills,
₅
once hidden, are revealed. The evergreens are sharply isolated. The bare, deciduous branches show lavender against the background.

1. A. NO CHANGE
   B. For example, there is
   C. For example, take
   D. On the one hand,

2. F. NO CHANGE
   G. Another example, there is
   H. Another example is
   J. On the other hand,

3. A. NO CHANGE
   B. that death will bring new birth in the spring
   C. that death will mean life in the spring
   D. of new life in the spring

4. F. NO CHANGE
   G. and opposing Shelley's
   H. as opposed to Shelley's
   J. which is opposed to Shelley's

5. A. NO CHANGE
   B. had fallen
   C. have fallen,
   D. fell

Passage 2

At first there was a gradual growth of interest in <u>skiing, starting in</u> the thirties, it
$$1$$
spread naturally to a few geographically suitable areas. In the forties and early fifties, release bindings were just becoming available, and skiers no longer had to rent the old-fashioned wooden skis <u>that tied the foot in like a clamp.</u> Then came
$$2$$
the explosion in the late sixties and early <u>seventies, new skis, new lifts, new areas,</u>
$$3$$
new clothes and boots every year or two. New learning methods <u>were attracting</u>
$$4$$
busloads and carloads of skiers from the cities <u>to be lost</u> among the complexity of
$$5$$
equipment and lessons and dangerous slopes.

1. A. NO CHANGE
   B. skiing, which started in
   C. skiing. Starting in
   D. skiing. In

2. F. NO CHANGE
   G. that, like a clamp, tied the foot in
   H. that secured the feet with straps
   J. holding the foot

3. A. NO CHANGE
   B. seventies, having new
   C. seventies, there being new
   D. seventies with the necessity for new

4. F. NO CHANGE
   G. had been attracting
   H. attract
   J. attracted

5. A. NO CHANGE
   B. whose neophytes were soon lost
   C. who were soon lost
   D. whose occupants quickly were lost

Passage 3

<u>There are two childhood fantasies</u>
___
1
<u>connected with Superman, and they make</u>
___
1
the figure more interesting than most comic

book characters. The first fantasy, and the

<u>most</u> obvious of the two, centers on
___
2
Superman's great strength and his <u>flight.</u> In a
___
3
sense, this fantasy is shortlived because a

child quickly learns that <u>it is</u> impossible
___
4
without a plane or a rocket. The second

fantasy is more subtle because it concerns

<u>hiding Superman's identity under the weak</u>
___
5
<u>disguise of Clark Kent.</u>
___
5

1. A. NO CHANGE
   B. Two childhood fantasies about
      Superman make
   C. There are two childhood fantasies
      about Superman that make
   D. There are two childhood fantasies
      about Superman making

2. F. NO CHANGE
   G. clearly
   H. more
   J. explicitly

3. A. NO CHANGE
   B. flying
   C. ability to fly
   D. speed in flight

4. F. NO CHANGE
   G. flying is
   H. they are
   J. both are

5. A. NO CHANGE
   B. Superman's disguise as the weakling
      Clark Kent.
   C. identifying Superman with Clark
      Kent.
   D. hiding Superman behind the calm
      exterior of Clark Kent.

Passage 4

The creative experience has been

compared to <u>the religious experience of</u>
___
1
Christian Revelation or to Zen *satori,*

which share a sense of the free soul,

<u>a sense of light</u> shining on the dark corners
___
2
of experience. Chaotic emotions and

disorderly images are given form and order,

<u>therefore</u> releasing the mind from excessive
___
3
self-consciousness. An artist may feel that he

or she has "conceived," <u>like a mother her</u>
___
4
<u>child,</u> but to perfect his or her work,
___
4
<u>it is necessary to work at it.</u> A scientist also
___
5
finds that, once a hypothesis is firm, he or

she must still struggle through experiments

and refinements before the work can be

accepted by the scientific community.

1. A. NO CHANGE
    B. the religious experiences of
    C. the religious feelings of
    D. OMIT

2. F. NO CHANGE
    G. there is a sense of light
    H. being a light
    J. and a light

3. A. NO CHANGE
    B. thereby
    C. moreover
    D. rather

4. F. NO CHANGE
    G. as a mother her child
    H. like a mother conceives her child
    J. as parents their children

5. A. NO CHANGE
    B. it is necessary to labor at it
    C. a great deal of labor is required.
    D. much work is required.

Passage 5

In our rush to find new ways to teach reading and writing, we may have lost some valuable lessons that our grandfathers learned. Not that we should whip young
                                        1
students through Latin at an early age, although some recent educational
            2
articles have suggested a revival of strong discipline as a learning aid. We might, however, return to the good old five-paragraph essay or classical dissertation, it
                                                3
is comprised of three central paragraphs
4

arguing for, against, and on the middle ground of an issue, with initial and closing
                                        5
paragraphs to introduce and conclude.
                5

1. A. NO CHANGE
    B. We might
    C. We probably can't
    D. We should not perhaps

2. F. NO CHANGE
    G. age; although
    H. age. Although
    J. age although

3. A. NO CHANGE
    B. dissertation, which
    C. dissertation. it
    D. dissertation and

4. F. NO CHANGE
    G. is made of
    H. composes
    J. comprises

5. A. NO CHANGE
    B. opening, introducing and closing,
    C. introductory and concluding
       paragraphs.
    D. an opening paragraph that intro-
       duces and a closing paragraph that
       concludes

Now check your answers.

Passage 1

1. The correct answer is B. This avoids the fragmented original and the colloquial abruptness of "take" that does not fit the tone of the passage.
2. The correct answer is H. This avoids the original's fragment. G is an impossible structure.
3. The correct answer is D. Parallelism requires another prepositional phrase beginning with "of."
4. The correct answer is H. This alone, among the alternatives, is correct idiomatic phrasing.
5. The correct answer is C. The word *after* in the beginning of this sentence tells us that the leaves have already fallen and are not in the process of doing so. Therefore, we need the present perfect tense, suggesting a state achieved sometime in the near past and continuing into the present.

Passage 2

1. The correct answer is C. This solves the problem of the run-on construction with the comma splices after "skiing" and "thirties."
2. The correct answer is H. Don't mix metaphors by starting with "tied," which implies ropes, strings, or something else, and ending with "clamp," which would require another verb.
3. The correct answer is D. This avoids the comma splice of the original, the dangling participle of choice B, and the awkwardness of choice C.
4. The correct answer is J. Simple past tense does the job here, as is suggested by "came" in the previous sentence.

5. The correct answer is B. "To be lost" is a floating infinitive without a proper antecedent in the main part of the sentence.

Passage 3

1. The correct answer is B. This choice eliminates the "there are" construction, which is usually unnecessary, and is weak construction, especially in a topic sentence.
2. The correct answer is H. Never use the superlative case with only two items—the comparative case is necessary. For example, "Of the two, George is better," but "Of the three, George is best."
3. The correct answer is C. "Flight" suggests cowardice. The fantasy would normally involve the ability to fly, not the speed (choice D) of Superman's flight.
4. The correct answer is G. This clears up any ambiguity that "it" might create, as a result of confusing "strength" and "flight." The clue to what "it" is are the words "plane" and "rocket"—both vehicles of flight. Avoid using pronouns with vague or ambiguous antecedents.
5. The correct answer is B. Using a noun, "disguise," as the subject of "concerns" is stronger and more definite than using a gerund like "hiding" or identifying."

Passage 4

1. The correct answer is D. Revelation and satori are religious experiences by definition; therefore, the underlined phrase is redundant.
2. The correct answer is F. This is an acceptable elliptical construction. We have left out the phrase "and also" to avoid annoying repetition.

3. The correct answer is B. "Thereby" indicates that through the agency of one thing, another thing has happened or is about to happen.

4. The correct answer is G. "As" is usually used with clauses. The original and choice H misuse "like" which should be used only as a preposition. The classic violation is an old cigarette commercial that stated, "So-and-so [cigarette brand] tastes good *like* a cigarette should."

5. The correct answer is C. "It" in its two different uses should not be repeated in such proximity. "Work" is also repeated awkwardly; "labor" continues the reference to human conception.

Passage 5

1. The correct answer is C. This eliminates the underlined fragment and catches the right tone—that we can't return to certain things that we have outgrown.

2. The correct answer is F. When a subordinate clause (here it is adverbial) comes after the main verb, it is set off by a comma only if there is a significant pause before it (as before "and" in its coordinate function).

3. The correct answer is B. This subordinates the material that follows in a nonrestrictive clause (adding nonessential material), set off by a comma. Choice C makes a new sentence, which would be choppy here. Choice D does not make sense.

4. The correct answer is J. A whole "comprises" its parts; it is not "comprised of" its parts; conversely, the parts "compose" the whole.

5. The correct answer is C. This provides the desired meaning without verbosity.

Most of the principles involved in answering these questions involve the basic rules of grammar, as well as some common sense. Often, by saying the phrases out loud (or out loud in your head, during the test), you will be able to eliminate those choices that sound wrong to you. However, there is no way to escape an understanding of the principles of grammar. The next section of the book will detail these principles, as well as provide you with numerous samples and explanations. Take your time reading through this section, or just skim through it if you want to understand more fully the explanation of an answer.

Unit 1

USAGE REVIEW

PARTS OF SPEECH

NOUN

A NOUN is the name of a person, place, or thing.

> *actor,   city,   lamp*

There are three kinds of nouns, according to the type of person, place, or thing the noun names.

(1) A *common* noun refers to a general type: girl, park, army.

(2) A *proper* noun refers to a particular person, place, or thing, and always begins with a capital letter: Mary, Central Park, U.S. Army.

(3) A *collective* noun signifies a number of individuals organized into one group: team, crowd, Congress.

Singular/Plural

Every noun has number. That means every noun is either singular or plural. The singular means only one; the plural means more than one. There are four ways to form the plurals of nouns:

(1) by adding *s* to the singular (horses, kites, rivers)

(2) by adding *es* to the singular (buses, churches, dishes, boxes, buzzes)

(3) by changing the singular (*man* becomes *men*, *woman* becomes *women*, *child* becomes *children*, *baby* becomes *babies*, *alumnus* becomes *alumni*)

(4) by leaving the singular as it is (moose, deer, and sheep are all plural as well as singular).

Note: When forming the plural of letters and numbers, add 's: A's, 150's. Otherwise, 's denotes possession.

Case

Nouns also have case, which indicates the function of the noun in the sentence. There are three cases—the nominative case, the objective case, and the possessive case.

(1) Nominative Case

A noun is in the nominative case when it is the subject of a sentence: The *book* fell off the table. The *boys* and *girls* ran outside.

The subject of a sentence is the person, place, or thing that the sentence is about. Thus, the *book* fell off the table is about the book.

A noun is in the nominative case when it is a predicate noun. This is a noun used after a linking verb. In such cases, the predicate noun means the same as the subject.

> Einstein was a *scientist*. (Einstein = scientist)

> Judith was a brilliant scholar and gifted teacher. (Judith = scholar and teacher)

A noun is in the nominative case when it is used in direct address. A noun in direct address shows that someone or something is being spoken to directly. This noun is set off by commas.

Claudel, please answer the phone.

Go home, *Fido*, before you get hit by a car.

A noun is in the nominative case when it is a nominative absolute. This is a noun with a participle (see verbs) that stands as an independent idea but is part of a sentence.

The *rain* having stopped, we went out to play.

The *bike* having crashed, the race was stopped.

A noun is in the nominative case when it is a nominative in apposition. This is one of a pair of nouns. Both nouns are equal in meaning and are next to each other. The noun in apposition is set off from the rest of the sentence by commas.

Steve, *my son*, is going to college.

That man is Syd, the *musician*.

(2) Objective Case

A noun is in the objective case when it is the direct object of a verb. A direct object is the receiver of the action of a verb. A verb that has a direct object is called a transitive verb.

The team elected *David*.

The team won the *game*.

A noun is in the objective case when it is the indirect object of a verb. This is a noun that shows *to* whom or *for* whom the action is taking place. The words *to* and *for* may not actually appear in the sentence, but they are understood. An indirect object *must* be accompanied by a direct object.

Pedro threw *Mario* the ball. (Pedro threw the ball to Mario).

Anya bought her *mother* a gift. (Anya bought a gift for her mother).

A noun is in the objective case when it is an objective complement. An objective complement is a noun that explains the direct object. The word *complement* indicates that this noun *completes* the meaning of the direct object.

The team elected Terry *captain*.

A noun is in the objective case when it is an objective by apposition. An objective by apposition is very much like a nominative in apposition. Again we have a pair of nouns that are equal in meaning and are next to each other. The noun in apposition explains the other noun, but now the noun being explained is in the objective case. Therefore, the noun in apposition is called the objective by apposition. The objective by apposition is set off from the rest of the sentence by commas.

The bully pushed Steve, the little *toddler*, into the sandbox.

He gave the money to Sam, the *banker*.

A noun is in the objective case when it is an adverbial objective. This is a noun that denotes distance or time.

The storm lasted an *hour*.

The troops walked five *miles*.

A noun is in the objective case when it is an object of a preposition.

The stick fell into the *well*. (*Into* is the preposition.)

The picture fell on the *table*. (*On* is the preposition.)

See the section on prepositions.

(3) Possessive Case

A noun is in the possessive case when it shows ownership. The correct use of the possessive case is often tested on the exam. The following rules will help you answer such questions correctly.

A. The possessive case of most nouns is formed by adding an apostrophe and s to the singular.

The *boy's* book

Emile's coat

B. If the singular ends in *s* add an apostrophe, or apostrophe *s*.

The *bus's* wheels.

or

The *bus'* wheels.

Charles' books.

or

Charles's books.

C. The possessive case of plural nouns ending in *s* is formed by adding just an apostrophe.

The *dogs'* bones.

Note: If *dog* was singular, the possessive case would be *dog's*.

D. If the plural noun does not end in *s* then add an apostrophe and *s*.

The *children's* toys.

The *men's* boots.

E. The possessive case of compound nouns is formed by adding an apostrophe and *s* to the last word if it is singular, or by adding an *s* and an apostrophe if the word is plural.

My *brother-in-law's* house.

My *two brothers'* house.

F. To show individual ownership, add an apostrophe and *s* to each owner.

Joe's and *Jim's* boats. (They each own their own boat.)

G. To show joint ownership, add an apostrophe and *s* to the last name.

Joe and *Jim's* boat. (They both own the same boat.)

PRONOUNS

A pronoun is used in place of a noun. The noun for which a pronoun is used is called the *antecedent*. The use of pronouns, particularly the relationship between a pronoun and its antecedent, is one of the most common items found on the test. Always make sure a pronoun has a clear antecedent.

John had a candy bar and a cookie. He ate *it* quickly. (Ambiguous) (What is the antecedent of *it* — *candy bar* or *cookie*?)

The boy rode his bike through the hedge, *which* was very large. (Ambiguous) (What was very large — the *bike* or the *hedge*?)

The captain was very popular. *They* all liked him. (Ambiguous) (Who liked him? *They* has no antecedent.)

There are ten kinds of pronouns:

(1) Expletive pronoun. The words *it* and *there* followed by the subject of the sentence are expletive pronouns.

> *There* were only a few tickets left.
>
> *It* was a long list of chores.

When using an expletive, the verb agrees with the subject.

> There *remains* one *child* on the bus.
>
> There *remain* many *children* on the bus.

(2) Intensive pronoun. This is a pronoun, ending in *self* or *selves*, which follows its antecedent and emphasizes it.

> He *himself* will go.
>
> The package was delivered to the boys *themselves*.

(3) A reflexive pronoun. This is a pronoun, ending in *self* or *selves*, which is usually the object of a verb or preposition, or the complement of a verb.

> I hate *myself*.
>
> They always laugh at *themselves*.

Myself, yourself, himself, herself, and *itself* are all singular. *Ourselves, yourselves,* and *themselves* are all plural. There is no such pronoun as hisself or theirselves. Do not use *myself* instead of *I* or *me*.

(4) Demonstrative pronoun. This is used in place of a noun and points out the noun. Common demonstrative pronouns are *this, that, these, those*.

> I want *those*.

(5) Indefinite pronoun. This pronoun refers to any number of persons or objects. Following is a list of some singular and plural indefinite pronouns.

> SINGULAR
>
> anybody, anyone, each, everybody, everyone, no one, nobody, none, somebody, someone
>
> PLURAL
>
> all, any, many, several, some

If the singular form is used as a subject, the verb must be singular.

> *Everyone* of *them* sings. (One person sings.)

If the singular form is used as an antecedent, its pronoun must be singular.

> Did *anybody* on any of the teams lose *his* sneakers? (One person lost *his* sneakers.)

(6) Interrogative pronoun. This pronoun is used in asking a question. Such pronouns are *who, whose, whom, what,* and *which. Whose* shows possession. *Whom* is in the objective case. *Whom* is used only when an object pronoun is needed.

(7) Reciprocal pronoun. This pronoun is used when referring to mutual relations. The reciprocal pronouns are *each other* and *one another*.

> They love *one another*.
>
> They often visit *each other's* houses.

Note that the possessive is formed by an *'s* after the word *other*.

(8) Possessive pronoun. This pronoun refers to a noun that owns something. The possessive pronouns are as follows:

> SINGULAR
>
> mine (my), yours, his, hers, its
>
> PLURAL
>
> ours, yours, theirs

Notice that possessive pronouns do not use an 's. *It's* is a contraction meaning *it is*; *its* denotes possession.

(9) Relative pronoun.

> Nominative case — who, that, which
>
> Objective case — whom, that, which
>
> Possessive case — whose

A relative pronoun used as the *subject* of a dependent clause is in the nominative case.

> I know *who* stole the car.
>
> Give the prize to *whoever* won it.

A relative pronoun used as the *object* of a dependent clause is in the objective case.

> He is the thief *whom* I know. (Object of verb *know*)

Note that the difficulty always comes between choosing *who* or *whom*. Remember that *who* is in the nominative case and is used for the appropriate situations discussed under nominative case in the section on nouns. *Whom* is in the objective case and is used for the appropriate situations discussed under objective case in the section on nouns.

> Who is coming? (*Who* is the subject.)
>
> Whom are you going with? (*Whom* is the object of the preposition *with*.)

The relative pronoun in the possessive case is *whose*. Notice there is no apostrophe in this word. The contraction *who's* means *who is*.

> I know *whose* book it is. (Denotes possession)
>
> I know *who's* on first base. (*who's* means *who is*)

(10) Personal pronouns

	Singular	Plural
NOMINATIVE CASE		
First person	I	we
Second person	you	you
Third person	he, she, it	they
OBJECTIVE CASE		
First person	me	us
Second person	you	you
Third person	him, her, it	them
POSSESSIVE CASE		
First person	mine (my)	ours (our)
Second person	yours (your)	yours (your)
Third person	his, hers, its (his, her, its)	theirs (their)

Personal pronouns denote what is called *person*. First-person pronouns show the person or thing that is speaking.

> I am going. (First person speaking)

Second-person pronouns show the person or thing being spoken to.

> *You* are my friend. (Second person spoken to)

Third-person pronouns show the person or thing being spoken about.

> Bea did not see *her*. (Third person spoken about)

IMPORTANT FOR EXAM

Pronouns must agree with their antecedents in person, number, and gender.

1. *Who* refers to persons only.

2. *Which* refers to animals or objects.

3. *That* refers to persons, animals, or objects.

> I don't know *who* the actor is. (Person)
>
> They missed their dog, *which* died. (Animal)
>
> I finished the book *which* (or *that*) you recommended. (Object)
>
> They are the people *who* started the fight. (Person)
>
> That is the tiger *that* ran loose. (Animal)
>
> The light *that* failed was broken. (Object)

Note that the singular indefinite antecedents always take a singular pronoun.

> *Everyone* of the girls lost *her* hat.
>
> *None* of the boys lost *his*.
>
> *Someone* left *his* bike outside.

Note that collective singular nouns take singular pronouns; collective plural nouns take plural pronouns.

> The choir sang *its* part beautifully.
>
> The choirs sang *their* parts beautifully.

Note that two or more antecedents joined by *and* take a plural pronoun.

> Dave *and* Steve lost *their* way.

Note that two or more singular antecedents joined by *or* or *nor* take a singular pronoun.

> Tanya or Charita may use *her* ball.
>
> Neither Tanya nor Charita may use *her* ball.

If two antecedents are joined by *or* or *nor*, and if one is plural and the other is singular, the pronoun agrees in number with the nearer antecedent.

> Neither the *ball* nor the *rackets* were in *their* place.

Case

Remember that pronouns must also be in the correct case.

(1) A pronoun must be in the nominative case when it is the subject of a sentence.

> James and *I* went to the airport.
>
> *We* freshmen helped the seniors.
>
> Peter calls her more than *I* do.
>
> Peter calls her more than *I*. (Here, the verb *do* is understood, and *I* is the subject of the understood verb *do*.)

(2) A pronoun is in the objective case when it is a direct object of the verb.

> Leaving James and *me*, they ran away.
>
> John hit *them*.
>
> The freshman helped *us* seniors.

A pronoun is in the objective case when it is the indirect object of a verb.

> Give *us* the ball.

(3) A pronoun is in the objective case when it is an object of a preposition.

>To Ben and *me*
>
>With Sheila and *her*
>
>Between you and *them*

(4) A pronoun is in the possessive case when it shows ownership.

>*Her* car broke down.
>
>*Theirs* did also.

A pronoun is in the possessive case when it appears before a gerund (see verbals).

>*His* going was a sad event.

For a more detailed analysis of the three cases, see the section on cases of nouns.

ADJECTIVES

An adjective describes or modifies a noun or a pronoun. An adjective usually answers the question *which one*? Or *what kind*? Or *how many*? There are a number of types of adjectives you should know.

(1) Articles (a, an, the)

An article must agree in number with the noun or pronoun it modifies.

>*A* boy
>
>*An* apple
>
>*The* girls

If the noun or pronoun begins with a consonant, use *a*. If the noun or pronoun begins with a vowel, use *an*.

>*A* pear
>
>*An* orange

(2) Limiting adjectives point out definite nouns or tell how many there are.

>*Those* books belong to John.
>
>The *three* boys didn't see *any* birds.

(3) Descriptive adjectives describe or give a quality of the noun or pronoun they modify.

>The *large* chair
>
>The *sad* song

(4) Possessive, demonstrative, and indefinite adjectives look like the pronouns of the same name. However, the adjective does not stand alone. It describes a noun or pronoun.

>*This* is *mine*. (Demonstrative and possessive pronouns)
>
>*This* book is *my* father's. (Demonstrative and possessive adjectives)

(5) Interrogative and relative adjectives look the same, but they function differently. Interrogative adjectives ask questions.

>*Which* way should I go?
>
>*Whose* book is this?
>
>*What* time is John coming?

Relative adjectives join two clauses and modify some word in the dependent clause.

>I don't know *whose* book it is.

IMPORTANT FOR EXAM

An adjective is used as a predicate adjective after a linking verb. If the modifier is describing the verb (a non-linking verb) we must use an adverb.

The boy is *happy*. (Adjective)
Joe appeared *angry*. (Adjective)
The soup tasted *spicy*. (Adjective)
Joe looked *angrily* at the dog. (Adverb — *angrily* modifies *looked*)

Positive, Comparative, and Superlative Adjectives

(1) The positive degree states the quality of an object.

(2) The comparative degree compares two things. It is formed by using *less* or *more* or adding *er* to the positive.

(3) The superlative degree compares three or more things. It is formed by using *least* or *most* or adding *est* to the positive.

Positive	Comparative	Superlative
Easy	easier; more easy; less easy	easiest; most easy; least easy
Pretty	prettier; more pretty; less pretty	prettiest; least pretty; most pretty

Do Not Use Two Forms Together

She is the most prettiest. (Incorrect)
She is the prettiest. (Correct)
She is the most pretty. (Correct)

VERBS

A verb either denotes action or a state of being. There are four major types of verbs: transitive, intransitive, linking, and auxiliary.

(1) Transitive verbs are action words that must take a direct object. The direct object, which receives the action of the verb, is in the objective case.

Joe *hit* the ball. (*Ball* is the direct object of *hit*.)

Joe *killed* Bill. (*Bill* is the direct object of *killed*.)

(2) Intransitive verbs denote action but do not take a direct object.

The glass *broke*.

The boy *fell*.

IMPORTANT FOR EXAM

Set, lay, and *raise* are always transitive and take an object. *Sit, lie*, and *rise* are always intransitive and do not take a direct object.

Set the book down, *lay* the pencil down, and *raise* your hands. (*Book, pencil*, and *hands* are direct objects of *set, lay*, and *raise*.)

Sit in the chair.

She *lies* in bed all day.

The sun also *rises*.

The same verb can be transitive or intransitive, depending on the sentence.

The pitcher *threw* wildly. (Intransitive)

The pitcher *threw* the ball wildly. (Transitive)

(3) Linking verbs have no action. They denote a state of being. Linking verbs mean "equal." Here are some examples: *is, are, was, were, be, been, am* (any form of the verb *to be*), *smell, taste, feel, look, seem, become, appear*.

Sometimes, these verbs are confusing because they can be linking verbs in one sentence and action verbs in another. You can tell if the verb is a linking verb if it means equal in the sentence.

He felt nervous. (*He* equals *nervous*.)
He felt nervously for the door bell. (*He* does not equal *door bell*.)

Linking verbs take a predicate nominative or predicate adjective. (See sections on nouns, pronouns, and adjectives.)

It *is I*.
It *is she*.

(4) Auxiliary verbs are sometimes called "helping" verbs. These verbs are used with an infinitive verb (*to* plus the verb) or a participle to form a verb phrase.

The common auxiliary verbs are:

> All forms of *to be, to have, to do, to keep.*
>
> The verbs *can, may, must, ought to, shall, will, would, should.*

> > He *has to go.* (Auxiliary *has* plus the infinitive *to go*)
> >
> > He *was going.* (Auxiliary *was* plus the present participle *going*)
> >
> > He *has gone.* (Auxiliary *has* plus the past participle *gone*)

There is no such form as *had ought.* Use *ought to have* or *should have.*

> He *ought to have gone.*
>
> He *should have gone.*

Every verb can change its form according to five categories. Each category adds meaning to the verb. The five categories are: *tense, mood, voice, number,* and *person.*

Tense: This indicates the *time,* or *when* the verb occurs. There are six tenses. They are:

present   past   future
present perfect   past perfect   future perfect

Three principal parts of the verb — the present, the past, and the past participle — are used to form all the tenses.

The *present tense* shows that the action is taking place in the present.

> The dog *sees* the car and *jumps* out of the way.

The present tense of a regular verb looks like this:

	SINGULAR	PLURAL
First person	I jump	We jump
Second person	You jump	You jump
Third person	He, she, it jumps	They jump

Notice that an *s* is added to the third-person singular.

The *past tense* shows that the action took place in the past.

> The dog *saw* the car and *jumped* out of the way.

The past tense of a regular verb looks like this:

	SINGULAR	PLURAL
First person	I jumped	We jumped
Second person	You jumped	You jumped
Third person	He, she, it jumped	They jumped

Notice that *ed* is added to the verb. Sometimes just *d* is added, as in the verb *used,* for example. In regular verbs the past participle has the same form as the past tense, but it is used with an auxiliary verb.

> The dog *had jumped.*

The *future tense* shows that the action is going to take place in the future. The future tense needs the auxiliary verbs *will* or *shall.*

> The dog *will see* the car and *will jump* out of the way.

The future tense of a regular verb looks like this:

	SINGULAR	PLURAL
First person	I shall jump	We shall jump
Second person	You will jump	You will jump
Third person	He, she, it will jump	They will jump

Notice that *shall* is used in the first person of the future tense.

To form the *three perfect tenses,* the verb *to have* and the past participle are used.

- The present tense of *to have* is used to form the *present perfect.*

  The dog *has seen* the car and *has jumped* out of the way.

- The present perfect tense shows that the action has started in the past and is continuing or has just been implemented in the present.

- The past tense of *to have* is used to form the *past perfect.*

  The dog *had seen* the car and *jumped* out of the way.

- The past perfect tense shows that the action had been completed in the past.

- The future tense of *to have* is used to form the *future perfect.*

  The dog *will have seen* the car and *will have jumped* out of the way.

- The future perfect tense shows that an action will have been completed before a definite time in the future.

Following is a table that shows the present, past, and future tenses of *to have*.

PRESENT TENSE		
	SINGULAR	PLURAL
First person	I have	We have
Second person	You have	You have
Third person	He, she, it has	They have

PAST TENSE		
	SINGULAR	PLURAL
First person	I had	We had
Second person	You had	You had
Third person	He, she, it had	They had

FUTURE TENSE		
	SINGULAR	PLURAL
First person	I shall have	We shall have
Second person	You will have	You shall have
Third person	He, she, it will have	They shall have

The perfect tenses all use the past participle. Therefore, you must know the past participle of all the verbs. As we said, the past participle usually is formed by adding *d* or *ed* to the verb. However, there are many irregular verbs. Following is a table of the principal parts of some irregular verbs.

PRESENT	PAST	PAST PARTICIPLE
arise	arose	arisen
awake	awoke, awaked	awoke, awaked, awakened
awaken	awakened	awakened
be	was	been
bear	bore	borne
beat	beat	beaten
become	became	become
begin	began	begun
bend	bent	bent
bet	bet	bet
bid (command)	bade, bid	bidden, bid
bind	bound	bound
bite	bit	bitten
bleed	bled	bled
blow	blew	blown
break	broke	broken
bring	brought	brought
build	built	built
burn	burned	burned, burnt
burst	burst	burst
buy	bought	bought
catch	caught	caught
choose	chose	chosen
come	came	come
cost	cost	cost
dig	dug	dug
dive	dived, dove	dived
do	did	done
draw	drew	drawn
dream	dreamed	dreamed
drink	drank	drunk
drive	drove	driven
eat	ate	eaten
fall	fell	fallen
fight	fought	fought
fit	fitted	fitted
fly	flew	flown
forget	forgot	forgotten, forgot
freeze	froze	frozen
get	got	got, gotten
give	gave	given
go	went	gone
grow	grew	grown
hang (kill)	hanged	hanged
hang (sus- pended)	hung	hung
hide	hid	hidden
hold	held	held
know	knew	known
lay	laid	laid
lead	led	led

PRESENT	PAST	PAST PARTICIPLE
lend	lent	lent
lie (recline)	lay	lain
lie (untruth)	lied	lied
light	lit	lit
pay	paid	paid
raise (take up)	raised	raised
read	read	read
rid	rid	rid
ride	rode	ridden
ring	rang	rung
rise (go up)	rose	risen
run	ran	run
saw (cut)	sawed	sawed
say	said	said
see	saw	seen
set	set	set
shake	shook	shaken
shine (light)	shone	shone
shine (to polish)	shined	shined
show	showed	shown, showed
shrink	shrank	shrunk, shrunken
sing	sang	sung
sit	sat	sat
slay	slew	slain
speak	spoke	spoken
spend	spent	spent
spit	spat, spit	spat, spit
spring	sprang	sprung
stand	stood	stood
steal	stole	stolen
swear	swore	sworn
swim	swam	swum
swing	swung	swung
take	took	taken
teach	taught	taught
tear	tore	torn
throw	threw	thrown
wake	waked, woke	waked, woken
wear	wore	worn
weave	wove, weaved	woven, weaved
weep	wept	wept
win	won	won
write	wrote	written

Another aspect of tense that appears on the test is the *correct sequence* or *order of tenses. Be sure if you change tense you know why you are doing so. Following are some rules to help you.*

95

When using the perfect tenses remember:

- The present perfect tense goes with the present tense.

  present

  As Dave *steps* up to the mound,

  present perfect

  the pitcher *has thrown* the ball to

  present perfect

  first and I *have caught* it.

- The past perfect tense goes with the past tense.

  past

  Before Dave *stepped* up to the

  past perfect

  mound, the pitcher *had thrown*

  past perfect

  the ball to first and I *had caught* it.

- The future perfect goes with the future tense.

  future

  Before Dave *will step* up to the mound, the pitcher

  future perfect

  will have thrown the ball to first

  future perfect

  and I *shall have caught* it.

- The present participle (verb + *ing*) is used when its action occurs at the same time as the action of the main verb.

  John, *answering* the bell, *knocked* over the plant. (*Answering* and *knocked* occur at the same time.)

- The past participle is used when its action occurs before the main verb.

  The elves, *dressed* in costumes, will *march* proudly to the shoemaker. (The elves dressed *before* they will march.)

Mood

The mood or mode of a verb shows the manner of the action. There are three moods.

1. The *indicative mood* shows the sentence is factual. Most of what we way is in the indicative mode.

2. The *subjunctive mood* is used for conditions contrary to fact or for strong desires. The use of the subjunctive mood for the verb *to be* is a test item.

Following is the conjugation (list of forms) of the verb *to be* in the subjunctive mood:

	PRESENT TENSE	
	SINGULAR	PLURAL
First person	I be	We be
Second person	You be	You be
Third person	He, she, it be	They be

	PAST TENSE	
	SINGULAR	PLURAL
First person	I were	We were
Second person	You were	You were
Third person	He, she, it were	They were

If I *be* wrong, then punish me.

If he *were* king, he would pardon me.

Also, *shall* and *should* are used for the subjunctive mood.

If he *shall* fail, he will cry.

If you *should* win, don't forget us.

3. The *imperative mood* is used for commands.

> Go at once!

If strong feelings are expressed, the command ends with an exclamation point. In commands, the subject *you* is not stated but is understood.

Voice

There are two voices of verbs. The active voice shows that the subject is acting upon something or doing something *to* something else. The active voice has a direct object.

> subject   object
> The *car* hit the *boy*.

The passive voice shows that the subject is acted upon *by* something. Something was done *to* the subject. The direct object becomes the subject. The verb *to be* plus the past participle is used in the passive voice.

> subject
> The *boy* was hit by the car.

Number

This, as before, means singular or plural. A verb must agree with its subject in number.

> The *list was* long. (Singular)
> The *lists were* long. (Plural)

Nouns appearing between subject and verb do not change subject/verb agreement.

> The *list* of chores *was* long. (Singular)
> The *lists* of chores *were* long. (Plural)

Subjects joined by *and* are singular if the subject is one person or unit.

> My *friend and colleague has* decided to leave. (Singular)
> *Five and five is* ten. (Singular)
> *Tea and milk is* my favorite drink. (Singular)

Singular subjects joined by *or, either-or,* and *neither-nor* take singular verbs.

> Either Alvin or Lynette *goes* to the movies.

If one subject is singular and one is plural, the verb agrees with the nearer subject.

> Either Alvin or the girls *go* to the movies.

The use of the expletive pronouns *there* and *it* do not change subject/verb agreement.

> There *is no one* here.
> There *are snakes* in the grass.

> Think: No one is there; snakes are in the grass.

A relative pronoun takes a verb that agrees in number with the pronoun's antecedent.

> It is the *electrician who suggests* new wiring. (Singular)
> It is the *electricians who suggest* new wiring. (Plural)

Singular indefinite pronouns take singular verbs.

> Everybody *buys* tickets.

It is hard to tell if some nouns are singular. Following is a list of tricky nouns that take singular verbs.

> Collective nouns — *army, class, committee, team*

Singular nouns in plural form — *news, economics, mathematics, measles, mumps, news, politics*

Titles, although plural in form, refer to a single work — *The New York Times*, Henry James's *The Ambassadors*

> The *army is* coming.
> *News travels* fast.
> *Jaws is* a good movie.

Don't (do not) is incorrect for third-person singular. *Doesn't (does not)* is correct.

> He *doesn't* agree.

Person

Person, as before, refers to first person (speaking), second person (spoken to), and third person (spoken about). A verb must agree with its subject in person.

> I study. (First person)
> He studies. (Third person)

Intervening nouns or pronouns do not change subject/verb agreement.

> *He* as well as I *is* going. (Third person)

If there are two or more subjects joined by *or* or *nor*, the verb agrees with the nearer subject.

> Either John or *we are* going. (First-person plural)

ADVERBS

An adverb describes or modifies a verb, an adjective, or another adverb. Adverbs usually answer the questions *why?, where?, when?, how? to what degree?* Many adverbs end in *ly*. There are two types of adverbs similar in use to the same type of adjective.

- *Interrogative adverbs* ask questions.

  > *Where* are you going?
  > *When* will you be home?

- *Relative adverbs* join two clauses and modify some word in the dependent clause.

  > No liquor is sold *where* I live.

As with adjectives, there are three degrees of comparison for adverbs, and a corresponding form for each.

1. The positive degree is often formed by adding *ly* to the adjective.

   > She was *angry*. (Adjective)
   > She screamed *angrily*. (Adverb)

2. The *comparative* is formed by using *more* or *less* or adding *er* to the positive.

3. The *superlative* is formed by using *most* or *least* or adding *est* to the positive.

Here are two typical adverbs:

POSITIVE DEGREE	COMPARATIVE DEGREE	SUPERLATIVE DEGREE
easily	easier, more easily, less easily	easiest, most easily, least easily
happily	happier, more happily, less happily	happiest, most happily, least happily

CONJUNCTIONS

Conjunctions connect words, phrases, or clauses. Conjunctions can connect equal parts of speech.

and
but
for
or

Some conjunctions are used in pairs:

> either . . . or
> neither . . . nor
> not only . . . but also

Here are some phrases and clauses using conjunctions:

> John *or* Mary (Nouns are connected.)
> On the wall *and* in the window (Phrases are connected.)
> Mark had gone *but* I had not. (Clauses are connected)
> *Either* you go *or* I will. (Clauses are connected.)

If the conjunction connects two long clauses, a comma is used in front of the coordinating conjunction:

> Julio had gone to the game in the afternoon, but Pedro had not.

Some conjunctions are transitional:

> therefore
> however
> moreover
> finally
> nevertheless

These conjunctions connect the meaning of two clauses or sentences.

IMPORTANT FOR EXAM

Be aware of *comma splices*. Comma splices occur when one connects two independent clauses with a comma, rather than with a semicolon or with a comma followed by a coordinating conjunction. An independent clause is a clause that can stand alone as a complete sentence.

> His bike was broken; therefore, he could not ride. (Correct)

> His bike was broken. Therefore he could not ride. (Correct)

> His bike was broken, and, therefore, he could not ride. (Correct)

> His bike was broken, therefore, he could not ride. (Incorrect)

> He found his wallet, however he still left the auction. (Incorrect)

The last two sentences are comma splices and are incorrect. *Remember, two independent clauses cannot be connected by a comma.*

PREPOSITIONS

A preposition shows the relationship between a noun or pronoun and some other word in the sentence.

The following are all prepositions:

about	for	through
above	in	to
across	inside	under
around	into	up
behind	of	upon
beneath	off	within
during	over	without

Sometimes groups of words are treated as single prepositions. Here are some examples:

> according to
> ahead of
> in front of
> in between

The preposition together with the noun or pronoun it introduces is called a prepositional phrase.

> *Under* the table
> *In front of* the oil painting
> *Behind* the glass jar
> *Along* the waterfront
> *Beside* the canal

Very often on the test, idiomatic expressions are given that depend upon prepositions to be correct. Following is a list of idioms showing the correct preposition to use:

Abhorrence of: He showed an *abhorrence of* violence.

Abound in (or *with*): The lake *abounded with* fish.

Accompanied by (a person): He was *accompanied by* his friend.

Accompanied with: He *accompanied* his visit *with* a house gift.

Accused by, of: He was *accused by* a person *of* a crime.

Adept in: He is *adept in* jogging.

Agree to (an offer): I *agree to* the terms of the contract.

Agree with (a person): I *agree with* my son.

Agree upon (or *on*) (a plan): I *agree upon* that approach to the problem.

Angry at (a situation): I was *angry at* the delay.

Available for (a purpose): I am *available for* tutoring.

Available to (a person): Those machines are *available to* the tenants.

Burden with: I won't *burden* you *with* my problems.

Centered on (or *in*): His efforts *centered on* winning.

Compare to (shows similarity): An orange can be *compared to* a grapefruit.

Compare with (shows difference): An orange can't be *compared with* a desk.

Conform to (or *with*): He does not *conform to* the rules.

Differ with (an opinion): I *differ with* his judgement.

Differ from (a thing): The boss's car *differs from* the worker's car.

Different from: His book is *different from* mine. (Use *different than* with a clause.)

Employed at (salary): He is *employed at* $25 a day.

Employed in (work): He is *employed in* building houses.

Envious of: She is *envious of* her sister.

Fearful of: She is *fearful of* thunder.

Free of: She will soon be *free of* her burden.

Hatred of: He has a *hatred of* violence.

Hint at: They *hinted at* a surprise.

Identical with: Your dress is *identical with* mine.

Independent of: I am *independent of* my parents.

In search of: He went in *search of* truth.

Interest in: He was not *interested in* his friends.

Jealous of: He was *jealous of* them.

Negligent of: He was *negligent of* his responsibilities.

Object to: I *object to* waiting so long.

Privilege of: He had the *privilege of* being born a millionaire.

Proficient in: You will be *proficient in* grammar.

Wait for: We will *wait for* them.

Wait on (service): The maid *waited on* them.

Like is used as a preposition. He wanted his dog to act *like* Lassie.

VERBALS

Sometimes verbs can change their form and be used as nouns, adverbs, or adjectives. These forms are called verbals.

1. The infinitive is formed by adding *to* in front of the verb. The infinitive may act as a noun, adjective, or adverb.

    > I love *to sing*. (Noun)
    >
    > Music *to sing* is my favorite kind. (Adjective)
    >
    > He went *to sing* in the choir. (Adverb)

    An infinitive phrase is used as a noun, adjective, or adverb.

    > I love *to sing songs*. (Noun)
    > Music *to sing easily* is my favorite. (Adjective)
    > He went *to sing very often*. (Adverb)

2. The participle can be either present or past. The present participle is usually formed by adding *ing* to a verb. The past participle is usually formed by adding *n, en, d,* or *ed* to a verb. The participle is used as an adjective.

    > The *swaying* crane struck the *fallen* boy.
    >
    > (*Swaying* is a present participle; *fallen* is a past participle.)

    A participle phrase is used as an adjective.

    > *Blowing the crane fiercely*, the wind caused much danger.

IMPORTANT FOR EXAM

Beware of dangling participle phrases.

> *Blowing the crane fiercely*, the crowd ran.
>
> (The wind is blowing the crane, not the crowd.)

3. The gerund is formed by adding *ing* to a verb. Although the gerund may look like a present participle, it is used only as a noun.

    > *Seeing* clearly is important for good *driving*.
    >
    > (*Seeing* is the subject; *driving* is the object of the preposition *for*.)
    >
    > A participle phrase is used as a noun.
    >
    > *Seeing traffic signals* is important for good driving.

PHRASES

A prepositional phrase begins with a preposition. A prepositional phrase can also be a noun phrase or an adjective phrase or an adverbial phrase.

> *"Over the hill"* was the slogan of the geriatric club. (Noun phrase)
>
> The top *of the statue* was broken. (Adjective phrase)
>
> The owl sat *in the nest*. (Adverbial phrase)

See the previous section on *verbals* for infinitive phrases, participle phrases, and gerund phrases.

IMPORTANT FOR EXAM

A dangling or misplaced modifier is a word or phrase acting as a modifier that does not refer clearly to the word or phrase it modifies.

A bright light blinded his eyes *over the door*. (Misplaced modifier — his eyes were not over the door.)

Blowing the crane fiercely, the crowd ran. (Misplaced participle phrase — the crowd was not blowing the crane.)

Watching television, cookies were eaten. (Dangling gerund phrase — cookies were not watching television.)

Not able to stop, the man jumped out of my way. (Dangling infinitive phrase — is it the man who could not stop?)

The following modifying phrases clearly show what they modify.

A bright light over the door blinded his eyes.

Because the wind was blowing the crane fiercely, the crowd ran.

Watching television, Laura ate the cookies.

Since I was not able to stop, the man jumped out of my way.

CLAUSES

Clauses are groups of words that contain a subject and a predicate (verb part of the sentence). There are two main kinds of clauses. One kind is the *independent clause*, which makes sense when it stands alone. Independent clauses are joined by coordinating conjunctions.

I know how to clean silver, *but* I never learned how to clean copper.

(The two independent clauses could stand alone as complete sentences.)

I know how to clean silver. I never learned how to clean copper.

The other kind of clause is a *dependent or subordinate clause*. Although this type of clause has a subject and a predicate, it cannot stand alone.

When I learn to clean copper, I will keep my pots sparkling.

When I learn to clean copper, by itself, does not make sense. Dependent clauses are always used as a single part of speech in a sentence. They function as nouns or adjectives or adverbs. When they function as nouns they are called *noun clauses*. When they function as adjectives they are called *adjective clauses*. When they are adverbs, they are called *adverbial clauses*. Since a dependent or subordinate clause cannot stand alone, it must be joined with an independent clause to make a sentence. A *subordinating conjunction* does this job. A relative pronoun (*who, that, which, what, whose,* and *whom*) may act as the subordinating conjunction. For adjective and adverbial clauses, a relative adverb (*while, when*) may act as the subordinating conjunction.

I noticed *that he was very pale*.

That he was very pale is a noun clause — the object of the verb *noticed*. *That* is the subordinating conjunction.

Who was guilty is not known.

Who was guilty is a noun clause — subject of the verb *is*. *Who* is the subordinating conjunction.

She lost the belt *which was a present*.

Which was a present is an adjective clause — describing *belt*. *Which* is the subordinating conjunction.

She lost the belt *when she dropped the bag*.

When she dropped the bag is an adverbial clause answering the question *when* about the predicate. *When* is the subordinating conjunction.

Clauses should refer clearly and logically to the part of the sentence they modify.

We bought a dress at Bloomingdale's *which was expensive.*

(Misplaced adjective clause. Did the writer mean Bloomingdale's was expensive?)

Correct: We bought a dress *which was expensive* at Bloomingdale's.

When finally discovered, not a sound was heard.

(Misplaced adverbial clause. Who or what is discovered?)

Correct: *When finally discovered*, the boys didn't make a sound.

SENTENCES

A sentence is a group of words that express a complete thought. An independent clause can stand by itself and may or may not be a complete sentence.

Beth and Terry rode the Ferris wheel; they enjoyed the ride. (Two independent clauses connected by a semicolon)

Beth and Terry rode the Ferris wheel. They enjoyed the ride. (Two independent clauses — each is a sentence)

1. A simple sentence has one independent clause. A dependent clause is never a sentence by itself. Here are some simple sentences:

   John and Fred played.

   John laughed and sang.

   John and Fred ate hot dogs and drank beer.

The following is not an independent clause:

   Fred said. (Incorrect — *said* is a transitive verb. It needs a direct object.)

   Fred said hello. (Correct)

2. A compound sentence has at least two independent clauses.

   Darryl bought the meat, and *Laverne bought the potatoes.*

3. A complex sentence has one independent clause and at least one dependent clause.

   Because she left early, she missed the end.

   (*Because she left early* is the dependent clause. *She missed the end* is an independent clause.)

4. A compound-complex sentence has two independent clauses and one or more dependent clauses.

   You prefer math and I prefer music, although I am the math major.

   (*You prefer math* and *I prefer music* are the independent clauses. The dependent clause is *although I am a math major.*)

COMMON SENTENCE ERRORS

SENTENCE FRAGMENTS

These are parts of sentences that are incorrectly written with the capitals and punctuation of a sentence.

Around the corner.
Because she left early.
Going to the movies.
A terrible tragedy.

Remember that sentences must have at least a subject and a verb.

RUN-ON SENTENCES

These are sentences that are linked incorrectly.

The rain was heavy, lightning was crackling he could not row the boat. (Incorrect)

Because the rain was heavy and lightning was crackling, he could not row the boat. (Correct)

The rain was heavy. Lightning was crackling. He could not row the boat. (Correct)

FAULTY PARALLELISM

Elements of equal importance within a sentence should have parallel structure or similar form.

To sing, *dancing*, and to laugh make life happy. (Incorrect)

To sing, to dance, and to laugh make life happy. (Correct)

He wants health, wealth, and *to be happy*. (Incorrect)

He wants health, wealth, and happiness. (Correct)

WATCH ARBITRARY TENSE SHIFTS

He *complained* while his father *listens*. (Incorrect)

He *complained* while his father *listened*. (Correct)

WATCH NOUN-PRONOUN AGREEMENTS

A *person* may pass if *they* study. (Incorrect)

A *person* may pass if *he* studies. (Correct)

WATCH THESE DON'TS

DON'T use *being that*; use *since* or *because*.

DON'T use *could of, should of, would of*; use *could have, should have, would have*.

DON'T use the preposition *of* in the following: off *of* the table, inside *of* the house.

DON'T use *this here* or *that there*; use just *this* or *that*.

DON'T misuse *then* as a coordinating conjunction; use *than* instead.

He is better *than* he used to be. (Correct)

He is better *then* he used to be. (Incorrect)

CAPITALIZATION

1. Capitalize all proper nouns.

   Capitalize names of specific people, places, things, peoples, and their languages: Americans, America, Spanish. Note: Henry takes Spanish three times a week. Henry takes math three times a week.

2. Capitalize religions and holy books: Islam, Koran, Bible

3. Capitalize calendar words: Monday, April

4. Capitalize historical periods and events: Renaissance, Civil War

5. Always capitalize the first word in a sentence: It is Henry.

6. Capitalize the first word in a letter salutation: Dear John, Dear Sir

7. Capitalize the first word of a letter closing: Very truly yours,

8. Capitalize the first word in a direct quote: He said, "Go away."

9. Capitalize the first, last, and important words in titles: *The Man Without a Country*

   Note: *A, an, and, the* are usually not capitalized unless they are the first word.

   Note also that conjunctions and prepositions with less than five letters are usually not capitalized.

10. Capitalize words used as part of a proper noun: Hudson Street, Uncle Fritz

11. Capitalize specific regions: I want to move to the South.

12. Capitalize abbreviations of capitalized words: D. B. Edelson

13. Capitalize acronyms formed from capitalized words: NASA, NATO

14. Capitalize the pronoun *I*: I beseech you to hear my prayer.

    Note that capitals are not used for seasons (summer, winter).

    Note that capitals are not used for compass directions (east, northeast).

    Note that capitals are not used for the second part of a quote: "I see," she said, "how smart Henry is."

PUNCTUATION

THE PERIOD

1. Use the period to end full sentences.

   Harry loves candy.

   Although John knew the course was difficult, he did not expect to fail.

2. Use the period with abbreviations:

   Mr.

   Ph.D.

   C.I.A.

THE QUESTION MARK

Use the question mark to end a direct question:

   Are you going to the store?

Note that indirect questions end with a period:

   He asked how Sue knew the right answer.

THE EXCLAMATION POINT

Use the exclamation point to denote strong feeling:

   Act now!

THE COLON

1. The colon can introduce a series or an explanation, but it must always follow an independent clause.

   The following sciences are commonly taught in college: biology, chemistry, and physics. (Correct)

   The sciences are: biology, chemistry, and physics. (Incorrect)

   The sciences are is not an independent clause.

2. The colon is used after the salutation in a business letter.

Dear Sir:

3. The colon is used to express the time:

It is 1:45.

THE SEMICOLON

1. The semicolon is used to link related independent clauses not linked by *and, but, or, nor, for, so,* or *yet*:

No person is born prejudiced; prejudice must be taught.

2. The semicolon is used before conjunctive adverbs and transitional phrases placed between independent clauses:

No person is born prejudiced; however, he has been taught well.

No person is born prejudiced; nevertheless, he has always appeared bigoted.

3. The semicolon is used to separate a series that already contains commas:

The team had John, the pitcher; Paul, the catcher; and Peter, the shortstop.

THE COMMA

1. The comma is used before long independent clauses linked by *and, but, or, nor, for, so,* or *yet*:

No person is born prejudiced, but some people learn quickly.

2. The comma is used following clauses, phrases, or expressions that introduce a sentence:

As I was eating, the waiter cleared the table.

In a great country like ours, people enjoy traveling.

3. The comma is used with nonrestrictive, or parenthetical, expressions (not essential to the meaning of the main clause).

He pulled the ice cream sundae, topped with whipped cream, toward him.

John is afraid of all women who carry hand grenades. *Notice there is no comma*. John is not afraid of all women. He is afraid of all women who carry hand grenades (restrictive clauses).

4. Use commas between items in a series:

Beth loves cake, candy, cookies, and ice cream.

5. Use the comma in direct address:

Pearl, come here.

6. Use the comma before and after terms in apposition:

Give it to Pearl, our good friend.

7. Use the comma in dates or addresses:

June 3, 1996

Freeport, Long Island

8. Use the comma after the salutation in a friendly letter:

Dear Henry,

9. Use the comma after the closing in letters:

Sincerely yours,

10. Use a comma between a direct quotation and the rest of the sentence:

"Our fudge," the cook bragged, "is the best in town."

11. Be sure to use two commas when needed:

    A good dancer, generally speaking, loves to dance.

12. Do not separate subjects and verbs with a comma:

    Students and teachers, receive rewards. (Incorrect)

13. Do not separate verbs and their objects with a comma:

    He scolded and punished, the boys. (Incorrect)

THE APOSTROPHE

1. Use the apostrophe to denote possession (see nouns).

    John's friend

2. Use the apostrophe in contractions:

    Didn't (did not)

    There's (there is)

3. Do not use an apostrophe with his, hers, ours, yours, theirs, or whose. Use an apostrophe with *its* if *its* is a contraction:

    The dog chewed *its* bone; *it's* hard for a little dog to chew such a big bone. (*It's* means it is; *its* is a pronoun that denotes possession.)

QUOTATION MARKS

1. Use quotation marks in direct quotes:

    "Get up," she said.

2. Use single quotes for a quote within a quote:

    Mark said, "Denise keeps saying 'I love you' to Ralph."

PARENTHESES

Use parentheses to set off nonrestrictive or unnecessary parts of a sentence:

This book (an excellent review tool) will help students.

THE DASH

1. Use the dash instead of parentheses:

    This book—an excellent review—will help students.

2. Use the dash to show interruption in thought:

    There are eight—remember, eight—parts of speech.

RHETORICAL REVIEW

STYLE

Good writing is clear and economical.

1. AVOID AMBIGUOUS PRONOUN REFERENCES

Tom killed Jerry. I feel sorry for *him*. (Who is *him*? Tom? Jerry?)

Burt is a nice man. I don't know why *they* insulted him. (Who does *they* refer to?)

2. AVOID CLICHÉS

Betty is *sharp as a tack*.

The math exam was *easy as pie*.

It will be *a cold day in August* before I eat dinner with Louisa again.

3. AVOID REDUNDANCY

Harry is a man who loves to gamble. (Redundant—we know that Harry is a man.)

Harry loves to gamble. (Correct)

Claire is a strange one. (Redundant—one is not necessary.)

Claire is strange.

This July has been particularly hot in terms of weather. (Redundant—*in terms of weather* is not necessary.)

This July has been particularly hot. (Correct)

4. AVOID WORDINESS

The phrases on the left are wordy. Use the word on the right.

WORDY	PREFERABLE
the reason why is that	because
the question as to whether	whether
in a hasty manner	hastily
be aware of the fact that	know
due to the fact that	because
in light of the fact that	since
regardless of the fact that	although
for the purpose of	to

5. AVOID VAGUE WORDS OR PHRASES

It is always preferable to use specific, concrete language rather than vague words and phrases:

The reality of the situation necessitated action. (Vague)

Bill shot the burglar before the burglar could shoot him. (Specific)

6. BE ARTICULATE. USE THE APPROPRIATE WORD OR PHRASE

The following are words or phrases that are commonly misused:

1. Accept: to receive or agree to (verb)
   I *accept* your offer.

   Except: preposition that means to leave out
   They all left *except* Dave.

2. Adapt: to change (verb)
   We must *adapt* to the new ways.

   Adopt: to take as one's own, to incorporate (verb)
   We will *adopt* a child.

3. Affect: to influence (verb)
   Their attitude may well *affect* mine.

   Effect: result (noun)
   What is the *effect* of their attitude?

4. Allusion: a reference to something (noun)
   The teacher made an *allusion* to Milton.

   Illusion: a false idea (noun)
   He had the *illusion* that he was king.

5. Among: use with more than two items (preposition)
   They pushed *among* the soldiers.

   Between: use with two items (preposition)
   They pushed *between* both soldiers.

6. Amount: cannot be counted (noun)
Sue has a large *amount* of pride.

Number: can be counted (noun)
Sue bought a *number* of apples.

7. Apt: capable (adjective)
She is an *apt* student.

Likely: probably (adjective)
We are *likely* to receive the prize.

8. Beside: at the side of (preposition)
He sat *beside* me.

Besides: in addition to (preposition)
There were others there *besides* Joe.

9. Bring: toward the speaker (verb)
Bring that to me.

Take: away from the speaker (verb)
Take that to him.

10. Can: to be able to (verb)
I *can* ride a bike.

May: permission (verb)
May I ride my bike?

11. Famous: well known (adjective)
He is a *famous* movie star.

Infamous: well known but not for anything good (adjective)
He is the *infamous* criminal.

12. Fewer: can be counted (adjective)
I have *fewer* pennies than John.

Less: cannot be counted (adjective)
I have *less* pride than John.

13. Imply: the speaker or writer is making a hint or suggestion (verb)
He *implied* in his book that women were inferior.

Infer: to draw a conclusion from the speaker or writer (verb)
The audience *inferred* that he was a woman-hater.

14. In: something is already there (preposition)
He is *in* the kitchen.

Into: something is going there (preposition)
He is on his way *into* the kitchen.

15. Irritate: to annoy (verb)
His whining *irritated* me.

Aggravate: to make worse (verb)
The soap *aggravated* his rash.

16. Teach: to provide knowledge (verb)
She *taught* him how to swim.

Learn: to acquire knowledge (verb)
He *learned* how to swim from her.

17. Un-interested: bored (adjective)
She is *uninterested* in everything.

Dis-interested: impartial (adjective)
He wanted a *disinterested* jury at his trial.

ORGANIZATION

A paragraph, like an essay, must have some organization plan. Each paragraph should represent the development of some point the author is making. Learn to recognize topic sentences, which often come at the beginning or end of a paragraph. Topic sentences tell the reader the main point of the paragraph.

Here are some sample topic sentences:

De Tocqueville is also concerned with the conflict between individual liberty and equality.

Another of the social institutions that leads to disaster in *Candide* is the aristocracy.

The Fortinbras subplot is the final subplot that points to Hamlet's procrastination.

Read the following paragraph and answer the appropriate questions.

1) Throughout history, writers and poets have created countless works of art. 2) The result is Paul's failure to pursue Clara and establish a meaningful relationship with her. 3) Paul's mother loves him, but the love is smothering and overprotective. 4) Although Paul feels free to tell his mother almost everything, he fails to tell her he is sexually attracted to Clara. 5) His feelings for Clara obviously make him feel he is betraying his mother. 6) Paul Morel's relationship with his mother in *Sons and Lovers* interferes with his relationship with Clara.

A. Which sentence does not belong in the above paragraph?

Answer: The first sentence is inappropriate to the idea of the paragraph, which concerns Paul's relationship with his mother and with Clara. The first sentence is also vague and virtually meaningless. Obviously, many works of art have been created throughout history. So what?

B. Unscramble the above paragraph and put the sentences in the correct order.

a. 2, 4, 3, 6, 5
b. 6, 5, 2, 4, 3
c. 3, 4, 5, 6, 2
d. 6, 3, 4, 5, 2

Answer: d. Obviously, sentence 1 does not fit the paragraph. Sentence 6 mentions Paul by his full name, the name of the work, and his relationships with both women, all of which are covered in the paragraph. It is the topic sentence. Sentence 2 sums up the paragraph; the clue is in the phrase "the result is." Logically sentence 2 should end the paragraph. Since the paragraph concerns Paul's relationship with his mother and its effect on his relationship with Clara, the other sentences should fall in place.

This section has covered a lot of the basic rules of grammar. It is primarily a reference section and you will not be expected to know everything on the exam. However, we suggest you use this section as a handy guide to help you understand many of the answers that might involve certain grammar principles with which you may not be familiar. Feel free to highlight certain portions of these principles so you can go back to them from time to time, especially when confronted with more difficult explanations of some of the problems both in the Strategy section as well as in any of the exams in the book.

RED ALERT

GENERAL SUGGESTIONS

Much of the success in test-taking comes from being comfortable both physically and mentally with the test you are taking. Physical comfort is very easy to achieve. Just remember a few important points:

1. **Be on time.** Actually, to be a few minutes early doesn't hurt. No one is helped by feeling rushed when beginning a test.

2. **Have a supply of pencils (#2) with good erasers.** There will be no time for borrowing or sharpening a pencil once the test begins.

3. **Wear comfortable clothing.** Layers of clothing are best, since they can be removed or put on, depending upon the temperature of the room. Don't wear shoes that pinch or a too-tight belt!

4. **Get a good rest the night before.** Cramming right before an ACT is not helpful and can sometimes lead to panic and confusion.

5. **Calculators are permitted** for the math test only, but not required. Contact ACT to find out which calculators are permitted.

Mental comfort is a little more difficult to achieve. *Preparation* is the key and comes with study and practice in the weeks and months before the test. Mental comfort is gained by becoming familiar with the test format, instructions, and types of problems that will appear.

Know the Test Format and Instructions

The Math section of the ACT consists of a total of 60 questions. 40% of the test (24 questions) is made up of questions from Pre-algebra and Elementary Algebra. 30% of the test (18 questions) is drawn from Intermediate Algebra and Coordinate Geometry. Finally, 30% of the test (18 questions) consists of Plane Geometry and Trigonometry questions. All questions are in the multiple-choice format, with 5 answer choices. Remember that on the ACT there is no penalty for wrong answers, so you should answer every question, even if you have to guess.

You will receive four scores for the mathematics portion of the ACT: a total test score based on all 60 questions, and subscores for Pre-algebra/Elementary Algebra, Intermediate Algebra/Coordinate Geometry, and Plane Geometry/Trigonometry.

Be sure that you have taken enough sample tests to be thoroughly familiar with the instructions. The instructions are part of the timed test. Do not spend valuable time reading them as if you had never seen them before. Of course, you can read them quickly to refresh your mind each time you start a new section of the test.

Pace Yourself

You are allowed 60 minutes for the entire math section. If you spend too much time on each question, you will not complete enough questions to receive a good score. Many very intelligent students work too slowly and spend too much time on details or neatness. As a result, they score lower than they should. As you work, put a mark by problems that take too long and a different mark by those you do not know how to solve, so you can go back to them later if you have time.

Bring a watch to the test and thus eliminate worry about how much time is left. When time is almost up, you should look over the rest of the problems and work those you know you can do most quickly.

All questions are equally weighted. Allot your time accordingly. Remember that hard questions count the same as easy ones. Don't miss out on one that might be easy for you by stubbornly sticking to one that might be more difficult.

Use the Test Booklet Scratch Area

For many problems, a simple sketch drawn in the scratch area of the test booklet will make the solution readily apparent and will thus save time. Also, do not attempt to do all computation work in your head. Remember to use the scratch area of the test booklet; mark only answers on the answer sheet.

Specific Suggestions

All of the general suggestions given will not help you if you are not prepared to solve the problems and arrive at the correct answers.

The examination questions require knowledge of pre-algebra, elementary and intermediate algebra, plane and coordinate geometry, and trigonometry. Most of the problems require some insight and originality—that is, you will need to know not only *how* to perform certain operations but also *when* to perform them. Very rarely will you be required to do a plain computation or find a routine solution.

Vocabulary is very important. A problem that asks you to find a *quotient* will be hard to do if you do not know the meaning of this term. Some basic terms you should know:

sum: the answer to an addition problem

product: the answer to a multiplication problem

quotient: the answer to a division problem

difference: the answer to a subtraction problem

integer: a whole number, either positive or negative or 0

prime number: a number with no factors other than 1 and itself

even integers: 2, 4, 6, 8, etc.

odd integers: 1, 3, 5, 7, etc.

consecutive integers: numbers in order, 1, 2, 3, or 7, 8, 9, etc.

Different types of problems call for different attacks. Of course, the most desirable situation is to know how to do all problems, work them out, and then fill in the letter space for the correct answer. But what if the answer you get is not among the choices, or you don't know how to do the problem in the first place? Then perhaps the following suggestions will help. However, remember these are only suggested methods for problem solving. Always do a problem your way if you are more comfortable with it and if it will solve the problem just as quickly.

Look for Shortcuts

Rarely will a problem on the ACT involve a long, cumbersome computation. If you find yourself caught up in a maze of large numbers, you have probably missed a shortcut.

Example:

Which is larger?

$$\frac{5}{23} \times \frac{7}{33} \quad \text{or} \quad \frac{7}{23} \times \frac{5}{31}$$

Solution:

Examination of the problem will let you see that after multiplying, in each case the numerators of the resulting fractions will be the same ($5 \cdot 7$ and $7 \cdot 5$). When the numerators of two fractions are the same, the fraction with the smaller denominator will be the larger fraction. In this case, the denominators are $23 \cdot 33$ and $23 \cdot 31$. It is not necessary to do the actual multiplication to see that $23 \cdot 31$ will be the smaller product (or denominator), making the larger fraction.

Example:

If $6 \times 6 \times (x) = 12 \times 12 \times 12$, then $x =$

(A) 6 **(B)** 12 **(C)** 18 **(D)** 24 **(E)** 48

Solution:

Use factoring and cancellation to eliminate the need to cube 12 and then divide by 36 ($6 \cdot 6$). Factor and cancel:

$$x = \frac{\overset{2}{\cancel{12}} \cdot \overset{2}{\cancel{12}} \cdot 12}{\underset{1}{\cancel{6}} \cdot \underset{1}{\cancel{6}}} = 48$$

The correct answer is E.

Estimate

On any timed competitive examination, it is necessary that you be able to estimate. Sometimes it is helpful to round off all numbers to a convenient power of 10 and estimate the answer. This will often enable you to pick the correct answer quickly without performing a lot of time-consuming computations. In some cases it will eliminate one or more of the answers right away, thus improving your chances if you have to guess.

Example:

Which of the following is closest to the value of

$$\frac{3654 \cdot 248}{1756}?$$

(A) 50 **(B)** 500 **(C)** 5,000 **(D)** 5 **(E)** 50,000

Solution:

3,654 is about 4,000. 248 is about 200 (or 300) and 1,756 is about 2,000. The problem then becomes:

$$\frac{\overset{2}{\cancel{4000}} \cdot 200}{\underset{1}{\cancel{2000}}} \cong 400$$

Therefore, choose answer B.

Substitute

Change confusing problems to more meaningful ones by substituting simple numbers for letters. Many students get confused by problems containing letters in place of numbers. These letters are called variables. Just remember that the letters stand for numbers; therefore, the same operations can be performed on them. Just think of how you would do the problem if there were numbers, and then perform the same operations on the letters.

Example:

If John's allowance is x a week and he saves m a week, what part of his allowance does he spend?

Solution:

Substituting some numbers for the letters in the problem, we get: If John's allowance is $5 a week and he saves $1 a week, then he spends $5 − $1, or $4 a week. This represents $4 (part) out of $5 (whole) or $\frac{4}{5}$ of his allowance.

Transferring the number computation to the original problem, we get:

$\frac{5-1}{5}$ or $\frac{x-m}{x}$ for the correct answer.

Example:

If a man was x years old y years ago, how many years old will he be z years from now?

Solution:

Substitute small numbers for the letters. If a man was 20 years old 5 years ago, how many years old will he be 8 years from now? The man is now 25 years old (20 + 5). Eight years from now he will be 20 + 5 + 8, or 33 years old. Back in the original problem, substitute letters for numbers in your solution:

$20 + 5 + 8 = x + y + z$

Work Backward

Some experts advise against this, but in some cases it can be advantageous for you to look at the answers first. You can save valuable time by knowing that all the answers are in common fractional or decimal form. Then you will want to work only in the form in which the answers are given.

Are all the answers the same except for one digit or placement of a decimal? Knowing this can save you time.

Example:

The square root of 106.09 is exactly:

(A) .103 **(B)** 1.03 **(C)** 10.3 **(D)** 103 **(E)** 1030

Solution:

Don't use your time to find the square root of 106.09. Work backward from the answers, which are all the same except for the placement of the decimal. Using the definition of square root (the number that when multiplied by itself will produce a given number), you can see that answer C is the only one that will give an answer of 106.09 when multiplied by itself.

Another type of problem in which it is helpful to work backward is the problem that contains an equation to solve. Trying each answer in the equation to see which one fits will help, especially if you are unsure of how to solve the equation.

Example:

$x\sqrt{.16} = 4$. Find the value of x:

(A) .1   **(B)** 1   **(C)** .4   **(D)** .64   **(E)** 10

Solution:

Examination of the equation reveals that it is really $.4x = 4$ ($\sqrt{.16} = .4$). Checking each answer will reveal that $10 \cdot .4 = 4$, therefore, E is the correct answer.

Answer the Question

Always check to see if you have answered the question asked. You can be sure, for instance, that if you are doing a problem involving two angles, the values for both angles will be among the answers listed. Be sure that you have found the right value.

Example:

If $3x + 2 = 12$, find $x - \dfrac{1}{3}$

(A) $3\dfrac{1}{3}$ (B) 3   (C) 10   (D) 4   (E) $5\dfrac{2}{3}$

Solution:

Solving the equation:
add −2 to both sides

$$3x + 2 = 12$$
$$\underline{ - 2 = -2}$$
$$3x = 10$$

Divide by 3

$$x = \dfrac{10}{3} = 3\dfrac{1}{3}$$

Notice that $x = 3\dfrac{1}{3}$ and that this answer is choice A. However, the problem asked us to find $x - \dfrac{1}{3}$. Therefore, the correct answer is B.

Guess

Remember that there is no penalty for a wrong answer. Thus, you should leave no question unanswered. If you are not sure how to solve a problem, see if you can eliminate two or more answers by any of the previously discussed strategies. Then guess from the remaining possibilities.

SPECIAL HELP FOR PROBLEM AREAS

Fractions

Comparing Fractions

Many problems will require that you know how to compare fractions. A few simple steps will ensure that you can do this.

1. If the *denominators* of two fractions are the *same,* the fraction with the *larger numerator* will be the fraction with the *larger* value.

   Example:

   Compare $\dfrac{3}{5}$ and $\dfrac{2}{5}$

   Solution:

   $3 > 2$, therefore $\dfrac{3}{5} > \dfrac{2}{5}$

2. If the *numerators* of two fractions are the *same,* the fraction with the *larger denominator* will be the *smaller* fraction.

   Example:

   Compare $\dfrac{2}{13}$ and $\dfrac{2}{15}$

   Solution:

   $13 < 15$, therefore $\dfrac{2}{13} > \dfrac{2}{15}$

3. If the numerators and denominators are different, the fractions can be compared by cross-multiplying. Cross-multiplying eliminates the need to find a common denominator in order to use method 1.

Example:

Compare $\dfrac{9}{13}$ and $\dfrac{11}{15}$

Solution:

Cross-multiply, putting the products above the numerators used in the products.

$135 < 143$, therefore $\dfrac{9}{13} < \dfrac{11}{15}$

Complex Fractions

If complex fractions (a fraction within a fraction) cause your mind to go blank, try this little routine. Whenever you have a complex fraction, find the least common denominator for all the denominators within the fraction and multiply all *terms* by this denominator. This will reduce the complex fraction to a simple one and make it easier to handle.

Example:

$$\dfrac{\dfrac{2}{3} + \dfrac{3}{4}}{1 - \dfrac{1}{3}}$$

Solution:

The least common denominator is 12. Multiply all terms by 12.

$$\dfrac{12\left(\dfrac{2}{3}\right) + \left(\dfrac{3}{4}\right)12}{12(1) - \dfrac{1}{3}(12)} = \dfrac{8 + 9}{12 - 4} = \dfrac{17}{8} = 2\dfrac{1}{8}$$

This routine can also be of use if the complex fraction contains letters or variables.

Example:

Simplify

$$\dfrac{1 - \dfrac{1}{x}}{1 + \dfrac{1}{x}}$$

Solution:

The least common denominator is x. Multiply all *terms* by x.

$$\dfrac{x(1) - \dfrac{1}{x}(x)}{x(1) + \dfrac{1}{x}(x)} = \dfrac{x - 1}{x + 1}$$

Percent

Percent problems are another source of trouble for many students. First, you should be sure you know how to change a decimal to a percent (multiply by 100) and to change a percent to a decimal or common fraction (divide by 100).

Examples:

$.35 = 35\% \ (.35 \cdot 100)$

$6\dfrac{1}{2}\% = 6.5\% = .065$

$(6\dfrac{1}{2}\% \div 100 = .065)$ or $(6.5\% \div 100 = 0.65)$

It is also a good idea to memorize the equivalent fractions for certain percents. This will save you time, as they will typically come up several times on the ACT.

$\frac{1}{2} = .50 = 50\%$ $\qquad$ $\frac{1}{6} = .16\frac{2}{3} = 16\frac{2}{3}\%$

$\frac{1}{4} = .25 = 25\%$ $\qquad$ $\frac{5}{6} = .83\frac{1}{3} = 83\frac{1}{3}\%$

$\frac{3}{4} = .75 = 75\%$ $\qquad$ $\frac{1}{8} = .12\frac{1}{2} = 12\frac{1}{2}\%$

$\frac{1}{5} = .20 = 20\%$ $\qquad$ $\frac{3}{8} = .37\frac{1}{2} = 37\frac{1}{2}\%$

$\frac{2}{5} = .40 = 40\%$ $\qquad$ $\frac{5}{8} = .62\frac{1}{2} = 62\frac{1}{2}\%$

$\frac{3}{5} = .60 = 60\%$ $\qquad$ $\frac{7}{8} = .87\frac{1}{2} = 87\frac{1}{2}\%$

$\frac{4}{5} = .80 = 80\%$ $\qquad$ $\frac{1}{10} = .10 = 10\%$

$\frac{1}{3} = .33\frac{1}{3} = 33\frac{1}{3}\%$ $\qquad$ $\frac{3}{10} = .30 = 30\%$

$\frac{2}{3} = .66\frac{2}{3} = 66\frac{2}{3}\%$ $\qquad$ $\frac{7}{10} = .70 = 70\%$

$1 = 100\%$ $\qquad$ $\frac{9}{10} = .90 = 90\%$

Remembering that *of* in a mathematical problem usually means that you have to multiply, algebraic equations can then be set up to solve the three types of percent problems.

Example:

What is 15% of 32?

Solution:

$x = 15\% \times 32$
$x = (.15)(32)$ (change 15% to a decimal fraction)
$x = 4.80$

Example:

9 is 30% of what number?

Solution:

$9 = 30\% \times x$
(a) $9 = (.30)x$ (change 30% to a decimal fraction)
or (b) $9 = \left(\frac{3}{10}\right)x$ (change 30% to a common fraction)
(a) $30 = x$ (divide by .3)
or (b) $30 = x$ (multiply by $\frac{10}{3}$)

Example:

12 is what percent of 72?

Solution:

$12 = x\% \cdot 72$
$12 = \left(\frac{x}{100}\right)72$ (change $x\%$ to a fraction)
$\frac{12}{72} = \frac{x}{100}$ (divide by 72)
$\frac{1}{6} = \frac{x}{100}$ (reduce $\frac{12}{72}$ to $\frac{1}{6}$)
$100 = 6x$ (cross-multiply)
$16\frac{2}{3} = x$ (divide by 6)

or, if you have memorized your fractional equivalent chart, you will know that $16\frac{2}{3}\% = \frac{1}{6}$.

Geometry

Many of the questions in the geometry area of the ACT will require recall of the numerical relationships learned in an informal geometry course. You will not be asked to do a formal proof! If you are thoroughly familiar with these relationships, you should not find the geometry questions difficult.

Be very careful with units, especially when finding area, perimeter, or volume. Change all dimensions to a common unit before doing the calculations.

Important Properties and Formulas

Memorize the following geometric properties to help speed your ability to solve the problems.

Properties of a Triangle

The sum of the angles of a triangle equals 180°.

An exterior angle of a triangle is equal to the sum of the remote interior angles.

An equilateral triangle has equal sides and all angles equal to 60°.

An isosceles triangle has two equal sides. The angles opposite these sides are also equal.

In a right triangle, $a^2 + b^2 = c^2$, where a and b are the legs and c is the hypotenuse (Pythagorean theorem).

Properties of Parallel Lines

Pairs of alternate interior angles are equal.

Pairs of corresponding angles are equal.

Pairs of interior angles on the same side of the transversal are supplementary (their sum is 180°).

Properties of a Parallelogram

Opposite sides are parallel.

Opposite sides are congruent.

Opposite angles are congruent.

Diagonals bisect each other.

Properties of a Rectangle

The same properties as a parallelogram, plus:

All angles are right angles.

The diagonals are congruent.

Properties of a Rhombus

The same properties as a parallelogram, plus:

All sides are congruent.

The diagonals are perpendicular to each other.

The diagonals bisect the angles.

Properties of a Square

The same properties as a parallelogram, plus those of a rectangle plus those of a rhombus.

Properties of a Circle

Know the different types of angles formed in a circle and their relationships to their arcs.

A central angle is equal in degrees to the measure of its intercepted arc.

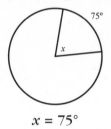

$$x = 75°$$

An inscribed angle is equal in degrees to one-half its intercepted arc.

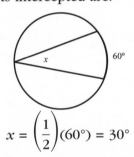

$$x = \left(\frac{1}{2}\right)(60°) = 30°$$

An angle formed by two chords intersecting in a circle is equal in degrees to one-half the sum of its intercepted arcs.

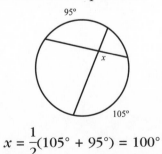

$$x = \frac{1}{2}(105° + 95°) = 100°$$

An angle outside the circle formed by two secants, a secant and a tangent, or two tangents is equal in degrees to one-half the difference of its intercepted arcs.

Two tangent segments drawn to a circle from the same external point are congruent.

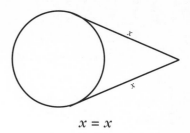

$$x = x$$

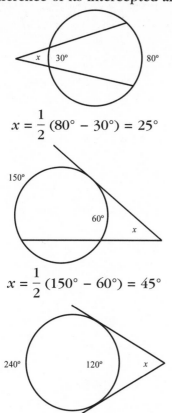

$$x = \frac{1}{2}(80° - 30°) = 25°$$

$$x = \frac{1}{2}(150° - 60°) = 45°$$

$$x = \frac{1}{2}(240° - 120°) = 60°$$

Important Area Formulas

Area of a triangle:	$A = \frac{1}{2}bh$	(b is the base, h is the height)
Area of a parallelogram:	$A = bh$	(b is the base, h is the height)
Area of a square:	$A = s^2$	(s is a side of the square)
Area of a circle:	$A = \pi r^2$	(r is the radius of the circle)
Area of a rectangle:	$A = lw$	(l is the length, w is the width)
or	$A = bh$	(since a rectangle is a parallelogram)
Area of a trapezoid:	$A = \frac{1}{2}h(b_1 + b_2)$	(h is the height, b_1 and b_2 are the bases)

Volumes

The volume of most solids is found by finding the area of the base and multiplying by the height.

Volume of a rectangular solid:	$V = lwh$	(base is a rectangle)
Volume of a cube:	$V = s^3$	(base is a square)
Volume of a cylinder:	$V = \pi r^2 h$	(base is a circle)

If you learn to recognize the relationships and formulas given above and the cases in which they apply, you will have the key to doing most of the problems involving geometry on the ACT.

Unit 2

ARITHMETIC

Whole Numbers

Definitions

The set of numbers {1, 2, 3, 4, . . .} is called the set of *counting numbers* and/or natural numbers, and/or sometimes the set *of positive integers.* (The notation, { }, means "set" or collection, and the three dots after the number 4 indicate that the list continues without end.) *Zero* is usually not considered one of the counting numbers. Together the counting numbers and zero make up the set of *whole numbers.*

Place Value

Whole numbers are expressed in a system of tens, called the *decimal* system. Ten *digits*—0, 1, 2, 3, 4, 5, 6, 7, 8, and 9—are used. Each digit differs not only in *face* value but also in *place* value, depending on where it stands in the number.

Example 1

237 means:

$$(2 \cdot 100) + (3 \cdot 10) + (7 \cdot 1)$$

The digit 2 has face value 2 but place value of 200.

Example 2

35,412 can be written as:

$$(3 \cdot 10{,}000) + (5 \cdot 1000) + (4 \cdot 100) + (1 \cdot 10) + (2 \cdot 1)$$

The digit in the last place on the right is said to be in the units or ones place; the digit to the left of that in the tens place; the next digit to the left of that in the hundreds place; and so on.

Odd and Even Numbers

A whole number is *even* if it is divisible by 2; it is *odd* if it is not divisible by 2. Zero is thus an even number.

Example

2, 4, 6, 8, and 320 are even numbers; 3, 7, 9, 21, and 45 are odd numbers.

Prime Numbers

The positive integer p is said to be a prime number (or simply *a prime*) if $p = 1$ and the only positive divisors of p are itself and 1. The positive integer 1 is called a *unit.* The first ten primes are 2, 3, 5, 7, 11, 13, 17, 19, 23, and 29. All other positive integers that are neither 1 nor prime are *composite numbers.* Composite numbers can be *factored,* that is, expressed as products of their divisors or factors; for example, $56 = 7 \cdot 8 = 7 \cdot 4 \cdot 2$. In particular, composite numbers can be expressed as products of their *prime* factors in just one way (except for order).

To factor a composite number into its prime factors, proceed as follows. First try to divide the number by the prime number 2. If this is successful, continue to divide by 2 until an odd number is obtained. Then attempt to divide the last quotient by the prime number 3 and by 3 again, as many times as possible. Then move on to dividing by the prime number 5, and other successive primes until a prime quotient is obtained. Express the original number as a product of all its prime divisors.

Example

Find the prime factors of 210.

2)210
3)105
5) 35
   7

Therefore:

$210 = 2 \cdot 3 \cdot 5 \cdot 7$ (written in any order) and 210 is an integer multiple of 2, of 3, of 5, and of 7.

Consecutive Whole Numbers

Numbers are consecutive if each number is the successor of the number that precedes it. In a consecutive series of whole numbers, an odd number is always followed by an even number, and an even number by an odd. If three consecutive whole numbers are given, either two of them are odd and one is even or two are even and one is odd.

Example 1

7, 8, 9, 10, and 11 are consecutive whole numbers.

Example 2

8, 10, 12, and 14 are consecutive even numbers.

Example 3

21, 23, 25, and 27 are consecutive odd numbers.

Example 4

21, 23, and 27 are *not* consecutive odd numbers because 25 is missing.

The Number Line

A useful method of representing numbers geometrically makes it easier to understand numbers. It is called the *number line*. Draw a horizontal line, considered to extend without end in both directions. Select some point on the line and label it with the number 0. This point is called the *origin*. Choose some convenient distance as a unit of length. Take the point on the number line that lies one unit to the right of the origin and label it with the number 1. The point on the number line that is one unit to the right of 1 is labeled 2, and so on. In this way, every whole number is associated with one point on the line, but it is not true that every point on the line represents a whole number.

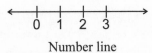

Number line

Ordering of Whole Numbers

On the number line the point representing 8 lies to the right of the point representing 5, and we say $8 > 5$ (read "8 is greater than 5"). One can also say $5 < 8$ ("5 is less than 8"). For any two whole numbers *a* and *b*, there are always three possibilities:

$$a < b, \qquad a = b, \qquad \text{or} \qquad a > b.$$

If $a = b$, the points representing the numbers *a* and *b* coincide on the number line.

Operations with Whole Numbers

The basic operations on whole numbers are addition (+), subtraction (−), multiplication (· or ×), and division (÷). These are all *binary* operations—that is, one works with two numbers at a time in order to get a unique answer. The operations of addition and multiplication on whole numbers are said to be *closed* because the answer in each case is also a whole number. The operations of subtraction and division on whole numbers are not closed because the unique answer is not necessarily a member of the set of whole numbers.

Examples

$$3 + 4 = 7 \quad \text{a whole number}$$
$$4 \cdot 3 = 12 \quad \text{a whole number}$$
$$2 - 5 = -3 \quad \text{not a whole number}$$
$$3 \div 8 = \frac{3}{8} \quad \text{not a whole number}$$

Addition

If addition is a binary operation, how are three numbers—say, 3, 4, and 8—added? One way is to write:

$$(3 + 4) + 8 = 7 + 8 = 15$$

Another way is to write:

$$3 + (4 + 8) = 3 + 12 = 15$$

The parentheses merely group the numbers together. The fact that the same answer, 15, is obtained either way illustrates the *associative property* of addition:

$$(r + s) + t = r + (s + t)$$

The order in which whole numbers are added is immaterial—that is, 3 + 4 = 4 + 3. This principle is called the *commutative property* of addition. Most people use this property without realizing it when they add a column of numbers from the top down and then check their result by beginning over again from the bottom. (Even though there may be a long column of numbers, only two numbers are added at a time.)

If 0 is added to any whole number, the whole number is unchanged. Zero is called the *identity element* for addition.

Subtraction

Subtraction is the inverse of addition. The order in which the numbers are written is important; there is no commutative property for subtraction.

$$4 - 3 \neq 3 - 4$$

The ≠ is read "not equal."

Multiplication

Multiplication is a commutative operation:

$$43 \cdot 73 = 73 \cdot 43$$

The result or answer in a multiplication problem is called the *product*.

If a number is multiplied by 1, the number is unchanged; the *identity element* for multiplication is 1.

Zero times any number is 0:

$$42 \cdot 0 = 0$$

Multiplication can be expressed with several different symbols:

$$9 \cdot 7 \cdot 3 = 9 \times 7 \times 3 = 9(7)(3)$$

Besides being commutative, multiplication is *associative:*

$$(9 \cdot 7) \cdot 3 = 63 \cdot 3 = 189$$

and

$$9 \cdot (7 \cdot 3) = 9 \cdot 21 = 189$$

A number can be quickly multiplied by 10 by adding a zero at the right of the number. Similarly, a number can be multiplied by 100 by adding two zeros at the right:

$$38 \cdot 10 = 380$$

and

$$100 \cdot 76 = 7600$$

Division

Division is the inverse of multiplication. It is not commutative:

$$8 \div 4 \neq 4 \div 8$$

The parts of a division example are named as follows:

$$\text{divisor} \overline{)\,\text{dividend}}^{\,\text{quotient}}$$

If a number is divided by 1, the quotient is the original number.

Division by 0 is not defined (has no meaning). Zero divided by any number other than 0 is 0:

$$0 \div 56 = 0$$

Divisors and Multiples

The whole number b *divides* the whole number a if there exists a whole number k such that $a = bk$. The whole number a is then said to be an integer *multiple* of b, and b is called a *divisor* (or *factor*) of a.

Example 1

3 divides 15 because $15 = 3 \cdot 5$. Thus, 3 is a divisor of 15 (and so is 5), and 15 is an integer multiple of 3 (and of 5).

Example 2

3 does not divide 8 because $8 \neq 3k$ for a whole number k.

Example 3

Divisors of 28 are 1, 2, 4, 7, 14, and 28.

Example 4

Multiples of 3 are 3, 6, 9, 12, 15, ...

Whole Number Problems

1. What is the prime factorization of 78?
2. What are the divisors of 56?
3. Which property is illustrated by the following statement?

   $(3 + 5) + 8 = 3 + (5 + 8)$

4. Which property is illustrated by the following statement?

   $(5 \cdot 7) \cdot 3 = (7 \cdot 5) \cdot 3$

5. Find the first five multiples of 7.

Solutions:

1. $78 = 2 \cdot 39 = 2 \cdot 3 \cdot 13$
2. The divisors of 56 are 1, 2, 4, 7, 8, 14, 28, 56
3. The Associative Property of Addition
4. The Commutative Property of Multiplication
5. 7, 14, 21, 28, 35

Fractions

Definitions

If a and b are whole numbers and $b \neq 0$, the symbol $\dfrac{a}{b}$ (or a/b) is called a fraction. The upper part, a, is called the *numerator,* and the lower part, b, is called the *denominator.* The denominator indicates into how many parts something is divided, and the numerator tells how many of these parts are taken. A fraction indicates division:

$$\frac{7}{8} = 8\overline{)7}$$

If the numerator of a fraction is 0, the value of the fraction is 0. If the denominator of a fraction is 0, the fraction is not defined (has no meaning):

$$\frac{0}{17} = 0 \qquad \frac{17}{0} \text{ not defined}$$
$$\text{(has no meaning)}$$

If the denominator of a fraction is 1, the value of the fraction is the same as the numerator:

$$\frac{18}{1} = 18$$

If the numerator and denominator are the same number, the value of the fraction is 1:

$$\frac{7}{7} = 1$$

Equivalent Fractions

Fractions that represent the same number are said to be *equivalent*. If m is a counting number and $\dfrac{a}{b}$ is a fraction, then:

$$\frac{m \times a}{m \times b} = \frac{a}{b}$$

because $\dfrac{m}{m} = 1$ and $1 \times \dfrac{a}{b} = \dfrac{a}{b}$

Example

$$\frac{2}{3} = \frac{4}{6} = \frac{6}{9} = \frac{8}{12}$$

These fractions are all equivalent.

Inequality of Fractions

If two fractions are not equivalent, one is smaller than the other. The ideas of "less than" and "greater than" were previously defined and used for whole numbers.

For the fractions $\dfrac{a}{b}$ and $\dfrac{c}{b}$:

$$\frac{a}{b} < \frac{c}{b} \text{ if } a < c$$

That is, if two fractions have the same denominator, the one with the smaller numerator has the smaller value.

If two fractions have different denominators, find a common denominator by multiplying one denominator by the other. Then use the common denominator to compare numerators.

Example

Which is smaller, $\dfrac{5}{8}$ or $\dfrac{4}{7}$?

$8 \cdot 7 = 56 =$ common denominator

$$\frac{5}{8} \times \frac{7}{7} = \frac{35}{56} \qquad \frac{4}{7} \times \frac{8}{8} = \frac{32}{56}$$

Since $32 < 35$,

$$\frac{32}{56} < \frac{35}{56} \text{ and } \frac{4}{7} < \frac{5}{8}$$

Reducing to Lowest Terms

The principle that

$$\frac{m \times a}{m \times b} = \frac{a}{b}$$

can be particularly useful in reducing fractions to lowest terms. Fractions are expressed in *lowest terms* when the numerator and denominator have no common factor except 1. To reduce a fraction to an equivalent fraction in lowest terms, express the numerator and denominator as products of their prime factors. Each time a prime appears in the numerator over the same prime in the denominator, $\dfrac{p}{p}$, substitute its equal value, 1.

Example

Reduce $\dfrac{30}{42}$ to an equivalent fraction in lowest terms:

$$\frac{30}{42} = \frac{2 \cdot 3 \cdot 5}{2 \cdot 3 \cdot 7} = 1 \cdot 1 \cdot \frac{5}{7} = \frac{5}{7}$$

In practice, this can be done even more quickly by dividing numerator and denominator by any number, prime or not, which will divide both evenly. Repeat this process until there is no prime factor remaining that is common to both numerator and denominator:

$$\frac{30}{42} = \frac{15}{21} = \frac{5}{7}$$

Proper Fractions, Improper Fractions, and Mixed Numbers

Definitions

A *proper fraction* is a fraction whose numerator is smaller than its denominator. Proper fractions always have a value less than 1:

$$\frac{3}{4} \qquad \frac{5}{8} \qquad \frac{121}{132} \qquad \frac{0}{1}$$

An *improper fraction* is a fraction with numerator equal to or greater than the denominator. Improper fractions always have a value equal to or greater than 1:

$$\frac{3}{2} \qquad \frac{17}{17} \qquad \frac{9}{1} \qquad \frac{15}{14}$$

A *mixed number* is a number composed of a whole number and a proper fraction. It is always greater than 1 in value:

$$3\frac{7}{8} \qquad 5\frac{1}{4} \qquad 11\frac{3}{14}$$

The symbol $3\frac{7}{8}$ means $3 + \frac{7}{8}$ and is read "three and seven-eighths."

To Change a Mixed Number into an Improper Fraction

Multiply the denominator by the whole number and add this product to the numerator. Use the sum so obtained as the new numerator, and keep the original denominator.

Example

Write $9\frac{4}{11}$ as an improper fraction:

$$9\frac{4}{11} = \frac{(11 \times 9) + 4}{11} = \frac{99 + 4}{11} = \frac{103}{11}$$

Note: In any calculations with mixed numbers, first change the mixed numbers to improper fractions.

To Change an Improper Fraction into a Mixed Number

Divide the numerator by the denominator. The result is the whole-number part of the mixed number. If there is a remainder in the division process because the division does not come out evenly, put the remainder over the denominator (divisor). This gives the fractional part of the mixed number:

$$\frac{20}{3} = 3\overline{)20} \qquad = 6\frac{2}{3}$$
$$\underline{18}$$
$$2 \text{ remainder}$$

Multiplication

Proper and Improper Fractions

Multiply the two numerators and then multiply the two denominators. If the numerator obtained is larger than the denominator, divide the numerator of the resulting fraction by its denominator:

$$\frac{3}{8} \times \frac{15}{11} = \frac{45}{88} \qquad \frac{3}{8} \times \frac{22}{7} = \frac{66}{56} = 1\frac{10}{56}$$

Multiplication of fractions is commutative.

Three or more fractions are multiplied in the same way; two numerators are done at a time and the result multiplied by the next numerator.

The product in the multiplication of fractions is usually expressed in lowest terms.

Canceling

In multiplying fractions, if any of the numerators and denominators have a common divisor (factor), divide each of them by this common factor and the value of the fraction remains the same. This process is called *canceling* or *cancellation*.

Example

$$\frac{\overset{9}{\cancel{27}}}{\underset{2}{\cancel{18}}} \times \frac{\overset{\cancel{90}}{\cancel{90}}}{\underset{100}{\cancel{300}}} = ?$$

$$\frac{27}{18} \times \frac{90}{300} = \frac{27}{18} \times \frac{9}{30}$$ Divide second

fraction by $\dfrac{10}{10}$

$$= \frac{\overset{9}{\cancel{27}}}{\underset{2}{\cancel{18}}} \times \frac{\overset{1}{\cancel{9}}}{\underset{10}{\cancel{30}}}$$ Cancel: 18 and 9 each divisible by 9; 27 and 30 each divisible by 3

$$= \frac{9 \times 1}{2 \times 10} = \frac{9}{20}$$ Multiply numerators; multiply denominators

Another method:

$$\frac{\overset{3}{\cancel{27}}}{\underset{2}{\cancel{18}}} \times \frac{\overset{3}{\cancel{9}}}{\underset{10}{\cancel{30}}} = \frac{3 \times 3}{2 \times 10} = \frac{9}{20}$$

Cancel: 27 and 18 have common factor 9; 9 and 30 have common factor 3

Note: Canceling can take place only between a numerator and a denominator, in the same or a different fraction, never between two numerators or between two denominators.

Mixed Numbers

Mixed numbers should be changed to improper fractions before multiplying. Then multiply as described above.

Example

To multiply

$$\frac{4}{7} \times 3\frac{5}{8}$$

change $3\frac{5}{8}$ to an improper fraction:

$$3\frac{5}{8} = \frac{(8 \times 3) + 5}{8} = \frac{24 + 5}{8} = \frac{29}{8}$$

Multiply

$$\frac{\overset{1}{\cancel{4}}}{7} \times \frac{29}{\underset{2}{\cancel{8}}} = \frac{29}{14}$$

The answer can be left in this form or changed to a mixed number: $2\frac{1}{14}$

Fractions with Whole Numbers

Write the whole number as a fraction with a denominator of 1 and then multiply:

$$\frac{3}{4} \times 7 = \frac{3}{4} \times \frac{7}{1} = \frac{21}{4} = 5\frac{1}{4}$$

Note: When any fraction is multiplied by 1, its value remains unchanged. When any fraction is multiplied by 0, the product is 0.

Division

Reciprocals

Division of fractions involves reciprocals. One fraction is the *reciprocal* of another if the product of the fractions is 1.

Example 1

$\dfrac{3}{4}$ and $\dfrac{4}{3}$ are reciprocals since

$$\frac{\overset{1}{\cancel{3}}}{\underset{1}{\cancel{4}}} \times \frac{\overset{1}{\cancel{4}}}{\underset{1}{\cancel{3}}} = \frac{1 \times 1}{1 \times 1} = 1$$

Example 2

$\dfrac{1}{3}$ and 3 are reciprocals since

$$\frac{1}{\underset{1}{\cancel{3}}} \times \frac{\overset{1}{\cancel{3}}}{1} = 1$$

To find the reciprocal of a fraction, interchange the numerator and denominator—that is, invert the fraction, or turn it upside down.

Proper and Improper Fractions

Multiply the first fraction (dividend) by the reciprocal of the second fraction (divisor). Reduce by cancellation if possible. If you wish to, change the answer to a mixed number when possible:

Example

$$\frac{9}{2} \div \frac{4}{7} = \frac{9}{2} \times \frac{7}{4}$$ The reciprocal of $\frac{4}{7}$ is $\frac{7}{4}$

because $\frac{4}{7} \times \frac{7}{4} = 1$

$$= \frac{63}{8}$$

$$= 7\frac{7}{8}$$

Mixed Numbers and/or Whole Numbers

Both mixed numbers and whole numbers must first be changed to equivalent improper fractions. Then proceed as described above.

Note: If a fraction or a mixed number is divided by 1, its value is unchanged. Division of a fraction or a mixed number by 0 is not defined. If a fraction is divided by itself or an equivalent fraction, the quotient is 1:

$$\frac{19}{7} \div \frac{19}{7} = \frac{19}{7} \times \frac{7}{19}$$ Reciprocal of $\frac{19}{7}$ is $\frac{7}{19}$

$$= 1 \times 1 = 1$$

Addition

Fractions can be added only if their denominators are the same (called the *common denominator*). Add the numerators; the denominator remains the same. Reduce the sum to the lowest terms:

$$\frac{3}{8} + \frac{2}{8} + \frac{1}{8} = \frac{3 + 2 + 1}{8} = \frac{6}{8} = \frac{3}{4}$$

When the fractions have different denominators, you must find a common denominator. One way of doing this is to find the product of the different denominators.

Example

$$\frac{5}{6} + \frac{1}{4} = ?$$

A common denominator is $6 \cdot 4 = 24$.

$$\frac{5}{6} \times \frac{4}{4} = \frac{20}{24} \quad \text{and} \quad \frac{1}{4} \times \frac{6}{6} = \frac{6}{24}$$

$$\frac{5}{6} + \frac{1}{4} = \frac{20}{24} + \frac{6}{24}$$

$$= \frac{20 + 6}{24}$$

$$= \frac{26}{24}$$

$$= \frac{13}{12}$$

$$= 1\frac{1}{12}$$

Least-Common Denominator

A denominator can often be found that is smaller than the product of the different denominators. If the denominator of each fraction will divide into such a number evenly and it is the *smallest* such number, it is called the *least* (or *lowest*) *common denominator*, abbreviated as LCD. Finding a least-common denominator may make it unnecessary to reduce the answer and enables one to work with smaller numbers. There are two common methods.

First Method: By Inspection

$$\frac{5}{6} + \frac{1}{4} = ?$$

LCD = 12 because 12 is the smallest number into which 6 and 4 divide evenly. Therefore:

$$12 \div 6 = 2 \qquad \text{multiply } \frac{5}{6} \times \frac{2}{2} = \frac{10}{12}$$

$$12 \div 4 = 3 \qquad \text{multiply } \frac{1}{4} \times \frac{3}{3} = \frac{3}{12}$$

Then:

$$\frac{5}{6} + \frac{1}{4} = \frac{10}{12} + \frac{3}{12}$$
$$= \frac{13}{12}$$
$$= 1\frac{1}{12}$$

Second Method: By Factoring

This method can be used when the LCD is not recognized by inspection. Factor each denominator into its prime factors. The LCD is the product of the highest power of each separate factor, where *power* refers to the number of times a factor occurs.

Example

$$\frac{5}{6} + \frac{1}{4} = ?$$

Factoring denominators gives:

$$6 = 2 \cdot 3 \quad \text{and} \quad 4 = 2 \cdot 2$$
$$\text{LCD} = 2 \cdot 2 \cdot 3$$
$$= 12$$

Convert to LCD:

$$\frac{5}{6} \times \frac{2}{2} = \frac{10}{12} \qquad \frac{1}{4} \times \frac{3}{3} = 12$$
$$\frac{5}{6} + \frac{1}{4} = \frac{10}{12} + \frac{3}{12}$$
$$= \frac{13}{12}$$
$$= 1\frac{1}{12}$$

The denominators 4 and 6 factor into $2 \cdot 2$ and $2 \cdot 3$, respectively. Although the factor 2 *appears* three times, its power is 2^2 from factoring 4. The factor 3 appears once, so its power is 3^1. Therefore, the LCD as a *product* of the *highest power of each separate factor* is $2 \times 2 \times 3$.

The factoring method of adding fractions can be extended to three or more fractions.

Example

$$\frac{1}{4} + \frac{3}{8} + \frac{1}{12} = ?$$

Factoring denominators gives:

$$4 = 2 \cdot 2 \qquad 8 = 2 \cdot 2 \cdot 2 \qquad 12 = 2 \cdot 2 \cdot 3$$
$$\text{LCD} = 2 \cdot 2 \cdot 2 \cdot 3$$
$$= 24$$

Convert to LCD:

$$\frac{1}{4} \times \frac{6}{6} = \frac{6}{24} \qquad \frac{3}{8} \times \frac{3}{3} = \frac{9}{24}$$
$$\frac{1}{12} \times \frac{2}{2} = \frac{2}{24}$$
$$\frac{1}{4} + \frac{3}{8} + \frac{1}{12} = \frac{6}{24} + \frac{9}{24} + \frac{2}{24}$$
$$= \frac{6 + 9 + 2}{24}$$
$$= \frac{17}{24}$$

Addition of Mixed Numbers

Change any mixed numbers to fractions. If the fractions have the same denominator, add the numerators. If the fractions have different denominators, find the LCD of the several denominators and then add numerators. Reduce the answer if possible. Write the answer as a mixed number if you wish.

Example

$$2\frac{2}{3} + 5\frac{1}{2} + 1\frac{2}{9} = ?$$

Factoring denominators gives:

$$3 = 3 \qquad 2 = 2 \qquad 9 = 3 \cdot 3$$

$$\text{LCD} = 2 \cdot 3 \cdot 3$$
$$= 18$$

Convert to LCD:

$$\frac{8}{3} \times \frac{6}{6} = \frac{48}{18} \qquad \frac{11}{2} \times \frac{9}{9} = \frac{99}{18}$$

$$\frac{11}{9} \times \frac{2}{2} = \frac{22}{18}$$

$$2\frac{2}{3} + 5\frac{1}{2} + 1\frac{2}{9} = \frac{8}{3} + \frac{11}{2} + \frac{11}{9}$$

$$= \frac{48}{18} + \frac{99}{18} + \frac{22}{18}$$

$$= \frac{48 + 99 + 22}{18}$$

$$= \frac{169}{18} = 9\frac{7}{18}$$

Subtraction

Fractions can be subtracted only if the denominators are the same. If the denominators are the same, find the difference between the numerators. The denominator remains unchanged.

Example

$$\frac{19}{3} - \frac{2}{3} = ?$$

$$= \frac{19 - 2}{3}$$

$$= \frac{17}{3}$$

$$= 5\frac{2}{3}$$

When fractions have different denominators, find equivalent fractions with a common denominator, and then subtract numerators.

Example

$$\frac{7}{8} - \frac{3}{4} = ?$$

Factoring denominators gives:

$$8 = 2 \cdot 2 \cdot 2 \qquad 4 = 2 \cdot 2$$

$$\text{LCD} = 2 \cdot 2 \cdot 2$$
$$= 8$$

Convert to LCD:

$$\frac{7}{8} = \frac{7}{8} \qquad \frac{3}{4} \times \frac{2}{2} = \frac{6}{8}$$

$$\frac{7}{8} - \frac{3}{4} = \frac{7}{8} - \frac{6}{8}$$

$$= \frac{7 - 6}{8}$$

$$= \frac{1}{8}$$

Mixed Numbers

To subtract mixed numbers, change each mixed number to a fraction. Find the LCD for the fractions. Write each fraction as an equivalent fraction whose denominator is the common denominator. Find the difference between the numerators.

Example

$$3\frac{3}{8} - 2\frac{5}{6} = ?$$

$$\text{LCD} = 24$$

$$3\frac{3}{8} - 2\frac{5}{6} = \frac{27}{8} - \frac{17}{6}$$

$$= \frac{81}{24} - \frac{68}{24}$$

$$= \frac{13}{24}$$

If zero is subtracted from a fraction, the result is the original fraction:

$$\frac{3}{4} - 0 = \frac{3}{4} - \frac{0}{4} = \frac{3}{4}$$

Fraction Problems

In the following problems, perform the indicated operations and reduce the answers to lowest terms.

1. $\dfrac{5}{12} \times \dfrac{4}{15}$

2. $\dfrac{1}{2} \div \dfrac{3}{8}$

3. $\dfrac{5}{12} + \dfrac{2}{3}$

4. $\dfrac{2}{3} - \dfrac{5}{11}$

5. $3\dfrac{1}{3} \times \dfrac{4}{5}$

6. $7\dfrac{4}{5} - 2\dfrac{1}{3}$

Solutions:

1. $\dfrac{5}{12} \times \dfrac{4}{15} = \dfrac{\overset{1}{\cancel{5}}}{\underset{3}{\cancel{12}}} \times \dfrac{\overset{1}{\cancel{4}}}{\underset{3}{\cancel{15}}} = \dfrac{1}{9}$

2. $\dfrac{1}{2} \div \dfrac{3}{8} = \dfrac{1}{2} \times \dfrac{8}{3} = \dfrac{1}{2} \times \dfrac{\overset{4}{\cancel{8}}}{3} \underset{1}{} = \dfrac{4}{3}$

3. $\dfrac{5}{12} + \dfrac{2}{3} = \dfrac{5}{12} + \dfrac{8}{12} = \dfrac{13}{12} = 1\dfrac{1}{12}$

4. $\dfrac{2}{3} - \dfrac{5}{11} = \dfrac{22}{33} - \dfrac{15}{33} = \dfrac{7}{33}$

5. $3\dfrac{1}{3} \times \dfrac{4}{5} = \dfrac{10}{3} \times \dfrac{4}{5} = \dfrac{\overset{2}{\cancel{10}}}{3} \times \dfrac{4}{\underset{1}{\cancel{5}}} = \dfrac{8}{3} = 2\dfrac{2}{3}$

6. $7\dfrac{4}{5} - 2\dfrac{1}{3} = \dfrac{39}{5} - \dfrac{7}{3} = \dfrac{117}{15} - \dfrac{35}{15} = \dfrac{82}{15} = 5\dfrac{7}{15}$

Decimals

Earlier, we stated that whole numbers are expressed in a system of tens, or the decimal system, using the digits from 0 to 9. This system can be extended to fractions by using a period called a *decimal point*. The digits after a decimal point form a *decimal fraction*. Decimal fractions are smaller than 1—for example, .3, .37, .372, and .105. The first position to the right of the decimal point is called the *tenths' place* since the digit in that position tells how many tenths there are. The second digit to the right of the decimal point is in the *hundredths' place*. The third digit to the right of the decimal point is in the *thousandths' place*, and so on.

Example 1

.3 is a decimal fraction that means

$$3 \times \dfrac{1}{10} = \dfrac{3}{10}$$

read "three-tenths."

Example 2

The decimal fraction of .37 means

$$3 \times \dfrac{1}{10} + 7 \times \dfrac{1}{100} = 3 \times \dfrac{10}{100} + 7 \times \dfrac{1}{100}$$

$$= \dfrac{30}{100} + \dfrac{7}{100} = \dfrac{37}{100}$$

read "thirty-seven hundredths."

Example 3

The decimal fraction .372 means

$$\frac{300}{1000} + \frac{70}{1000} + \frac{2}{1000} = \frac{372}{1000}$$

read "three hundred seventy-two thousandths."

Whole numbers have an understood (unwritten) decimal point to the right of the last digit (i.e., 4 = 4.0). Decimal fractions can be combined with whole numbers to make *decimals*—for example, 3.246, 10.85, and 4.7.

Note: Adding zeros to the right of a decimal after the last digit does not change the value of the decimal.

Rounding Off

Sometimes a decimal is expressed with more digits than desired. As the number of digits to the right of the decimal point increases, the number increases in accuracy, but a high degree of accuracy is not always needed. Then, the number can be "rounded off" to a certain decimal place.

To round off, identify the place to be rounded off. If the digit to the right of it is 0, 1, 2, 3, or 4, the round-off place digit remains the same. If the digit to the right is 5, 6, 7, 8, or 9, add 1 to the round-off place digit.

Example 1

Round off .6384 to the nearest thousandth. The digit in the thousandths' place is 8. The digit to the right in the ten-thousandths' place is 4, so the 8 stays the same.

Example 2

.6386 rounded to the nearest thousandth is .639, rounded to the nearest hundredth is .64, and rounded to the nearest tenth is .6. After a decimal fraction has been rounded off to a particular decimal place, all the digits to the right of that place will be 0.

Note: Rounding off whole numbers can be done by a similar method. It is less common but is sometimes used to get approximate answers quickly.

Example

Round 32,756 to the nearest *hundred*. This means, to find the multiple of 100 that is nearest the given number. The number in the hundreds' place is 7. The number immediately to the right is 5, so 32,756 rounds to 32,800.

Decimals and Fractions

Changing a Decimal to a Fraction

Place the digits to the right of the decimal point over the value of the place in which the last digit appears and reduce if possible. The whole number remains the same.

Example

Change 2.14 to a fraction or mixed number. Observe that 4 is the last digit and is in the hundredths' place.

$$.14 = \frac{14}{100} = \frac{7}{50}$$

Therefore:

$$2.14 = 2\frac{7}{50}$$

Changing a Fraction to a Decimal

Divide the numerator of the fraction by the denominator. First put a decimal point followed by zeros to the right of the number in the numerator. Add and divide until there is no remainder. The decimal point in the quotient is aligned directly above the decimal point in the dividend.

Example

Change $\frac{3}{8}$ to a decimal.

Divide

$$
\begin{array}{r}
.375 \\
8\overline{)3.000} \\
\underline{24} \\
60 \\
\underline{56} \\
40 \\
\underline{40} \\
\end{array}
$$

When the division does not terminate with a 0 remainder, two courses are possible.

First Method: Divide to three decimal places.

Example

Change $\frac{5}{6}$ to a decimal.

$$
\begin{array}{r}
.833 \\
6\overline{)5.000} \\
\underline{48} \\
20 \\
\underline{18} \\
20 \\
\underline{18} \\
2 \\
\end{array}
$$

The 3 in the quotient will be repeated indefinitely. It is called an *infinite decimal* and is written .833 . . . .

Second Method: Divide until there are two decimal places in the quotient and then write the remainder over the divisor.

Example

Change $\frac{5}{6}$ to a decimal.

$$
\begin{array}{r}
.833 \\
6\overline{)5.000} = .83\tfrac{1}{3} \\
\underline{48} \\
20 \\
\underline{18} \\
20 \\
\end{array}
$$

Addition

Addition of decimals is both commutative and associative. Decimals are simpler to add than fractions. Place the decimals in a column with the decimal points aligned under each other. Add in the usual way. The decimal point of the answer is also aligned under the other decimal points.

Example

$43 + 2.73 + .9 + 3.01 = ?$

$$
\begin{array}{r}
43. \\
2.73 \\
.9 \\
\underline{3.01} \\
49.64 \\
\end{array}
$$

Subtraction

For subtraction, the decimal points must be aligned under each other. Add zeros to the right of the decimal point if desired. Subtract as with whole numbers.

Examples

$$
\begin{array}{rrr}
21.567 & 21.567 & 39.00 \\
\underline{-9.4} & \underline{-9.48} & \underline{-17.48} \\
12.167 & 13.087 & 21.52 \\
\end{array}
$$

Multiplication

Multiplication of decimals is commutative and associative:

$$5.39 \times .04 = .04 \times 5.39$$
$$(.7 \times .02) \times .1 = .7 \cdot (.02 \times .1)$$

Multiply the decimals as if they were whole numbers. The total number of decimal places in the product is the sum of the number of places (to the right of the decimal point) in all of the numbers multiplied.

Example

$8.64 \times .003 = ?$

8.64	2 places to right of decimal point
$\times\ .003$	$+ 3$ places to right of decimal point
.02592	5 places to right of decimal point

A zero had to be added to the left of the product before writing the decimal point to ensure that there would be five decimal places in the product.

Note: To multiply a decimal by 10, simply move the decimal point one place to the right; to multiply by 100, move the decimal point two places to the right.

Division

To divide one decimal (the dividend) by another (the divisor), move the decimal point in the divisor as many places as necessary to the right to make the divisor a whole number. Then move the decimal point in the dividend (expressed or understood) a corresponding number of places, adding zeros if necessary. Then divide as with whole numbers. The decimal point in the quotient is placed above the decimal point in the dividend after the decimal point has been moved.

Example

Divide 7.6 by .32.

$$
.32\overline{)7.60} = 32\overline{)760.00}^{\displaystyle 23.75}
$$

```
        23.75
.32)7.60 = 32)760.00
              64
             120
              96
             240
             224
             160
             160
```

Note: "Divide 7.6 by .32" can be written as $\dfrac{7.6}{.32}$. If this fraction is multiplied by $\dfrac{100}{100}$, an equivalent fraction is obtained with a whole number in the denominator:

$$\frac{7.6}{.32} \times \frac{100}{100} = \frac{760}{32}$$

Moving the decimal point two places to the right in both divisor and dividend is equivalent to multiplying each number by 100.

Special Cases

If the dividend has a decimal point and the divisor does not, divide as with whole numbers and place the decimal point of the quotient above the decimal point in the divisor.

If both dividend and divisor are whole numbers but the quotient is a decimal, place a decimal point after the last digit of the dividend and add zeros as necessary to get the required degree of accuracy. (*See* Changing a Fraction to a Decimal, page 133).

Note: To divide any number by 10, simply move its decimal point (understood to be after the last digit for a whole number) one place to the left; to divide by 100, move the decimal point two places to the left; and so on.

Percents

Percents, like fractions and decimals, are ways of expressing parts of whole numbers, as 93%, 50%, and 22.4%. Percents are expressions of hundredths—that is, of fractions whose denominator is 100. The symbol for percent is "%".

Example

$25\% = $ twenty-five hundredths $= \dfrac{25}{100} = \dfrac{1}{4}$

The word *percent* means *per hundred*. Its main use is in comparing fractions with equal denominators of 100.

Relationship with Fractions and Decimals

Changing Percent into Decimal

Divide the percent by 100 and drop the symbol for percent. Add zeros to the left when necessary:

$30\% = .30 \qquad 1\% = .01$

Remember that the short method of dividing by 100 is to move the decimal point two places to the left.

Changing Decimal into Percent

Multiply the decimal by 100 by moving the decimal point two places to the right, and add the symbol for percent:

$.375 = 37.5\% \qquad .001 = .1\%$

Decimal Problems

1. Change the following decimals into fractions, and reduce.
   a. 1.16
   b. 15.05

2. Change the following fractions into decimals.
   a. $\dfrac{3}{8}$
   b. $\dfrac{2}{3}$

In the following problems, perform the indicated operations.

3. $3.762 + 23.43$

4. $1.368 - .559$

5. $8.7 \times .8$

6. $.045 \div .5$

Solutions:

1. a. $1.16 = 1\dfrac{16}{100} = 1\dfrac{8}{50} = 1\dfrac{4}{25}$

  b. $15.05 = 15\dfrac{5}{100} = 15\dfrac{1}{20}$

2. a. $\dfrac{3}{8} = 8\overline{)3.000}$ = .375

$$\begin{array}{r} .375 \\ 8\overline{)3.000} \\ \underline{24} \\ 60 \\ \underline{-56} \\ 40 \end{array}$$

  b. $\dfrac{2}{3} = 3\overline{)2.00}$ = .666...

$$\begin{array}{r} .666... \\ 3\overline{)2.00} \\ \underline{18} \\ 20 \\ \underline{-18} \\ 20 \end{array}$$

3.
$$\begin{array}{r} 3.762 \\ +23.43 \\ \hline 27.192 \end{array}$$

4.
$$\begin{array}{r} 1.368 \\ -.559 \\ \hline .809 \end{array}$$

5.
$$\begin{array}{r} 8.7 \\ \times .8 \\ \hline 6.96 \end{array}$$

6.
$$\begin{array}{r} 0.09 \\ .5\overline{)0.0.45} \end{array}$$

Changing Percent into Fraction

Drop the percent sign. Write the number as a numerator over a denominator of 100. If the numerator has a decimal point, move the decimal point to the right the necessary number of places to make the numerator a whole number. Add the same number of zeros to the right of the denominator as you moved places to the right in the numerator. Reduce where possible.

Examples

$$20\% = \frac{20}{100} = \frac{2}{10} = \frac{1}{5}$$

$$36.5\% = \frac{36.5}{100} = \frac{365}{1000} = \frac{73}{200}$$

Changing a Fraction into Percent

Use either of two methods.

First Method: Change the fraction into an equivalent fraction with a denominator of 100. Drop the denominator (equivalent to multiplying by 100) and add the % sign.

Example

Express $\frac{6}{20}$ as a percent.

$$\frac{6}{20} \times \frac{5}{5} = \frac{30}{100} = 30\%$$

Second Method: Divide the numerator by the denominator to get a decimal with two places (express the remainder as a fraction if necessary). Change the decimal to a percent.

Example

Express $\frac{6}{20}$ as a percent.

$$\frac{6}{20} = 20\overline{)6.00} = 30\%$$
$$\underline{60}$$
(with .30 above)

Percent Problems

1. Change the following percents into decimals:

   a. 37.5%   b. 0.5%

2. Change the following decimals into percents:

   a. 0.625   b. 3.75

3. Change the following fractions into percents:

   a. $\frac{7}{8}$ b. $\frac{73}{200}$

4. Change the following percents into fractions:

   a. 87.5%   b. 0.02%

Solutions:

1. a. 37.5% = 0.375

   b. 00.5% = 0.005

2. a. 0.625 = 62.5%

   b. 3.75 = 375%

3. a. $\frac{7}{8} = 8\overline{)7.000} = 87.5\%$ (0.875)

   b. $\frac{73}{200} = 200\overline{)73.000} = 36.5\%$ (0.365)

4. a. $87.5\% = 0.875 = \frac{875}{1,000} = \frac{35}{40} = \frac{7}{8}$

   b. $0.02\% = 0.0002 = \frac{2}{10,000} = \frac{1}{5,000}$

Word Problems

When doing percent problems, it is usually easier to change the percent to a decimal or a fraction before computing. When we take a percent of a certain number, that number is called the *base,* the percent we take is called the *rate,* and the result is called the *percentage* or *part.* If we let B represent the base, R the rate, and P the part, the relationship between these quantities is expressed by the following formula:

$$P = R \cdot B$$

All percent problems can be done with the help of this formula.

Example 1

In a class of 24 students, 25% received an A. How many students received an A? The number of students (24) is the base, and 25% is the rate. Change the rate to a fraction for ease of handling and apply the formula.

$$25\% = \frac{25}{100} = \frac{1}{4}$$

$$P = R \times B$$

$$= \frac{1}{\cancel{4}_1} \times \frac{\cancel{24}^{\,6}}{1}$$

$$= 6 \text{ students}$$

To choose between changing the percent (rate) to a decimal or a fraction, simply decide which would be easier to work with. In Example 1, the fraction was easier to work with because cancellation was possible. In Example 2, the situation is the same except for a different rate. This time the decimal form is easier.

Example 2

In a class of 24 students, 29.17% received an A. How many students received an A? Changing the rate to a fraction yields

$$\frac{29.17}{100} = \frac{2917}{10,000}$$

You can quickly see that the decimal is the better choice.

$$29.17\% = .2917$$

$$P = R \times B$$

$$= .2917 \times 24$$

$$= 7 \text{ students}$$

$$\begin{array}{r} .2917 \\ \times\ \ 24 \\ \hline 1.1668 \\ 5.834\ \ \\ \hline 7.0008 \end{array}$$

Example 3

What percent of a 40-hour week is a 16-hour schedule?

40 hours is the base and 16 hours is the part. $P = R \cdot B$

$$16 = R \cdot 40$$

Divide each side of the equation by 40.

$$\frac{16}{40} = R$$

$$\frac{2}{5} = R$$

$$40\% = R$$

Example 4

A woman paid $15,000 as a down payment on a house. If this amount was 20% of the price, what did the house cost?

The part (or percentage) is $15,000, the rate is 20%, and we must find the base. Change the rate to a fraction.

$$20\% = \frac{1}{5}$$

$$P = R \times B$$

$$\$15,000 = \frac{1}{5} \times B$$

Multiply each side of the equation by 5.

$$\$75,000 = B = \text{cost of house}$$

Percent of Increase or Decrease

This kind of problem is not really new but follows immediately from the previous problems. First calculate the *amount* of increase or decrease. This amount is the P (percentage or part) from the formula $P = R \cdot B$. The base, B, is the original amount, regardless of whether there was a loss or gain.

Example

By what percent does Mary's salary increase if her present salary is $20,000 and she accepts a new job at a salary of $28,000?

Amount of increase is:

$28,000 − $20,000 = $8000

$$P = R \cdot B$$

$$\$8000 = R \cdot \$20,000$$

Divide each side of the equation by $20,000. Then:

$$\frac{\overset{40}{\cancel{8000}}}{\underset{100}{\cancel{20,000}}} = \frac{40}{100} = R = 40\% \text{ increase}$$

Discount and Interest

These special kinds of percent problems require no new methods of attack.

Discount: The amount of discount is the difference between the original price and the sale, or discount, price. The rate of discount is usually given as a fraction or as a percent. Use the formula of the percent problems $P = R \cdot B$, but now P stands for the part or discount, R is the rate, and B, the base, is the original price.

Example 1

A table listed at $160 is marked 20% off. What is the sale price?

$$P = R \cdot B$$
$$= .20 \cdot \$160 = \$32$$

This is the amount of discount or how much must be subtracted from the original price. Then:

$160 − $32 = $128 sale price

Example 2

A car priced at $9000 was sold for $7200. What was the rate of discount?

$$\text{Amount of discount} = \$9000 − \$7200$$
$$= \$1800$$

Discount = rate · original price
$$\$1800 = R \cdot \$9000$$

Divide each side of the equation by $9000:

$$\frac{\overset{20}{\cancel{1800}}}{\underset{100}{\cancel{9000}}} = \frac{20}{100} = R = 20\%$$

Successive Discounting: When an item is discounted more than once, it is called successive discounting.

Example 1

In one store, a dress tagged at $40 was discounted 15%. When it did not sell at the lower price, it was discounted an additional 10%. What was the final selling price?

$$\text{Discount} = R \cdot \text{original price}$$
$$\text{First discount} = .15 \cdot \$40 = \$6$$
$$\$40 − \$6 = \$34 \text{ selling price after}$$
first discount

Second
$$\text{discount} = .10 \cdot \$34 = \$3.40$$
$$\$34 − \$3.40 = \$30.60 \text{ final selling price}$$

Example 2

In another store, an identical dress was also tagged at $40. When it did not sell, it was discounted 25% all at once. Is the final selling price lower or higher than in Example 1?

$$\text{Discount} = R \cdot \text{original price}$$
$$= .25 \cdot \$40$$
$$= \$10$$

$40 − $10 = $30 final selling price

This is a lower selling price than in Example 1, where two successive discounts were taken. Although the two discounts from Example 1 add up to the discount of Example 2, the final selling price is not the same.

Interest: Interest problems are similar to discount and percent problems. If money is left in the bank for a year and the interest is calculated at the end of the year, the usual formula $P = R \cdot B$ can be used, where P is the *interest*, R is the *rate*, and B is the *principal* (original amount of money borrowed or loaned).

Example 1

A certain bank pays interest on savings accounts at the rate of 4% per year. If a man has $6700 on deposit, find the interest earned after 1 year.

$$P = R \cdot B$$
$$\text{Interest} = \text{rate} \cdot \text{principal}$$
$$P = .04 \cdot \$6700 = \$268 \text{ interest}$$

Interest problems frequently involve more or less time than 1 year. Then the formula becomes:

Interest = rate · principal · time

Example 2

If the money is left in the bank for 3 years at simple interest (the kind we are discussing), the interest is

$3 \cdot \$268 = \$804$

Example 3

Suppose $6700 is deposited in the bank at 4% interest for 3 months. How much interest is earned?

Interest = rate · principal · time

Here the 4% rate is for 1 year. Since 3 months is $\dfrac{3}{12} = \dfrac{1}{4}$

Interest $= .04 \cdot \$6700 \cdot \dfrac{1}{4} = \$67$

Percent Word Problems

1. Janet received a rent increase of 15%. If her rent was $785 monthly before the increase, what is her new rent?

2. School bus fares rose from $25 per month to $30 per month. Find the percent of increase.

3. A dress originally priced at $90 is marked down 35%, then discounted a further 10%. What is the new, reduced price?

4. Dave delivers flowers for a salary of $45 a day, plus a 12% commission on all sales. One day his sales amounted to $220. How much money did he earn that day?

5. A certain bank pays interest on money market accounts at a rate of 6% a year. If Brett deposits $7,200, find the interest earned after one year.

Solutions:

1. Amount of increase = $785 × 15%
   = $785 × .15 = $117.75

   New rent = $902.75

2. Amount of increase = $30 − $25 = $5

   Percent of increase $= \dfrac{5}{25} = \dfrac{1}{5} = 20\%$

3. Amount of first markdown = $90 × 35%
= $90 × .35 = $31.50

Reduced price = $90 − $31.50 = $58.50

Amount of second markdown = $58.50
× 10% = $58.50 × .1 = $5.85

Final price = $58.50 − $5.85 = $52.65

4. Commission = $220 × 12% = $220
× .12 = $26.40

Money earned = $45 + $26.40 = $71.40

5. Interest = $7,200 × 6% = $7,200 × .06 =
$432

Signed Numbers

In describing subtraction of whole numbers, we said that the operation was not closed—that is, 4 − 6 will yield a number that is not a member of the set of counting numbers and zero. The set of *integers* was developed to give meaning to such expressions as 4 − 6. The set of integers is the set of all *signed* whole numbers and zero. It is the set {..., −4, −3, −2, −1, 0, 1, 2, 3, 4, ...}

The first three dots symbolize the fact that the negative integers go on indefinitely, just as the positive integers do. Integers preceded by a minus sign (called *negative integers*) appear to the left of 0 on a number line.

Decimals, fractions, and mixed numbers can also have negative signs. Together with positive fractions and decimals, they appear on the number line in this fashion:

All numbers to the right of 0 are called *positive numbers.* They have the sign +, whether it is actually written or not. Business gains or losses, feet above or below sea level, and temperature above and below zero can all be expressed by means of signed numbers.

Addition

If the numbers to be added have the same sign, add the numbers (integers, fractions, decimals) as usual and use their common sign in the answer:

$$+9 + (+8) + (+2) = +19 \text{ or } 19$$
$$−4 + (−11) + (−7) + (−1) = −23$$

If the numbers to be added have different signs, add the positive numbers and then the negative numbers. Ignore the signs and subtract the smaller total from the larger total. If the larger total is positive, the answer will be positive; if the larger total is negative, the answer will be negative. The answer may be zero. Zero is neither positive nor negative and has no sign.

Example

$$+3 + (−5) + (−8) + (+2) = ?$$
$$+3 + (+2) = +5$$
$$−5 + (−8) = −13$$
$$13 − 5 = 8$$

Since the larger total (13) has a negative sign, the answer is −8.

Subtraction

The second number in a subtraction problem is called the *subtrahend.* In order to subtract, change the sign of the subtrahend and then continue as if you were *adding* signed numbers. If there is no sign in front of the subtrahend, it is assumed to be positive.

Examples

Subtract the subtrahend (bottom number) from the top number.

15	5	−35	−35	42
5	15	−42	42	35
10	−10	7	−77	7

Multiplication

If two and only two signed numbers are to be multiplied, multiply the numbers as you would if they were not signed. Then, if the two numbers have the *same sign,* the product is *positive.* If the two numbers have *different signs,* the product is *negative.* If more than two numbers are being multiplied, proceed two at a time in the same way as before, finding the signed product of the first two numbers, then multiplying that product by the next number, and so on. The product has a positive sign if all the factors are positive or there is an even number of negative factors. The product has a negative sign if there is an odd number of negative factors.

Example

$-3 \cdot (+5) \cdot (-11) \cdot (-2) = -330$

The answer is negative because there is an odd number (three) of negative factors.

The product of a signed number and zero is zero. The product of a signed number and 1 is the original number. The product of a signed number and −1 is the original number with its sign changed.

Examples

$$-5 \cdot 0 = 0$$
$$-5 \cdot 1 = -5$$
$$-5 \cdot (-1) = +5$$

Division

If the divisor and the dividend have the same sign, the answer is positive. Divide the numbers as you normally would. If the divisor and the dividend have different signs, the answer is negative. Divide the numbers as you normally would.

Examples

$$-3 \div (-2) = \frac{3}{2} = 1\frac{1}{2}$$
$$8 \div (-.2) = -40$$

If zero is divided by a signed number, the answer is zero. If a signed number is divided by zero, the answer does not exist. If a signed number is divided by 1, the number remains the same. If a signed number is divided by −1, the quotient is the original number with its sign changed.

Examples

$$0 \div (-2) = 0$$

$$-\frac{4}{3} \div 0 \qquad \text{not defined}$$

$$\frac{2}{3} \div 1 = \frac{2}{3}$$

$$4 \div -1 = -4$$

Signed Numbers Problems

Perform the indicated operations:

1. $+ 6 + (-5) + (+2) + (-8) =$
2. $- 5 - (-4) + (-2) - (+6) =$
3. $-3 \cdot (+5) \cdot (-7) \cdot (-2) =$
4. $9 \div (-.3) =$

Solutions:

1. $+6 + (-5) = +1$
   $+1 + (+2) = +3$
   $+3 + (-8) = -5$
2. $-5 -(-4) = -5 + 4 = -1$
   $-1 + (-2) = -3$
   $-3 - (+6) = -9$
3. $-3 \cdot (+5) = -15$
   $-15 \cdot (-7) = +105$
   $+105 \cdot (-2) = -210$
4. $9 \div (-.3) = -30$

Powers, Exponents, and Roots

Exponents

The product $10 \cdot 10 \cdot 10$ can be written 10^3. We say 10 is raised to the *third power*. In general, $a \times a \times a \dots a$ n times is written a^n. The *base a* is raised to the *n*th power, and *n* is called the *exponent*.

Examples

$3^2 = 3 \cdot 3$ read "3 squared"

$2^3 = 2 \cdot 2 \cdot 2$ read "2 cubed"

$5^4 = 5 \cdot 5 \cdot 5 \cdot 5$ read "5 to the fourth power"

If the exponent is 1, it is usually understood and not written; thus, $a^1 = a$. Since

$a^2 = a \times a$ and $a^3 = a \times a \times a$

then

$a^2 \times a^3 = (a \times a)(a \times a \times a) = a^5$

There are three rules for exponents. In general, if k and m are any counting numbers or zero, and a is any number,

Rule 1: $a^k \times a^m = a^{k+m}$

Rule 2: $a^m \cdot b^m = (ab)^m$

Rule 3: $(a^k)^n = a^{kn}$

Examples

Rule 1: $2^2 \cdot 2^3 = 4 \times 8 = 32$
and $2^2 \times 2^3 = 2^5 = 32$

Rule 2: $3^2 \times 4^2 = 9 \times 16 = 144$
and $3^2 \times 4^2 = (3 \times 4)^2 = 12^2 = 144$

Rule 3: $(3^2)^3 = 9^3 = 729$
and $(3^2)^3 = 3^6 = 729$

Roots

The definition of roots is based on exponents. If $a^n = c$, where a is the base and n the exponent, a is called the *n*th *root* of *c*. This is written $a = \sqrt[n]{c}$. The symbol $\sqrt{}$ is called a *radical sign*. Since $5^4 = 625$, $\sqrt[4]{625}$ = 5 and 5 is the fourth root of 625. The most frequently used roots are the second (called the square) root and the third (called the cube) root. The square root is written $\sqrt{}$ and the cube root is written $\sqrt[3]{}$.

Square Roots

If c is a positive number, there are two values, one negative and one positive, which when multiplied together will produce c.

Example

$+4 \cdot (+4) = 16$ and $-4 \cdot (-4) = 16$

The positive square root of a positive number c is called the *principal* square root of c (briefly, the *square root* of c) and is denoted by $\sqrt{c}$:

$$\sqrt{144} = 12$$

If $c = 0$, there is only one square root, 0. If c is a negative number, there is no real number that is the square root of c:

$$\sqrt{-4} \text{ is not a real number}$$

Cube Roots

Both positive and negative numbers have real cube roots. The cube root of 0 is 0. The cube root of a positive number is positive; that of a negative number is negative.

Examples

$2 \cdot 2 \cdot 2 = 8$

Therefore $\sqrt[3]{8} = 2$

$-3 \cdot (-3) \cdot (-3) = -27$

Therefore $\sqrt[3]{-27} = -3$

Each number has only one real cube root.

Fractional Exponents

The values of k, m, and n from the three exponent rules can be expanded to include positive and negative fractions. In particular, roots can be expressed as fractional exponents. In Rule 3, $(a^k)^n = a^{kn}$.

Let $k = \dfrac{1}{n}$. Then $(a^{\frac{1}{n}})^n = a^1 = a$ and $a^{\frac{1}{n}}$ is the nth root of a. Rule 2, $a^m \times b^m = (a \times b)^m$, which is true when a and b are any numbers and n is an integer, can be extended to include the case in which the exponent is a fraction. Suppose $m = \dfrac{1}{k}$. Then:

$$a^{\frac{1}{k}} \times b^{\frac{1}{k}} = (a \times b)^{\frac{1}{k}}$$

$$\text{or } \sqrt[k]{a \times b} = \sqrt[k]{a} \times \sqrt[k]{b}$$

This last formulation justifies the simplification of square roots. If the number under the radical sign is a square number, the process will terminate in a number without the radical sign. If the number is not square, the process should terminate when the number remaining under the radical sign no longer contains a square.

Example 1

Simplify $\sqrt{98}$

$$\sqrt{98} = \sqrt{2 \times 49}$$

$$= \sqrt{2} \times \sqrt{49} \quad \text{where 49 is a square number}$$

$$= \sqrt{2} \times 7$$

Therefore, $\sqrt{98} = 7\sqrt{2}$ and the process terminates because there is no whole number whose square is 2. $7\sqrt{2}$ is called a radical expression or simply a *radical*.

Example 2

Which is larger, $\left(\sqrt{96}\right)^2$ or $\sqrt{2^{14}}$?

$$\left(\sqrt{96}\right)^2 = \sqrt{96} \times \sqrt{96} = \sqrt{96 \times 96}$$
$$= 96$$

$$\sqrt{2^{14}} = 2^7 = 128 \quad \text{because } 2^{14} = 2^7 \times 2^7$$
$$\text{by}$$

Rule 1 or because $\sqrt{2^{14}} = (2^{14})^{1/2} = 2^7$
by Rule 3

Since $128 > 96$,

$$\sqrt{2^{14}} > \left(\sqrt{96}\right)^2$$

Example 3

Which is larger, $2\sqrt{75}$ or $6\sqrt{12}$?

These numbers can be compared if the same number appears under the radical sign. Then the greater number is the one with the larger number in front of the radical sign.

$$\sqrt{75} = \sqrt{25 \times 3} = \sqrt{25} \times \sqrt{3} = 5\sqrt{3}$$

Therefore:

$$2\sqrt{75} = 2(5\sqrt{3}) = 10\sqrt{3}$$

$$\sqrt{12} = \sqrt{4 \times 3} = \sqrt{4} \times \sqrt{3} = 2\sqrt{3}$$

Therefore:

$$6\sqrt{12} = 6(2\sqrt{3}) = 12\sqrt{3}$$

Since $12\sqrt{3} > 10\sqrt{3}$,

$$6\sqrt{12} > 2\sqrt{75}$$

Note: Numbers such as $\sqrt{2}$ and $\sqrt{3}$ are called *irrational* numbers to distinguish them from *rational* numbers, which include the integers and the fractions. Irrational numbers also have places on the number line. They may have positive or negative signs. The combination of rational and irrational numbers, all the numbers we have used so far, make up the *real* numbers. Arithmetic, algebra, and geometry deal with real numbers. The number π, the ratio of the circumference of a circle to its diameter, is also a real number; it is irrational, although it is approximated by 3.14159.... Instructions for taking the ACT say that the numbers used are real numbers. This means that answers may be expressed as fractions, decimals, radicals, or integers, whatever is required.

Radicals can be added and subtracted only if they have the same number under the radical sign. Otherwise, they must be reduced to expressions having the same number under the radical sign.

Example

Add $2\sqrt{18} + 4\sqrt{8} - \sqrt{2}$.

$\sqrt{18} = \sqrt{9 \times 2} = \sqrt{9} \times \sqrt{2} = 3\sqrt{2}$

therefore $2\sqrt{18} = 2(3\sqrt{2}) = 6\sqrt{2}$

and $\sqrt{8} = \sqrt{4 \times 2} = \sqrt{4} \times \sqrt{2} = 2\sqrt{2}$

therefore $4\sqrt{8} = 4(2\sqrt{2}) = 8\sqrt{2}$

giving $2\sqrt{18} + 4\sqrt{8} - \sqrt{2}$

$= 6\sqrt{2} + 8\sqrt{2} - \sqrt{2} = 13\sqrt{2}$

Radicals are multiplied using the rule that

$$\sqrt[k]{a \times b} = \sqrt[k]{a} \times \sqrt[k]{b}$$

Example

$\sqrt{2}\left(\sqrt{2} - 5\sqrt{3}\right) = \sqrt{4} - 5\sqrt{6}$
$= 2 - 5\sqrt{6}$

A quotient rule for radicals similar to the product rule is:

$$\sqrt[k]{\frac{a}{b}} = \frac{\sqrt[k]{a}}{\sqrt[k]{b}}$$

Example

$$\sqrt{\frac{9}{4}} = \frac{\sqrt{9}}{\sqrt{4}} = \frac{3}{2}$$

Exponents, Powers, and Roots Problems

1. Simplify $\sqrt{162}$

2. Find the sum of $\sqrt{75}$ and $\sqrt{12}$

3. Combine $\sqrt{80} + \sqrt{45} - \sqrt{20}$

4. Simplify $\sqrt{5}(2\sqrt{2} - 3\sqrt{5})$

5. Divide and simplify $\dfrac{15\sqrt{96}}{5\sqrt{2}}$

6. Calculate $5^2 \times 2^3$

Solutions:

1. $\sqrt{162} = \sqrt{2 \cdot 81} = \sqrt{2} \cdot \sqrt{81} = 9\sqrt{2}$

2. $\sqrt{75} + \sqrt{12} = 5\sqrt{3} + 2\sqrt{3} = 7\sqrt{3}$

3. $\sqrt{80} + \sqrt{45} - \sqrt{20}$
   $= 4\sqrt{5} + 3\sqrt{5} - 2\sqrt{5} = 5\sqrt{5}$

4. $\sqrt{5}\left(2\sqrt{2} - 3\sqrt{5}\right)$
   $= 2\sqrt{10} - 3\sqrt{25} = 2\sqrt{10} - 3(5)$
   $= 2\sqrt{10} - 15$

5. $\dfrac{15\sqrt{96}}{5\sqrt{2}} = \dfrac{15(4\sqrt{6})}{5\sqrt{2}} = \dfrac{60\sqrt{6}}{5\sqrt{2}} = 12\sqrt{3}$

6. $5^2 \times 2^3 = 25 \times 8 = 200$

ALGEBRA

Algebra is a generalization of arithmetic. It provides methods for solving problems that cannot be done by arithmetic alone or that can be done by arithmetic only after long computations. Algebra provides a shorthand way of reducing long verbal statements to brief formulas, expressions, or equations. After the verbal statements have been reduced, the resulting algebraic expressions can be simplified. Suppose that a room is 12 feet wide and 20 feet long. Its perimeter (measurement around the outside) can be expressed as:

$12 + 20 + 12 + 20$ or $2(12 + 20)$

If the width of the room remains 12 feet but the letter l is used to symbolize length, the perimeter is:

$$12 + l + 12 + l \text{ or } 2(12 + l)$$

Further, if w is used for width, the perimeter of *any* rectangular room can be written as $2(w + l)$. This same room has an area of 12 feet by 20 feet or $12 \cdot 20$. If l is substituted for 20, any room of width 12 has area equal to $12l$. If w is substituted for the number 12, the area of any rectangular room is given by wl or lw. Expressions such as wl and $2(w + l)$ are called *algebraic expressions*. An *equation* is a statement that two algebraic expressions are equal. A *formula* is a special type of equation.

Evaluating Formulas

If we are given an expression and numerical values to be assigned to each letter, the expression can be evaluated.

Example

Evaluate $2x + 3y - 7$ if $x = 2$ and $y = -4$.
Substitute given values
$2(2) + 3(-4) - 7 = ?$

Multiply numbers using rules for signed numbers
$4 + -12 - 7 = ?$

Collect numbers
$4 - 19 = -15$

We have already evaluated formulas in arithmetic when solving percent, discount, and interest problems.

Example

The formula for temperature conversion is:

$$F = \frac{9}{5} C + 32$$

where C stands for the temperature in degrees Celsius and F for degrees Fahrenheit. Find the Fahrenheit temperature that is equivalent to 20°C.

$$F = \frac{9}{5} (20°C) + 32 = 36 + 32 = 68°F$$

Algebraic Expressions

Formulation

A more difficult problem than evaluating an expression or formula is to translate from a verbal expression to an algebraic one:

Verbal	Algebraic
Thirteen more than x	$x + 13$
Six less than twice x	$2x - 6$
The square of the sum of x and 5	$(x + 5)^2$
The sum of the square of x and the square of 5	$x^2 + 5^2$
The distance traveled by a car going 50 miles an hour for x hours	$50x$
The average of 70, 80, 85, and x	$\dfrac{70 + 80 + 85 + x}{4}$

Simplification

After algebraic expressions have been formulated, they can usually be simplified by means of the laws of exponents and the common operations of addition, subtraction, multiplication, and division. These techniques will be described in the next section. Algebraic expressions and equations frequently contain parentheses, which are removed in the process of simplifying. If an expression contains more than one set of parentheses, remove the inner set first and then the outer set. Brackets, [ ], which are often used instead of parentheses, are treated the same way. Parentheses are used to indicate multiplication. Thus $3(x + y)$ means that 3 is to be multiplied by the sum of x and y. The *distributive law* is used to accomplish this:

$$a(b + c) = ab + ac$$

The expression in front of the parentheses is multiplied by each term inside. Rules for signed numbers apply.

Example

Simplify $3[4(2 - 8) - 5(4 + 2)]$.

This can be done in two ways.

Method 1: Combine the numbers inside the parentheses first:

$$3[4(2 - 8) - 5(4 + 2)] = 3[4(-6) - 5(6)]$$
$$= 3[-24 - 30]$$
$$= 3[-54] = -162$$

Method 2: Use the distributive law:

$$3[4(2 - 8) - 5(4 + 2)] = 3[8 - 32 - 20 - 10]$$
$$= 3[8 - 62]$$
$$= 3[-54] = -162$$

If there is a (+) before the parentheses, the signs of the terms inside the parentheses remain the same when the parentheses are removed. If there is a (−) before the parentheses, the sign of each term inside the parentheses changes when the parentheses are removed.

Once parentheses have been removed, the order of operations is multiplication and division, then addition and subtraction from left to right.

Example

$(-15 + 17) \cdot 3 - [(4 \cdot 9) \div 6] = ?$

Work inside the parentheses first:
$(2) \cdot 3 - [36 \div 6] = ?$

Then work inside the brackets:
$2 \cdot 3 - [6] = ?$

Multiply first, then subtract, proceeding from left to right:
$6 - 6 = 0$

The placement of parentheses and brackets is important. Using the same numbers as above with the parentheses and brackets placed in different positions can give many different answers.

Example

$-15 + [(17 \cdot 3) - (4 \cdot 9)] \div 6 = ?$

Work inside the parentheses first:
$-15 + [(51) - (36)] \div 6 = ?$

Then work inside the brackets:
$-15 + [15] \div 6 = ?$

Since there are no more parentheses or brackets, proceed from left to right, dividing before adding:

$$-15 + 2\frac{1}{2} = -12\frac{1}{2}$$

Operations

When letter symbols and numbers are combined with the operations of arithmetic (+, −, ·, ÷) and with certain other mathematical operations, we have an *algebraic expression*. Algebraic expressions are made up of several parts connected by a plus or a minus sign; each part is called a *term*. Terms with the same letter part are called *like terms.* Since algebraic expressions represent numbers, they can be added, subtracted, multiplied, and divided.

When we defined the commutative law of addition in arithmetic by writing $a + b = b + a$, we meant that a and b could represent any number. The expression $a + b = b + a$ is an *identity* because it is true for all numbers. The expression $n + 5 = 14$ is not an identity because it is not true for all numbers; it becomes true only when the number 9 is substituted for n. Letters used to represent numbers are called *variables*. If a number stands alone (the 5 or 14 in $n + 5 = 14$), it is called a *constant* because its value is constant or unchanging. If a number appears in front of a variable, it is called a *coefficient.* Because the letter x is frequently used to represent a variable, or *unknown,* the times sign ×, which can be confused with it in handwriting, is rarely used to express multiplication in algebra. Other expressions used for multiplication are a dot, parentheses, or simply writing a number and letter together:

$5 \cdot 4$ or $5(4)$ or $5a$

Of course, 54 still means fifty-four.

Addition and Subtraction

Only like terms can be combined. Add or subtract the coefficients of like terms, using the rules for signed numbers.

Example 1

Add $x + 2y - 2x + 3y$.

$x - 2x + 2y + 3y = -x + 5y$

Example 2

Perform the subtraction:

$$-30a - 15b + 4c$$
$$- (- 5a + 3b - c + d)$$

Change the sign of each term in the subtrahend and then add, using the rules for signed numbers:

$$-30a - 15b + 4c$$
$$\underline{5a - 3b + c - d}$$
$$-25a - 18b + 5c - d$$

Multiplication

Multiplication is accomplished by using the *distributive property.* If the multiplier has only one term, then

$a(b + c) = ab + bc$

Example

$9x(5m + 9q) = (9x)(5m) + (9x)(9q)$
$= 45mx + 81qx$

When the multiplier contains more than one term and you are multiplying two expressions, multiply each term of the first expression by each term of the second and then add like terms. Follow the rules for signed numbers and exponents at all times.

Example

$(3x + 8)(4x^2 + 2x + 1)$
$= 3x(4x^2 + 2x + 1) + 8(4x^2 + 2x + 1)$
$= 12x^3 + 6x^2 + 3x + 32x^2 + 16x + 8$
$= 12x^3 + 38x^2 + 19x + 8$

If more than two expressions are to be multiplied, multiply the first two, then multiply the product by the third factor, and so on, until all factors have been used.

Algebraic expressions can be multiplied by themselves (squared) or raised to any power.

Example 1

$(a + b)^2 = (a + b)(a + b)$
$= a(a + b) + b(a + b)$
$= a^2 + ab + ba + b^2$
$= a^2 + 2ab + b^2$

since $ab = ba$ by the commutative law

Example 2

$$(a + b)(a - b) = a(a - b) + b(a - b)$$
$$= a^2 - ab + ba - b^2$$
$$= a^2 - b^2$$

Factoring

When two or more algebraic expressions are multiplied, each is called a factor and the result is the *product*. The reverse process of finding the factors when given the product is called *factoring*. A product can often be factored in more than one way. Factoring is useful in multiplication, division, and solving equations.

One way to factor an expression is to remove any single-term factor that is common to each of the terms and write it outside the parentheses. It is the distributive law that permits this.

Example

$$3x^3 + 6x^2 + 9x = 3x(x^2 + 2x + 3)$$

The result can be checked by multiplication.

Expressions containing squares can sometimes be factored into expressions containing letters raised to the first power only, called *linear factors*. We have seen that

$$(a + b)(a - b) = a^2 - b^2$$

Therefore, if we have an expression in the form of a difference of two squares, it can be factored as:

$$a^2 - b^2 = (a + b)(a - b)$$

Example

Factor $4x^2 - 9$.

$$4x^2 - 9 = (2x)^2 - (3)^2 = (2x + 3)(2x - 3)$$

Again, the result can be checked by multiplication.

A third type of expression that can be factored is one containing three terms, such as $x^2 + 5x + 6$. Since

$$(x + a)(x + b) = x(x + b) + a(x + b)$$
$$= x^2 + xb + ax + ab$$
$$= x^2 + (a + b)x + ab$$

an expression in the form $x^2 + (a + b)x + ab$ can be factored into two factors of the form $(x + a)$ and $(x + b)$. We must find two numbers whose product is the constant in the given expression and whose sum is the coefficient of the term containing x.

Example 1

Find factors of $x^2 + 5x + 6$.

First find two numbers which, when multiplied, have +6 as a product. Possibilities are 2 and 3, −2 and −3, 1 and 6, −1 and −6. From these select the one pair whose sum is 5. The pair 2 and 3 is the only possible selection, and so:

$$x^2 + 5x + 6 = (x + 2)(x + 3) \quad \text{written in either order}$$

Example 2

Factor $x^2 - 5x - 6$.

Possible factors of −6 are −1 and 6, 1 and −6, 2 and −3, −2 and 3. We must select the pair whose sum is −5. The only pair whose sum is −5 is + 1 and −6, and so

$$x^2 - 5x - 6 = (x + 1)(x - 6)$$

In factoring expressions of this type, notice that if the last sign is plus, both a and b have the same sign and it is the same as the sign of the middle term. If the last sign is minus, the numbers have opposite signs.

Many expressions cannot be factored.

Division

$$\frac{36mx^2}{9m^2x} = 4m^{1-2}x^{2-1}$$

$$= 4m^{-1}x^1 = \frac{4x}{m}$$

Method 2: Cancellation

$$\frac{36mx^2}{9m^2x} = \frac{\overset{4}{\cancel{36}}\cancel{m}x\cancel{x}}{\underset{1}{\cancel{9}\cancel{m}\cancel{m}\cancel{x}}} = \frac{4x}{m}$$

This is acceptable because

$$\frac{ab}{bc} = \frac{a}{b}\left(\frac{c}{c}\right) \text{ and } \frac{c}{c} = 1$$

so that $\dfrac{ac}{bc} = \dfrac{a}{b}$

    If the divisor contains only one term and the dividend is a sum, divide each term in the dividend by the divisor and simplify as you did in Method 2.

$$\frac{9x^3 + 3x^2 + 6x}{3x} = \frac{\overset{3x^2}{\cancel{9x^3}}}{\cancel{3x}} + \frac{\overset{x}{\cancel{3x^2}}}{\cancel{3x}} + \frac{\overset{2}{\cancel{6x}}}{\cancel{3x}}$$

$$= 3x^2 + x + 2$$

Example

This method cannot be followed if there are two terms or more in the denominator since

$$\frac{a}{b+c} \neq \frac{a}{b} + \frac{a}{c}$$

In this case, write the example as a fraction. Factor the numerator and denominator if possible. Then use laws of exponents or cancel.

Example

Divide $x^3 - 9x$ by $x^3 + 6x^2 + 9x$.

Write as:

$$\frac{x^3 - 9x}{x^3 + 6x^2 + 9x}$$

Both numerator and denominator can be factored to give:

$$\frac{x(x^2 - 9)}{x(x^2 + 6x + 9)} = \frac{\cancel{x}(x+3)(x-3)}{\cancel{x}(x+3)(x+3)} = \frac{x-3}{x+3}$$

Algebra Problems

1. Simplify: $4[2(3-7) - 4(2+6)]$
2. Subtract: $(-25x + 4y - 12z)$
   $- (4x - 8y - 13z)$
3. Multiply: $(5x + 2)(3x^2 - 2x + 1)$
4. Factor completely: $2x^3 + 8x^2 - 90x$
5. Factor completely: $32x^2 - 98$
6. Divide: $\dfrac{x^2 + 2x - 8}{x^2 - x - 20}$

Solutions:

1. $4[2(3-7) - 4(2+6)] = 4[2(-4)-4(8)]$
   $= 4[-8 - 32] = 4(-40) = -160$
2. $(-25x + 4y - 12z) - (4x - 8y - 13z)$
   $= -25x + 4y - 12z - 4x + 8y + 13z$
   $= -29x + 12y + z$
3. $(5x + 2)(3x^2 - 2x + 1)$
   $= 5x(3x^2 - 2x + 1) + 2(3x^2 - 2x + 1)$
   $= 15x^3 - 10x^2 + 5x + 6x^2 - 4x + 2$
   $= 15x^3 - 4x^2 + x + 2$
4. $2x^3 + 8x^2 - 90x = 2x(x^2 + 4x - 45)$
   $= 2x(x + 9)(x - 5)$
5. $32x^2 - 98 = 2(16x^2 - 49)$
   $= 2(4x - 7)(4x + 7)$
6. $\dfrac{x^2 + 2x - 8}{x^2 - x - 20} = \dfrac{(x + 4)(x - 2)}{(x - 5)(x + 4)}$

$$= \frac{\overset{1}{\cancel{(x+4)}}(x - 2)}{(x - 5)\underset{1}{\cancel{(x+4)}}} = \frac{x-2}{x-5}$$

Equations

Solving equations is one of the major objectives in algebra. If a variable x in an equation is replaced by a value or expression that makes the equation a true statement, the value or expression is called a *solution* of the equation. (Remember that an equation is a mathematical statement that one algebraic expression is equal to another.)

An equation may contain one or more variables. We begin with one variable. Certain rules apply to equations whether there are one or more variables. The following rules are applied to give equivalent equations that are simpler than the original:

Addition: If $s = t$, then $s + c = t + c$.
Subtraction: If $s + c = t + c$, then $s = t$.
Multiplication: If $s = t$, then $cs = ct$.
Division: If $cs = ct$ and $c \neq 0$, then $s = t$.

To solve for x in an equation in the form $ax = b$ with $a \neq 0$, divide each side of the equation by a:

$$\frac{ax}{a} = \frac{b}{a} \quad \text{yielding} \quad x = \frac{b}{a}$$

Then, $\frac{b}{a}$ is the solution to the equation.

Example 1

Solve $4x = 8$.

Write $\dfrac{4x}{4} = \dfrac{8}{4}$

$\qquad\qquad x = 2$

Example 2

Solve $2x - (x - 4) = 5(x + 2)$ for x.

$2x - (x - 4) = 5(x + 2)$

$2x - x + 4 = 5x + 10$ Remove parentheses by distributive law.

$x + 4 = 5x + 10$ Combine like terms.

$x = 5x + 6$ Subtract 4 from each side.

$-4x = 6$ Subtract $5x$ from each side.

$x = \dfrac{6}{-4}$ Divide each side by -4.

$= -\dfrac{3}{2}$ Reduce fraction to lowest terms. Negative sign now applies to the entire fraction.

Check the solution for accuracy by substituting in the original equation:

$$2\left(-\frac{3}{2}\right) - \left(-\frac{3}{2} - 4\right) \overset{?}{=} 5\left(-\frac{3}{2} + 2\right)$$

$$-3 - \left(-\frac{11}{2}\right) \overset{?}{=} 5\left(\frac{1}{2}\right)$$

$$-3 + \frac{11}{2} \overset{?}{=} \frac{5}{2}$$

$$-\frac{6}{2} + \frac{11}{2} \overset{?}{=} \frac{5}{2} \quad \text{check}$$

Equations Problems

Solve the following equations for x:

1. $3x - 5 = 3 + 2x$

2. $3(2x - 2) = 12$

3. $4(x - 2) = 2x + 10$

4. $7 - 4(2x - 1) = 3 + 4(4 - x)$

Solutions:

1. $3x - 5 = 3 + 2x$

$$\frac{-2x \qquad\qquad -2x}{x - 5 = 3}$$

$$\frac{+5 \quad +5}{x = 8}$$

2. $3(2x - 2) = 12$

$6x - 6 = 12$

$6x = 18$

$x = 3$

3. $4(x - 2) = 2x + 10$

$4x - 8 = 2x + 10$

$4x = 2x + 18$

$2x = 18$

$x = 9$

4. $7 - 4(2x - 1) = 3 + 4(4 - x)$

$7 - 8x + 4 = 3 + 16 - 4x$

$11 - 8x = 19 - 4x$

$11 = 19 + 4x$

$-8 = 4x$

$x = -2$

Word Problems Involving One Unknown

In many cases, if you read a word problem carefully, assign a letter to the quantity to be found, and understand the relationships between known and unknown quantities, you can formulate an equation in one unknown.

Number Problems and Age Problems

These two kinds of problems are similar to each other.

Example

One number is 3 times another, and their sum is 48. Find the two numbers.

Let x = second number. Then the first is $3x$. Since their sum is 48,

$3x + x = 48$

$4x = 48$

$x = 12$

Therefore, the first number is $3x = 36$.

$36 + 12 = 48$ check

Distance Problems

The basic concept is:

Distance = rate · time

Example

In a mileage test, a man drives a truck at a fixed rate of speed for 1 hour. Then he increases the speed by 20 miles per hour and drives at that rate for 2 hours. He then reduces that speed by 5 miles per hour and drives at that rate for 3 hours. If the distance traveled was 295 miles, what are the rates of speed over each part of the test?

Let x be the first speed, $x + 20$ the second, and $x + (20 - 5) = x + 15$ the third. Because distance = rate · time, multiply these rates by the time and formulate the equation by separating the two equal expressions for distance by an equals sign:

$1x + 2(x + 20) + 3(x + 15) = 295$

$x + 2x + 3x + 40 + 45 = 295$

$6x = 210$

$x = 35$

The speeds are 35, 55, and 50 miles per hour.

Consecutive Number Problems

This type usually involves only one unknown. Two numbers are consecutive if one is the successor of the other. Three consecutive numbers are of the form x, $x + 1$, and $x + 2$. Since an even number is divisible by 2, consecutive even numbers are of the form $2x$, $2x + 2$, and $2x + 4$. An odd number is of the form $2x + 1$.

Example

Find three consecutive whole numbers whose sum is 75.

Let the first number be x, the second $x + 1$, and the third $x + 2$. Then:

$$x + (x + 1) + (x + 2) = 75$$
$$3x + 3 = 75$$
$$3x = 72$$
$$x = 24$$

The numbers whose sum is 75 are 24, 25, and 26. Many versions of this problem have no solution. For example, no three consecutive whole numbers have a sum of 74.

Work Problems

These problems concern the speed with which work can be accomplished and the time necessary to perform a task if the size of the work force is changed.

Example

If Joe can type a chapter alone in 6 days and Ann can type the same chapter in 8 days, how long will it take them to type the chapter if they both work on it?

We let x = number of days required if they work together, and then put our information into tabular form:

	Joe	Ann	Together
Days to type chapter	6	8	x
Part typed in 1 day	$\dfrac{1}{6}$	$\dfrac{1}{8}$	$\dfrac{1}{x}$

Since the part done by Joe in 1 day plus the part done by Ann in 1 day equals the part done by both in 1 day, we have

$$\frac{1}{6} + \frac{1}{8} = \frac{1}{x}$$

Next we multiply each member by $48x$ to clear the fractions, giving:

$$8x + 6x = 48$$
$$14x = 48$$
$$x = 3\frac{3}{7} \text{ days}$$

Word Problems in One Unknown Problems

1. If 18 is subtracted from six times a certain number, the result is 96. Find the number.

2. A 63-foot rope is cut into two pieces. If one piece is twice as long as the other, how long is each piece?

3. Peter is now three times as old as Jillian. In six years, he will be twice as old as she will be then. How old is Peter now?

4. Lauren can clean the kitchen in 30 minutes. It takes Kathleen 20 minutes to complete the same job. How long would it take to clean the kitchen if they both worked together?

5. A train travels 120 miles at an average rate of 40 mph, and it returns along the same route at an average rate of 60 mph. What is the average rate of speed for the entire trip?

6. The sum of two consecutive odd integers is 68. Find the integers.

Solutions:

1. Let x = the number.

Then, $6x - 18 = 96$

$$6x = 114$$
$$x = 19$$

The number is 19.

2. Let x = the length of the short piece.

Then, $2x$ = the length of the longer piece.

And, $x + 2x = 63$

$$3x = 63$$
$$x = 21$$
$$2x = 42$$

The pieces are 21 feet and 42 feet.

3. Let J = Jillian's age now;

$\quad$ 3J = Peter's age now;

$\quad$ J + 6 = Jillian's age in 6 years;

$\quad$ 3J + 6 = Peter's age in 6 years.

Then,

$3J + 6 = 2 (J + 6)$

$3J + 6 = 2J + 12$

$\quad 3J = 2J + 6$

$\quad\quad J = 6$

$\quad 3J = 18$

Peter is currently 18 years old.

4. Let x = the number of minutes to do the job working together.

Lauren does $x/30$ of the job.

Kathleen does $x/20$ of the job.

$x/30 + x/20 = 1$ (Multiply by 60)

$\quad 2x + 3x = 60$

$\quad\quad 5x = 60$

$\quad\quad\quad x = 12$

It would take 12 minutes to do the job together.

5. The train takes $120/40 = 3$ hours out, and

the train takes $120/60 = 2$ hours back.

The total trip takes 5 hours.

The total distance traveled is 240 miles.

Then,

Rate = Distance/Time = $240/5 = 48$

The average rate is 48 mph.

6. Let x = the first odd integer.

Then, $x + 2$ = the second odd integer, and,

$x + x + 2 = 68$

$\quad 2x + 2 = 68$

$\quad\quad 2x = 66$

$\quad\quad\quad x = 33$

$x + 2 = 35$

The numbers are 33 and 35.

Literal Equations

An equation may have other letters in it besides the variable (or variables). Such an equation is called a *literal equation*. An illustration is $x + b = a$, with x the variable. The solution of such an equation will not be a specific number but will involve letter symbols. Literal equations are solved by exactly the same methods as those involving numbers, but we must know which of the letters in the equation is to be considered the variable. Then the other letters are treated as constants.

Example 1

Solve $ax - 2bc = d$ for x.

$ax = d + 2bc$

$$x = \frac{d + 2bc}{a} \text{ if } a \neq 0$$

Example 2

Solve $ay - by = a^2 - b^2$ for y.

$y(a - b) = a^2 - b^2 \quad$ Factor out common term.

$y(a - b) = (a + b)(a - b) \quad$ Factor expression on right side.

$\quad\quad y = a + b \quad$ Divide each side by $a - b$ if $a \neq b$.

Example 3

Solve for S the equation

$$\frac{1}{R} = \frac{1}{S} + \frac{1}{T}$$

Multiply every term by RST, the LCD:

$$ST = RT + RS$$
$$ST - RS = RT$$
$$S(T - R) = RT$$
$$S = \frac{RT}{T - R} \qquad \text{If } T \neq R$$

Quadratic Equations

An equation containing the square of an unknown quantity is called a *quadratic* equation. One way of solving such an equation is by factoring. If the product of two expressions is zero, at least one of the expressions must be zero.

Example 1

Solve $y^2 + 2y = 0$.

$y(y + 2) = 0$ Remove common factor

$y = 0$ or $y + 2 = 0$ Since product is 0, at least one of factors must be 0.

$y = 0$ or $y = -2$

Check by substituting both values in the original equation:

$$(0)^2 + 2(0) = 0$$
$$(-2)^2 + 2(-2) = 4 - 4 = 0$$

In this case there are two solutions.

Example 2

Solve $x^2 + 7x + 10 = 0$.

$x^2 + 7x + 10 = (x + 5)\,(x + 2) = 0$

$x + 5 = 0 \qquad$ or $x + 2 = 0$

$x = -5 \quad$ or $\qquad x = -2$

Check:

$$(-5)^2 + 7(-5) + 10 = 25 - 35 + 10 = 0$$
$$(-2)^2 + 7(-2) + 10 = \ \ 4 - 14 + 10 = 0$$

Not all quadratic equations can be factored using only integers, but solutions can usually be found by means of a formula. A quadratic equation may have two solutions, one solution, or occasionally no real solutions. If the quadratic equation is in the form $Ax^2 + Bx + C = 0$, x can be found from the following formula:

$$x = \frac{-B \pm \sqrt{B^2 - 4AC}}{2A}$$

Example

Solve $2y^2 + 5y + 2 = 0$ by formula. Assume $A = 2$, $B = 5$, and $C = 2$.

$$x = \frac{-5 \pm \sqrt{5^2 - 4(2)(2)}}{2(2)}$$
$$= \frac{-5 \pm \sqrt{25 - 16}}{4}$$
$$= \frac{-5 \pm \sqrt{9}}{4}$$
$$= \frac{-5 \pm 3}{4}$$

This yields two solutions:

$$x = \frac{-5 + 3}{4} = \frac{-2}{4} = \frac{-1}{2} \text{ and}$$
$$x = \frac{-5 - 3}{4} = \frac{-8}{4} = -2$$

So far, each quadratic we have solved has had two distinct answers, but an equation may have a single answer (repeated), as in

$$x^2 + 4x + 4 = 0$$
$$(x + 2)(x + 2) = 0$$
$$x + 2 = 0 \text{ and } x + 2 = 0$$
$$x = -2 \text{ and } x = -2$$

The only solution is -2.

It is also possible for a quadratic equation to have no real solution at all.

Example

If we attempt to solve $x^2 + x + 1 = 0$, by formula, we get:

$$x = \frac{-1 \pm \sqrt{1 - 4(1)(1)}}{2} = \frac{-1 \pm \sqrt{-3}}{2}$$

Since $\sqrt{-3}$ is not defined, this quadratic has no real answer.

Rewriting Equations

Certain equations written with a variable in the denominator can be rewritten as quadratics.

Example

Solve $-\dfrac{4}{x} + 5 = x$

$-4 + 5x = x^2$ Multiply both sides by $x \neq 0$.

$-x^2 + 5x - 4 = 0$ Collect terms on one side of equals and set sum equal to 0.

$x^2 - 5x + 4 = 0$ Multiply both sides by -1.

$(x - 4)(x - 1) = 0$ Factor

$x - 4 = 0$ or $x - 1 = 0$

$x = 4$ or $x = 1$

Check the result by substitution:

$-\dfrac{4}{4} + 5 \overset{?}{=} 4$ and $-\dfrac{4}{1} + 5 \overset{?}{=} 1$

$-1 + 5 = 4 \qquad -4 + 5 = 1$

Some equations containing a radical sign can also be converted into a quadratic equation. The solution of this type of problem depends on the principle that

If $A = B$ then $A^2 = B^2$

and If $A^2 = B^2$ then $A = B$ or $A = -B$

Example

Solve $y = \sqrt{3y + 4}$

$$y = \sqrt{3y + 4}$$
$$y^2 = 3y + 4$$
$$y^2 - 3y - 4 = 0$$
$$(y - 4)(y + 1) = 0$$
$$y = 4 \text{ or } y = -1$$

Check by substituting values into the original equation:

$4 \overset{?}{=} \sqrt{3(4) + 4}$ and

$-1 = \sqrt{3(-1) + 4}$

$4 \overset{?}{=} \sqrt{16} \quad -1 \overset{?}{=} \sqrt{1}$

$4 = 4 \quad -1 \neq 1$

The single solution is $y = 4$: the false root $y = -1$ was introduced when the original equation was squared.

Equation Solving Problems

Solve the following equations for the variable indicated:

1. Solve for W: $P = 2L + 2W$

2. Solve for x: $ax + b = cx + d$

3. Solve for x: $8x^2 - 4x = 0$

4. Solve for x: $x^2 - 4x = 21$

5. Solve for y: $\sqrt{y + 1} - 3 = 7$

Solutions:

1. $P = 2L + 2W$

$2W = P - 2L$

$W = \dfrac{P - 2L}{2}$

2. $ax + b = cx + d$

$ax = cx + d - b$

$ax - cx = d - b$

$x(a - c) = d - b$

$x = \dfrac{d - b}{a - c}$

3. $8x^2 - 4x = 0$

$4x(x - 2) = 0$

$x = 0, 2$

4. $x^2 - 4x = 21$

$x^2 - 4x - 21 = 0$

$(x - 7)(x + 3) = 0$

$x = 7, -3$

5. $\sqrt{y + 1} - 3 = 7$

$\sqrt{y + 1} = 10$

$(\sqrt{y + 1})^2 = 10^2$

$y + 1 = 100$

$y = 99$

Linear Inequalities

For each of the sets of numbers we have considered, we have established an ordering of the members of the set by defining what it means to say that one number is greater than the other. Every number we have considered can be represented by a point on a number line.

An *algebraic inequality* is a statement that one algebraic expression is greater than (or less than) another algebraic expression. If all the variables in the inequality are raised to the first power, the inequality is said to be a *linear inequality*. We solve the inequality by reducing it to a simpler inequality whose solution is apparent. The answer is not unique, as it is in an equation, since a great number of values may satisfy the inequality.

There are three rules for producing equivalent inequalities:

1. The same quantity can be added or sub-tracted from each side of an inequality.

2. Each side of an inequality can be multiplied or divided by the same *positive* quantity.

3. If each side of an inequality is multiplied or divided by the same *negative* quantity, the sign of the inequality must be reversed so that the new inequality is equivalent to the first.

Example 1

Solve $5x - 5 > -9 + 3x$.

$5x > -4 + 3x$ Add 5 to each side.

$2x > -4$ Subtract $3x$ from each side.

$x > -2$ Divide by $+2$.

Any number greater than -2 is a solution to this inequality.

Example 2

Solve $2x - 12 < 5x - 3$.

$2x < 5x + 9$ Add 12 to each side.

$-3x < 9$ Subtract $5x$ from each side.

$x > -3$ Divide each side by -3, changing sign of inequality.

Any number greater than -3—for example, $-2\frac{1}{2}$, 0, 1, or 4—is a solution to this inequality.

Linear Equations in Two Unknowns

Graphing Equations

The number line is useful in picturing the values of one variable. When two variables are involved, a coordinate system is effective. The Cartesian coordinate system is constructed by placing a vertical number line and a horizontal number line on a plane so that the lines intersect at their zero points. This meeting place is called the *origin*. The horizontal number line is called the x axis, and the vertical number line (with positive numbers above the x axis) is called the y axis. Points in the plane correspond to ordered pairs of real numbers.

Example

The points in this example are:

x	y
0	0
1	1
3	−1
−2	−2
−2	1

A first-degree equation in two variables is an equation that can be written in the form $ax + by = c$, where a, b, and c are constants. *First-degree* means that x and y appear to the first power. *Linear* refers to the graph of the solutions (x, y) of the equation, which is a straight line. We have already discussed linear equations of one variable.

Example

Graph the line $y = 2x - 4$.
First make a table and select small integral values of x. Find the value of each corresponding y and write it in the table:

x	y
0	−4
1	−2
2	0
3	2

If $x = 1$, for example, $y = 2(1) - 4 = -2$. Then plot the four points on a coordinate system. It is not necessary to have four points; two would do since two points determine a line, but plotting three or more points reduces the possibility of error.

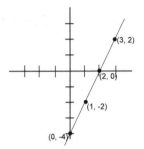

After the points have been plotted (placed on the graph), draw a line through the points and extend it in both directions. This line represents the equation $y = 2x - 4$.

Solving Simultaneous Linear Equations

Two linear equations can be solved together (simultaneously) to yield an answer (x, y) if it exists. On the coordinate system, this amounts to drawing the graphs of two lines and finding their point of intersection. If the lines are parallel and therefore never meet, no solution exists.

Simultaneous linear equations can be solved in the following manner without drawing graphs. From the first equation find the value of one variable in terms of the other; substitute this value in the second equation. The second equation is now a linear equation in one variable and can be solved. After the numerical value of the one variable has been found, substitute that value into the first equation to find the value of the second variable. Check the results by putting both values into the second equation.

Example 1

Solve the system

$2x + y = 3$
$4x - y = 0$

From the first equation, $y = 3 - 2x$. Substitute this value of y into the second equation to get

$4x - (3 - 2x) = 0$
$4x - 3 + 2x = 0$
$6x = 3$
$x = \dfrac{1}{2}$

Substitute $x = \dfrac{1}{2}$ in the first of the original equations:

$2\left(\dfrac{1}{2}\right) + y = 3$
$1 + y = 3$
$y = 2$

Check by substituting both x and y values into the second equation:

$4\left(\dfrac{1}{2}\right) - 2 = 0$
$2 - 2 = 0$

Example 2

A change-making machine contains $30 in dimes and quarters. There are 150 coins in the machine. Find the number of each type of coin.

Let x = number of dimes and y = number of quarters. Then:

$x + y = 150$

Since $.25y$ is the product of a quarter of a dollar and the number of quarters and $.10x$ is the amount of money in dimes,

$.10x + .25y = 30$

Multiply the last equation by 100 to eliminate the decimal points:

$10x + 25y = 3000$

From the first equation, $y = 150 - x$. Substitute this value in the equivalent form of the second equation.

$10x + 25(150 - x) = 3000$
$-15x = -750$
$x = 50$

This is the number of dimes. Substitute this value in $x + y = 150$ to find the number of quarters, $y = 100$.

Check:

$.10(50) + .25(100) = 30$
$\$5 + \$25 = \$30$

Linear Inequalities and Equations Problems

1. Solve for x: $12x < 5(2x + 4)$

2. Solve for y: $6y + 2 < 8y + 14$

3. Find the common solution:
   $x - 3y = 3$
   $2x + 9y = 11$

4. A coin collection consisting of quarters and nickels has a value of $4.50. The total number of coins is 26. Find the number of quarters and the number of nickels in the collection.

5. Mr. Linnell bought 3 cans of corn and 5 cans of tomatoes for $3.75. The next week, he bought 4 cans of corn and 2 cans of tomatoes for $2.90. Find the cost of a can of corn.

Solutions:

1. $12x < 5(2x + 4)$
   $12x < 10x + 20$
   $2x < 20$
   $x < 10$

2. $6y + 2 < 8y + 14$
   $6y < 8y + 12$
   $-2y < 12$
   $y > -6$

3. $x - 3y = 3$
$2x + 9y = 11$

Multiply the first equation by 3.

$3(x - 3y) = 3(3)$
$2x + 9y = 11$

$3x - 9y = 9$
$\underline{2x + 9y = 11}$
$5x = 20$
$x = 4$

Now substitute this answer for x in the second equation.

$2(4) + 9y = 11$
$8 + 9y = 11$
$9y = 3$
$y = 1/3$

4. Let Q = the number of quarters in the collection.
Let N = the number of nickels in the collection.
Then, $.25Q + .05N = 4.50$
$Q + N = 26$

Multiply the top equation by 100 to clear the decimals:

$25Q + 5N = 450$
$Q + N = 26$

Multiply the bottom equation by −5 and add:

$25Q + 5N = 450$
$\underline{-5Q - 5N = -130}$
$20Q = 320$
$Q = 16$
$N = 10$
There are 16 quarters and 10 nickels.

5. Let c = the cost of a can of corn
t = the cost of a can of tomatoes
Then,

$3c + 5t = 3.75$
$4c + 2t = 2.90$

Multiply the top equation by 2, the bottom one by −5, and add:

$6c + 10t = 7.50$
$\underline{-20c - 10t = -14.50}$
$-14c = -7.00$
$c = .50$
A can of corn costs 50¢.

Ratio and Proportion

Many problems in arithmetic and algebra can be solved using the concept of *ratio* to compare numbers. The ratio of a to b is the fraction $\frac{a}{b}$. If the two ratios $\frac{a}{b}$ and $\frac{c}{d}$ represent the same comparison, we write:

$$\frac{a}{b} = \frac{c}{d}$$

This equation (statement of equality) is called a *proportion*. A proportion states the equivalence of two different expressions for the same ratio.

Example 1

In a class of 39 students, 17 are men. Find the ratio of men to women.
39 students − 17 men = 22 women
Ratio of men to women is 17/22, also written $17 : 22$.

Example 2

A fertilizer contains 3 parts nitrogen, 2 parts potash, and 2 parts phosphate by weight. How many pounds of fertilizer will contain 60 pounds of nitrogen?

The ratio of pounds of nitrogen to pounds of fertilizer is 3 to $3 + 2 + 2 = 3/7$. Let x be the number of pounds of mixture. Then:

$$\frac{3}{7} = \frac{60}{x}$$

Multiply both sides of the equation by $7x$ to get:

$3x = 420$
$x = 140$ pounds

Computing Averages and Medians

Mean

Several statistical measures are used frequently. One of them is the *average* or *arithmetic mean*. To find the average of N numbers, add the numbers and divide their sum by N.

Example 1

Seven students attained test scores of 62, 80, 60, 30, 50, 90, and 20. What was the average test score for the group?

$$62 + 80 + 60 + 30 + 50 + 90 + 20 = 392$$

Since there are 7 scores, the average score is

$$\frac{392}{7} = 56$$

Example 2

Joan allotted herself a budget of $50 a week, on the average, for expenses. One week she spent $35, the next $60, and the third $40. How much can she spend in the fourth week without exceeding her budget?

Let x be the amount spent in the fourth week. Then:

$$\frac{35 + 60 + 40 + x}{4} = 50$$

$$35 + 60 + 40 + x = 200$$

$$135 + x = 200$$

$$x = 65$$

She can spend $65 in the fourth week.

Median

If a set of numbers is arranged in order, the number in the middle is called the *median*.

Example

Find the median test score of 62, 80, 60, 30, 50, 90, and 20. Arrange the numbers in increasing (or decreasing) order
20, 30, 50, 60, 62, 80, 90
Since 60 is the number in the middle, it is the median. It is not the same as the arithmetic mean, which is 56.

If number of scores is an even number, the median is the arithmetic mean of the middle two scores.

COORDINATE GEOMETRY

We have already seen that a coordinate system is an effective way to picture relationships involving two variables. In this section, we will learn more about the study of geometry using coordinate methods.

Lines

Recall that the general equation of a line has the following form:

$$Ax + By + C = 0,$$

where A and B are constants and are not both 0. This means that if you were to find all of the points (x, y) that satisfy the above equation, they would all lie on the same line as graphed on a coordinate axis.

If the value of B is not 0, a little algebra can be used to rewrite the equation in the form

$$y = mx + b,$$

where m and b are two constants. Since the two numbers m and b determine this line, let's see what their geometric meaning is. First of all, note that the point $(0, b)$ satisfies the above equation. This means that the point $(0, b)$ is one of the points on the line; in other words, the line crosses the y-axis at the point b. For this reason, the number b is called the *y-intercept* of the line.

To interpret the meaning of m, choose any two points on the line. Let us call these points $(x_1, y_1,)$ and (x_2, y_2). Both of these points must satisfy the equation of the line above, and so:

$$y_1 = mx_1 + b \text{ and } y_2 = mx_2 + b.$$

If we subtract the first equation from the second we obtain

$$y_2 - y_1 = m(x_2 - x_1),$$

and solving for m, we find

$$m = (y_2 - y_1)/(x_2 - x_1).$$

The above equation tells us that the number m in the equation $y = mx + b$ is the ratio of the difference of the y-coordinates to the difference of the x-coordinates. This number is called the *slope* of the line. Therefore, the ratio $m = (y_2 - y_1)/(x_2 - x_1)$ is a measure of the number of units the line rises (or falls) in the y direction for each unit moved in the x direction. Another way to say this is that the slope of a line is a measure of the rate at which the line rises (or falls). Intuitively, a line with a positive slope rises from left to right; one with a negative slope falls from left to right.

Because the equation $y = mx + b$ contains both the slope and the y-intercept, it is called the *slope-intercept* form of the equation of the line. This, however, is not the only form in which the equation of the line can be written.

If the line contains the point (x_1, y_1), its equation can also be written as:

$$y - y_1 = m(x - x_1).$$

This form of the equation of a line is called the *point-slope* form of the equation of a line, since it contains the slope and the coordinates of one of the points on the line.

Two lines are parallel if and only if they have the same slope. Two lines are perpendicular if and only if their slopes are negative inverses of each other. This means that if a line has a slope m, any line perpendicular to this line must have a slope of $-1/m$. Also note that a horizontal line has a slope of 0. For such a line, the slope-intercept form of the equation reduces to $y = b$.

Finally, note that if $B = 0$ in the equation $Ax + By + C = 0$, the equation simplifies to

$$Ax + C = 0,$$

and represents a vertical line (a line parallel to the y-axis) that crosses the x-axis at $-C/A$. Such a line is said to have no slope.

Example 1

Find the slope and the y-intercept of the following lines.

a. $y = 5x - 7$

b. $3x + 4y = 5$

a. $y = 5x - 7$ is already in slope-intercept form. The slope is 5, and the y-intercept is -7.

b. Write $3x + 4y = 5$ in slope-intercept form:

$$4y = -3x + 5$$

$$y = (-3/4)x + (5/4)$$

The slope is $-3/4$, and the y-intercept is $5/4$. This means that the line crosses the y-axis at the point $5/4$, and for every 3 units moved in the x-direction, the line falls 4 units in the y-direction.

Example 2

Find the equations of the following lines:

a. the line containing the points (4, 5) and (7,11)

b. the line containing the point (6, 3) and having slope 2

c. the line containing the point (5, 2) and parallel to $y = 4x + 7$

d. the line containing the point (−2, 8) and perpendicular to $y = -2x + 9$

Solutions

a. First, we need to determine the slope of the line.

$$m = (11 - 5)/(7 - 4) = 6/3 = 2.$$

Now, using the point-slope form: $y - 5 = 2(x - 4)$. If desired, you can change this to the slope-intercept form: $y = 2x - 3$.

b. Since we know the slope and a point on the line, we can simply plug into the point-slope form: $y - 3 = m (x - 6)$ to obtain $y - 3 = 2(x - 6)$.

c. The line $y = 4x + 7$ has a slope of 4. Thus, the desired line can be written as $y - 2 = 4(x - 5)$.

d. The line $y = -2x + 9$ has a slope of -2. The line perpendicular to this one has a slope of 1/2. The desired line can be written as $y - 8 = (1/2)(x + 2)$.

Circles

From a geometric point of view, a circle is the set of points in the plane, each of whose members is the same distance from a particular point called the center of the circle. We can determine the equation of a circle by manipulating the distance formula.

Suppose that we have a circle whose radius is a given positive number r, and whose center lies at the point (h, k). If (x, y) is a point on the circle, then its distance from the center of the circle would be

$$\sqrt{(x - h)^2 + (y - k)^2},$$

and since this distance is r, we can say

$$\sqrt{(x - h)^2 + (y - k)^2} = r.$$

Squaring both sides, we get the following result: the equation of a circle whose center is at (h, k) and whose radius is r is given by:

$$(x - h)^2 + (y - k)^2 = r^2$$

Example

Find the equation of the circle with radius 7, and center at $(0, -5)$.

Substituting into the formula above, we obtain $x^2 + (y + 5)^2 = 49$.

Example

Describe the set of points (x, y) with the property that $x^2 + y^2 > 25$.

The equation $x^2 + y^2 = 25$ describes a circle, centered at the origin, with radius 5. The given set contains all of the points that are *outside* this circle.

Coordinate Geometry Problems

1. Find the y-intercept of the line
$3x - 5y = 15$

2. Find the equation of the line whose slope is -2 and whose y-intercept is 5.

3. Find the slope of the line $2x + 3y = 8$

4. Find the equation of the line containing the points $(2, 4)$ and $(10, 9)$.

5. Find the equation of the line containing the point $(6, 3)$ and parallel to $y = 6x - 8$.

6. Find the equation of the line containing the point $(2, 3)$ and perpendicular to $y = -\frac{1}{3}x + 7$.

7. Find the equation of the circle centered at $(-2, 3)$ with radius 7.

Solutions:

1. A line crosses the y-axis at the point where $x = 0$.
$$3(0) - 5y = 15$$
$$-5y = 15$$
$$y = -3$$
The y-intercept is $(0, -3)$.

2. sing the slope-intercept formula for the equation of a line: $y = -2x + 5$.

3. Put the equation in slope-intercept form:
$$2x + 3y = 8$$
$$3y = -2x + 8$$
$$y = -\frac{2}{3}x + \frac{8}{3}$$
The slope is $-\frac{2}{3}$

4. The slope of the line would be
$\frac{9 - 4}{10 - 2} = \frac{5}{8}$ Using the point-slope form:
$$(y - 4) = \frac{5}{8}(x - 2)$$
$$8(y - 4) = 5(x - 2)$$
$$8y - 32 = 5x - 10$$
$$5x - 8y = -22$$

5. The slope of $y = 6x - 8$ is 6.
Using the point-slope form:
$$y - 3 = 6(x - 6)$$
$$y - 3 = 6x - 36$$
$$6x - y = 33$$

6. The slope of $y = -\frac{1}{3}x + 7$ is $-\frac{1}{3}$.
The slope of the perpendicular line would be 3.
Using the point-slope formula:
$$y - 3 = 3(x - 2)$$
$$y - 3 = 3x - 6$$
$$3x - y = 3$$

7. Using the general formula for the equation of a circle:
$$(x - (-2))^2 + (y - 3)^2 = 7^2$$
$$\text{or } (x + 2)^2 + (y - 3)^2 = 49$$

PLANE GEOMETRY

Plane geometry is the science of measurement. Certain assumptions are made about undefined quantities called points, lines, and planes, and then logical deductions about relationships between figures composed of lines, angles and portions of planes are made, based on these assumptions. The process of making the logical deduction is called a *proof.* In this summary we are not making any proofs but are giving the definitions frequently used in geometry and stating relationships that are the results of proofs.

Lines and Angles

Angles

A line in geometry is always a straight line. When two straight lines meet at a point, they form an *angle.* The lines are called *sides* or *rays* of the angle, and the point is called the *vertex.* The symbol for angle is ∠. When no other angle shares the same vertex, the name of the angle is the name given to the vertex, as in angle *A:*

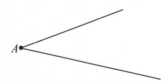

An angle may be named with three letters. Following, for example, *B* is a point on one side and *C* is a point on the other. In this case the name of the vertex must be the middle letter, and we have angle *BAC.*

Occasionally an angle is named by a number or small letter placed in the angle.

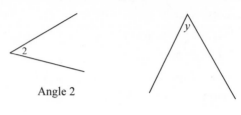

Angle 2

Angle *y*

Angles are usually measured in degrees. An angle of 30 degrees, written 30°, is an angle whose measure is 30 degrees. Degrees are divided into minutes; 60′ (read "minutes") = 1°. Minutes are further divided into seconds; 60″ (read "seconds") = 1′.

Vertical Angles

When two lines intersect, four angles are formed. The angles opposite each other are called *vertical angles* and are equal to each other.

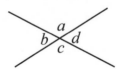

a and *c* are vertical angles.
∠*a* = ∠c
b and *d* are vertical angles.
∠*b* = ∠d

Straight Angle

A *straight angle* has its sides lying along a straight line. It is always equal to 180°.

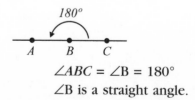

∠*ABC* = ∠B = 180°
∠B is a straight angle.

164

Adjacent Angles

Two angles are *adjacent* if they share the same vertex and a common side but no angle is inside another angle. $\angle ABC$ and $\angle CBD$ are adjacent angles. Even though they share a common vertex B and a common side AB, $\angle ABD$ and $\angle ABC$ are not adjacent angles because one angle is inside the other.

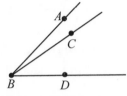

Supplementary Angles

If the sum of two angles is a straight angle (180°), the two angles are *supplementary* and each angle is the supplement of the other.

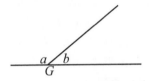

$\angle G$ is a straight angle = 180°.
$\angle a + \angle b = 180°$
$\angle a$ and $\angle b$ are supplementary angles.

Right Angles

If two supplementary angles are equal, they are both *right* angles. A *right* angle is one-half a straight angle. Its measure is 90°. A right angle is symbolized by ⌐.

$\angle G$ is a straight angle.
$\angle b + \angle a = \angle G$, and $\angle a = \angle b$. $\angle a$ and $\angle b$ are right angles.

Complementary Angles

Complementary angles are two angles whose sum is a right angle (90°).

$\angle Y$ is a right angle.
$\angle a + \angle b = \angle Y = 90°$.
$\angle a$ and $\angle b$ are complementary angles.

Acute Angles

Acute angles are angles whose measure is less than 90°. No two acute angles can be supplementary angles. Two acute angles can be complementary angles.

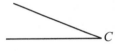

$\angle C$ is an acute angle.

Obtuse Angles

Obtuse angles are angles that are greater than 90° and less than 180°.

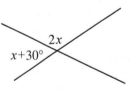

$\angle D$ is an obtuse angle.

Example 1

In the figure, what is the value of x?

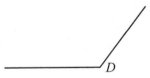

Since the two labeled angles are supplementary angles, their sum is 180°.

$$(x + 30°) + 2x = 180°$$
$$3x = 150°$$
$$x = 50°$$

Example 2

Find the value of x in the figure.

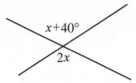

Since the two labeled angles are vertical angles, they are equal.

$x + 40° = 2x$

$40° = x$

Example 3

If angle Y is a right angle and angle b measures $30°15'$, what does angle a measure?

Since angle Y is a right angle, angles a and b are complementary angles and their sum is $90°$.

$\angle a + \angle b = 90°$

$\angle a + 30°15' = 90°$

$\angle a = 59°45'$

Lines

A *line* in geometry is always assumed to be a straight line. It extends infinitely far in both directions. It is determined if two of its points are known. It can be expressed in terms of the two points, which are written as capital letters. The following line is called *AB*.

Or, a line may be given one name with a small letter. The following line is called line *k*.

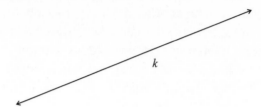

A *line segment* is a part of a line between two *endpoints*. It is named by its endpoints, for example, A and B.

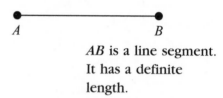

AB is a line segment. It has a definite length.

If point P is on the line and is the same distance from A as from B, then P is the *midpoint* of segment *AB*. When we say *AP = PB*, we mean that the two line segments have the same length.

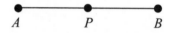

A part of a line with one endpoint is called a *ray*. *AC* is a ray of which A is an endpoint. The ray extends infinitely far in the direction away from the endpoint.

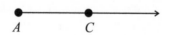

Parallel Lines

Two lines meet or intersect if there is one point that is on both lines. Two different lines may either intersect in one point or never meet, but they can never meet in more than one point.

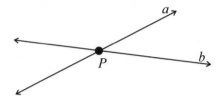

Two lines in the same plane that never meet no matter how far they are extended are said to be *parallel*, for which the symbol is ∥. In the following diagram $a \parallel b$.

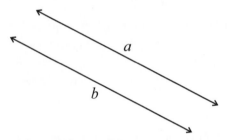

If two lines in the same plane are parallel to a third line, they are parallel to each other. Since $a \parallel b$ and $b \parallel c$, we know that $a \parallel c$.

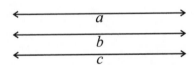

Two lines that meet each other at right angles are said to be *perpendicular*, for which the symbol is ⊥. Line *a* is perpendicular to line *b*.

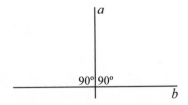

Two lines in the same plane that are perpendicular to the same line are parallel to each other.

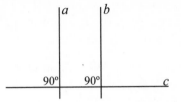

Line $a \perp$ line *c* and line $b \perp$ line *c*.
Therefore, $a \parallel b$.

A line intersecting two other lines is called a *transversal*. Line *c* is a transversal intersecting lines *a* and *b*.

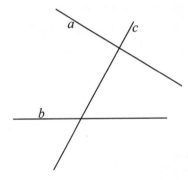

The transversal and the two given lines form eight angles. The four angles between the given lines are called *interior angles;* the four angles outside the given lines are called *exterior angles*. If two angles are on opposite sides of the transversal, they are called *alternate angles*.

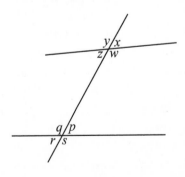

$\angle z$, $\angle w$, $\angle q$, and $\angle p$ are interior angles.

$\angle y$, $\angle x$, $\angle s$, and $\angle r$ are exterior angles.

$\angle z$ and $\angle p$ are alternate interior angles; so are $\angle w$ and $\angle q$.

$\angle y$ and $\angle s$ are alternate exterior angles; so are $\angle x$ and $\angle r$.

Pairs of *corresponding* angles are y and $\angle q$; $\angle z$ and $\angle r$; $\angle x$ and $\angle p$; $\angle w$ and $\angle s$. Corresponding angles are sometimes called exterior-interior angles.

When the two given lines cut by a transversal are parallel lines:

1. the corresponding angles are equal.
2. the alternate interior angles are equal.
3. the alternate exterior angles are equal.
4. interior angles on the same side of the transversal are supplementary.

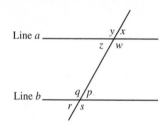

If line *a* is parallel to line *b:*

1. $\angle y = \angle q$, $\angle z = \angle r$, $\angle x = \angle p$, and $\angle w = \angle s$.
2. $\angle z = \angle p$ and $\angle w = \angle q$.
3. $\angle y = \angle s$ and $\angle x = \angle r$.
4. $\angle z + \angle q = 180°$, and $\angle p + \angle w = 180°$

Because vertical angles are equal, $\angle p = \angle r$, $\angle q = \angle s$, $\angle y = \angle w$, and $\angle x = \angle z$. If any one of the four conditions for equality of angles holds true, the lines are parallel; that is, if two lines are cut by a transversal and one pair of the corresponding angles is equal, the lines are parallel. If a pair of alternate interior angles or a pair of alternate exterior angles is equal, the lines are parallel. If interior angles on the same side of the transversal are supplementary, the lines are parallel.

Example

In the figure, two parallel lines are cut by a transversal. Find the measure of angle y.

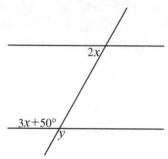

The two labeled angles are supplementary.

$$2x + (3x + 50°) = 180°$$
$$5x = 130°$$
$$x = 26°$$

Since $\angle y$ is vertical to the angle whose measure is $3x + 50°$, it has the same measure.

$$y = 3x + 50° = 3(26°) + 50° = 128°$$

Polygons

A *polygon* is a closed plane figure composed of line segments joined together at points called *vertices* (singular, *vertex*). A polygon is usually named by giving its vertices in order.

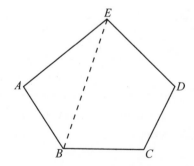

Polygon *ABCDE*

In the figure, points *A*, *B*, *C*, *D*, and *E* are the vertices, and the sides are *AB*, *BC*, *CD*, *DE*, and *EA*. *AB* and *BC* are *adjacent* sides, and *A* and *B* are adjacent vertices. A *diagonal* of a polygon is a line segment joining any two nonadjacent vertices. *EB* is a diagonal.

Polygons are named according to the number of sides or angles. A *triangle* is a polygon with three sides, a *quadrilateral* a polygon with four sides, a *pentagon* a polygon with five sides, and a *hexagon* a polygon with six sides. The number of sides is always equal to the number of angles.

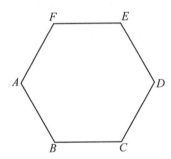

Hexagon

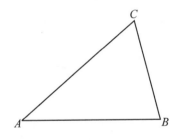

Triangle

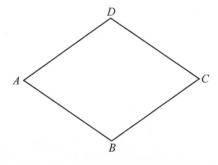

Quadrilateral

The *perimeter* of a polygon is the sum of the lengths of its sides. If the polygon is regular (all sides equal and all angles equal), the perimeter is the product of the length of *one* side and the number of sides.

Congruent and Similar Polygons

If two polygons have equal corresponding angles and equal corresponding sides, they are said to be *congruent*. Congruent polygons have the same size and shape. They are the same in all respects except possibly position. The symbol for congruence is ≅.

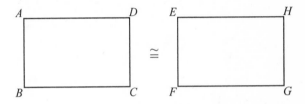

When two sides of congruent or different polygons are equal, we indicate the fact by drawing the same number of short lines through the equal sides.

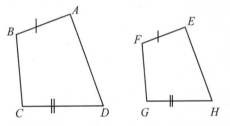

This indicates that *AB* = *EF* and *CD* = *GH*.

Two polygons with equal corresponding angles and corresponding sides in proportion are said to be *similar*. The symbol for similar is ∼.

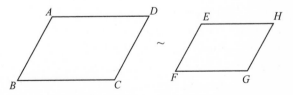

Similar figures have the same shape but not necessarily the same size.

A *regular polygon* is a polygon whose sides are equal and whose angles are equal.

Triangles

A *triangle* is a polygon of three sides. Triangles are classified by measuring their sides and angles. The sum of the angles of a plane triangle is always 180°. The symbol for a triangle is $\triangle$. The sum of any two sides of a triangle is always greater than the third side.

Equilateral

Equilateral triangles have equal sides and equal angles. Each angle measures 60° because $\frac{1}{3}(180°) = 60°$.

$AB = AC = BC$.
$\angle A = \angle B = \angle C = 60°$.

Isosceles

Isosceles triangles have two sides equal. The angles opposite the equal sides are equal. The two equal angles are sometimes called the *base* angles and the third angle is called the *vertex* angle. Note that an equilateral triangle is isosceles.

$FG = FH$.
$FG \neq GH$.
$\angle G = \angle H$.
$\angle F$ is vertex angle.
$\angle G$ and $\angle H$ are base angles.

Scalene

Scalene triangles have all three sides of different length and all angles of different measure. In scalene triangles, the shortest side is opposite the angle of smallest measure, and the longest side is opposite the angle of greatest measure.

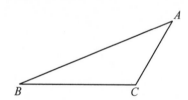

$AB > BC > CA$; therefore $\angle C > \angle A > \angle B$.

Right

Right triangles contain one right angle. Since the right angle is 90°, the other two angles are complementary. They may or may not be equal to each other. The side of a right triangle opposite the right angle is called the *hypotenuse.* The other two sides are called *legs.* The *Pythagorean theorem* states that the square of the length of the hypotenuse is equal to the sum of the squares of the lengths of the legs.

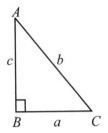

AC is the hypotenuse.
AB and BC are legs.
$\angle B = 90°$.
$\angle A + \angle C = 90°$.
$a^2 + c^2 = b^2$.

Examples

If ABC is a right triangle with right angle at B, and if AB = 6 and BC = 8, what is the length of AC?

$AB^2 + BC^2 = AC^2$

$6^2 + 8^2 = 36 + 64 = 100 = AC^2$

$AC = 10$

If the measure of angle A is 30°, what is the measure of angle C ?

Since angles A and C are complementary:

$30° + C = 90°$

$C = 60°$

If the lengths of the three sides of a triangle are *a, b,* and *c* and the relation $a^2 + b^2 = c^2$ holds, the triangle is a right triangle and side *c* is the hypotenuse.

Example

Show that a triangle of sides 5, 12, and 13 is a right triangle.

The triangle will be a right triangle if $a^2 + b^2 = c^2$.

$5^2 + 12^2 = 13^2$

$25 + 144 = 169$

Therefore, the triangle is a right triangle and 13 is the length of the hypotenuse.

Area of a Triangle

An *altitude* (or height) of a triangle is a line segment dropped as a perpendicular from any vertex to the opposite side. The area of a triangle is the product of one-half the altitude and the base of the triangle. (The base is the side opposite the vertex from which the perpendicular was drawn.)

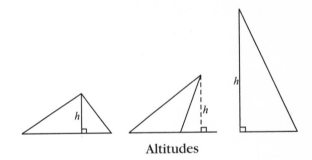

Altitudes

Example

Find the area A of the following isosceles triangle.

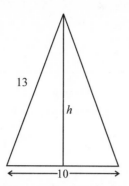

In an isosceles triangle the altitude from the vertex angle bisects the base (cuts it in half).

The first step is to find the altitude. By the Pythagorean theorem, $a^2 + b^2 = c^2$; $c = 13$, $a = h$, and $b = \frac{1}{2}(10) = 5$.

$$b^2 + 5^2 = 13^2$$
$$b^2 + 25 = 169$$
$$b^2 = 144$$
$$b = 12$$
$$A = \frac{1}{2} \cdot \text{base} \cdot \text{height}$$
$$= \frac{1}{2} \cdot 10 \cdot 12$$
$$= 60$$

Similarity

Two triangles are *similar* if all three pairs of corresponding angles are equal. The sum of the three angles of a triangle is 180°; therefore, if two angles of triangle I equal two corresponding angles of triangle II, the third angle of triangle I must be equal to the third angle of triangle II and the triangles are similar. The lengths of the sides of similar triangles are in proportion to each other. A line drawn parallel to one side of a triangle divides the triangle into two portions, one of which is a triangle. The new triangle is similar to the original triangle.

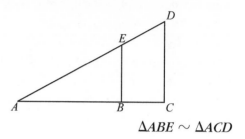

$$\triangle ABE \sim \triangle ACD$$

Example

In the following figure, if $AC = 28$ feet, $AB = 35$ feet, $BC = 21$ feet, and $EC = 12$ feet, find the length of DC if $DE \parallel AB$.

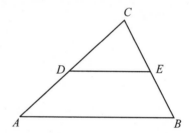

Because $DE \parallel AB$, $\triangle CDE \sim \triangle CAB$. Since the triangles are similar, their sides are in proportion:

$$\frac{DC}{AC} = \frac{EC}{BC}$$
$$\frac{DC}{28} = \frac{12}{21}$$
$$DC = \frac{12 \cdot 28}{21} = 16 \text{ feet}$$

Quadrilaterals

A quadrilateral is a polygon of four sides. The sum of the angles of a quadrilateral is 360°. If the opposite sides of a quadrilateral are parallel, the quadrilateral is a *parallelogram*. Opposite sides of a parallelogram are equal and so are opposite angles. Any two consecutive angles of a parallelogram are supplementary. A diagonal of a parallelogram divides the parallelogram into congruent triangles. The diagonals of a parallelogram bisect each other.

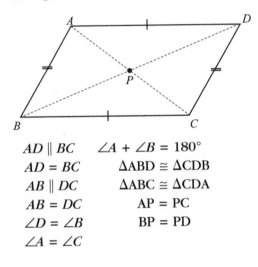

$AD \parallel BC$	$\angle A + \angle B = 180°$
$AD = BC$	$\triangle ABD \cong \triangle CDB$
$AB \parallel DC$	$\triangle ABC \cong \triangle CDA$
$AB = DC$	$AP = PC$
$\angle D = \angle B$	$BP = PD$
$\angle A = \angle C$	

Definitions

A *rhombus* is a parallelogram with four equal sides. The diagonals of a rhombus are perpendicular to each other.

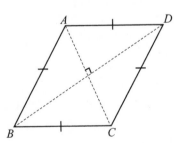

A *rectangle* is a parallelogram with four right angles. The diagonals of a rectangle are equal and can be found using the Pythagorean theorem if the sides of the rectangle are known.

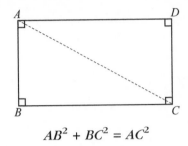

$$AB^2 + BC^2 = AC^2$$

A *square* is a rectangle with four equal sides.

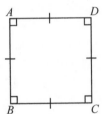

A *trapezoid* is a quadrilateral with only one pair of parallel sides, called *bases*. The nonparallel sides are called *legs*.

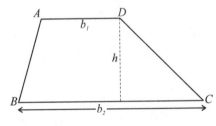

$AD \parallel BC$.
AD and BC are bases.
AB and DC are legs.
h = altitude

173

Finding Areas

The area of any *parallelogram* is the product of the base and the height, where the height is the length of an altitude, a line segment drawn from a vertex perpendicular to the base.

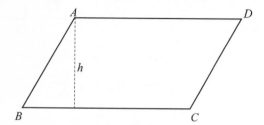

Since rectangles and squares are also parallelograms, their areas follow the same formula. For a *rectangle,* the altitude is one of the sides, and the formula is length times width. Since a *square* is a rectangle for which length and width are the same, the area of a square is the square of its side.

The area of a *trapezoid* is the height times the average of the two bases. The formula is:

$$A = h\frac{b_1 + b_2}{2}$$

The bases are the parallel sides, and the height is the length of an altitude to one of the bases.

Example 1

Find the area of a square whose diagonal is 12 feet. Let s = side of square. By the Pythagorean theorem:

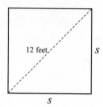

$$s^2 + s^2 = 12^2$$
$$2s^2 = 144$$
$$s^2 = 72$$
$$s = \sqrt{72}$$

Use only positive value because this is the side of a square.

Since $A = s^2$

$A = 72$ square feet

Example 2

Find the altitude of a rectangle if its area is 320 and its base is 5 times its altitude. Let altitude = h. Then base = $5h$. Since $A = bh$,

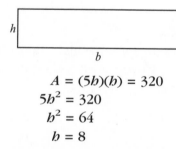

$$A = (5h)(h) = 320$$
$$5h^2 = 320$$
$$h^2 = 64$$
$$h = 8$$

If a quadrilateral is not a parallelogram or trapezoid but is irregularly shaped, its area can be found by dividing it into triangles, attempting to find the area of each, and adding the results.

Circles

Definitions

Circles are closed plane curves with all points on the curve equally distant from a fixed point called the *center.* The symbol ⊙ indicates a circle. A circle is usually named by its center. A line segment from the center to any point on the circle is called the *radius* (plural, radii). All radii of the same circle are equal.

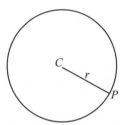

C = center

CP = radius = *r*

A *chord* is a line segment whose endpoints are on the circle. A *diameter* of a circle is a chord that passes through the center of the circle. A diameter, the longest distance between two points on the circle, is twice the length of the radius. A diameter perpendicular to a chord bisects that chord.

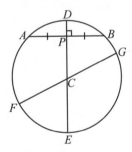

AB is a chord.
C is the center.
DCE is a diameter.
FCG is a diameter.
AB ⊥ DCE so AP = PB.

A *central angle* is an angle whose vertex is the center of a circle and whose sides are radii of the circle. An *inscribed angle* is an angle whose vertex is on the circle and whose sides are chords of the circle.

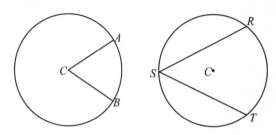

∠ACB is a central angle

∠RST is an inscribed angle

An *arc* is a portion of a circle. The symbol ⌒ is used to indicate an arc. Arcs are usually measured in degrees. Since the entire circle is 360°, a semicircle (half a circle) is an arc of 180°, and a quarter of a circle is an arc of 90°

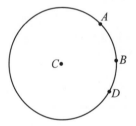

⌒
ABD is an arc.

⌒
AB is an arc.

⌒
BD is an arc.

A central angle is equal in measure to its intercepted arc.

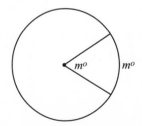

An inscribed angle is equal in measure to one-half its intercepted arc. An angle inscribed in a semicircle is a right angle because the semicircle has a measure of 180°, and the measure of the inscribed angle is one-half of that.

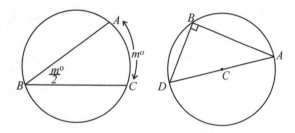

$\overset{\frown}{DA} = 180°$; therefore,

$\angle DBA = 90°$.

Perimeter and Area

The perimeter of a circle is called the *circumference*. The length of the circumference is πd, where d is the diameter, or $2\pi r$, where r is the radius. The number π is irrational and can be approximated by 3.14159..., but in problems dealing with circles it is best to leave π in the answer. There is no fraction exactly equal to π.

Example

If the circumference of a circle is 8π feet, what is the radius?

Since $C = 2\pi r = 8\pi$, $r = 4$ feet.

The length of an arc of a circle can be found if the central angle and radius are known. Then, the length of arc is $\dfrac{n°}{360°}(2\pi r)$, where the central angle of the arc is $n°$. This is true because of the proportion:

$$\frac{\text{Arc}}{\text{Circumference}} = \frac{\text{central angle}}{360°}$$

Example

If a circle of radius 3 feet has a central angle of 60°, find the length of the arc intercepted by this central angle.

$$\text{Arc} = \frac{60°}{360°}(2\pi 3) = \pi \text{ feet}$$

The area A of a circle is πr^2, where r is the radius. If the diameter is given instead of the radius,

$$A = \pi\left(\frac{d}{2}\right)^2 = \frac{\pi d^2}{4}.$$

Example 1

Find the area of a circular ring formed by two concentric circles of radii 6 and 8 inches, respectively. (Concentric circles are circles with the same center.)

The area of the ring will equal the area of the large circle minus the area of the small circle.

$$\text{Area of ring} = \pi 8^2 - \pi 6^2$$
$$= \pi(64 - 36)$$
$$= 28\pi \text{ square inches}$$

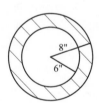

Example 2

A square is inscribed in a circle whose diameter is 10 inches. Find the difference between the area of the circle and that of the square.

If a square is inscribed in a circle, the diagonal of the square is the diameter of the circle. If the diagonal of the square is 10 inches, then, by the Pythagorean theorem,

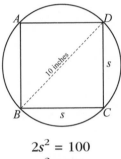

$$2s^2 = 100$$
$$s^2 = 50$$

The side of the square s is $\sqrt{50}$, and the area of the square is 50 square inches. If the diameter of the circle is 10, its radius is 5 and the area of the circle is $\pi 5^2 = 25\pi$ square inches. Then, the difference between the area of the circle and the area of the square is:

$25\pi - 50$ square inches
$= 25\ (\pi - 2)$ square inches

Distance Formula

In the arithmetic section, we described the Cartesian coordinate system when explaining how to draw graphs representing linear equations. If two points are plotted in the Cartesian coordinate system, it is useful to know how to find the distance between them. If the two points have coordinates (a, b) and (p, q), the distance between them is:

$$d = \sqrt{(a - p)^2 + (b - q)^2}$$

This formula makes use of the Pythagorean theorem.

Example

Find the distance between the two points $(-3, 2)$ and $(1, -1)$.

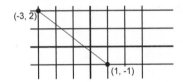

Let $(a, b) = (-3, 2)$ and $(p, q) = (1, -1)$.

Then:

$$d = \sqrt{(-3-1)^2 + [2 - (-1)]^2}$$
$$= \sqrt{(-4)^2 + (2 + 1)^2}$$
$$= \sqrt{(-4)^2 + 3^2}$$
$$= \sqrt{16 + 9} = \sqrt{25} = 5$$

Plane Geometry Problems

1. In triangle QRS, $\angle Q = \angle R$ and $\angle S = 64°$. Find the measures of $\angle Q$ and $\angle R$.
2. In parallelogram ABCD, $\angle A$ and $\angle C$ are opposite angles. If $\angle A = 12x°$ and $\angle C = (10x + 12)°$, find the measures of $\angle A$ and $\angle C$.

3. What is the area of a trapezoid whose height is 5 feet, and whose bases are 7 feet and 9 feet?

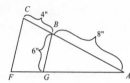

4. In the preceding figure, CF ∥ BG. Find the length of CF.

5. The hypotenuse of a right triangle is 25 feet. If one leg is 15 feet, find the length of the other leg.

6. Find the area of a circle whose diameter is 16 inches.

7. Find the distance between the points $(-1, -2)$ and $(5, 7)$.

Solutions:

1. $\angle Q + \angle R + \angle S = 180°$
$\angle Q + \angle R + 64° = 180°$
$\angle Q + \angle R = 116°$

Since $\angle Q = \angle R$, they must each have measures of 58°.

2. The opposite angles in a parallelogram are equal. Thus,
$12x = 10x + 12$
$2x = 12$
$x = 6$

Thus, $12x = 12(6) = 72$.
$\angle A$ and $\angle C$ both measure 72°.

3. $A = h\left(\dfrac{b_1 + b_2}{2}\right)$
$= 5\left(\dfrac{7 + 9}{2}\right) = 5\left(\dfrac{16}{2}\right) = 5(8) = 40$

The area of the trapezoid is 40.

4. Since CF ∥ BG, $\triangle ACF \sim \triangle ABG$.
Therefore, $\dfrac{6}{CF} = \dfrac{8}{12}$
$8\ CF = 72$
$CF = 9$ inches.

5. Using the Pythagorean theorem,
$a^2 + 15^2 = 25^2$
$a^2 + 225 = 625$
$a^2 = 400$
$a = \sqrt{400} = 20$

The length of the other leg is 20.

6. If d = 16, r = 8. $A = \pi r^2 = \pi(8)^2 = 64\pi$
The area of the triangle is 64π.

7. $d = \sqrt{(5 - (-1))^2 + (7 - (-2))^2}$
$= \sqrt{6^2 + 9^2} = \sqrt{36 + 81} = \sqrt{117}$

The distance between the points is equal to $\sqrt{117}$.

TABLES AND GRAPHS

Tables and graphs give visual comparisons of amount. They show relationships between two or more sets of information. It is essential to be able to read tables and graphs correctly.

Tables

Tables present data corresponding to classifications by row and column. Tables always state the units (thousands of people, years, millions of dollars, for example) in which the numbers are expressed. Sometimes the units are percents. Both specific and general questions can be answered by using the information in the table.

Example 1

What language is spoken at home by almost one-half of those not speaking English at home?

Spanish; 8,768/17,985 is about 48%.

Example 2

What language has the highest percent of its speakers in the 45-to-64-year-old age bracket?

Polish, with 45.7%.

Example 3

How many persons between the ages of 18 and 24 speak Korean at home?

There are 191,000 of all ages speaking Korean, of which 17.8% are between 18 and 24:

.178 × 191,000 = 33,998 persons

Persons 5 Years Old and Over Speaking Various Languages at Home, by Age: November 1995

(Numbers in thousands: civilian noninstitutional population)

Language spoken at home	Persons 5 years old and over	Total %	5 to 13 years	14 to 17 years	18 to 24 years	25 to 44 years	45 to 64 years	65 to 74 years	75 years and over
Total	200,812	*	30,414	15,955	27,988	59,385	43,498	15,053	8,519
Percent	*	100.0	15.1	7.9	13.9	29.6	21.7	7.5	4.2
Speaking English only	176,319	100.0	15.4	8.0	14.1	29.5	21.5	7.4	4.0
Speaking other language	17,985	100.0	14.4	6.9	12.6	30.8	21.8	7.5	6.0
Chinese	514	100.0	12.5	5.8	15.8	34.8	21.2	6.8	3.1
French	987	100.0	8.1	5.5	10.2	29.9	30.4	9.9	6.0
German	1,261	100.0	5.4	7.1	10.8	24.3	27.4	12.8	12.2
Greek	365	100.0	16.7	4.9	10.4	38.1	21.9	4.4	3.6
Italian	1,354	100.0	7.5	4.9	8.1	19.3	31.5	15.1	13.7
Japanese	265	100.0	7.9	6.8	7.9	27.2	36.6	9.4	3.8
Korean	191	100.0	16.2	5.8	17.8	35.6	19.9	3.7	1.0
Philippine languages	419	100.0	10.7	5.3	8.6	40.8	20.3	7.2	6.9
Polish	731	100.0	2.7	1.4	3.7	13.8	45.7	21.6	10.9
Portuguese	245	100.0	15.9	8.6	12.2	33.9	22.0	3.7	3.3
Spanish	8,768	100.0	20.2	8.8	15.4	34.6	15.8	3.1	2.2
Yiddish	234	100.0	8.5	0.4	3.0	15.8	20.9	29.1	21.8
Other	2,651	100.0	10.0	4.9	10.8	30.3	23.3	10.1	10.6
Not reported	6,508	100.0	11.1	8.4	13.5	26.9	25.1	9.5	5.6

(Notice that in this table the numbers are given in thousands, so that the number speaking German at home, for example, is not 1261 but 1,261,000.)

Graphs

Bar Graphs

Bar graphs may be horizontal or vertical, but both axes are designed to give information. The height (or width) of the bar is proportional to the number or percent represented. Bar graphs are less accurate than tables but give a quick comparison of information. There may be only two variables, as in the following graph. One is the year and the other is the percentage of the labor force made up of women.

WOMEN AS A PERCENTAGE OF THE LABOR FORCE

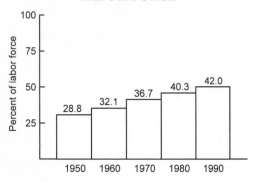

Example

Between which 10 years does the chart show the greatest percent increase of women in the labor force?

For each of the 10-year periods there is some increase. Subtract each percent from the one to the right of it; four subtractions. The greatest increase, 4.6%, occurs between 1960 and 1970.

In this bar graph, percents are written at the top of each bar. This is not always the case. If the numbers are not given, you must read across, using a ruler or card, to the relevant axis and estimate the height.

Bar graphs such as the following can compare two sets of data for varying years. This graph shows, for example, that 86.8% of the male population 16 years old and over was in the labor force in 1950. In that same year, 33.9% of the female population was in the labor force. It gives different information from the previous graph.

PERCENTAGE OF POPULATION 16 YEARS OLD AND OVER IN THE LABOR FORCE

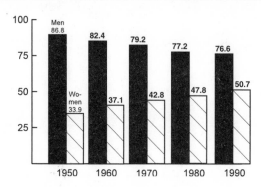

Example

Explain the apparent discrepancy for the year 1980 between the percentage for women in this graph (47.8%) and that in the previous graph (40.3%).

This graph shows that 47.8% of all women were in the labor force in 1980—that is, 47.8% of 100 women were working. The previous graph showed that 40.3% of 100 *workers,* or 40.3%, were women. There is no discrepancy. The populations are different.

Cumulative Bar Graphs

These graphs are similar to bar graphs, but each bar contains more than one kind of information and the total height is the sum of the various components. The following graph gives percentages for college graduates on the bottom and high school graduates on the top. There might well be other gradations, such as "some college" above the college section and "some high school" above the high school section.

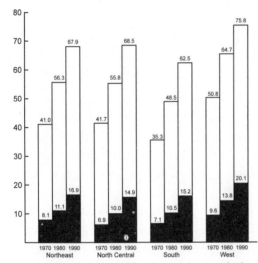

Percent of persons 25 years old and over who were high school graduates and college graduates, by region: 1970, 1980, and 1990

Example 1

For each of the 3 years, which region consistently has the lowest percentage of college graduates?

North Central

Example 2

Which region has the lowest *total* educational attainment for each of the 3 years?

The South

Example 3

In 1990, which region had the highest percentage of high school graduates, and what was it?

For 1990, subtract the percent for college graduates from the total percent; four subtractions. The highest is the West, with 75.8% − 20.1% = 55.7%.

Example 4

Which region had the greatest percentage increase of college graduates between 1980 and 1990?

The West, with 20.1% − 13.8% = 6.3%.

Circle Graphs

Circle graphs, also known as pie charts, show the breakdown of an entire quantity, such as a college budget, into its component parts. The circle representing 100% of the quantity is cut into pieces, each piece having a certain percentage value. The sum of the pieces is 100%. The size of the piece is proportional to the size of the percent. To make a circle graph, you must have an instrument called a protractor which measures degrees. Suppose the measured quantity is 10% of the whole. Because 10%

of 360° is 36°, a central angle of 36° must be measured and radii drawn. This piece now has an area of 10% of the circle. When answering questions on circle graphs, compare percentages.

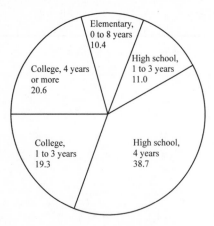

Years of school completed

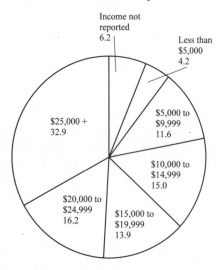

Family Income
(restricted to persons living in primary families)

Percent distribution of voters in the last election by years of school completed and family income

Example 1

Of those who voted in the last election, what percentage attended college at some time?

This information is in the first graph. Add 20.6% to 19.3% to get 39.9%.

Example 2

Of those who voted in the last election and who reported their income levels, what percentage had a family income below $10,000?

This information is in the second graph. Add 4.2% to 11.6% to get 15.8%.

Line Graphs

Like bar graphs, line graphs follow vertical and horizontal information axes, but the line graph is continuous. There may be a single broken line or there may be several, comparing three or four stocks or incomes or, as in the case of this graph, numbers of workers in selected occupations. The line graph shows trends: increasing, decreasing, or not changing.

MILLIONS OF WORKERS IN SELECTED OCCUPATIONS

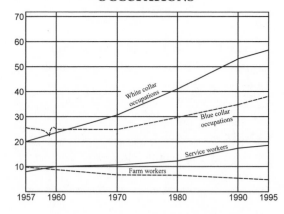

In this graph, the actual number of people in an occupation in a given year must be estimated. For example, the number of service workers in 1980 seems to be 14 million, and the number of white-collar workers for the same year about 40 million.

Example

In 1990, what was the total number of workers in all four occupations?

Estimate each number by comparison with the values at the left. Then add the four. Estimates: farm workers 3 million, service workers 18 million, blue-collar workers 33 million, and white-collar workers 52 million, total 106 million.

Since the scale on graphs is usually marked in large increments, since the lines used are often thick, and since the estimates must often be made on the side of the graph far from the scale, use whole numbers as much as possible when estimating. Use only the fraction one-half (1/2) if your judgment tells you something less than a whole number should be used. Because all the information must be estimated, units less than one-half will not significantly affect your answer. Do not spend time trying to figure the precise number on the scale. A reasonable estimate should let your answer be within 1 or 2 percent on either side of the correct answer choice. As part of your strategy for dealing with graphs, look at the answer choices to get an idea of the magnitude of your estimate before doing the estimating. Choose the answer choice closest to your estimate.

Example

If your estimate is 97 million and the answer choices are 3 million, 0.5 million, 90 million, 103 million, and 98 million, choose 98 million as your answer.

Tables and Graphs Problems

Use this bar graph to answer the following questions:

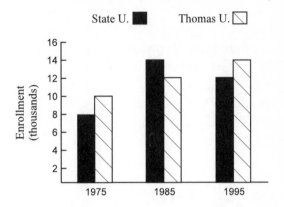

STUDENT ENROLLMENTS: STATE U. VS. THOMAS U.

1. What was the enrollment at State U. in 1975?
2. In 1985, how many more students were enrolled at State U. than at Thomas U.?
3. If the average tuition at State U. in 1995 was $6,500, what was the total revenue received in tuition at State U. that year?
4. In 1985, 74% of the students enrolled at State U. were males. How many males attended State U. in 1985?
5. Find the percent of increase in enrollment at Thomas U. from 1975 to 1985.

Solutions:

1. 8,000 students
2. 14,000 − 12,000 = 2,000 students
3. 12,000 × $6,500 = $78,000,000
4. 14,000 × 74% = 14,000 × .74 = 10,360 students
5. Increase in enrollment = 12,000 − 10,000 = 2,000
   Percent of increase in enrollment = 2,000 ÷ 10,000 = 1/5 = 20%

TRIGONOMETRY

Trigonometry enables you to solve problems that involve finding measures of unknown lengths and angles.

The Trigonometric Ratios

Every right triangle contains two acute angles. With respect to each of these angles, it is possible to define six ratios, called the trigonometric ratios, each involving the lengths of two of the sides of the triangle. For example, consider the following triangle *ABC*.

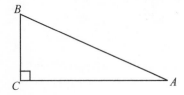

In this triangle, side *AC* is called the side adjacent to angle *A,* and side *BC* is called the side opposite angle *A.* Similarly, side *AC* is called the side opposite angle *B,* and side *BC* is called the side adjacent to angle *B.* Of course, side *AB* is referred to as the hypotenuse with respect to both angles *A* and *B.*

The six trigonometric ratios with respect to angle *A,* along with their standard abbreviations, are given below:

Sine of angle *A* = sin *A*
= opposite/hypotenuse = *BC/AB*

Cosine of angle *A* = cos *A*
= adjacent/hypotenuse = *AC/AB*

Tangent of angle *A* = tan *A*
= opposite/adjacent = *BC/AC*

Cotangent of angle *A* = cot *A*
= adjacent/opposite = *AC/AB*

Secant of angle *A* = sec *A*
= hypotenuse/adjacent = *AB/AC*

Cosecant of angle *A* = csc *A*
= hypotenuse/opposite = *AB/BC*

The last three ratios are actually the reciprocals of the first three, in particular:

cot *A* = 1/tan *A*

sec *A* = 1/cos *A*

csc *A* = 1/sin *A*

Also note that:

sin *A*/cos *A* = tan *A*, and
cos *A*/sin *A* = cot *A*.

In order to remember which of the trigonometric ratios is which, you can memorize the well-known acronym: **SOH–CAH–TOA** ("Sock it to her"). This stands for: **S**ine is **O**pposite over **H**ypotenuse, **C**osine is **A**djacent over **H**ypotenuse, **T**angent is **O**pposite over **A**djacent.

Example

Consider right triangle *DEF* below, whose sides have the lengths indicated. Find sin *D*, cos *D*, tan *D*, sin *E*, cos *E*, and tan *E*.

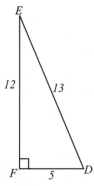

$$\sin D = EF/ED = \frac{12}{13} \qquad \sin E = DF/ED = \frac{5}{13}$$

$$\cos D = DF/ED = \frac{5}{13} \qquad \cos E = EF/ED = \frac{12}{13}$$

$$\tan D = EF/DF = \frac{12}{5} \qquad \tan E = DF/EF = \frac{5}{12}$$

Note that the sine of *D* is equal to the cosine of *E*, and the cosine of *D* is equal to the sine of *E*.

Example

In right triangle ABC, $\sin A = \dfrac{4}{5}$. Find the values of the other five trigonometric ratios.

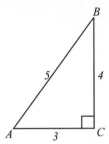

Since the sine of A = opposite over hypotenuse = $\dfrac{4}{5}$, we know that $BC = 4$, and $AB = 5$. We can use the Pythagorean theorem to determine that $AC = 3$. Then:

$$\cos A = \frac{3}{5}, \ \tan A = \frac{4}{3}, \ \cot A = \frac{3}{4},$$

$$\sec A = \frac{5}{3}, \ \csc A = \frac{5}{4}.$$

Trigonometric Ratios for Special Angles

The actual values for the trigonometric ratios for most angles are irrational numbers, whose values can most easily be found by looking in a trig table or using a calculator. On the ACT, you will not need to find the values for such trig functions; you can simply leave the answer in terms of the ratio. For example, if the answer to a word problem is $35 \tan 37°$, the correct answer choice will be, in fact, $35 \tan$ $37°$. There are, however, a few angles whose ratios can be obtained exactly. The ratios for $30°$, $45°$, and $60°$ can be determined from the properties of the 30-60-90 right triangle and the 45-45-90 right triangle. First of all, note that the Pythagorean theorem can be used to determine the following side and angle relationships in 30-60-90 and 45-45-90 triangles:

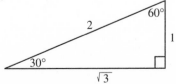

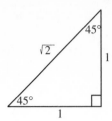

From these diagrams, it is easy to see that:

$$\sin 30° = 1/2, \ \cos 30° = \frac{\sqrt{3}}{2}$$

$$\tan 30° = 1/\sqrt{3} = \sqrt{3}/3$$

$$\sin 60° = \sqrt{3}/2, \ \cos 60° = 1/2,$$

$$\tan 60° = \sqrt{3}$$

$$\sin 45° = \cos 45° = 1/\sqrt{2} = \sqrt{2}/2,$$

$$\tan 45° = 1$$

Example

From a point A, which is directly across from point B on the opposite sides of the banks of a straight river, the measure of angle BAC to a point C, 35 meters upstream from B, is 30. How wide is the river?

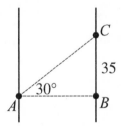

To solve this problem, note that $\tan A =$ opposite/adjacent = $BC/AB = 35/AB$. Since the measure of angle A is $30°$, we have $\tan 30° = 35/AB$. Then:

$$AB = 35/\tan 30° = 35/\sqrt{3}/3 = 105/\sqrt{3}.$$

Therefore, the width of the river is $\dfrac{105}{\sqrt{3}}$ meters, or approximately 60 meters wide.

The Pythagorean Identities:

There are three fundamental relationships involving the trigonometric ratios that are true for all angles, and are helpful when solving problems. They are:

$$\sin^2 A + \cos^2 A = 1$$
$$\tan^2 A + 1 = \sec^2 A$$
$$\cot^2 A + 1 = \csc^2 A$$

These three identifies are called the Pythagorean identities since they can be derived from the Pythagorean theorem. For example, in triangle *ABC* below

$$a^2 + b^2 = c^2$$

Dividing by c^2, we obtain,

$$a^2/c^2 + b^2/c^2 = 1, \text{ or}$$
$$(a/c)^2 + (b/c)^2 = 1.$$

Now, note that $a/c = \sin A$ and $b/c = \cos A$. Substituting these values in, we obtain $\sin^2 A + \cos^2 A = 1$. The other two identities are similarly obtained.

Example

If, in triangle ABC, sin A = 7/9, what are the values of cos A and tan A?

Using the first of the trigonometric identities, we obtain:

$$(7/9)^2 + \cos^2 A = 1$$
$$49/81 + \cos^2 A = 1$$
$$\cos^2 A = 1 - 49/81$$
$$\cos A = \sqrt{32/81} = 4\sqrt{2}/9.$$

Then, since tan *A* = sin *A*/cos *A*, we have tan *A* = (7/9)/(4√2/9) = 7/4√2 = 7√2/8.

Trigonometry Problems

1. In right triangle ABC, tan A = 4/3. Find the value of sin A and sec A.
2. Find the value of sin 30° + tan 45° + cos 60°.
3. If, in right triangle DEF, cos D = 11/16, find the value of csc D and cot D.
4. The road to a bridge above a highway is 500 feet long. The road makes an angle of 30° with the horizontal. Find the height of the bridge.

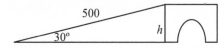

5. At a point 15 feet from the base of a tree, the angle of elevation to its top is 60°. Find the height of the tree.
6. A ladder leans against a building, touching it at a point 18 feet above the ground. If the ladder makes an angle of 45° with the ground, how long is the ladder?

Solutions

1.

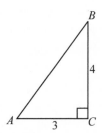

$$\tan A = \frac{4}{3} = \frac{\text{opposite}}{\text{adjacent}}$$

From the Pythagorean theorem, we can determine that the hypotenuse is 5.

$$\text{Then, } \sin A = \frac{\text{opposite}}{\text{hypotenuse}} = \frac{4}{5}$$
$$\sec A = \frac{\text{hypotenuse}}{\text{adjacent}} = \frac{5}{3}$$

2. Sin 30° + tan 45° + cos 60°
   = 1/2 + 1 + 1/2 = 2.

3.

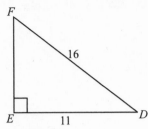

$$\cos D = \frac{\text{adjacent}}{\text{hypotenuse}} = \frac{11}{16}$$

To find FE, use the Pythagorean theorem.

$$11^2 + (FE)^2 = 16^2$$
$$121 + (FE)^2 = 256$$
$$(FE)^2 = 135$$
$$FE = \sqrt{135} = 3\sqrt{15}$$

Then, $\csc D = \dfrac{\text{hypotenuse}}{\text{opposite}}$

$$= \frac{16}{3\sqrt{15}} = \frac{16}{3\sqrt{15}} \cdot \frac{\sqrt{15}}{\sqrt{15}} = \frac{16\sqrt{15}}{45}$$

$$\cot D = \frac{\text{adjacent}}{\text{opposite}}$$

$$= \frac{11}{3\sqrt{15}} = \frac{11}{3\sqrt{15}} \cdot \frac{\sqrt{15}}{\sqrt{15}} = \frac{11\sqrt{15}}{45}$$

4.

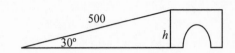

sin 30° = h/500
Thus, h = 500 sin 30° = 500 (1/2) = 250
The bridge is 250 feet high.

5.

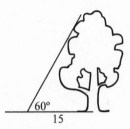

tan 60° = h/15
Thus, 15 tan 60° = h
and h = 15 ($\sqrt{3}$).
The height of the tree is 15 $\sqrt{3}$ feet.

6.

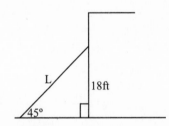

sin 45° = 18/L

Thus, $L = \dfrac{18}{\sin 45°} = \dfrac{18}{\dfrac{\sqrt{2}}{2}} = \dfrac{36}{\sqrt{2}} = \dfrac{36\sqrt{2}}{2}$

$= 18\sqrt{2}$
The ladder is 18$\sqrt{2}$ feet long.

RED ALERT

The Reading section of the ACT is a 35-minute, 40-question test of your ability to read and comprehend fiction, social science, natural science, and humanities reading passages. The questions asked in the reading section can be broken down into two main categories: (1) questions that ask you for information specifically presented in the passage, and (2) questions that ask you to draw inferences from the passage—that is, to answer questions based on what is implied rather than stated in the passage.

You will receive an overall reading score for this section of the test plus two subscores: one based on your reading of the social science and physical science sections and one based on your prose fiction and humanities scores.

In the Reading section, you will read four passages, each of which is followed by ten multiple-choice questions. The passages are selected to represent the level of reading encountered by first-year college students. The reading passages are drawn from the following subject areas:

Social Sciences: history, political science, economics, anthropology, psychology, and sociology.

Natural Science: biology, chemistry, physics, and physical sciences.

Humanities: art, music, philosophy, theater, architecture, and dance.

Prose Fiction: intact short stories or excerpts from short stories or novels.

Don't expect the passages to be familiar to you; even the specific subjects may not be familiar to you, but you may feel more comfortable with a natural science passage, for example—even on an unfamiliar topic—if you have focused on science in your high school studies.

Before we look more specifically at the kinds of questions you will encounter on the test, let's discuss certain strategies you will need to practice and use on the Reading section of the ACT.

TEST-TAKING STRATEGIES

We will discuss **relying on information within the passage**, **choosing the order of the passages**, **pacing yourself**, **annotating the passage**, and **practicing specific reading strategies**.

Relying on information within the passage. Occasionally you may encounter a reading passage that discusses a subject you have studied. While this can make the passage easier to read, it can also tempt you to rely on your own knowledge about the subject. You must rely solely on the information presented in the passage for your answers—in fact, sometimes the "wrong answers" for the questions are based on true information about the subject not given in the passage. Since the test makers are testing your reading ability (rather than your general knowledge), an answer based on information not contained in the passage is considered incorrect. Thus, if you are reading a passage discussing Pavlov's famous experiments with dogs (which you have studied), be sure you don't base your answers to the questions on information not presented in the reading passage. Even if it is true of Pavlov's experiments, it will be counted as a wrong answer.

Choosing the order of the passages. The test makers have arranged the reading passages in an order that may not be the best order for you. Before you start reading the passages, quickly look through them and choose which order will work best for you. For example, if you find the fiction-reading passage easiest, you may want to start with that passage even though the fiction passage may be placed after the humanities and social sciences passages. Don't forget to do all four passages, however.

If you read the passages out of order, you may want to transfer the answers to the answer sheet after you have finished all the passages, since you will be reading the questions in a different order from the one set up on the answer sheet. (You will need to pace yourself so that you have time to transfer the answers at the end.) If you choose to transfer the answers as you go, be sure you're marking the answers for the correct numbers—if the fiction section is third, it will begin with question number 21, not question number 1.

Pacing yourself. In order to complete the test in 35 minutes, you will need to practice pacing yourself. Make sure you don't spend so much time on some of the passages that you don't have time to complete all four passages. You will have about 8½ minutes to read one passage and answer the 10 ques-tions—that breaks down to between 2 and 3 minutes to read the passage and between 30 and 40 seconds per question.

Since you need to make every second count, be sure you don't waste any time—by reading the directions, for example. We'll discuss them right now so that you know what they say: "There are four passages in this test. Each passage is followed by several questions. After reading a passage, choose the best answer to each question and fill in the corresponding oval on your answer document. You may refer to the passages as often as necessary."

You also need to avoid working too long on any one question or any one passage—if it's hard, go on. If you have time at the end, go back and work on it some more.

You may need to increase your reading speed in order to complete the test in the allotted time. (Although reading speed doesn't necessarily correspond to intelligence or to reading ability, on a timed test your reading speed will affect your score.) Since you have only 35 minutes to read four passages and answer 40 questions, you need to read at least 250 words per minute in order to complete the test.

Let's find out your reading speed now. First, have someone time you as you read for one minute at a comfortable speed. (You can begin reading after studying the follow-ing formula.) Mark where you begin and end. Count the number of words on three full lines of text. Divide the number of words by 3. This will give you the average number of words per line. Count the number of lines you read, and multiply that by the average number of words per line. The answer is your reading speed per minute. (See the following formula.)

$$\frac{\text{words on 3 lines}}{3} = \text{average words/line}$$

average words per line × lines read in 1 minute = words per minute

If your reading speed is below 250 words per minute, you will need to practice reading more quickly in order to complete this section of the test. The simplest method of improving your reading speed is to move your index finger along the line you are reading at a slightly faster pace than feels comfortable. Some of you may want to practice using a pencil, since a pencil comes in handy for marking the passage as you go.

To improve your speed using this method, be sure to read every day, using your finger or pencil to force yourself to read at a faster pace than usual.

If you need more help to increase your reading speed, books on speed reading should be available at your local library (and may even be available at your school library). Courses in speedreading may also be available at your local community or state college.

Many students fear that if they read more quickly, they will not understand what they are reading; however, reading more quickly actually can help increase your comprehension. When you read, you are trying to form in your mind the idea the author had when writing, so the more slowly you read, the longer it takes for you to create that mental image of what the author is saying. Thus, when you read more slowly, you are making it harder to under-stand the author's ideas.

Annotating. Since you will need to refer back to the reading passages to answer the questions, you need to annotate, or mark up, the passage to help you find specific elements in the passage. Many high school students have been taught not to write in their textbooks because they are school property and must be returned in good condition. However, annotation is a skill worth practicing. When you take the test, you will not be able to use highlighter pens, so you should practice using a pencil. You will want to use different kinds of marks to mean different things—if you just use underlining, your marks won't help you quickly find the elements in the passage that you need. Here are some suggestions: circle names of people, historic periods, etc.; underline words in lists; draw a line down the left margin to mark the line numbers specifically mentioned in a question. (We'll try annotation on a example passage later.)

In addition to marking up the passage, especially if you use the reading strategy of reading the *question stems* first, mark the key words in the question stems, too—they may tell you where in the passage to look for information or which kind of question you are being asked. (The question stem is the introductory part of the question, not the possible answers. For example, the question stem might say, "According to the passage, Einstein wanted to prove which of the following theories?")

If you decide to skip a question and return to it later, mark the question, perhaps by circling the question number, so you can find it easily later—like this:

②. According to the passage, Martha Graham's dance style could best be called which of the following?

Eliminating wrong answers. If you find after taking the pretest that you can quickly and accurately tell which are the right answers, don't change your strategy. However, many students find they are doing poorly on the test because they decide too quickly which is the correct answer without considering all the choices. Also, even students who usually choose correctly find this strategy helpful when they are stumped by a question: eliminate the wrong answers first. As you eliminate each answer, mark it—perhaps with a slash through the letter so that you don't have to remember which ones you've eliminated—like this:

A. Life is for the living.

Often, one of the choices is clearly weaker than another. By eliminating that choice, you increase your chances of making a correct choice by 25 percent. The weakest choice often has nothing to do with the passage or presents a clichéd truism about life—such an answer can be eliminated quickly. Often other wrong answers refer to information listed in the passage in other places. It won't be completely off the topic, but it will not relate to the portion of the passage being discussed in the question.

If you eliminate a second wrong answer, you have increased your chance of answering the question correctly by another 25 percent. Other types of wrong answers to look out for are answers that are partially true, that are too broad, or that rely on information outside the passage.

With practice, you should usually be able to eliminate three wrong answers, leaving you with the right answer. But even if you can't eliminate three wrong answers, eliminate as many as possible—then guess.

Reading strategies. We will discuss three main reading strategies. You will need to try them all and choose which ones work best for you. You may find some work better than others or that certain ones work best for certain types of passages.

The **first strategy** is to read the passage first, annotating as you go; then answer the questions. This strategy will probably be most useful for the fiction passages, but for the other passages it's probably the weakest choice. (However, if you find it works best for you, stick with it.)

For the **second strategy**, read the question stems first, annotating them as you go. After reading the question stems, read the passage.

This method helps guide your reading, so you focus only on those parts of the reading passage that help you answer the questions.

The **third strategy** is often the most useful, though it may take a bit of time to become used to it. We'll call it PQR, which stands for Preview the passage, read the Question stems, then Read the passage. This method is very helpful because you get a brief picture of the passage first, then a look at what the questions will be, and finally, as you read the passage, you can look for the answers to the questions. However, you will need to work quickly to be able to use this method. (Try using it timed so that you don't spend more than 8½ minutes reading and answering the questions for any one passage.)

To Preview, quickly skim the first paragraph of the selection—or if the first paragraph is long, read just the first and last sentences. Now quickly read the first sentence of all the subsequent paragraphs, and the last sentence of the final paragraph. This Preview should give you a sense of the subject of the passage and an idea of what each paragraph is about.

The next step is the Q step—quickly read the question stems, annotating them as needed. Now go back to the passage and read it quickly all the way through, annotating as you find the answers to the questions. Now answer the questions. Although this method is the most difficult to get used to, it is worth practicing, since it can be so helpful.

As you take the practice tests in this book, try using these three methods to determine which works best for you. For example, you may find that for the fiction passage, you like the first reading strategy, reading the passage first. For passages in subjects in which you feel some familiarity, you might be more comfortable reading the question stems first, then reading the passage. For the passages you feel most unsure of, you may want to use the PQR method.

Question Types

Now let's look more specifically at the kinds of questions you will encounter on the test. The natural science, social science, and humanities reading passages are all similar to one another; they are informative passages such as you might expect to encounter in textbooks. The following example passage is a natural science selection. We will use it to illustrate the types of questions used for the natural science, social science, and humanities passages. We'll also start using annotation. Because we will discuss each question in depth, you should read the passage first, annotating as you go, then answer the questions. The following passage is about half the length of an actual reading passage on the test. Read it now, using your finger or pencil to force you to read at a slightly faster pace than is comfortable. Annotate the passage as you read it, marking what seems to you to be the most important information.

Line One of the surprises of modern biochemistry is the discovery of the incredibly sophisticated devices used by microorganisms to survive in inhospi-
5   table environments. It seems anthropo-morphic to refer to these survival mechanisms as strategies, yet they so resemble some of the most clever kinds of schemes we can devise that it is hard
10   to find a more appropriate word. Indeed, when the study of life teaches new useful methods, we utilize the knowledge of bionics, the science of designing systems or instruments
15   modeled after organisms.

An example of a cellular strategy is the mining of iron by bacteria. The element is one of the most plentiful on earth, consisting of about 5 percent of
20   rocks. Because of the high atmospheric concentration of oxygen, most iron exists as very insoluble ferric oxides and hydroxides. Therefore, even given the substantial total quantity of the
25   metal, the concentration in soluble form needed by organisms is extremely low, somewhere around one part per hundred million in the oceans. Never-theless, iron is an essential element for
30   most cellular processes, and a given bacterium can survive only if it some-how manages to extract such atoms from its environment. . . .

Living systems have a . . . subtle,
35   low-temperature, atom-by-atom method of solving the problem. The bacterium synthesizes and excretes into its surroundings molecules that have an extremely high affinity for binding iron
40   at a very specific site. Such compounds are called chelators (from the Greek word for *claw*) because of the strength with which they scavenge every available free iron atom. This shifts the
45   equilibrium and leads to the solubiliza-tion of the plentiful oxides. The next step in the process is carried out by a transport system in the cell membrane that pumps the complexed metal back
50   into the cell. Within the cytoplasm the chelator retains the iron so that it is unavailable for biochemical reactions. Two different schemes are used to pry the iron loose from the molecular claw.
55   In one of these, the enzymes digest the binding structure. This is a high price to pay, for the cell must synthesize replacement molecules to get more iron. In the other method, the iron is

60 chemically reduced to the ferrous form, which is then released. In either case, the metal atom is free within the cell where it is quickly utilized in making various ferroproteins. . . .

Factual questions. Now that you have read the passage, let's begin by looking at the kinds of factual questions you can expect to see: simple facts, complex facts, negative questions, and puzzle questions. With fact questions, the correct answer is stated either in the exact words from the passage or in words that are almost identical to the words in the passage. But note that wrong answers for these questions usually are also taken right from the passage but fail to answer the question.

The following question illustrates a simple fact question:

1. According to the passage, iron is plentiful:

   A. in the ocean.
   B. in the air.
   C. in bacteria.
   D. in rocks.

The information for this question is specifically stated in the passage, in lines 17–20—"The element [iron] is one of the most plentiful on earth, consisting of about 5 percent of rocks." For such a simple question, it may not even be necessary to eliminate choices A, B, and C. It is clear that the answer is D.

But sometimes the fact questions are more complex, requiring you to combine facts or glean information from more than one place in the passage. For example:

2. According to the passage, one method of "prying the iron loose from the molecular claw":

   F. allows the metal atom to be free within the cell.
   G. keeps the iron unavailable for biochemical reactions.
   H. reduces the iron chemically to the ferrous form.
   J. uses the iron to make various ferroproteins.

This question is more complex because you are being asked to identify which of these answers is true of only one of the different methods for prying the iron loose, as described in lines 53–54. We can eliminate choice G because this is the opposite of the correct answer. The methods of prying the iron loose are what make it available for use. Choices F and J are true of both methods, so H is correct since it pertains to only one method.

Sometimes fact questions are presented as negative questions: you are asked to choose which of the choices is not correct. Negative questions can be identified because the question stem always contains the word EXCEPT, in all caps. Here is an example:

3. All of the following information from the passage would be useful to a scientist interested in bionics EXCEPT which choice?

   A. A chelator allows bacteria to bind and transport iron into the cytoplasm.
   B. Iron is one of the most plentiful elements on earth.
   C. Iron must be removed from the chelator before it is usable in the cell.
   D. Bacteria must extract iron from their environment in order to survive.

For this kind of question, you may want to use the same strategy as for other questions—eliminate the wrong answer. But for negative questions, the wrong answer is the answer you want! Here it is the answer that won't be useful to bionic science.

However, let's imagine you can't identify the "wrong" answer—then eliminate "right" answers. Since lines 13-15 explains that bionics is "the science of designing systems or instruments modeled after organisms," A, C, and D—which all describe something about organisms—would be likely to help bionic scientists; B is the only answer that does *not* relate to organisms, so it is the correct answer to this negative fact question.

Another tricky fact question is the "logic puzzle" type. Let's look at one of these:

4. According to the passage, which of the following statements explain why organisms must develop strategies to mine iron?

    I. It is needed in substantial quantities.

    II. It is not readily available in soluble form.

    III. It is found in about 5 percent of rocks.

    F. III only
    G. II only
    H. I and III only
    J. I, II, and III

Although this type of question looks intimidating, answering it only requires a refinement of the technique of eliminating wrong answers. Here, rather than eliminating the letter choice—F, G, etc.—we eliminate the Roman numerals, but with this type of question, we don't know whether just one of the Roman numeral choices is

correct, whether two are, or whether all three are correct.

Let's begin by identifying which Roman numeral choices are clearly incorrect. I is clearly wrong, since the passage notes that there are "substantial" quantities of iron on earth, lines 24-25, not that it's needed in substantial quantities by bacteria. Thus, choices H and J are incorrect. Now we must choose between Roman numerals II and III, since no letter option gives us the choice of both of them. Although Roman numeral III gives accurate information from the passage, it does not as clearly suggest a reason why bacteria have to mine iron, so we can eliminate choice F. That leaves us with Roman numeral II, choice G, that bacteria must mine iron because so little is available in soluble form—see lines 17-20.

Inference questions. Fact and inference questions can be very similar to each other, but with inference questions, the answer is either stated in different terms from the words used in the passage or is only implied or suggested by the passage. Let's look at an example:

5. It can be inferred from the passage that when the chelator binds the iron, the iron:

    A. becomes soluble.
    B. is in a usable form.
    C. is no longer an oxide.
    D. becomes a chelator.

To answer this question, we look again at the portion of the passage that describes what happens when the chelator binds the iron, lines 36-46. "The bacterium synthesizes and excretes into its surroundings molecules that have an extremely high affinity for binding iron at a very specific site. Such compounds are called chelators (from the Greek word for *claw*) because of the strength with which they scavenge every available free iron atom. This shifts the equilibrium and leads to the solubilization of the plentiful oxides." We can immediately eliminate D, since nothing is said about the bound iron becoming a chelator. We can also eliminate C, since the passage is describing the iron oxides. Later in the passage we read that even after the iron is inside the bacteria, it isn't useable until it has been removed from the chelator, so B is also incorrect, leaving A that it becomes soluble—note the phrase "solubilizations of the plentiful [iron] oxides."

Another type of inference question asks about the meaning of words or phrases in the passage. Often you will be asked to identify the meaning of a word you don't know at all or that you may have encountered before but can't define. In these cases, you will need to rely on clues provided in the passage to help you identify the best word choice. Let's consider the following example:

6. In the context of the passage, the word *anthropomorphic* means:

    F.   contradictory and irrational.
    G. anthropologically sound.
    H. ascribing human qualities to something nonhuman
    J.   deriving from plants.

Begin by looking at where in the passage the word *anthropomorphic* is used, lines 5–6: "It seems anthropomorphic to refer to these survival mechanisms as strategies, yet they so resemble some of the most clever kinds of schemes we can devise that it is hard to find a more appropriate word." If you know that the Greek root *anthro-* means "human," you will probably be able to immediately eliminate choices F and J.

But let's assume you don't know that. Substitute the choices to see which one sounds best in context. If you were to paraphrase the sentence, you might say, "Although it seems 'anthropomorphic' to call these things 'strategies,' they seem so similar to what we do that it's hard to find a better way to say it." "Deriving from plants" does not fit the sense of the sentence at all, eliminating J. And why would it be "contradictory" or "irrational" to call these survival mechanisms by a name similar to "what we do"? Thus, F is another unlikely choice that can be eliminated.

Choice G is an answer set up to catch the unwary—since it also begins with the root *anthro-*, you may be tempted to choose it, but since anthropology is the study of humans, this is an unlikely choice for a passage on microorganisms, leaving H, "ascribing human qualities to something nonhuman."

Notice here that the correct choice is also the longest answer. Often, though not always, the longest vocabulary answer is the correct one—since the test makers must describe the word precisely. If you are unable to eliminate wrong answers or can't eliminate all the wrong answers, you may want to try applying the "rule of thumb" that the longest answer is most likely to be correct.

Questions regarding phrases require this same kind of attention to the context given in the passage.

Questions about the main idea of a paragraph or the subject of a passage are similar as well. Your task here is to come up with the answer that best summarizes or encompasses what the paragraph or passage says. Here's an example:

7. The main point of the second paragraph (lines 16–33) is that:

A. iron is an essential element for bacteria.
B. iron is one of the most plentiful elements on earth.
C. bacteria use incredibly sophisticated survival mechanisms.
D. bacteria must extract iron from the environment to survive.

As with the other questions, you should begin by looking at the second paragraph, lines 16–33. You should quickly eliminate C because it is not mentioned in the paragraph. Although B is mentioned in the paragraph, it is unlikely to be correct since it describes only one sentence in the paragraph, and it is too general. A is a better possibility, but it is less complete than D, the answer that encompasses the idea of a survival strategy that relates to iron.

Now we will look at a fiction passage to see how it is similar to and different from the informative passages. The fiction passages usually contain only a few characters and usually don't present an entire story; the passages may not even present a single clear episode. They usually contain some dialogue. Characters that don't appear in the passage may be mentioned or discussed.

As with the informative passages, you will be asked "factual" questions about elements of the passage, that is, you will be asked for information that actually appears in the passage. You may be asked questions regarding who the characters are—their ages, relationships to each other, their appearance, and so on. You may be asked questions about the plot—the order of events in the passage or what events occurred.

Certain inference questions will be similar to those you encounter in informative passages: vocabulary and phrase questions, for example. But you may also be asked to decide a character's attitude or emotional state. These kinds of questions are based on information you learn from clues in the passage, but they are usually not specifically stated by the author. Let's look at the following example—the length of a complete fiction passage. Don't forget to annotate!

Line "My aunt will be down presently, Mr. Nuttel," said a very self-possessed young lady of fifteen; "in the meantime you must put up with me."
5 Framton Nuttel endeavoured to say the correct something which should duly flatter the niece of the moment without unduly discounting the aunt that was to come. Privately he doubted
10 more than ever whether these formal visits on a succession of total strangers would do much towards helping the nerve cure which he was supposed to be undergoing.
15 "I know how it will be," his sister had said when he was preparing to migrate to his rural retreat; "you will bury yourself down there and not speak to a living soul, and your nerves will be
20 worse than ever from moping. I shall just give you letters of introduction to all the people I know there. Some of them, as far as I can remember, were quite nice."
25 Framton wondered whether Mrs. Sappleton, the lady to whom he was presenting one of the letters of introduction, came into the nice division.
  "Do you know many people
30 round here?" asked the niece, when

she judged that they had had sufficient silent communion.''

''Hardly a soul,'' said Framton. ''My sister was staying here, at the rectory, you know, some four years ago, and she gave me letters of introduction to some of the people here.''

He made the last statement in a tone of distinct regret.

''Then you know practically nothing about my aunt?'' pursued the self-possessed young lady.

''Only her name and address,'' admitted the caller. He was wondering whether Mrs. Sappleton was in the married or widowed state. An undefinable something about the room seemed to suggest masculine habitation.

''Her great tragedy happened just three years ago,'' said the child; ''that would be since your sister's time.''

''Her tragedy?'' asked Framton; somehow in this restful country spot tragedies seemed out of place.

''You may wonder why we keep that window wide open on an October afternoon,'' said the niece, indicating a large French window that opened on to a lawn.

''It is quite warm for the time of the year,'' said Framton; ''but has that window got anything to do with the tragedy?''

''Out through that window, three years ago to a day, her husband and her two young brothers went off for their day's shooting. They never came back. In crossing the moor to their favorite snipe-shooting ground they were all three engulfed in a treacherous piece of bog. It had been that dreadful wet summer, you know, and places that were safe in other years gave way suddenly without warning. Their bodies were never recovered. That was the dreadful part of it.'' Here the child's voice lost its self-possessed note and became falteringly human. ''Poor aunt always thinks that they will come back some day, they and the little brown spaniel that was lost with them, and walk in at that window just as they used to do. That is why the window is kept open every evening till it is quite dusk. Poor dear aunt, she has often told me how they went out, her husband with his white waterproof coat over his arm, and Ronnie, her younger brother, singing, 'Bertie, why do you bound?' as he always did to tease her, because she said it got on her nerves. Do you know, sometimes on still, quiet evenings like this, I almost get a creepy feeling that they will all walk in through that window—''

She broke off with a little shudder. It was a relief to Framton when the aunt bustled into the room with a whirl of apologies for being late in making her appearance.

''I hope Vera has been amusing you,'' she said.

''She has been very interesting,'' said Framton.

''I hope you don't mind the open window,'' said Mrs. Sappleton briskly; ''my husband and brothers will be home directly from shooting, and they always come in this way. They've been out for snipe in the marshes today, so they'll make a fine mess over my poor carpets. So like you men-folk, isn't it?'

She rattled on cheerfully about the shooting and the scarcity of birds, and the prospects for duck in the winter. To Framton it was all purely horrible. He made a desperate but only partially successful effort to turn the talk on to a

less ghastly topic; he was conscious
120 that his hostess was giving him only a
fragment of her attention, and her eyes
were constantly straying past him to
the open window and the lawn
beyond. It was certainly an unfortunate
125 coincidence that he should have paid
his visit on this tragic anniversary.

Now let's look at some factual questions for this fiction passage:

1. According to the passage, Ronnie is:

   A. Mrs. Sappleton's son.
   B. Vera's younger brother.
   C. Mr. Nuttel's sister.
   D. Mrs. Sappleton's brother.

To answer this question, let's find Ronnie in the passage—did you circle the name? Look at line 88, where Vera states that "Ronnie, her younger brother" left on the shooting expedition. This helps us eliminate A and C. We may be unclear about whose younger brother this is, but if we look at the beginning of the same sentence, we see that Vera is speaking about her aunt, Mrs. Sappleton, so we can eliminate B. The answer is D, Ronnie is Mrs. Sappleton's younger brother.

Here's a more complex fact question:

2. Vera's and Mrs. Sappleton's accounts of why the window is open differ from each other in what way?

   F. Mrs. Sappleton's explanation is longer.
   G. Mrs. Sappleton does not believe the men will return.
   H. Vera does not believe the men are dead.
   J. Mrs. Sappleton claims the men went out that day.

To begin, let's eliminate the answers we can remember without referring back to the story. Vera says that her aunt can't accept the men's deaths, so we can eliminate H. Mrs. Sappleton doesn't pay complete attention to Framton because she keeps looking out the window, apparently expecting the men to return, so G is unlikely. Lines 78-85 are Vera's explanation; lines 105-109 are Mrs. Sappleton's, clearly shorter, so we can eliminate F. That leaves J; Mrs. Sappleton says in lines 109-110, "They've been out for snipe in the marshes today."

Here's an example of a factual question about plot:

3. According to the passage, when does Framton try to change the subject?

   A. In the middle of Vera's description of the tragedy.
   B. When Mrs. Sappleton is discussing the hunting prospects.
   C. As soon as Mrs. Sappleton enters the room.
   D. When Vera first asks him who he knows in the area.

If we can find where Framton "made a desperate but only partially successful effort to turn the talk," lines 117-119, we see that it's in the paragraph where Mrs. Sappleton is talking about shooting birds, and we can immediately eliminate A, C, and D, leaving B.

Inference questions. The inference questions for the fiction section are similar to those on the informative passages; however, there's one additional type: inferring mood, character, or feeling. Here is an example:

4. Framton's emotional state during his visit may best be described as:

    F. thoughtless.
    G. relaxed.
    H. uneasy.
    J. offensive.

This question asks you to rely on clues found throughout the passage. You may remember that Framton "doubts" the visits will help him; he feels it's "unfortunate" that he visited on the anniversary of the tragedy, etc. Clearly, "relaxed," G, does not apply, nor does J, "offensive." "Thoughtless," F seems less appropriate than "uneasy" H.

STRATEGIES AFTER PRACTICE TESTS

Once you've taken the pretest, and after each practice test, there are additional strategies you should use to help you improve your score on the Reading section.

First, for each question you got wrong, you should explain to someone else—or to yourself—why the book's answer is better than your answer. You may need to refer to the explanations in order to understand why the book's answer is correct. (It's human nature to want to justify your answer, but if you explain why the book's answer is right, you will begin to think like the test makers, and you'll be more likely to answer similar types of questions correctly in the future.)

Also, analyze what kinds of errors you're making: Do you mostly miss inference questions? Do have a hard time finding the facts in the passage? Do you struggle with the fiction passages but not with the informative ones? Once you analyze these problems, you can focus your attention on refining your skills with those particular kinds of questions.

Finally, if you're getting more than half the questions in a passage wrong, take one of the practice tests without worrying about the time limit. (But notice how long it takes you—it might take you an hour, for example.) This will give you a chance to become at ease with the types of questions asked, and you'll probably do much better going slowly. Then take another practice test, at a slightly faster pace, 45 minutes, for example. (Be sure to work on your reading speed as well.) Finally, try taking a practice test in the allotted time so that on the actual test you will be used to the 35-minute limit.

One final word: Try all the strategies and use them all to do your best on the Reading section of the ACT. And make sure you practice, practice, practice, In fact, we've given you some additional problems following this section so you can practice until you're completely comfortable with your ability to answer these types of questions quickly and correctly.

Unit 3

Use the following passages to practice your strategies and reading techniques. Each passage is followed by the answers. The questions test some of the basic skills you will be tested on in the actual ACT exam: referring to what is explicitly stated; and reasoning to determine implicit meanings and to draw conclusions, comparisons, and generalizations. The passages also cover a variety of topics: social studies, science, prose fiction, and humanities.

Passage 1

Line Australia has the distinction of being the only inhabited continent that lies completely south of the equator. Its location causes seasons that are the direct opposite
5 of those lands that lie completely north of the equator.

Australia is divided into six major geographic regions: the Humid Southeast, the great Dividing Range, the Black Slope,
10 the Mediterranean Coastal Strip, the Northern Tropical Lands, and the Dead Heart. The Great Dividing Range separates Australia's plains from its plateau, serving as its continental divide. There are no rivers
15 flowing through this region. Rivers to the east of the Dividing Range flow eastward to the ocean. Those rivers to the west of the Dividing Range empty out into the western lakes. Very little rainfall is received in the
20 Black Slope region. Nevertheless, it is good farmland because irrigation is provided by neighboring rivers.

Geography can play strange tricks on the region's climate. Australia is essentially
25 a very dry continent, even though it lies in the midst of vast oceans. Rainfall is limited to coastal areas. Generally speaking, Australia has only two seasons: one hot and one cool. The hot season usually occurs

30 during the months between September and March, with the average temperature ranging from 70 to 90 degrees. The northern coast of the continent is the warmest region, since it lies closest to the
35 equator.

Australia is plagued with many problems, one of which is insufficient population. The southeastern region is the area with the highest population. Inad-
40 equate transportation is another major problem. The geography of the interior of the continent is not conducive to the building of railroad or highway facilities, and there is hardly any river transportation.
45 The Great Barrier Reef along Australia's coast makes sea transportation in the area extremely difficult. The most efficient methods of transportation are by air and overland routes.
50 Australia today retains its pioneering spirit. The people continue to develop its natural resources in the hope of a more abundant future.

1. It can be inferred from the passage that Australia receives its nickname, "The Land Down Under," as a result of its:

   A. once being submerged underwater
   B. geographic location
   C. varying climate
   D. isolation from the rest of the world

2. Australia is characterized by its:

   F. two-season climate
   G. lack of variation in topography
   H. well-developed interior
   J. varying topography

3. The most productive farmland in Australia is located in:

   A. the Humid Southeast
   B. the Great Dividing Range
   C. the Black Slope
   D. the Dead Heart

4. Because of the peculiar geographical conditions of Australia:

   F. it would not be surprising to find out that Australians are lazy
   G. the majority of the population are farmers
   H. merchant seafaring and trading are chief occupations
   J. the people of Australia are adventurous

Answers to Passage 1

1. The correct answer is B. This can be inferred from the opening sentence: "The only inhabited continent that lies completely south of the equator."

2. The correct answer is F. Reread the third paragraph to verify this choice. Choice J is a possible answer. However, varying topography is characteristic of most continents, and not all that unusual. The word "characterized" in the question implies something unique, and the fact that Australia has only two seasons is a unique characteristic.

3. The correct answer is C. The last two sentences in paragraph 2 provide the answer.

4. The correct answer is J. This answer is implied by the last paragraph. Choice H can be eliminated immediately, since paragraph 4 states that because of the Great Barrier Reef, seas transportation is extremely difficult. Given the hardships that people face in Australia, it is not likely that they are a lazy people, so you

can eliminate choice F. Nothing in the passage implies that the majority of the people are farmers, and therefore you can also eliminate choice G.

Passage 2

Line Despite the modern desire to be easy and casual, Americans from time to time give thought to the language they use—to grammar, vocabulary, and gobbledygook.
5 And, as on other issues, they divide into two parties. The larger, which includes everybody from the proverbial plain man to the professional writer, takes for granted that there is a right way to use words and
10 construct sentences, and many wrong ways. The right way is believed to be clearer, simpler, more logical, and therefore more likely to prevent error and confusion. Good writing is easier to read; it offers a pleasant
15 combination of sound and sense.

    Against this majority view is the doctrine of an embattled minority, who make up for their small number by their great learning and their place of authority
20 in the school system and the world of scholarship. They are the professional linguists, who deny that there is such a thing as correctness. The language, they say, is what anybody and everybody speaks.
25 Hence, there must be no interference with what they regard as a product of nature. They denounce all attempts at guiding choice; their governing principle is epitomized in the title of a speech by a
30 member of the profession: "Can Native Speakers of a Language Make Mistakes?"

    Within the profession of linguists there are, of course, warring factions, but, on this conception of language as a natural
35 growth with which it is criminal to tamper, they are at one. In their arguments one finds appeals to democratic feelings of social equality (all words and forms are equally good) and individual freedom (one
40 may do what one likes with one's own speech). These assumptions further suggest that the desire for correctness, the very idea of better or worse in speech, is a hangover from aristocratic and oppressive

45 times. To the linguists, change is the only ruler to be obeyed. They equate it with life and accuse their critics of being clock-reversers, enemies of freedom, menaces to "life."

1. The larger of the two groups mentioned believes that:

    A. all language is natural

    B. good writing must be grammatical

    C. language has its right ways and its wrong ways

    D. language is democratic

2. According to the author, the professional writer is:

    F. a scholar

    G. a professional linguist

    H. part of the minority

    J. part of the majority

3. The professional linguists:

    A. deny there is such a thing as correctness

    B. epitomize their profession

    C. are at war

    D. never write articles

4. In the phrase "their governing principle is epitomized in," the word *epitomized* means:

    F. referred to

    G. denied

    H. summed up

    J. mentioned

5. The desire for correctness is equated by some with:

    A. liberalism

    B. a collapse of standards

    C. lack of freedom

    D. depression

6. The only ruler to be obeyed is:

    F. scholarship

    G. linguistic heritage

    H. scholarly standards

    J. change

Answers to Passage 2

1. The correct answer is C. This is stated in paragraph 1. Choices A, B, and D are not mentioned in the passage.

2. The correct answer is J. This is stated in paragraph 1. Choices F, G, and H are the opposite of the correct answer.

3. The correct answer is A. This is directly stated in paragraph 2. The other choices are not mentioned.

4. The correct answer is H. This is a vocabulary question, and this is the one definition of the word.

5. The correct answer is C. This can be inferred from the tone of the last three sentences in paragraph 3. The use of the phrases "oppressive times," "only ruler to be obeyed," and "enemies of freedom" are the clues.

6. The correct answer is J. The answer is clearly stated in the last paragraph. Choices F, G, and H are specific "rulers"; therefore, all three choices are the opposite of "change."

Passage 3

Line Early experimenters in chemistry identified a group of substances having certain properties in common. These substances, when dissolved in water, acted as electrical
5 conductors, reacted with metals such as zinc to liberate gas, were corrosive to the skin, turned blue litmus to red, and tasted sour. These substances were called acids. Further study and experimentation indi-
10 cated that acids release hydrogen ions in water solution.

Another group of substances has properties that contrast strongly with the properties of acids, with the exception of
15 the property of electrical conductivity. These substances change red litmus to blue, and, when added to an acid, cause the identifying properties of the acid and those of the added substance to disappear. The
20 one property that remains characteristic of the mixture is electrical conductivity. The substances in this second group are called bases. Again, further study and experimentation indicated that bases combine with
25 hydrogen ions. This combination forms water. The remaining portion of the acid and the base form a salt. So, when an acid and a base are combined, the chemical reaction results in the production of a salt
30 and water.

In order to understand the behavior of acids and bases, we have two definitions. The first comes from the laboratory determination of what an acid or a base
35 does; that is, how we can recognize the acid or the base. This is called an operational definition because it gives the measurements or operations used to classify a substance. The second type of definition
40 is a conceptual one. It helps to explain. It tries to answer the question "Why?" Neither is the complete or perfect definition. As chemical systems become more complicated, we have to expand these
45 definitions.

1. It can be inferred that bases:

   A. release hydrogen ions in small amounts
   B. use up hydrogen ions
   C. release hydrogen ions in large amounts
   D. taste sour

2. The electrical conductivity that remains as a property of the acid-base mixture is best explained as a characteristic of the:

   F. acid only
   G. base only
   H. acid and base
   J. salt

3. Which is a characteristic of an acid?

   I. It turns litmus blue.
   II. It releases hydrogen ions.
   III. electrical conductivity
   IV. It combines with hydrogen ions.

   A. only I and III
   B. only II and IV
   C. only II and III
   D. only III and IV

4. Which operational definition of an acid is most helpful in explaining why certain chemical reactions occur as they do?

   F. An acid reacts with zinc to produce hydrogen gas.
   G. An acid turns litmus red.
   H. An acid tastes sour.
   J. An acid is corrosive to the skin.

Answers to Passage 3

1. The correct answer is B. Since bases combine with hydrogen ions (paragraph 2), and acids release hydrogen ions (paragraph 1), then it can be inferred that bases use up hydrogen ions.

2. The correct answer is H. The selection indicates that in the acid-base mixture, the properties of the acid and the base disappear (except electrical conductivity). It follows that electrical conductivity is a property of the salt that is formed.

3. The correct answer is C. Acids release hydrogen ions and act as electrical conductors. Selection I is incorrect, since the passage states that acid turns blue litmus red, and therefore you can eliminate choice A. Paragraph 1 says that acids release hydrogen ions in water solution, and thus selection II is correct. That narrows down your choices to B and C. Since selection IV is the opposite of selection II, and Paragraph 2 says that bases combine with hydrogen ions, and thus you can eliminate selection IV and choice B.

4. The correct answer is F. An operational definition comes from what a substance does. Obviously, the one choice that best explains chemical reactions of acids is F. Other answers to this question are also operational definitions but do not refer to chemical reactions of acids.

Passage 4

Line   High audience loyalty is characteristic of radio stations. Often a listener turns on the same station day after day and keeps it turned on most of the day. There is little
5   switching. This is because of the programming policies of the stations. Programming policies determine the audiences. Some programs appeal to general and diversified audiences; others are beamed to identifiable
10   groups.

Most stations are strong on music, interspersed with newscasts, weather reports, and similar features. Each, however, is likely to feature a particular type of
15   programming. Stations and programs may

be categorized in several ways. Here are some typical examples:

Middle-of-the-road music. This type of music predominates. It features Broadway
20   and movie numbers, "oldies but goodies," and current popular tunes, except rock 'n' roll, rhythm and blues, country and western, jazz, classical, and sacred music, both orchestral and vocal.

25   *"Talk" Radio.* These stations devote a major portion of their programming to interviews and discussions on a wide variety of subjects. They often feature guests who are well-known authorities on
30   food, drama, public affairs, education, and other subjects. Many of the shows are interactive, and the public can telephone the host to express their own views.

Farm programs. Located usually in
35   rural areas, stations broadcasting this type of program devote few or many hours to subjects of interest to rural area families, including daily stock and crop quotations.

Ethnic stations. These stations devote
40   the entire broadcasting day or a large portion of the day to ethnic (African-American, Hispanic-American, Asian-American) music and performers. Especially in large metropolitan areas, they may divide
45   their time between ethnic programming and foreign-language programs.

Foreign-language stations. Programs on these stations are broadcast in one or more foreign languages. Some of these
50   stations devote only a few hours to a single language; others may have programs in as many as ten different languages.

Stations often owe their popularity not just to program content, but to
55   individual disc jockeys, newscasters, talk-show hosts, sportscasters, announcers, and other personalities.

1. The author states that audiences listen to the same station because they:

   A. don't switch stations
   B. belong to groups
   C. like the programs and personalities
   D. listen to music

2. Examples of stations programmed for specific groups are:

   F. news, ethnic, and music stations
   G. farm, music, and talk stations
   H. foreign-language, music, and news stations
   J. foreign-language, farm, and ethnic stations

3. The word *beamed* in paragraph 1 means:

   A. smiled
   B. lit up
   C. sent out
   D. flashed

4. In this selection the author:

   F. disapproves of present radio programming
   G. approves of present radio programming
   H. feels audiences are too easily satisfied
   J. described types of radio programming

5. Many radio listeners:

   A. switch stations constantly
   B. also watch television
   C. respond to radio advertisers
   D. keep their radios on all day

6. One type of programming not mentioned is:

   F. classical music
   G. oldies but goodies
   H. sacred music
   J. opera

Answers to Passage 4

1. The correct answer is C. The first and last paragraphs indicate that programming policies determine the audiences (paragraph 1), and that various types of radio personalities are responsible for stations' popularity (paragraph 8). Choice A is merely a repeat of the question. Choices B and D do not tell *why* audiences are loyal to one station.

2. The correct answer is J. Foreign-language, farm, and ethnic stations are meant for specific groups. News, talk, and music stations are meant for a general audience. F, G, and H are only partially correct. *Remember:* If part of an answer is incorrect, the entire answer is considered incorrect.

3. The correct answer is C. The word *beamed* in paragraph 1 refers to radio signals sent out to a receiver.

4. The correct answer is J. This selection is descriptive; the author makes no value judgments. Choices F, G, and H are incorrect, since the questions indicate opinions ("disapproves," "approves," "feels"), which cannot be inferred from the selection.

5. The correct answer is D. Paragraph 1 states that listeners turn on the same station and keep it turned on most of the day.

6. The correct answer is J. This is a good question in which to use the process of elimination. Choices F, G, and H are all mentioned in paragraph 3. Operas are not mentioned in the selection.

Passage 5

Line A prominent economist has conveniently
classified the five stages of economic
growth that all societies, past and present,
tend to pass through in their quest for
5   economic expansion. These stages include:
(1) traditional society, (2) preconditions for
take-off, (3) take-off, (4) drive to maturity,
and (5) the age of high mass consumption.
Another stage, one that goes beyond the
10   age of high mass consumption, would be
referred to as "the welfare state."

The traditional society is one in which
there is a ceiling on productivity, there is
no effective use of technology, and
15   labor-saving inventions are nonexistent. A
greater percentage of its human and natural
resources is diverted to agriculture and
other necessities of life.

Preconditions for take-off occur when
20   the society begins to change its attitude
toward economic growth. Some of its
resources are diverted from agriculture and
put to work on industrial expansion.

The take-off stage is a key one. Society
25   has reached the point where it has been
able to overcome political, social, and
moral obstacles to economic expansion.
This is a period when new sources of
energy—coal, petroleum, oil—are com-
30   bined with technological innovations to
introduce new industries. Heavy emphasis
is laid on communication and transportation, as was the case with the United States,
Japan, Russia, and Germany in the middle
35   and end of the nineteenth century. The
chemical and electrical industries have
contributed heavily to their phenomenal
rate of economic growth.

If all goes well during the take-off
40   stage, the sixty years following the initial
take-off should see the economy enter into
economic maturity. Ten to 20 percent of its
resources are now directed toward industry, transportation, and communication.
45   The society has reached a point where it
can generate new industries beyond what
already exists in the economy. There is an
eye for overseas markets to sell its goods.
This is also a period of an ever-growing
50   urban skilled and unskilled working class. A
new class of production managers takes
over from the giant entrepreneurs. Incomes, both monetary and real, begin to
surge upward.

55   The age of high mass consumption,
characteristic of the United States in the
twentieth century, is identified by a bulging
service-oriented economy. The art of mass
production has been sufficiently mastered.
60   Consumer goods and services take first
priority. This is a period of more leisure
time and early retirement. The automobile
and a host of electrical appliances were the
earmarks of this stage of economic growth
65   in the United States.

Beyond the age of high mass consumption looms the welfare state. Society
demands more social goods and services
from the government. It is said that 20 to
70   25 percent of the civilian population in the
United States is already employed by local,
state, and federal governments. Some
experts fear that increasing intervention by
the government in the economy of the
75   United States will lead to a subtle form of
dictatorship. Other experts believe that the
government is not doing enough to serve
the welfare of its citizens. Only time will
tell who is right.

1. An appropriate title for this passage would be:

   A. "The Disadvantage of Economic Growth"
   B. "The Advantages of Economic Growth"
   C. "The Stages of Economic Growth"
   D. "The Effects of Economic Growth"

2. According to the author, the difference between the take-off stage and economic maturity is that the latter:

   F. is a period in which only 5 to 10 percent of the society's resources is used for industry and transportation
   G. is a period in which more resources are used for the production of consumer goods
   H. is a period in which there continues to be political and social obstacles to growth
   J. is a period in which the economy can generate new industries beyond what already exists

3. According to the passage, the time it takes to go from one stage of growth to the next is

   A. fixed
   B. indeterminate
   C. determined by the priorities that societies give to economic growth
   D. determined by the amount of capital formation

4. On the whole, the tone of the selection appears to be:

   F. emotional
   G. opinionated
   H. objective
   J. narrative

5. According to experts, the United States economy is:

   A. becoming more consumer-goods-oriented
   B. becoming more capital-goods-oriented
   C. becoming more social-goods-oriented with decreased government intervention
   D. becoming more social-goods-oriented with increased government intervention

Answers to Passage 5

1. The correct answer is C. The passage is about all five stages of economic growth.
2. The correct answer is J. The fifth paragraph specifically provides this information.
3. The correct answer is C. Throughout the passage, the author implies that there are noneconomic determinants of economic growth (political and social attitudes) that contribute to an expanding economy.
4. The correct answer is H. The author describes the stages of growth for informational purposes. Words like *emotional*, and *opinionated*, in choices F and G, imply a subjective approach to the passage. Therefore, these two choices are similar and should be eliminated. The word *narrative* (choice J) is used to tell a story. This is a descriptive selection.

5. The correct answer is D. The last paragraph states that "society demands more social goods and services." Thus, choices A (consumer-goods-oriented) and B (capital-goods-oriented) can be eliminated. In the same paragraph, it states that "some experts fear increasing intervention by the government." You can then eliminate choice C (decreased government intervention).

Passage 6

Line Ours was the marsh country, down by the river, within, as the river wound, twenty miles of the sea. My first most vivid and broad impression of the identity of things,
5 seems to me to have been gained on a memorable raw afternoon towards evening. At such a time I found out for certain, that this bleak place overgrown with nettles was the churchyard; and that Philip Pirrip, late
10 of this parish, and also Georgiana, wife of the above, were dead and buried; and that Alexander, Bartholomew, Abraham, Tobias, and Roger, infant children of the aforesaid, were also dead and buried; and that the
15 dark flat wilderness beyond the churchyard, intersected with dykes and mounds and gates, with scattered cattle feeding on it, was the marshes; and that the low leaden line beyond was the river; and that the
20 distant savage lair from which the wind was rushing, was the sea; and that the small bundle of shivers growing afraid of it all and beginning to cry, was Pip.
"Hold your noise!" cried a terrible
25 voice, as a man started up from among the graves at the side of the church porch. "Keep still, you little devil, or I'll cut your throat!"
A fearful man, all in coarse gray, with
30 a great iron on his leg. A man with no hat, and with broken shoes, and with an old rag tied round his head. A man who had been soaked in water, and smothered in mud, and lamed by stones, and cut by flints, and
35 stung by nettles, and torn by briars; who limped, and shivered, and glared and

growled; and whose teeth chattered in his head as he seized me by the chin.
"Oh! Don't cut my throat, sir," I
40 pleaded in terror. "Pray don't do it, sir."
"Tell us your name!" said the man. "Quick!"
"Pip, sir."
"Once more," said the man, staring at
45 me. "Give it mouth!"
"Pip. Pip, Sir"
"Show us where you live," said the man. "Point out the place!"
I pointed to where our village lay, on
50 the flat inshore among the alder-trees and pollards, a mile or more from the church.
The man, after looking at me for a moment, turned me upside down, and emptied my pockets. There was nothing in
55 them but a piece of bread. When the church came to itself—for he was so sudden and strong that he made it go head over heels before me, and I saw the steeple under my feet—when the church came to
60 itself, I say, I was seated on a high tomb-stone, trembling, while he ate the bread ravenously.
"You young dog," said the man, licking his lips. "What fat cheeks you ha'
65 got."
I believe they were fat, though I was at that time undersized, for my years, and not strong.
"Darn me if I couldn't eat 'em," said
70 the man, with a threatening shake of his head, "and if I han't half a mind to't!"
I earnestly expressed my hope that he wouldn't, and held tighter to the tombstone on which he had put me; partly, to keep
75 myself upon it; partly, to keep myself from crying.
From: *Great Expectations* by Charles Dickens

1. The story takes place:

    A. in a graveyard
    B. within twenty miles of the sea
    C. in a country village
    D. in a church

2. The man was probably:

    F. a ghost
    G. a murderer
    H. a guard
    J. a convict

3. Pip is probably:

    A. a little boy imagining things
    B. an adult telling about his early experiences
    C. the fearful man
    D. a frightened child

Answers to Passage 6

1. The correct answer is A. The fearful man appeared among the graves; Pip sits on a tombstone. Choices B, C, and D are more general locations of the story. *Remember:* always choose the most specific answer.

2. The correct answer is J. The clue is "with a great iron on his leg." This refers to leg chains that convicts wear. F and H are not proven in the story. It is possible that the man might be a murderer, choice G, but we can only infer that he is a convict. There is nothing in the passage that states what his crime might have been.

3. The correct answer is B. The story is introduced by telling the reader of the storyteller's "first most vivid and broad impression of things." This statement, plus the use of the past tense, indicates the story is a retelling of the past.

We have presented a variety of different types of passages and question types for your review. If you have had any difficulty with these review passages, go back to the previous section and reread the strategies for answering these questions.

RED ALERT

The science reasoning test requires you to have a basic knowledge of the subject areas. The overviews should be helpful in refreshing your memory of the various subjects. However, this part of the ACT exam is not designed to test your ability to recall specific facts. Rather, it is designed to test your ability to recognize and solve problems in a logical and scientific manner. You may be asked to produce results based on different experimental designs, or to draw conclusions from information presented in seven different passages. Some of the information will be presented as data in graphs and tables, while other passages contain descriptive research summaries. You will also be asked to evaluate passages that present opposing points of view. In all cases, the questions will be designed to determine whether you (1) understand the information as it is presented, (2) can analyze and interpret the information presented, and (3) can draw general conclusions from the information presented. The questions testing understanding are often easier to answer than the questions that fall into the other two categories.

TEST FORMAT

All questions are multiple choice. There will be 40 questions. The possible choices for answers will be either A, B, C, and D, or F, G, H, and J. Following each passage there will be a group of 5 to 7 questions relating to that passage. You will have 35 minutes to answer all 40 questions. The questions may be from any science discipline, which includes astronomy, biology, chemistry, earth science, and physics.

In this part of the ACT exam, there are three question types: Data Interpretation, Conflicting Viewpoints, and Research Summaries. A detailed explanation of each of these follows, accompanied by actual questions and in-depth solutions to help you understand how to interpret and answer these types of questions.

PREPARATION

Because the Science Reasoning test is not based on knowledge of facts, cramming to memorize as many facts as possible won't be of much help. Your best preparation is to have a solid high school education in the various fields of science, with emphasis on those courses that required you to read, evaluate, and analyze various situations and topics. If you have experience using the scientific method, that will also be of help. Experience in planning experiments and interpreting and discussing the results is most useful. Many of these skills are developed in courses that have laboratories associated with them. In addition, following this strategy section is a brief overview of basic scientific principles of the four major areas that will be covered on the ACT exam: biology, chemistry, physics, and earth and space science.

Having a healthy curiosity and a willingness to evaluate and question the new ideas and facts that you encounter every day are your best allies. Do you try to learn more about the things you hear and read? Do articles on scientific topics catch your attention to the extent that you try to understand new developments or question reported findings? If so, you will probably be well prepared to deal with the types of questions you will be asked on this exam.

You may find it helpful to read recent articles about science topics: *Discover, Scientific American, Science Digest,* and *Popular Science* magazines will give you excellent practice in reading about a variety of scientific ideas, as well as presenting the material in differing formats. Evaluate the things you read carefully. Make sure you understand what was done and why. For example, if a graph or table is used to present data, you may have to identify the variables or controls. You will also have to be able to read and interpret data presented in these different formats. You may also be asked questions related to higher-level learning skills, such as synthesis and evaluation. Key words in these types of questions may include *explain, interpret, conclude, summarize, justify,* or *compare,* to name just a few. You may also have to demonstrate understanding of the significance of the information when relating it to other situations.

TEST-TAKING STRATEGIES

Base your answers strictly on the information presented in the passage. The questions are usually straightforward, without hidden meaning. Try not to look for subtle or obscure meanings. The questions are written to test your understanding of the passage.

Make sure you are familiar with the test format, as previously explained.

1. Scan the passage to see what its about; then reread it carefully.

2. You should first try to answer the questions that simply test to see if you know the facts. These are very straight-forward. Skip the hard questions and return to them later.

3. Make sure you read all of the choices carefully.

4. Cross out those choices that are clearly incorrect. The process of elimination is sometimes the best way to arrive at the correct answer.

Time yourself while taking the practice exams in this book. Remember that you will have just 35 minutes to complete all 40 questions. This allows just five minutes for each passage. You should be able to read the passage in about two minutes, and you will then have 30 seconds to answer each question. Estimate answers where possible. You may not have time to complete complex calculations.

Finally, make sure that you answer all the questions. Be careful not to select two answers for any questions, because it will be marked wrong. However, because there is no penalty for guessing, you may have to choose this as a last resort at the end of the exam.

PRACTICE

The following sample passages and questions will help you prepare for the exam. Each of the three types of science passages is explained, and examples are given to help you become familiar with them. Following this section are more passages for additional practice. Take the time to work on them and study the answers closely in order to understand fully the type of material you will surely encounter on the actual ACT exam.

RESEARCH SUMMARIES

Research summaries describe results of studies that are not presented graphically or in data tables. These summaries present data that are relative to the situation but may not always make sense in other situations. Still, these types of summaries provide information about patterns and trends that we can relate to everyday observations and experiences.

Research summaries describe experimental designs and procedures, as well as the results obtained. The summaries may also explain the hypotheses being tested.

Questions about research summaries may be related to experimental design, such as "What was tested?" or "Identify the experimental variables and controls." You may also be asked to predict results, which requires you to analyze trends from the information in the summaries. You may have to select the best hypothesis for a given situation, or you may have to develop or test a new hypothesis by changing an experimental design.

Passage 1

Studies were conducted to determine the effects of LoPressor, a drug developed for hypertension, on the spontaneous development of tumors in inbred mice.

Experiment 1

Four groups of ten mice each were given varied doses of LoPressor for six months. Each group had from one to six mice develop tumors. More mice developed tumors as the dosage of the drug dosage was increased.

Experiment 2

Four groups of mice given the same dosages of LoPressor as in Experiment 1, but for only three months, developed tumors only in the group receiving the highest dosage of the drug.

Experiment 3

Ten mice were subjected to all the same conditions as the mice tested in Experiments 1 and 2, such as food, water, light, air, and bedding. However, this group received no LoPressor. None of these mice developed tumors after three months or after six months of treatment.

1. Which experiment served as a control?

   A. Experiment 1
   B. Experiment 2
   C. Experiment 3
   D. There was no control.

   The answer is C. The control has all the same factors as the experimental group, except the control is not subjected to the experimental variables, such as dosage.

2. What conclusions can be drawn from Experiment 1 alone?

   F. Tumor development was dependent upon the strain of mouse used.
   G. Tumor development was dependent upon the length of treatment with LoPressor.
   H. Tumor development was triggered by the environment, regardless of treatment with LoPressor.
   J. The dosage of LoPressor affected the number of tumors that developed in the mice.

   The answer is J. The only variable discussed was dosage, and the number of tumors increased as dosage increased.

3. What effect did length of treatment have on tumor development?

   A. The rate of tumor development decreased over time.
   B. The rate of tumor development increased over time.
   C. The rate of tumor development was the same at all points in time.
   D. Time was not a test variable.

   The answer is B. Since more tumors were observed at all treatment dosages after six months than after three months, one must conclude that increasing length of treatment increases the incidence of tumor development.

4. Using only the data in Experiment 2, which of the following could be concluded?

   F. Only the highest dose of the drug caused tumor development.
   G. Time was not a factor in tumor development.
   H. The experimental control developed tumors.
   J. More mice should have been tested in each group.

   The correct answer is F. Using only the data in Experiment 2, this initial conclusion would be valid. However, any drug like this must be tested using many variables to determine the true effect.

5. What conclusions can be drawn from Experiment 3?

   A. Tumor development always occurred in this strain of mouse, regardless of treatment.
   B. Time was not a factor in tumor development.
   C. These mice were naturally immune to this type of tumor.
   D. This is the experimental control group.

   The correct answer is D. This is a typical control group, subjected to the same conditions as the experimental groups, except the experimental variables were omitted.

6. What conclusions can be drawn from all three experiments?

    F.   LoPressor caused a higher incidence of tumor development with increasing dosage and increasing time of treatment.

    G.   LoPressor did not cause tumor development.

    H.   Length of treatment was the only variable affecting tumor development.

    J.   No conclusion can be drawn because there were no experimental controls.

The correct answer is F. Data from all three experiments show only two factors that contributed to tumor development: (1) dosage, and (2) length of treatment. In each case, tumor incidence increased as the variable increased.

DATA REPRESENTATION

Results of scientific experiments, surveys, or studies can be presented in various ways. The common formats for data presentation are graphs, tables, or charts.

In data tables, the experimental variables are usually shown at the top of the columns. The rows may indicate which variables changed or the results (values) for each experimental variable tested. In graphs, variables are listed along the x and y coordinates. The actual graph shows the relationship between the variables. For example, when measuring bacterial growth using turbidometry, absorbance (on the y-axis) increases as the amount of culture time (along the x-axis) increases, but only up to a certain point. The resulting graph shows a line that increases absorbance with time, then levels off in a fairly flat line.

Maps, scatter charts, diagrams, and bar graphs may also be used effectively. You may want to look through some of the recommended reading materials or your science textbooks to make sure you understand how to read and interpret data presented in these different forms.

There are a number of things presented in graphs, tables, and charts in addition to the values or results obtained for the experimental variables. Pay attention to the units of measure listed along with the variables. For example, these may be listed as distance (km), weight (g, kg), absorbance (630 nm), or time (min), to name a few.

Sometimes you will be asked to look for trends in the data presented. These can be identified by a fairly steady increase or decrease in the values shown in a table or on a graph or chart. Sometimes there are also correlations between the variables. You can sometimes identify a correlation by noticing whether when one variable changes in a consistent pattern or trend, another variable changes in some consistent manner as well. For example, a table or graph may show that a certain species of grub is present in the soil in maximum numbers when the temperature is between 45 and 75 degrees Fahrenheit. The independent (or experimental) variable is the temperature. The dependent variable (or result) is the number of grubs present. A second column in the table or line on a graph may show the number of robins observed in the same area, and that the number varies with the temperature. There may or may not be a correlation between the number of grubs present and the number of robins observed. The correlation, if any, could be positive or negative. You would have to decide based on the actual data.

As you can see, there are a number of different things to keep in mind when interpreting the data representations. What are the variables, and what values were presented? What are the units for the values, and do the different values correlate with one another? Keeping these questions in mind should help you answer the various questions following each passage.

Passage 2

The modern view of an atom includes three "principal parts." A dense nucleus contains protons and neutrons, and an "orbiting cloud" of electrons. The atomic mass of an atom is the sum of the number of protons and neutrons (each of which has a relative mass of 1). Neutral atoms have no overall electric charge, because the number of protons (which carry a +1 charge) and the number of electrons (which carry a −1 charge) are equal. The neutron has no electric charge. The atomic number assigned to an element is the number of protons in its nucleus. Ions are formed when electrons are lost or gained resulting in an unequal number of protons and electrons. Isotopes are subsets of having different "neutron counts." These species remain electrically neutral, but are either lighter or heavier due to neutron loss or gain.

Examine the following table:

1. In the preceding table, what correctly completes the line describing the atomic "arrangement" for Al?

   A. Atomic mass = 13 Proton count = 13
   B. Atomic mass = 14 Proton count = 13
   C. Atomic mass = 27 Proton count = 13
   D. Atomic mass = 27 Proton count = 14

   The correct response is C. The number of protons *always* equal the atomic number (13). The atomic mass is the *sum* of the number of protons and neutrons (27).

2. In the line describing the Ba^{+2} ion, the correct number of electrons should be:

   F. 56
   G. 54
   H. 58
   J. 137

   The correct response is G. An ion is an "electrically charged particle" created by electron loss or gain. Since the symbol indicates a +2 charge, there must be 2 more positive components (protons) than negative components (electrons). Since there are 56 protons listed in the table, there must be 54 electrons.

Symbol	Atomic Number	Atomic Mass	Proton Count	Neutron Count	Electron Count	Ion or Isotope?
K	19	39.0	19	20	19	NO
Al	13			14	13	NO
Ba^{+2}	56	137.0	56			ION
		31.0	15		15	NO
F^{-1}	9			10		ION
Mg^{+2}	12	24.0		12		ION

3. In the line that shows an unknown species with an atomic mass of 31.0, the correct sequence of entries for Symbol, Atomic Number, and Neutron Count should be:

A. [P] [15] [16].
B. [P] [16] [16].
C. [P^3] [12] [16].
D. [P] [16] [15].

The correct response is A. Atomic number [15] is always the same as the number of protons which is listed in the table as [15]. In the Periodic Table, [P] is the symbol for the element with the atomic number of 15, and since the atomic mass (the sum of the protons and neutrons) is listed on the table as 31.0, the number of neutrons is [16] (31.0 − 15 = 16).

4. In the line describing the arrangement of the F^1 ion, the correct number of protons should be:

F. 10
G. 9
H. 8
J. 18

The correct response is G. The number of protons is *always* equal to the atomic number. Compare the atomic numbers and electron counts of those given: K and Al; they are equal.

5. The correct electron count that should be assigned to the species represented in the final line of the preceding table should be:

A. 9
B. 20
C. 22
D. 12

The correct response is B. Since the atomic number is listed in the table as 12, Mg^{+2} must have 12 protons. Since the electric charge is +2, there must be 10 electrons (12 − 10 = 2).

6. The correct atomic mass that should be inserted into the box describing F^1 in the preceding table is:

F. 9
G. 10
H. 18
J. 19

The correct response is J. The −1 charge in this problem has no effect on the atomic mass. The atomic mass is the sum of the number of protons and neutrons. The number of protons *always* equals the atomic number (in this case 9). Therefore, protons [9] + neutrons [10] = 19.0.

CONFLICTING VIEWPOINTS

The third type of passage you will be asked to analyze is the Conflicting Viewpoints question type. This type of analysis is based on the premise that the same set of facts may be interpreted in different ways, based on a person's understanding of those facts. A person's understanding can be limited when he or she doesn't have enough knowledge about the background of a subject, or when he or she doesn't have enough data to completely or accurately analyze the facts as they are presented.

In order to analyze this type of passage, you need to evaluate both the hypothesis and the data supporting it, based on each person's point of view. You may be asked to predict results based on these points of view. You may also have to determine what kinds of assumptions have been made by these individuals and whether or not these assumptions were justified. Finally, you may have to pick the best hypothesis or identify the best argument supporting it. Again, this requires you to understand and analyze the assumptions that were made.

These passages begin with a simple question or statement such as:

"Can living things arise from nonliving matter?" (abiogenesis vs. biogenesis)

In response, you will see some passages that represent opposing points of view about the topic in question, such as the following:

Scientist 1: Living things may arise spontaneously by massing the vital forces from nonliving matter. This is called abiogenesis or spontaneous generation. Examples include: (1) maggots growing on cooked meat or other food left out in the open because the vital forces in the meat provide the energy for maggots to appear spontaneously, and (2) microorganisms grow in broth left out in the open because the vital force of the broth reaches a mass that generates living microorganisms.

Scientist 2: Living things arise only from other living things of their same kind (biogenesis). While variables such as temperature and availability of nutrients and oxygen may affect this process, they cannot by themselves produce living things. Life begets life. Examples include: (1) flies must come in contact with meat or broth for maggots to appear, and maggots mature into flies, and (2) a broth grows microorganisms only when the broth is exposed directly to air or something else that contains microorganisms, even though we can't see them.

You will then be asked to answer questions based on certain data, using the conflicting points of view:

1. A piece of roast beef was thoroughly cooked, then left in a container on the counter. The container was covered with gauze to allow air and room temperature heat to reach the meat. According to the hypothesis of scientist 1, what will happen to the meat?

A. The meat will not produce maggots, because the meat is out in the open.
B. The meat cannot give rise to maggots when gauze is present.
C. The meat left out in the open will give rise to maggots from vital forces within the meat itself.
D. Cooking the meat destroys all vital forces that give rise to maggots.

Scientist 1 would expect the meat to produce maggots through spontaneous generation if the meat is left out in the open. The gauze and cooking should have no impact on this process according to his thinking. His hypothesis clearly eliminates answer A. The correct answer is C.

2. Based on question 1, what conclusions could scientist 2 reach that is consistent with his hypothesis?

F. The meat will produce maggots because it is out in the open and the gauze allows air to contact the meat.

G. The meat cannot give rise to maggots because the gauze keeps the flies away from it.

H. The vital forces in the meat will produce maggots with or without gauze present.

J. The meat was once living; therefore, it can produce other living things such as maggots.

Scientist 2 would conclude that the meat could not produce maggots if the gauze kept flies away from the meat. He does not support the hypothesis for spontaneous generation, which rules out F, H, and J. The correct answer is G.

3. Scientist 2 vigorously heated two containers of beef broth to destroy any living microorganisms. Then he kept the container loosely covered at room temperature. No microorganisms grew in either container. Scientist 1 would support his hypothesis by arguing that:

A. the broths cannot produce microorganisms when covered.

B. beef broth contains no vital forces and should not be used.

C. microorganisms will not grow in beef broth because they prefer chicken broth.

D. the heat destroyed the vital forces of the beef broth, so microorganisms cannot grow.

Scientist 1 would not choose answers B and C, because that would be inconsis-

tent with his hypothesis. If the reason his hypothesis includes "out in the open" as a condition for growth is because he assumes air is needed for growth to occur, then he should also reject answer A, since air could pass in and out of a loosely covered container. Scientist 1 would choose D.

4. Scientist 2 argued that some invisible organisms in the air were dropping into open containers of broth or food, giving rise to other microorganisms that caused the broths to turn cloudy and spoil. He passed air through chemically treated cotton wool to filter out these "invisible microorganisms." He then showed that broths exposed only to filtered air did not grow microorganisms. Scientist 1 would conclude that:

F. treatment of the air would be harmful to the process of spontaneous generation.

G. the treated air would support spontaneous generation.

H. the presence or absence of air is irrelevant to spontaneous generation.

J. spontaneous generation requires no air.

Answer G is not consistent with the outcome. Nothing grew. Scientist 1's hypothesis strongly implies that air is required for growth of microorganisms, ruling out H and J as likely answers. Scientist 1 would choose answer F.

5. Using the same argument and experimental data as in question 4, scientist 2 would conclude that:

   A. the treated filter trapped and destroyed microorganisms in the air that would have given rise to microorganisms in the broth.

   B. microorganisms would still grow in the broth over time.

   C. the treated filter would have no effect on the growth of microorganisms.

   D. air is not necessary for microorganisms to grow.

The correct answer is A. This was the whole point of the experiment.

6. Scientist 2 heated broth in two flasks to destroy any living microorganisms. One flask neck was left directly open to the air above it. The other flask neck was bent to the side in an S shape so that air could freely enter, but any microorganisms present in the air would be trapped in the neck, unable to reach the broth. His hypothesis would predict that:

   F. nothing could grow in either broth.

   G. the broth in the curved-neck flask would grow microorganisms because it got "clean" air.

   H. the broth in the straight-neck flask would grow microorganisms because they could fall directly into the broth.

   J. both broths would produce growth of microorganisms due to spontaneous generation.

Only answer H would be possible, since the experiment allowed free flow of air in both cases, but the S-necked flask would trap contaminants. Scientist 2 would not choose J, as he rejects the hypothesis of spontaneous generation.

Unit 4

This section will serve as a conceptual overview for the science section of the ACT Assessment. The major concepts sections review important ideas and information in the major science areas covered on this test: biology, chemistry, physics, and earth and space science. Even though the test items in the Science Reasoning section of the test *do not* require you to recall specific scientific facts, it is much easier to read and interpret a science passage and the accompanying questions if you have at least some basic understanding of the subject, as well as a familiarity with some of the terms.

You can skim the following material at your leisure, or use this section as a reference after you have answered the sample questions or the questions on the tests included in this book. It may help you better understand the explanations for the answers.

BIOLOGY

Life Functions

1. All living things carry out certain activities or functions in order to maintain life.
2. Nutrition is the process of ingesting and absorbing food to provide the energy for life, promote growth, and repair or replace worn or damaged tissues.
3. Transport involves movement of nutrients, water, ions, and other materials into and out of the various cells and tissues of organisms. This process includes absorption of small molecules across cell membranes and secretion of biochemicals such as enzymes, mucous, and hormones. In many species, the circulatory system plays an important role in transport.
4. Metabolism includes the process by which nutrients and simple molecules are used to form more complex molecules for growth, repair, and reproduction (anabolism). Metabolism also includes the process of breaking down complex molecules to release energy from chemical bonds (catabolism) and to provide small molecules such as simple sugars and amino acids as building blocks for more complex molecules (anabolism).
5. An internal balance in all aspects of metabolism and biological function is called homeostasis.
6. Digestion is a special form of catabolism that breaks food down into smaller molecules and releases energy.
7. Absorption allows small molecules to pass through cell membranes throughout the body tissues. This allows for gas exchange, and in some species such as plants and fungi, nutrients are obtained by absorption from soil and water.
8. The behavior of living things is a response to stimuli in the environment. These stimuli may include things such as light, chemical signals, noise, or a change in the seasons.
9. Excretion is the elimination of waste products.
10. Reproduction is the creation of offspring. Living things reproduce sexually, asexually, or both. Life comes from other living things.

Chemistry of Life

1. All living things are made up of the same elements, with the most abundant being carbon, hydrogen, nitrogen, oxygen, phosphorous, and sulfur. Trace elements and minerals are also essential components of all living things.

2. All species consume or absorb nutrients to carry out essential biological activities. Catabolic activities such as digestion provide the energy and building blocks for biosynthetic (anabolic) activities such as growth, repair, and reproduction.

3. Digestion in some species includes both a mechanical breakdown of food or nutrients (chewing), as well as absorption. In animals such as humans, the digestive tract is a system that is complex in both structure and function. In more primitive organisms, digestion may occur in a less specialized fashion. For example, some protozoa can absorb nutrients, then digest them within membrane-bound vacuoles that contain digestive enzymes. Some bivalves, such as clams and oysters, have gills within a mantle cavity that are used for gas exchange.

4. Regardless of their specific metabolic processes, all living things use enzymes to catalyze the chemical reactions of life. Whether consuming energy or releasing it, these chemical reactions are essential to all living things.

Photosynthesis and Respiration

1. Cellular respiration is a catabolic activity that breaks down carbohydrates, fats, and proteins to produce energy, in the form of ATP. This process consumes oxygen and produces carbon dioxide and water as by-products. In eukaryotic cells, cellular respiration takes place in the mitochondria. In prokaryotic cells, bacteria, this process takes place on the cell membrane, since bacteria do not contain mitochondria.

2. Respiration includes several metabolic pathways: Glycolysis, the Kreb's Cycle, and the Electron Transport Chain. These pathways can work together to completely oxidize one molecule of glucose, producing up to 38 molecules of ATP in the process. Synthesis of ATP is an anabolic process.

3. Photosynthesis occurs in plants and some other organisms, such as algae. These organisms use sunlight as a source of energy to synthesize carbohydrates, lipids, proteins, and other organic substances. Photosynthetic organisms are the producers of the biosphere.

4. Chloroplasts are the site of photosynthesis in plants and eukaryotic algae. Photosynthesis includes two separate processes. One stage of photosynthesis is the "light reactions" that convert solar energy to chemical energy. The second stage is the Calvin Cycle, which consumes carbon dioxide from the environment. This cycle uses ATP produced in the light reactions as a source of energy to produce carbohydrate from CO_2.

Genetics and Reproduction

1. Humans have 23 pairs of chromosomes in each cell. Each person has one pair of sex chromosomes, coded XX for females and XY for males. The sex chromosomes contain the genes that determine sex, as well as some other characteristics. The remaining 22 pairs of chromosomes are called autosomes. Other species have different numbers of chromosomes.

2. Each pair of chromosomes is a homologous pair. For each of the 23 pairs in humans, one chromosome of each pair is from the mother and one is from the father. The gametes, or sex cells, contain 23 single chromosomes each. When fertilization occurs, the fertilized egg, or zygote, then contains 23 pairs of chromosomes.

3. Chromosomes are made up of subunits called genes. Individual genes code for various traits or characteristics of all living things. Pairs of genes that have the same position on each member of a pair of chromosomes, and which can take alternate forms, are called alleles. Allele codes for dominant traits are assigned upper case letters, and recessive traits are assigned the same letter, but in lowercase form.

4. Dominant genes control the phenotype (appearance) of the individual. For example, assume that red flowers (R) are dominant and white flowers (r) are a recessive trait of peas. An individual with one dominant gene from one parent and one recessive gene from the other parent will have a genotype of Rr. The individual will express the dominant gene, and therefore will have red flowers. Individuals with a genotype of RR will also produce red flowers. In order to produce white flowers, the individual must inherit two recessive genes and have a genotype of rr.

5. Chromosomes are made up primarily of DNA (deoxyribonucleic acid). DNA occurs as a double-stranded molecule in cells. The subunits of DNA are bases called adenine (A), cytosine (C), guanine (G), and thymine (T). They always occur in pairs in DNA. The pairing is specific: A-T or T-A, and G-C or C-G. These are called complementary base pairs. When the bases bond to each other, they hold the two strands of DNA together. The DNA then coils to form a double helix.

6. When the strands of DNA separate to reproduce, the base pairs split apart. Each strand then binds to new complementary bases to form two identical daughter strands. Each new double strand of DNA contains one of the original strands and one new strand. This is called semiconservative replication.

7. RNA (ribonucleic acid) helps transcribe the genetic code in DNA and translates it into proteins. RNA, a single-stranded molecule, is also made up of nitrogen bases, except that it contains uracil (U) instead of thymine (T). If RNA were being produced using DNA as the template or code, the messenger RNA (mRNA) would contain a U instead of a T, and that U would be opposite or complementary to an A on the DNA strand. All other complementary pairs are the same as with two strands of DNA.

8. Codons are triplets of nucleotide bases (A, T, U, G, C) that code for specific amino acids. For example, UGU and UGC are both codons for the amino acid cysteine. There are 64 codons, but there are only 20 amino acids. Having more than one codon for most amino acids allows for some variation in the genetic code. Amino acids are the building blocks of proteins.

9. There are three types of RNA: (1) messenger RNA (mRNA), (2) transfer RNA (tRNA), and (3) ribosomal RNA (rRNA). These three work together in the cell cytoplasm to carry out protein synthesis. The mRNA carries the ''message'' or genetic code from the DNA. Ribosomes, made up of rRNA, serve as the site of protein synthesis. Ribosomes and tRNA work together to ''translate'' the message. The tRNA carries amino acids to the site of protein synthesis. The tRNA anticodon pairs with the codon on the mRNA to make sure that the correct amino acid is added to the protein being synthesized.

10. Mitosis is an asexual process whereby cells divide for the purpose of growth and repair. Two identical daughter cells are produced. Occasional differences may occur due to mutations. Each daughter cell contains the same number of chromosomes as the parent cells. Other types of asexual reproduction are budding and binary fission.

11. Meiosis is a process of cell division that produces gametes for sexual reproduction. Sexual reproduction combines genes from two different parents to produce offspring that are genetically diverse.

Molecular Genetics and Molecular Biology

1. Rapid advances in technology have greatly increased our knowledge of genetics at the molecular level. This has opened exciting new fields of study in genetic engineering and biotechnology. The technology can be applied to many disciplines, including agriculture, medicine, pharmaceuticals, consumer science, biology, forensic medicine and criminology, and biochemistry.

2. Genes can be manipulated to correct genetic defects. Genes can be transferred from one organism to another. Transgenic plants, bacteria, and animals containing genes from other species are being developed routinely.

3. Human gene products such as insulin and tissue plasminogen activator are now produced by inserting the genes into bacteria or yeast cells. These microbes are then grown in huge quantities, and the genes produce the desired ''product'' as the organisms grow. Many other therapeutic and industrial products are produced in a similar manner.

4. Bioremediation is a special area of biotechnology that uses microorganisms to destroy harmful materials in the environment, leaving harmless molecules as by-products. Some of these organisms are genetically engineered to perform certain tasks. They can clean up oil spills or toxic chemicals by breaking them down into harmless substances.

5. Animals and plants are genetically engineered (modified) to improve productivity, yield, nutrient content, appearance, and conceivably almost any trait one could imagine. This may become essential to increasing the food supply as populations increase and as farmland disappears. This technology is rapidly changing our ability to fight disease and genetic disorders.

6. The human genome project is being conducted to "map" the location and function of every gene on all of the human chromosomes. It is estimated that humans have approximately 100,000 genes.

7. There are many social and ethical issues relating to biotechnology, genetic engineering, and molecular biology. It will become increasingly important for the general public to be educated about these issues.

Evolution

1. Charles Darwin traveled throughout the Southern Hemisphere in the 1830s aboard the HMS *Beagle* in order to observe the abundant and unique life forms. He gathered evidence supporting the hypothesis of common descent—that all living things have a common ancestry. He also made observations and documented evidence that species adapt to changes in their environment, and these adaptations result in biological diversity.

2. Darwin, along with Alfred Russel Wallace, presented a joint paper hypothesizing that natural selection accounts for the origin of new biological species. The theory of natural selection proposes that adaptations occur due to constantly changing environment.

3. The theory of natural selection essentially states that (1) members of a species have different traits, which can be inherited; (2) all species produce more offspring than can reproduce or survive (survival of the fittest); (3) some individuals adapt to change, and they survive and reproduce more successfully than those that cannot adapt; (4) the offspring of subsequent generations inherit the adaptive characteristics; and (5) natural selection produces populations adapted to their particular environment.

4. Random mutations or changes also occur. In both cases, advances in molecular biology are making it possible to analyze the genetic relatedness of various species and to identify mutations that did not arise through adaptive change.

5. Humans and higher primates, such as apes and chimpanzees, are closely related genetically. This supports the hypothesis of common descent.

6. Adaptations may produce similarities or differences based on the environment. Some animals have developed similar features such as hooves or claws. However, there are different types of hooves for running, claws for defense or climbing, and so on.

Ecology

1. Ecology is the study of the interactions of organisms with their environment, both living (biotic) and nonliving (abiotic). That environment and all organisms and things within it are collectively called an ecosystem.

2. The biotic potential of a population is the maximum rate of growth that will occur under ideal conditions (food, space, etc.).

3. The carrying capacity of the environment limits the size of a given population. Variables such as the change of seasons may cause fluctuations in population size due to different capacities over time.

4. Communities contain a variety of populations. They interact in many ways, including competition, symbiosis, and predation. Competition for food, space, and other things limits population size. Natural predators help keep populations in balance within a community. Symbiosis is the close association of two species. It may be beneficial to one species (commensalism) or to both (mutualism). It may also harm one species while benefiting the other (parasitism).

5. A balanced ecosystem recycles dead and used materials, has an energy source, and includes producers (green plants), consumers (herbivores, carnivores, omnivores), decomposers (bacteria, fungi), and abiotic components.

6. Succession is a sequence of communities in an environment evolving from simple to complex. Each community is a seral stage, and the entire sequence is a sere. The first seral stage is a pioneer community. Climax communities are final seral stages. Succession from sand dunes to mature deciduous forests represents a sere typical of the mid-Atlantic coastal region of the United States.

7. Humans create waste and pollution that endanger the balance of ecosystems. Depletion of the ozone layer, for example, could increase the amount of ultraviolet light reaching the earth, which may cause mutations, and possibly extinction, of many species. Some scientists hypothesize that global warming is occurring due to the build-up of carbon dioxide (CO_2) from combustion of fossil fuels and wood from deforestation. An increase of global temperature of just a few degrees centigrade could cause a substantial increase in sea levels, as well as a marked change in the variety and numbers of various species.

8. Proper disposal and recycling of wastes, sustainable use of natural resources, and development of alternative energy sources (other than fossil fuels and wood) are but a few things needed to maintain life as we know it.

The Cell

1. All living things are made of cells. Surrounded by a cell membrane, each cell contains the genetic material that codes for the structure and function of the entire organism. Some organisms are unicellular, while most organisms are multicellular. Cells are surrounded by cell membranes. Some cells also have cell walls.

2. Cell membranes are selectively permeable, in that they control which molecules enter or leave the cell. This may include gases, nutrients, water, and wastes.

3. The cell membrane is a bilayer of phospholipids (a type of fat). Proteins imbedded in this bilayer sometimes help transport molecules across the bilayer by forming channels. These are called carrier proteins.

4. Some cells contain a nucleus (eukaryotes). The nucleus is surrounded by a porous membrane, and it contains chromosomes. The nucleus is the control center of the cell because it contains all the genetic information. Some cells (prokaryotes) have no nucleus. Bacteria are prokaryotes. They have only one chromosome, which is located in an area of their cytoplasm called a nucleoid.

5. All eukaryotic cells contain mitochondria. Mitochondria are the site of ATP production. They are the powerhouse of the cell. Prokaryotes produce ATP using cytochromes imbedded in their cell membrane.

6. Cytoplasm is a semifluid liquid that fills the cell and holds the components of a cell. It also holds dissolved nutrients such as amino acids and sugars.

7. Endoplasmic reticulum (ER) is a network of folded membranes that carry materials from the nucleus to the cytoplasm. The rough ER is studded with ribosomes, which are the site of protein synthesis. The smooth ER produces lipids and hormones. Ribosomes are also found free in the cytoplasm.

8. Lysosomes are membrane-bound vacuoles in the cytoplasm. They contain hydrolytic enzymes that digest materials that enter the cell. The enzymes are in vacuoles so that they don't destroy the cell itself.

9. The golgi apparatus is another series of folded membranes that has several functions. It receives materials from the endoplasmic reticulum for processing (modification), packaging (putting a membrane around a molecule), or secretion (leaving the cell).

10. Although each cell of an individual contains all the genetic information for its form and function, not every cell expresses all the information. In multicellular organisms, cells develop in different ways as the embryo develops. This unique ability for cellular differentiation allows development of specialized cellular organelles, cells, tissues, organs, and systems that make each member of a species unique.

11. The expression and the composition of the genetic material within each cell contribute to both the unity and diversity of living things.

CHEMISTRY

Basic Concepts

1. Chemistry can be described as being concerned with the composition of matter and the changes that it can undergo. There are several main ''branches'' of chemistry. Organic Chemistry is mostly concerned with the study of chemicals containing the element carbon. Inorganic Chemistry is the study of all elements and compounds other than organic compounds. Analytical Chemistry is the study of qualitative (what is present?) and quantitative (how much is present?) analysis of elements and compounds. Physical Chemistry is the study of reaction rates, mechanisms, bonding and structure, and thermodynamics. Biochemistry is the study of the chemical reactions that happen within the biological process.

2. Matter is defined as anything that has mass and occupies space. Mass is the quantity of matter in a particular body. Weight is the gravitational force of attraction between the body's mass and the mass of the planet (usually earth) on which it is weighed.

3. Energy is defined as the capacity to do work or to transfer heat.

4. In chemistry, there are three commonly employed temperature scales: Fahrenheit, Celsius, and Kelvin; only Celsius and Kelvin are accepted universally. The Kelvan and Celsius scales have identical degree increments, but different zeros. In particular, °Kelvin = °Celsius + 273, or °Celsius = °Kelvin − 273.

5. The calorie (cal), a unit of measurement for heat energy, is defined as the amount of heat required to raise the temperature of 1.00 g of water from 14.5 to 15.5 °C. The joule (J) is the unit of energy preferred in the SI system; 1 cal = 0.234 cal. Specific heat is defined in the metric system as the number of calories required to raise the temperature of 1.00 g of a substance 1 °C.

6. Density is defined as the mass of a substance occupying a unit volume, i.e.,

   Density = Mass / Volume

7. There are three physical states of matter—solids, liquids, and gases—although many chemists now recognize a fourth state, a plasma. Matter is further divided into two major subdivisions: homogeneous and heterogenous. Homogenous matter is uniform throughout, and heterogeneous matter is not uniform throughout.

8. Pure substances are divided into two groups: compounds and elements. A compound is a pure substance that can be broken down by various chemical means into two or more different substances. An element is a pure substance that cannot be decomposed into simpler substances by ordinary chemical means. The basic "building block" of a compound is a molecule. The basic "building block" of an element is an atom.

Atoms and Atomic Theory

1. The atom is a complex unit composed of various subatomic particles including electrons, protons, and neutrons.

2. The basic "shape" of an atom consists of a dense nucleus composed of neutrons and protons, and a "cloud" of orbiting electrons. The electrons orbit around the nucleus at various energy levels.

3. Electrons carry a negative electric charge and have almost negligible mass.

4. Protons have a relative mass of 1 (atomic mass unit) and carry a positive electric charge.

5. Like the proton, the neutron also has a relative mass of 1 (atomic mass unit), but the neutron carries no electric charge.

6. Atoms of different elements have a different combination of electrons, protons, and neutrons. Although a proton in a gold nucleus would "look like" a proton in a silver nucleus, the difference between gold and silver is in the *number* of protons found in the nuclei of these atoms. The nucleus of a gold atom contains 79 protons, and the nucleus of a silver atom contains 47 protons.

7. The mass of an atom is measured in atomic mass units (amu). The mass is almost entirely contained in the nucleus, but the atomic volume is almost completely outside the nucleus (defined by the orbiting electrons).

8. The atomic number of an element is the number of protons in the nucleus.

9. Since only protons and neutrons have significant mass, the atomic mass of an element is the sum of the number of protons and neutrons. Example: If an atom of gold has an atomic number of 79 and an atomic mass of 197 (amu), its nucleus must contain 79 protons and 118 neutrons.

10. Most elements exist as isotopes. An isotope of an element necessarily has the same number of protons, but a different number of neutrons. The actual atomic mass found on the Periodic Table is the average for the natural abundance of the atomic masses of the known isotopes.

11. Atomic mass numbers are based on the standard mass of 12.000 for a carbon atom.

12. Electrons can be found in distinct energy levels (called quantum levels) orbiting the nucleus. These energy levels are assigned letter designations such as K, L, M, N, O, etc.

13. Electrons can "jump" from one energy level to another, but cannot exist in between levels. Electrons absorb energy in order to move to higher levels, and emit energy upon moving to lower levels. The energy that is lost or gained is done so in discrete quantities known as quanta.

14. Elements may be identified by examining the spectral lines produced by the energy radiated or absorbed by electrons moving from one quantum level to another. Each element has its own identifying "fingerprint" of spectral lines.

15. The average path that an electron takes while traveling around the nucleus is known as its orbital. Orbitals vary in size, shape, and spacial orientation. Each electron occupies an orbital, and orbitals can hold no more than two electrons (Pauli Exclusion Principle). When a pair of electrons occupies a single orbital, they must have opposite "spin."

16. The electrons in the outermost principal energy level of an atom are known as the valence electrons.

17. Radiation is the disintegration of the nucleus of an atom with emission from its nuclear particles. Some elements are naturally radioactive, whereas others can have this property artificially induced.

18. Nuclear disintegration may produce alpha particles, beta particles, gamma rays, or a combination of these three.

19. Alpha particles are heavy, with a structure similar to a helium nucleus carrying a +2 charge.

20. Beta particles are essentially high-speed electrons.

21. Gamma rays are not particles but high-energy X rays.

22. The half-life of a radioactive isotope is the time required for one-half of the nuclei in a microscopic sample to disintegrate.

Periodic Classification of Elements

1. The modern Periodic Table is the evolution of work begun by a German chemist, Lothar Meyer (1830–1895) and a Russian chemist, Dmitri Mendeleev (1834–1906). Mendeleev is credited with much of the successes of the table, since he purposely left gaps in its construction to allow for the discovery of elements that had not yet been found, but had "predictable properties."

2. The table is arranged in an order consistent with increasing atomic number (number of protons).

3. Vertical columns in the Periodic Table are called *groups* or *families,* and they are elements with similar electron arrangements and similar chemical properties.

4. Elements with metallic properties are found on the left side of the table, while nonmetals are found on the right side of the table.

5. Metals tend to lose electrons (and form positive ions), while nonmetals tend to gain electrons (and form negative ions), or they can often share electrons with other nonmetals.

6. There are eight nonmetals that form homonuclear diatomic molecules when found naturally in the environment. An easy method to remember them is the phrase: *hydrogen* + *"the magic seven*!" Hydrogen, of course, is diatomic, existing as H_2 in the environment. To find the other seven diatomic elements, look at a Periodic Table. Find element number 7 (nitrogen) and, beginning with nitrogen, note that number 7 is formed on the table with the remaining diatomic elements! They are (forming the number 7) nitrogen, oxygen, fluorine, chlorine, bromine, iodine, and astatine! Their formulas would be written as $H_2 - N_2 - O_2 - F_2 - Cl_2 - Br_2 - I_2 - At_2$, respectfully. All other elements exist in nature as monatomic elements.

7. The elements in the vertical column headed by lithium (on many periodic tables hydrogen is placed here for "graphic balance") are known as *alkali metals.* Column II (headed by beryllium) contains the *alkali earth metals.* On the right side of the table the column headed by oxygen is often called the *chalcogen* family, while the column of elements headed by *fluorine* is known as the *Halogens.* All of the elements in the final column are very unreactive elements previously known as the Inert Gases, but now are called the *noble gases.*

8. The Periodic Table can be used to predict the number of valence electrons (and resulting oxidation number), which is helpful in writing chemical formulas. For example, in a chemical bonding situation, all of the Alkali Metals carry a charge of +1, the Alkali Earth Metals +2, and the Halogens −1.

9. A chemical bond forms by the transfer of an electron from one atom to another, or by the sharing of an electron of an electron pair.

10. Ionic bonds are formed when electrons are completely transferred. Ionic bonds are often formed when a metal from the left side of the Periodic Table transfers an electron to a nonmetal from the right side of the table. The number of electrons that transfer dictates the nature of the ionic bond and can be used to predict the formula of the compound. Examples: sodium (with one available valence electron to transfer) combines with chlorine (''looking'' for a valence electron) and forms the compound NaCl (sodium chloride). Magnesium (with two available valence electrons to transfer) then would need to combine with two chlorine atoms (each atom ''looking'' for one valence electron) to form the compound $MgCl_2$ (magnesium chloride).

11. Covalent bonds, found in chemicals such as carbon dioxide (CO_2) and sulfur trioxide (SO_3), involve the sharing of electrons rather than the transfer of electrons. Ionic bonds are usually stronger, forming chemicals with higher melting and boiling points.

12. When energy is absorbed, chemical bonds can be broken. When chemical bonds are formed, energy is released.

13. Chemical reactions involve changes in bonding energy, yet they conform to the Laws of Conservation of Mass and Conservation of Energy.

Chemical Nomenclature of Inorganic Compounds

1. Binary compounds result from the combination of a metal with a non-metal. Name the metal first, followed by the ''root'' of the nonmetal and add the ending ''ide.'' Examples: NaCl (sodium chloride), $MgCl_2$ (magnesium chloride), Al_2O_3 (aluminum oxide).

2. Binary compounds involving a transition metal combining with a nonmetal are slightly more complex. Transition metals can exist with different valences (oxidation numbers); this produces compounds with different chemical and physical properties, and this difference must be included in the nomenclature of the compound. For example, iron exists in two common forms (with different oxidation numbers). It can combine with chlorine, for example, as a Fe^{+2} ion or as a Fe^{+3} ion, producing $FeCl_2$ and $FeCl_3$, respectively. The first compound is named iron (II) chloride (indicating that the +2 form of iron was involved), and the latter compound is named iron (III) chloride (indicating that the +3 form of iron was used). This system of using numbers (Roman numerals) to indicate the valence of the metal involved in a bond has replaced an older system, which used (inconsistently) Latin suffixes such as ''ic'' and ''ous'' to correspond with valence numbers.

3. Binary compounds involving covalent bonds (usually nonmetals combining with nonmetals) use a series of prefixes to indicate how many atoms of each molecule are involved in the compound. Examples: sulfur can combine with oxygen in at least three different ways, depending on laboratory or environmental conditions. The compound SO is named sulfur monoxide, while SO_2 is named sulfur dioxide, and SO_3 would be named sulfur trioxide. Correspondingly, the chemical P_2O_5 is named *Diphosphorous pentoxide*. Note: these prefixes are used only in non-metal-nonmetal bonded chemicals.

4. A knowledge of *radicals* is essential in understanding the nomenclature of inorganic chemicals. Radicals are molecular fragment elements with a specific oxidation number. Radicals enter into chemical reactions without internal change in their own bonding. Examples: The hydroxide radical (OH^{-1}) "behaves" like a halogen when forming compounds. Combining a metal with hydroxide, such as Na, produces a compound with the formula NaOH, which is named sodium hydroxide. Magnesium combining with hydroxide produces the compound $Mg(OH)_2$, named magnesium hydroxide. *Note* that the parentheses around the (OH) in this case indicates there are two individual hydroxide radicals involved in the formation of this compound. The same Roman numeral "rules" for transition metals combining with radicals continue to apply. Thus, $Fe(OH)_3$ is named iron (III) hydroxide.

Stoichiometry Calculations

1. The basic unit for all chemical calculations is the *mole*.

2. A mole of *anything* contains Avogadro's number of particles (6.02 × 10^{23}). Therefore, if you had a mole of pencils, you would have 6.02 × 10^{23} pencils, but if you had a mole of gold, you would have a quantity of an element that contained 6.02 × 10^{23} atoms.

3. Atomic and molecular masses in grams are determined to be the mass at one mole of atoms or molecules, respectively. Examples: 1 mole of gold contains 6.02 × 10^{23} atoms, and has a mass of 196.967g. 1 mole of sodium chloride contains 6.02 × 10^{23} molecules of NaCl and has a mass of 58.44 g (one adds the atomic masses of both sodium and chlorine together for this result).

4. For gases only: 1 mole of an ideal gas occupies a volume of 22.4 liters at STP (Standard Temperature and Pressure — 25° Celsius and 760 mm pressure).

5. In problems involving stoichiometric ratios, the balancing numbers (coefficients) in an equation are *moles*. Stoichiometry problems must be calculated in moles, and a thorough understanding of gram-to-mole conversions is needed.

6. An important formula to remember: *moles = grams / molecular mass.* For example:

   65.8 grams of sodium chloride = how many moles?

   moles = (65.8 grams given in the problem) *divided* by (58.4 grams/mole — the molecular mass)

   moles = 1.1

7. All stoichiometry problems assume a *correctly balanced equation.* Example: Based on this correctly balanced equation: $N_2 + 3H_2 \rightarrow 2NH_3$, how many moles of nitrogen are needed to react completely with 6 moles of hydrogen?

The solution is based on the ratio of the moles of nitrogen (1) and hydrogen (3) from the correctly balanced equation. Let "x" represent the moles of nitrogen. A ratio is established using the coefficients found in the balanced equation: $\frac{1}{3}\left(\frac{N_2}{H_2}\right)$ corresponds to $\frac{x}{6}\left(\frac{N_2}{H_2}\right)$, so solving for x, $x = 2$

8. The *molarity* of a solution is the number of moles of solute contained in 1 liter of solution. Other methods of calculating the concentration of solutions include *normality* and *molality.* The molarity calculation is the most widely recognized.

Solutions, Acids, and Bases

1. Electrolytes are substances that dissolve in water to form solutions that will conduct an electric current. Dissolved ions conduct current.

2. Acids have the following properties:

a. Acid solutions conduct electricity (i.e., acids are electrolytes).
b. Acids react with many active metals to liberate hydrogen gas.
c. Acids turn litmus paper red.
d. Acids form a salt and water when reacting with bases.
e. Acids have a sour taste.
f. Acids, when measured on the pH scale, have pH < 7.

g. An acid, as defined by Arrhenius in 1884, is a substance that yields a hydrogen ion H^+ when dissolved in water. Arrhenius's definition has since been expanded to include its producing a hydronium H_3O^+ ion.
h. Acids were defined in 1923 by Brønsted and Lowry to be *proton donors.*

3. Bases have the following properties:

a. Basic solutions conduct electricity (i.e., bases are electrolytes).
b. Basic solutions react with acids to form salts and water.
c. Bases turn litmus paper blue.
d. Bases have a bitter taste.
e. Bases feel "slippery" (caustic properties).
f. Bases, when measured on the pH scale, have pH > 7.
g. Bases were defined in 1923 by Brønsted and Lowry to be *proton acceptors.*
h. Most common bases contain the OH^- ion.

4. Some chemicals, such as water, are *amphiprotic*—that is, they can be either proton donors or acceptors (and thus can be considered as either an acid or a base).

5. Neutralization is the reaction by which equivalent quantities of an acid and a base react to form a salt and water. In the laboratory, *titration* is the procedure that is used to quantitatively mix acids and bases.

6. A salt results from the combination of an acid and a base. A salt is formed from the negative ion (anion) of the acid, and the positive ion (cation) of the base.

233

7. pH is a measure of the concentration of an acid or base. By definition, it is the negative of the common logarithm ($-\log_{\text{base 10}}$) of the hydrogen ion (actually the hydronium ion) concentration. On a practical basis, it is a scale from 0 to 14, with the number 7 being considered neutral. Acids have a pH < 7 and bases have a pH > 7. The scale is designed to measure the concentration of dilute acids and bases. Concentrated acids can have a pH *below* 0, and concentrated bases can have a pH *above* 14. A reciprocal scale, the pOH scale, is a measure of the concentration of OH^- ions in solution. In pH calculations, it is important to remember that pH + pOH = 14.

Electrochemistry

1. A knowledge of oxidation numbers is important in the understanding of electrochemistry and also in balancing complex oxidation/reduction (redox) equations.

2. An oxidation number is a "label" assigned to atoms that indicates the extent to which they have either lost or gained electrons. Assigning oxidation numbers is based on many complex considerations involving the type of bonding involved. Following are some general rules for assigning these numbers to atoms and some examples.

   a. The oxidation number for an element that is not in a multi-compound element is always zero:

   N_2 (each nitrogen has an oxidation number of zero)

   O_3 (each oxygen has an oxidation number of zero)

   Ca (the calcium atom has an oxidation number of zero)

   b. The oxidation number of an atom that is a monatomic ion in a compound is the same as the electrical charge on the ion (its valence).

   $MgBr_2$: This compound is formed from Mg^{+2} ions and Br^- ions, so the oxidation numbers are identical to the electrical ion charges. Mg = (+2) Br = (−1)

   Al_2O_3: This compound is formed from Al^{+3} ions and O^{-2} ions, so the oxidation numbers are identical to the electrical ion charges. Al = (+3) O = (−2)

   c. The oxidation number of H (hydrogen) is always +1 (except in salts, where hydrogen is bonded to a metal).

   d. The oxidation number of O (oxygen) is almost always −2 (except in peroxides and superoxides).

   e. The sum of all oxidation numbers in a compound must be ZERO. The sum of oxidation numbers in an ion must equal the charge of the ion.

Examples: H_3PO_4 The sum of the oxidation numbers must total zero. Using the rules above, hydrogen always carries a charge of +1, but there are 3 hydrogen atoms in the compound, resulting in an overall charge of +3. Oxygen always carries a charge of −2, but there are 4 oxygen atoms in the compound, resulting in an overall charge of −8. To balance the +3 (from the hydrogen) and the −8 (from the oxygen), an oxidation number must be assigned to phosphorus (P) to make the total equal zero. The number +5 results from phosphorus. (+3) + (+5) + (−8) = (0)

SO_3^{-2} (sulfite ion) In this case, the sum of the oxidation numbers must equal the assigned charge on the ion (−2). The oxidation number of oxygen is −2, but there are 3 oxygen atoms in the ion's formula, giving an overall charge of −6. A number (+4) must then be assigned to the sulfur atom to make the overall charge equal −2. (+4) + (−6) = (−2), the charge on the sulfite ion.

3. In an oxidation/reduction (redox) reaction, the electrons lost by one compound always equals the electrons gained by another.

4. The term *oxidation* describes a reaction in which the oxidation number increases (as you examine the reaction from the reactant to the product side). In other words, when an ion is oxidized, it loses electrons and becomes more positive.

$Fe^{+2} \rightarrow Fe^{+3} + e^-$ Note in this example that iron is changing from the +2 ion to the +3 ion. Its oxidation number is increasing; therefore, by definition, it is being oxidized.

5. The term *reduction* describes a reaction in which the oxidation number decreases. In other words, when an ion is reduced, it gains electrons and becomes more negative.

$Br_2 + 2e^- \rightarrow 2Br^-$ Note in this example that bromine is changing from an oxidation state of zero (by definition, all "free" elements have an oxidation number of zero), to a charge of −1 (of course, there are 2 bromine ions so the overall charge is −2). To accomplish this change, molecular bromine is needed to *gain* 2 electrons; thus, it is *reduced.*

6. In all *redox* reactions, the oxidation and reduction occur simultaneously. There is always a conservation of both mass and charge.

7. The particle that is being oxidized is also known as the *reducing agent;* conversely, the particle that is being reduced is known as the *oxidizing agent.* In an electrolytic cell (a battery), oxidation takes place at the positive electrode (called the cathode), while reduction takes place at the negative electrode (called the anode).

Chemical Equilibrium

1. Chemical reactions may either release heat (exothermic) or absorb heat (endothermic).

2. The series of chemical steps involved in a chemical reaction is known as the *reaction mechanism.*

3. The minimum amount of energy needed to initiate a chemical reaction is known as *the activation energy.*

4. The total amount of heat released or absorbed is known as the *heat of reaction.* This heat is usually measured in kJ/mol and is given the symbol ΔH (Delta H) in heat of reaction expressions. A negative value for a ΔH measurement is assigned to exothermic reactions, while a positive ΔH value is assigned to endothermic reactions.

5. The rate of a chemical reaction as well as the equilibrium between reactants and products is based on numerous factors, including temperature, concentration of reactants, pressure, and the presence of catalysts and/or inhibitors. A knowledge of Le Châtelier's Principles is important in understanding equilibrium situations.

6. Chemical equilibrium represents a state of balance between reactants and products. Altering any of the experimental conditions forces the system to shift and establish a new equilibrium.

PHYSICS

Units of Measure

The metric system:

mega-	1,000,000	(10^6)
kilo-	1,000	(10^3)
deci-	0.1	(10^{-1})
centi-	0.01	(10^{-2})
milli-	0.001	(10^{-3})
micro-	0.000001	(10^{-6})
nano-	0.000000001	(10^{-9})

Basic units of measurement:

Metric System		English System
length	meter	foot
mass	gram	slug
volume	liter	quart
weight	Newton	pound

Unit Conversions

1 meter = 100 centimeters = 1000 millimeters

1 inch = 2.54 centimeters

1 meter = 39.37 inches

1 gram = 1000 milligrams

1 kilogram = 1000 grams = 2.2 lbs.

1 liter = 1000 milliliters = 1.06 quarts

1 gallon = 3.78 liters

Derived Units

Newton = 1 kg · m/s^2 The force necessary to accelerate one kilogram of mass at the rate of one meter per second squared

Joule = 1 N · m The energy required to exert one Newton of force is exerted through a distance of one meter

Watt = 1 J/s The power corresponding to energy being expended at the rate of one joule per second

Pascal = 1 N/m^2 Pressure corresponding to one Newton of force being exerted over one square meter of area

Volt = 1 J/C The potential difference equal to one joule of work done per coulomb of charge

Ampere = 1 C/s A measure of electric current equal to one coulomb of charge per second

Ohm = 1 V/A The electric resistance in a conductor such that a potential difference of one volt is required to produce a current of one ampere

Mechanics

1. Velocity: the time rate of change of the displacement of an object in a specified direction

2. Acceleration: the time rate of change of velocity with regard to magnitude or direction

3. Momentum: a quantity expressing the motion of a body equal to the product of its mass and its velocity

4. Force: the time rate of change of the momentum of a body equal to its mass times its acceleration

5. Gravity: the gravitational force between two masses is proportional to the product of the two masses divided by the square of the distance between them.

6. Kinetic energy: the energy of a moving object equal to one half its mass times the square of its velocity

7. Potential energy: the energy of an object with respect to the position of the object

8. Newton's three laws of motion:

   a. *Inertia:* An object will continue with the same speed and direction unless acted upon by an outside force.

   b. *Force:* When a force acts upon a body, it produces a change in momentum equal to its mass times its acceleration.

   c. *Reaction:* When a force acts upon a body, that body simultaneously exerts an equal and opposite force.

Wave motion

1. Transverse waves: waves in which the medium through which the waves travel oscillates in a direction perpendicular to the direction of the wave (e.g., ocean waves)

2. Longitudinal waves: waves in which the medium through which the waves travel oscillates in a direction parallel to the direction of the wave (e.g., sound waves)

3. Wavelength: the distance from the crest of one wave to the crest of the next

4. Frequency: the number of cycles per unit time of a wave or oscillation

5. Wave velocity: the velocity of a wave through a medium equal to its frequency times its wavelength

Light

1. Visible light: electromagnetic radiation that can be perceived by the eye. This includes the colors of the rainbow that are, in order of increasing frequency: red, orange, yellow, green, blue, indigo, and violet.

2. The electromagnetic spectrum: the entire continuous spectrum of all forms of electromagnetic radiation. These are, in order of increasing frequency: radio waves, microwaves, infrared, visible light, ultraviolet, X rays, and gamma rays.

3. The law of reflection: When light impinges on a reflecting surface, the angle of incidence is equal to the angle of reflection.

4. Refraction: When light travels from one medium into another, the light beam can be bent. The refracted angle is smaller if the medium is a higher optical density and larger if the medium is of lower optical density.

5. Dispersion: As light travels through a prism, each frequency (or color) is refracted by a slightly different amount. Each color emerges from the prism at a slightly different angle and is separated from the others.

Electricity and Magnetism

1. Charge: A charge can be positive or negative. When two like charges approach each other, they experience a repulsive force. When two unlike charges approach each other, they experience an attractive force.

2. Electromagnetism: A phenomenon whereby a magnetic field is produced by the circular motion of electrons.

3. Magnet: A body, usually made of iron or steel, which contains a permanent magnetic field. The magnetic field has two poles, north and south. Each atom in the magnet produces a tiny magnetic field due to the motion of it electrons. In certain substances, such as iron, these atoms can be aligned in response to an external magnetic field, producing a magnet that is stable unless disrupted by outside influences, such as excessive heat.

4. Magnetic force: There is a force of attraction between unlike poles and a repulsive force between like poles.

5. Charge moving through a magnetic field: Whenever a charge moves at right angles through a magnetic field, it experiences a force perpendicular to both the velocity of the charge and the magnetic field. If the charge moves parallel to the field, then no force is experienced.

Sound

1. Sound waves: As sound waves travel through a medium, they cause a compression and refraction of the medium. The speed of sound through a medium depends on the density and the temperature of the medium.

2. Energy transmission: As sound waves pass through a medium, material is not transported; instead, energy is transported by the collision of one molecule with the next. The medium vibrates back and forth but does not travel with the wave.

EARTH AND SPACE SCIENCE

The field of earth science is broad and within it there are many disciplines or specialties. Geology is probably the largest area of earth science. Geology is the study of the solid Earth. There are many areas of geology related to the sciences of physics, chemistry, biology, and astronomy. Any science that seeks to understand the Earth or what it was like in the past can be considered an earth science. Earth scientists study the rocks that make up the Earth, the atmosphere, climate and meteorology, the history of life, how the Earth formed and its evolution, the Earth's place in the solar system, water, and the oceans.

Geology

1. The Earth is a zoned or layered body, with each layer having characteristic physical and chemical properties. The outermost layer is the crust: It is the thinnest layer, with a thickness of 5 to 75 km. It is composed of rocks made up predominantly of silicate (silicon and oxygen) minerals. It is also the least dense layer, with a density of from 2.5 to 3.0 g/cm^3. Below the crust is the mantle; it extends about halfway to the center of the Earth and is also composed of silicate minerals rich in magnesium and iron. It is denser than the crust, with a density of 3.3 to 5.0 g/cm^3. The next layer is the outer core; it is liquid and is composed mostly of iron and nickel. The inner core is also mostly iron and nickel but is solid, with a density of 12.6 to 13.0 g/cm^3.

2. Rocks are classified into three types: igneous, sedimentary, and metamorphic. Rocks exposed at the surface undergo the processes of weathering and erosion. Weathering is the process whereby rocks break down into smaller and smaller pieces. This process occurs as a result of mechanical action, such as water freezing and thawing in cracks of rocks, breaking them apart, or by chemical changes of the minerals, such as the formation of clay by the weathering of the mineral feldspar. The process of erosion occurs when water or wind transports the weathered material.

3. The first type of rock is igneous rock. Igneous rocks form from the crystallization of magma or molten rock. Magma erupted from volcanoes is termed lava and produces volcanic igneous rocks, which cool quickly and have a fine-grained texture. Basalt is such a volcanic rock, which is formed from lava erupted from a volcano. Magma that cools below the surface produces plutonic igneous rock, which has a coarser texture (with larger crystal size) than volcanic rocks. Granite is the most common type of plutonic rock.

4. An important product of weathered rocks is soils. Almost all life on land is dependent upon these materials, directly or indirectly. Soils are a mixture of weathering residues (primarily sand, silt, and clay), decaying organic matter, living creatures (bacteria, fungi, worms, and insects), air, and moisture. The thickness of soils can vary from a few centimeters to many meters thick. Factors that affect the type of soil formed are primarily the rock material from which it forms, the climate (temperature and moisture), and the terrain. Soils may take hun-

dreds to thousands of years to form and are very susceptible to degradation through poor management and use by human activity. Once severely damaged, a soil is virtually lost to any productive use. Desertification is the process, mostly from human use, whereby a productive soil in a semiarid area becomes unproductive and desert conditions prevail.

5. Sedimentary rocks are formed when sediments of gravel, sand, silt, and clay particles are deposited in layers and from compaction transforms sediment into sedimentary rocks. Plants and animals that were living at the time can be buried in the sediment, and parts of their anatomy can be preserved as fossils. Sedimentary rocks and any included fossils can yield information about the past depositional environment.

6. When heat and pressure are exerted on rocks, the result is metamorphic rock. When rocks undergo heating and pressurization, metamorphic rock results. For example, the sedimentary rock shale will become slate, or sandstone will become quartzite.

7. Plate tectonics is the theory of how the Earth operates and is a unifying theory of geology. It explains the formation of mountains and their location, as well as the shape and locations of the present continents. The outer shell of the Earth is relatively brittle and cold. It is broken into about nine major semi-rigid plates. There are two types of crust — continental and oceanic. Continental crust is less dense (2.7 g/cm^3) than oceanic crust (3.0 g/cm^3). Most geologic activity—such as earthquakes, igneous activity (volcanoes), and

mountain building—occurs along the plate boundaries. At the boundaries, plates spread apart, collide, or slide past each other. The outer crustal rocks are less dense than the underlying mantle rocks. Also, mantle rocks may more easily behave ductilely or plastically—that is, they deform by a type of flow rather than by breaking or cracking like most crustal rocks.

8. Faults are extensive cracks in rocks where they slip or slide past each other. This motion is not steady but occurs in sudden jolts. The result of one of these "slips" causes large vibrations and tremors at the surface of the Earth, producing an earthquake.

9. The continents all are ringed by continental margins, which are regions where the continents meet the oceans. The continental margins are in turn made up of a gently dipping continental slope, a more steeply inclined continental slope, and (in some locations) a more gently dipping continental rise. The continental slope extends outward from the coast to a depth of about 100 meters. There it gives way to the continental slope. The continental slope is the true edge of the continents, as the sea actually extends up onto the continents. Abyssal plains are locations that are of a relatively constant depth of about 4 to 5 km. Other common features of note on the sea floor include sea mounts, ridges, and plateaus. Sea mounts are submarine volcanic peaks: Should they reach above sea level, they form islands. Mid-ocean ridges form the longest linear feature on the planet surface. Typically, mid-ocean ridges rise about 2.5 km above the surrounding ocean floor and are 2,000 km wide. They are

a location of intense seismic and volcanic activity. It is here that new ocean crust is created as the sea floor spreads apart. Ocean trenches are features where the depth reaches 11,000 meters (averaging about 8,000 meters). Trenches are long and relatively narrow (about 100 km). They may be found along a continental margin—the Peru-Chile Trench extends along western South America—or they may be found away from the margins as, for example, the Marianas Trench in the western Pacific Ocean. At trenches, two plates of the Earth's crust are coming together, and one (always oceanic crust) is descending back into the mantle.

Hydrology

1. Hydrology is the study of water at the surface and in the ground. The hydrologic cycle describes the movement of water on and within the Earth. Reservoirs are locations where water is available for use. Ninety-eight percent of the water on Earth is found in the oceans. Most water that falls as precipitation comes ultimately from oceans. Water is taken into the atmosphere by evaporation in the form of water vapor. Condensation occurs when the air is saturated, vapor condenses to water, or freezes into ice crystals. The result is clouds and fog. Precipitation occurs when the droplets or ice crystals become too heavy to stay suspended in the atmosphere and they fall toward the surface. Precipitation over land has several fates. Some water will stay aboveground, where it collects together to form runoff. Eventually enough collects to form streams; these in turn

feed rivers. Some runoff may go into lakes. Water soaks into the ground by infiltration, and it becomes groundwater. The level below which water in the ground is saturated is termed the water table. The depth of the water table depends on the climate of the area, as well as the terrain and the nature of the rocks. In general, groundwater flows from areas of higher topography to areas of lower topography and flows toward the oceans, just as do rivers. The movement of groundwater is much slower than that of surface water. On the surface or from the soil, some water evaporates into the atmosphere again. In addition, plants take up water from the soil and lose water by transpiration through the stomates of leaves. Animals also lose water by respiration, perspiration, and urination. Evapotranspiration (evaporation plus transpiration) is the term describing the collective transfer of water back into the atmosphere over the land surface.

2. Layers of rock and sediment that contain water and allow it to be pumped out are called aquifers. An example might be a poorly cemented sandstone. An aquiclude is a rock through which water is unable to flow. Examples of an aquiclude are shale and granite. Because the movement of groundwater is so slow, aquifers are very susceptible to contamination from pollutants. Contamination of groundwater makes it unusable and very difficult to clean up. Most efforts involving groundwater contamination involve monitoring the movement of the contaminant and trying to control the spreading of it by studying the effects of pumping nearby wells.

The Solar System

1. The sun is the largest body of the solar system and is also the center of it. Its diameter is 109 Earth diameters, or 135 million km. Yet, because of the gaseous nature of the sun, its density is less than the solid Earth's, very closely approximating the density of water. The sun's composition is 90 percent hydrogen, almost 10 percent helium, and minor amounts of other, heavier elements. The sun has a surface temperature of 6000°C and an interior temperature estimated at 15×10^6 °C. The source of the sun's energy is nuclear fusion. In the interior of the sun, a nuclear reaction occurs, converting four hydrogen nuclei (protons) into a nucleus of helium. In this nuclear reaction, some of the mass of the hydrogen nuclei is converted into energy. This results in a tremendous amount of energy being released.

2. The formation of the solar system occurred approximately 5 billion years ago. The most accepted theory of the origin of the sun and planets of the solar system is the nebular hypothesis. This hypothesis holds that a nebula or cloud of gas existed, consisting of approximately 80 percent hydrogen, 15 percent helium, and a few percent of the heavier elements. This cloud began to collapse or condense together under the influence of its own gravity. At the same time, the cloud had a rotational component to it, and as its collapse continued, the rotational velocity became faster. This rotation caused the nebula to form a disklike structure, and within the disk, small nuclei developed from which the planets would eventually form. Most of the matter, however,

became concentrated in the center, where eventually the sun formed. As more and more matter collapsed inward, the temperature of this central mass began to rise due to compression of the gases. As the collapse continued, gravitational attraction got stronger, resulting in the compression of the hydrogen gas with the consequence of heating it. Eventually the temperature became hot enough to begin nuclear fusion. The sun contains 99.85 percent of the mass of the solar system. The rest is found within the planets, moons, asteroids, and comets.

3. There are nine planets in the solar system. They are, in order of increasing distance from the sun: Mercury, Venus, Earth, Mars, Jupiter, Saturn, Uranus, Neptune, and Pluto. Based upon their gross physical characteristics, the planets fall within two groups: the terrestrial planets (Mercury, Venus, Earth, and Mars) and the Jovian (Jupiterlike) planets (Jupiter, Saturn, Uranus, and Neptune). Pluto is not included in either category because its position at the far edge of the solar system and its small size make its true nature a mystery. The terrestrial planets are so called because of their Earthlike characteristics: all four are composed primarily of solid, rocky material. Size is the most obvious difference between the two groups. Earth, the largest terrestrial planet at a diameter of 12,751 km, is only one-quarter the size of the smallest Jovian planet, Neptune, at 46,500 km. Mercury is the smallest planet, with a diameter of 4854 km. The largest planet, Jupiter, has a diameter of 143,000 km.

4. Other characteristics in which the two groups markedly differ include mass, density, and composition. The Jovian planets are much more massive compared to the terrestrial planets. Earth is the most massive terrestrial planet. Venus is about 8/10 as massive. Mercury is the least massive planet at about 0.06 times the mass of Earth. Jupiter is the most massive planet at 318 times the Earth. Uranus is the least massive Jovian planet, at 14.6 times the mass of Earth. The densities of the terrestrial planets average about 5 g/cm^3, or five times the density of water. The Jovian planets, despite their large masses, have an average density of about 1.5 g/cm^3. Compositional variations are responsible for the differences in densities.

5. The materials of which both groups are composed can be divided into three groups. They are gases, rocks, and ices and are based upon their melting points. Gases are those materials with melting points close to absolute zero or $-273°C$ (Absolute zero is the lowest theoretical temperature). Hydrogen and helium are the gases. The rocky materials are made primarily of silicate minerals and iron and have melting points greater than 700°C. The ices have intermediate melting points and include ammonia (NH_4), carbon dioxide(CO_2), methane (CH_4), and water (H_2O).

6. The terrestrial planets consist mainly of rocky and metallic material with minor amounts of gases and ices. The Jovian planets consist of a large percentage of hydrogen and helium with varying amounts of ices. This composition accounts for their low densities. All the Jovian planets are thought to contain a core of rocky and metallic material as much as the terrestrial planets.

7. Finally, the atmospheres are the last major difference. The Jovian planets have thick, dense atmospheres of hydrogen and helium, while the terrestrial planets have comparatively thin atmospheres. Gravity on the Jovian planets is much greater than the terrestrial planets, so they have been able to hold on to the abundant hydrogen and helium. The terrestrial planets, however, have much weaker gravity fields and probably lost all their original hydrogen-helium atmospheres early in their history to the solar winds. On Earth, a second atmosphere formed from outgassing (loss of gases during volcanic activity).

The Atmosphere

1. Study of the Earth's atmosphere is a very important part of the earth sciences. All life on Earth is dependent on the atmosphere. The composition of the atmosphere is fairly simple. Nitrogen gas (N_2) comprises about 78 percent, oxygen (O_2) makes up about 21 percent, and argon (Ar) about 0.93 percent. One gas that forms a very small component in terms of abundance but has a big impact on weather and climate is carbon dioxide (CO_2). Its abundance is about 0.035 percent.

2. As mentioned before, carbon dioxide has a very low abundance but a big impact on weather and climate. Along with some other gases, it absorbs infrared radiation going from the Earth's surface out into space, resulting in the trapping of heat in the atmosphere. This process is known as the greenhouse effect. It is natural and is an important aspect of our atmosphere. Without it, our atmosphere would not be warm enough to sustain life as we know it, and our planet would probably be too cold for liquid water to exist. The problem is that human activity over the past century is increasing the amount of carbon dioxide in the atmosphere as a result of the extensive use of fossil fuels, such as petroleum and coal, and the burning of rainforests. Over the last fifty years, carbon dioxide levels have been rising. The threat is that this increase may cause the atmosphere to become warmer. This effect is termed *global warming*. If global warming is occurring, the changes could have significant consequences to human culture. Currently it appears that the temperature of the atmosphere is rising. It has not, however, been shown that this rise in temperature is completely the result of the increase of carbon dioxide or that it is out of the range of normal global temperature fluctuations. It also has not been shown what the impact will be of the continued use of fossil fuels and the resulting increase in carbon dioxide. Another way human activities have an impact upon the atmosphere concerns ozone (O_3). Ozone is a gas found in the upper atmosphere where it functions as a filter of harmful ultraviolet radiation from the sun. Without it, life could not exist on the surface of our planet. Human use of chemicals called chloroflourocarbons (CFCs) as refrigerants and as propellants for aerosol sprays has affected this layer. CFCs go into the stratosphere and cause the breakdown of ozone, thereby reducing its concentration. There have already been international treaties signed limiting the use of CFCs to reduce the threat to the ozone layer.

3. The Earth's atmosphere is divided into four layers based on temperature gradient. The bottom layer is known as the troposphere. It extends to an altitude of approximately 8 to 18 km and is characterized by an average decrease in temperature of 6.5°C per kilometer increase in altitude. It contains approximately 80 percent of the mass of the atmosphere. Virtually all clouds and precipitation form in and are restricted to this layer. The vertical mixing of this layer is extensive and is the layer in which "weather" occurs. Above the troposphere and extending to about 50 km is the stratosphere. Here the temperature remains constant with increasing altitude to about 20 km, then begins to increase with altitude. The stratosphere is important because it contains ozone (O_3), the gas that absorbs most ultraviolet light, keeping it from reaching the Earth's surface and protecting life on the surface. The mesosphere lies above the stratosphere and here again temperatures decrease with increasing altitude. At about 80 km the temperature is approximately −90°C. The layer above, with no well-defined upper limit, is the thermosphere. Here temperatures rise again due to the absorption of short wave radiation by air molecules. Temperatures rise to 1000 °C. Even though temperatures are very high, it would not feel hot if you were exposed to this air. Temperature is defined as the average kinetic energy of the atoms present in what is being measured. Molecules of air here are moving very fast with a high kinetic energy and therefore have a high temperature. However, here the air is so thin that anything exposed has very few molecules striking it, resulting in little transfer of energy.

4. Energy from the sun is the most important control over the weather and climate of the Earth. Solar radiation accounts for virtually all the energy that heats the surface of the Earth, drives the ocean currents, and creates winds. It is therefore necessary to understand what causes the time and space variations in the amount of solar radiation received in order to understand basic atmospheric processes. The Earth in space has two principal motions: rotation and revolution. Rotation is the spinning of the Earth about its axis—the line running through the poles. The Earth rotates once every 24 hours, producing the daily cycle of daylight and darkness. Half the Earth is always experiencing daylight, and the other half is always experiencing darkness. Revolution is the motion of the Earth orbiting around the sun. The distance between the Earth and sun averages about 150 million km. The Earth's orbit is not circular but is slightly elliptical. Each year on about January 3, the Earth is 147 km from the sun, closer than any other time of the year. On about July 4, the Earth is 152 km from the sun, farther away than any other time of the year. Even though the distance from the sun varies during the course of the year, this results in only slight variation in the amount of energy received from the sun and has little consequence when explaining major seasonal temperature variations. Consider that the Earth is closer to the sun during the Northern Hemisphere winter.

5. Probably the most noticeable aspect of seasonal variation is the difference in the length of daylight. Days are longest during the summer and shortest during the winter. However, this fact does not account fully for the seasons. Another factor that may not be as noticeable is the height above the horizon of the sun at noon. On the summer solstice, the sun is highest overhead at noon. It gradually retreats lower and lower in the sky from this day through the fall, until, on the winter solstice, it is at its lowest noon position in the sky. It then begins daily to get higher and higher in the sky again, repeating the cycle. This altitude of the sun affects the angle at which the sun's rays strike the surface of the Earth, resulting in a difference in the intensity of solar radiation received from the sun. This results in a seasonal variation in solar heating. The more direct rays of summer result in more energy being received on the Earth's surface in the hemisphere experiencing summer. In winter, when the rays are less direct, less energy is received in the winter hemisphere, for as the rays of the sun become less direct, the energy is spread over a greater area. This can be demonstrated with a flashlight, noting that the direct beam (of vertical rays) is brighter in a smaller area than an inclined beam, which is less bright, illuminating a larger area. Also, the oblique rays must travel through more atmosphere before reaching the Earth's surface, which means that they have more chance of being filtered, scattered, or reflected before reaching the Earth's surface.

6. What causes this yearly fluctuation in the angle of the sun? It is a result of the continual change in orientation of the Earth with respect to the sun. The Earth's axis is not perpendicular to the ecliptic (the plane of orbit around the sun), but is inclined at an angle of about 23½° from the perpendicular. As the Earth orbits around the sun, the axis of the Earth remains pointed in the same direction (toward the North Star). As a result, the angle at which the sun's rays strike a given location on the Earth is continually changing. On one day during the year (the summer solstice), the Northern Hemisphere is leaning 23½° toward the sun, and vertical rays of the noon sun strike the Tropic of Cancer, 23½° north latitude. Six months later (the winter solstice), it is leaning 23½° away from the sun, and vertical rays of the noon sun strike the Earth at the Tropic of Capricorn, 23½° south latitude. At the vernal and autumnal equinoxes (first day of spring and autumn, respectively), vertical rays of the noon sun strike at the equator.

7. Weather occurs as a result of the unequal heating of the Earth's surface. The strongest radiation from the sun is received around the equator and the poles receive the least. There is also a difference resulting from the fact that the oceans and continents do not heat up equally. The atmosphere is constantly acting to redistribute this energy from the equator toward the poles. Winds also result from the unequal heating of the surface, moving from areas of high pressure to areas of low pressure. High-pressure centers occur when cool air sinks toward the surface and spreads laterally outward. In low pressure centers, air is warmer and rises upward in the troposphere. Fronts form at the boundaries of air masses that have different temperature and moisture characteristics; fronts are generally sites of active weather, such as storms and precipitation.

8. All air contains some water vapor. In order for the water vapor to condense, it must become saturated in the air. Saturation occurs mainly as a result of air cooling in some way. Warm air can hold more moisture than can cold air. The cooling of air is accomplished mainly along fronts where warm air is pushed upward over cooler air, or cool air is shoved under warmer air. As air rises, it expands due to the decrease in pressure. As air expands, it also cools. If there is enough moisture, condensation will occur and clouds will form. Clouds are formed of tiny ice crystals or of water droplets suspended in the air. If the ice crystals or water droplets become large and heavy enough to fall through the air, precipitation may occur. Cooling of air can also occur

along mountain ranges where the air is forced upward to get over the mountain. This phenomenon is termed the *orographic effect.* It results in the windward side of the mountains receiving a greater amount of precipitation than the leeward side. The leeward, or desert side, is referred to as being in a rain shadow.

There is no need to memorize any of the preceding information. We have merely provided it for you as an overview of the basic areas of science that are covered on the ACT. It is helpful to read through this section at your leisure to have at least some understanding of terms that are used throughout the Science Reasoning portion of the test. It will also serve you well to check your answers against the appropriate material in this section if you are having a problem understanding some of the test material.

PRACTICE QUESTIONS

Now that you have reviewed the strategies for taking the test and have had a chance to analyze the different question types, it would be a good idea to practice with some additional questions. The following Science Reasoning questions are divided into the three basic types of questions: Research Summaries, Data Representation, and Conflicting Viewpoints. Answer all of the questions and then check your answers at the end of each section. The key to success on the ACT test or, for that matter, any test is to practice, practice, practice.

RESEARCH SUMMARY PRACTICE
Passage 1

To investigate the hypothesis that Ohm's law (V = IR) is obeyed at different temperatures, three experiments were performed:

Experiment 1

A circuit was set up in which a resistor of 6 ohms was connected to a battery of 12V. The current through the resistor was measured at 20 degrees Celsius and found to be 2 amps.

Experiment 2

Another circuit was set up in which various resistors were connected to a battery of 6V. The temperature was kept constant. It was found that the greater the resistance, the lower the current through the resistor. The current was found to be inversely proportional to the resistance.

Experiment 3

A third circuit was set up so that a resistor of 5 ohms was connected to a battery of 10V. The temperature was allowed to vary, and the current through the resistor was measured at each temperature. It was found that the higher the temperature, the lower the current.

1. What conclusion can be drawn from Experiment 1 alone?

    A. Ohm's law is obeyed, independent of temperature.
    B. Ohm's law is obeyed only at a temperature of 20 degrees.
    C. Ohm's law is obeyed for at least one temperature.
    D. Resistance varies with temperature.

2. From Experiment 3 alone, we can best conclude that:

    F. Ohm's law is obeyed at various temperatures
    G. Ohm's law is not obeyed at various temperatures
    H. as the temperature increases, the voltage across the battery decreases
    J. none of the above

3. Which would be considered a controlled variable in the experiments?

    A. the temperature
    B. the resistance
    C. the voltage
    D. the current

4. Which experiment served as a control?

   F. Experiment 1

   G. Experiment 2

   H. Experiment 3

   J. There was no control

5. From Experiments 2 and 3, it could be concluded that:

   A. Ohm's law is not obeyed at higher temperatures

   B. as the temperature of a resistor increases its resistance increases

   C. any circuit at 40 degrees will have a lower current than any circuit at 20 degrees

   D. current is directly proportional to resistance.

6. From all three experiments we can say that:

   F. for a given voltage as the resistance increases the current decreases

   G. the current is directly proportional to the temperature

   H. Ohm's law is invalid at high temperatures

   J. Ohm's law is not true

Passage 2

It has been observed that by various processes, sedimentary particles (gravel, sand, silt, and clay) get deposited in horizontal layers or strata. It is inferred that these layers later become lithified, or turned into sedimentary rock. Often animals and plants that were living at the time these layers were being deposited become buried, and their remains are turned into fossils. A distinctive unit of rock layers is called a formation. Fossils can be used to correlate layers from one location to another. Breaks in the sequence can be caused by intervals of erosion by wind, water, or glacial ice. A geologist studied the sequence of rocks at three locations to determine the succession of rock formations in an area. The findings are given in the following tables.

Table 1. Sequence of Rock Formations at Location 1

Layer	Description
Sandstone	No fossils
1′ gray ash bed	Distinctive volcanic deposit
Tan shale	
Limestone	Wide variety of marine animals

Table 2. Sequence of Rock Formations at Location 2 (5 miles from Location 1)

Layer	Description
Red sandstone	Reptile tracks
Black shale	Few marine fossils
Sandstone	No fossils
1′ gray ash bed	Distinctive volcanic deposit
Tan shale	

Table 3. Sequence of Rock Formations at Location 3 (10 miles from Location 1)

Layer	Description
Sandstone	No fossils
1′ gray ash bed	Distinctive volcanic deposit
Limestone	Wide variety of marine animals

7. From the sequence of rock formation at Locations 1 and 2, what might the sequence be for the area if all rocks were present?

A. tan shale, limestone, gray ash bed, sandstone, black shale, red sandstone

B. limestone, tan shale, gray ash bed, sandstone, black shale, red sandstone

C. limestone, tan shale, gray ash bed, sandstone, tan shale, sandstone

D. tan shale, gray ash bed, sandstone, black shale, red sandstone, limestone

8. The sequence of rocks in Location 3 is similar, but not identical to, the sequence in Locations 1 and 2. What might be a possible reason for the difference?

F. erosion

G. lithification

H. solution

J. compaction

9. You are at another location and you observe a sequence of rock formations with the sequence of sandstone, 1' gray ash bed, sandstone, and black shale. Would this sequence have been deposited at the same time as the sediment in the other locations?

A. No, because the sequence does not match exactly.

B. No, because even though there is the same ash bed, it could be from another volcano.

C. Yes, because the ash from the volcano would have been widely dispersed, making this sequence equivalent.

D. Yes, because they both contain sandstone and black shale.

10. What formation was most likely deposited on land?

F. black shale

G. limeston

H. gray ash bed

J. red sandstone

11. In order to better correlate strata from one location to another using fossils, it would be desirable for a fossil to have this characteristic:

A. a species that existed only for a short period of time before its extinction

B. a species that is very common and found around the world

C. a species that has existed for a long period of time before its extinction

D. It does not matter how long a species existed to use it for correlation.

12. If you wanted to find a level in the sequence that was deposited at one time, what rock formation would probably be the most likely one you could use?

F. limestone

G. black shale

H. red sandstone

J. gray ash bed

Passage 3

To investigate the nature of light and matter, and to determine if light and matter consist of waves or particles, the following experiments were performed.

Experiment 1

Red light (λ=700 nm) from a laser beam was allowed to pass through 2 slits simultaneously and projected onto a screen a known distance away. An interference pattern of alternating bright and dark fringes was seen. As the screen was moved farther away from the slits, the separation between the bright and dark fringes increased.

Experiment 2

Light of various wavelengths was allowed to pass through the same two slits and projected onto a screen. Throughout the experiment the screen was kept a fixed distance from the slits. It was noted that a similar pattern of light and dark fringes was seen on the screen as in Experiment 1. As the wavelength of the light got shorter and shorter, the distance beween the fringes got smaller and smaller. At very short wavelengths, the fringes are so close together that it is difficult to observe any dark fringes; instead, bright spots are observed opposite the slits.

Experiment 3

Electrons (low-mass particles) are sent through the same apparatus as in Experiment 2. A pattern of alternate bright and dark fringes is seen. Higher-mass particles such as protons are sent through the slits, and the separation between the fringes is seen to be much smaller. Very high-mass particles are sent through and no fringes are seen at all, but a bright spot on the screen opposite each slit is seen.

13. What conclusion can be drawn from Experiment 1?

   A.   Light is a wave. It showed wave characteristics such as interference.

   B.   Light may act as a wave or particle, depending on how widely separated the slits are.

   C.   Light is a particle. Its path was changed as it went through the slits.

   D.   The experiment was inconclusive with regard to the wave or particle nature of light.

14. Which experiment served as a control?

   F.   Experiment 1

   G.   Experiment 2

   H.   Experiment 3

   J.   There was no control.

15. What conclusion can be drawn from Experiments 1 and 2 alone?

   A.   Light acts like a wave.

   B.   Light acts as a particle.

   C.   The shorter the wavelength of light, the more it acts like a particle and less like a wave.

   D.   The shorter the wavelength of light, the more it acts like a wave and less like a particle.

16. From Experiment 3 we can conclude that:

   F.   electrons are waves

   G.   electrons act like waves, and protons act like particles

   H.   matter has a dual nature. The lower the mass, the more it acts like a wave and less like a particle.

   J.   No conclusion can be made regarding the wave or particle nature of subatomic particles.

17. In Experiment 3, if the screen was moved farther away from the slits you would expect:

   A. the bright and dark fringes to disappear

   B. the electrons to behave less like waves

   C. the fringes to be more widely separated

   D. the fringes to be more closely spaced

18. The best conclusion that can be drawn from all three experiments is that:

   F. there is no relation between light and matter

   G. matter is condensed light

   H. both matter and light have a particle nature and a wave nature

   J. neither matter nor light has a particle or a wave nature

ANSWERS TO RESEARCH SUMMARY PRACTICE QUESTIONS

1. The correct answer is C. Experiment 1 simply verified Ohm's law at one temperature. No conclusions can be reached for other temperatures.

2. The correct answer is J. Nothing is said in Experiment 3 about how much the current varied with temperature. You do not know if the resistance changed proportionately and the law was obeyed or if the law broke down.

3. The correct answer is C. The voltage is kept constant throughout all experiments.

4. The correct answer is F. Experiment 1 establishes that Ohm's law is valid for at least one temperature.

5. The correct answer is B. Experiment 2 shows that for a given voltage, as resistance increases current decreases. In Experiment 3, as the temperature increased, the current decreased, so it may be concluded that the current decreased because the resistance increased.

6. The correct answer is F. From all three experiments, it is shown that both higher resistance and higher temperature result in lower current. The resistance must increase as the temperature increases.

7. The correct answer is B. The order of rock formations overlaps at these two locations. By lining up the equivalent units, an overall sequence is determined.

8. The correct answer is F. If a unit is missing in an area, it could have been eroded before the deposition of the next unit.

9. The correct answer is C. Volcanic rocks are dispersed widely in an instant in geologic time. Layers of sedimentary rocks, though laterally greatly continuous, still may have taken 100,000 or even 1 million years to accumulate, making them poor indicators of a time line. Because the ash bed is so distinctive, it probably is equivalent to the other locations.

10. The correct answer is J. The red sandstone was probably deposited on land because it contains preserved reptile tracks.

11. The correct answer is A. In order to determine that two or more layers are correlated or deposited at the same time, you would want to use a species that existed only for a short time.

12. The correct answer is J; the gray ash bed for reasons stated in Table #3.

13. The correct answer is A. This experiment showed the wave nature of light. As the light went through the two slits, it diffracted and showed interference.

14. The correct answer is F.

15. The correct answer is C. As the wavelength of light got shorter, the interference pattern was less noticeable and the less the wave nature was evident.

16. The correct answer is H. Low-mass electrons clearly exhibited wave characteristics like interference, while this behavior became less evident with higher-mass objects.

17. The correct answer is C. Particles such as electrons clearly exhibited wave characteristics. As shown in Experiment 1, the farther the screen the greater the separation of the fringes.

18. The correct answer is H. From Experiment 2, the shorter the wavelength, the less wavelike light appeared. The longer the wavelength, the more wavelike light appeared. In Experiment 3, the lower the mass, the more wavelike matter appeared; the greater the mass, the more particlelike matter appeared.

DATA REPRESENTATION PRACTICE

Passage 1

The Iowa Department of Health was notified of a husband, wife, and son who had become ill about one hour after eating dinner. All three had symptoms that included nausea, vomiting, diarrhea, and fever. The three were treated and sent home. All three recovered within forty-eight hours of the onset of illness.

Table 1. Data on Food Eaten and Development of Food Poisoning

Food Eaten	Husband	Wife	Daughter	Son	Dog
Fish	x	x		x	x
Pasta	x	x	x		
Salad	x	x	x	x	
Wine	x	x		x	
Water	x	x	x	x	x
Ill	yes	yes	no	yes	yes

1. Which of the following was the likely cause of the illness?

   A. water
   B. pasta
   C. wine
   D. fish

2. If the dog had not become ill, what would be the likely conclusion?

   F. Dogs don't show the same signs and symptoms as people.
   G. The wine caused the illness.
   H. The fish caused the illness.
   J. The water caused the illness.

3. If the entire family and their dog had become ill, what would be the logical conclusion?

   A. The fish caused the illness.
   B. The pasta caused the illness.
   C. The salad caused the illness.
   D. The water caused the illness.

4. If the parents and children became ill but the dog did not, what would be the likely conclusion?

   F. The fish caused the illness.
   G. The pasta caused the illness.
   H. The wine caused the illness.
   J. The water caused the illness.

5. If the dog became ill but the parents and children did not, what would be the best conclusion?

A. The fish caused the illness.
B. The pasta caused the illness.
C. The combination of fish and water caused the illness.
D. The food and water did not cause the illness.

6. If the wife and son had consumed no wine, which of the following is the best conclusion?

F. The wine caused the illness.
G. The fish caused the illness.
H. The pasta caused the illness.
J. The water caused the illness.

Passage 2

Three test tubes, each of which contains an unknown solid (and a thermometer), are placed in an oil bath at 3.0 degrees Celsius and slowly heated to determine an approximate melting and boiling point for each substance. The following table represents thermometer readings in each of the test tubes (at 1-minute intervals) as the oil bath is heated. None of the unknown solids sublimes (heated into vapor and allowed to solidify again). On the Celsius scale, water melts at 0 degrees and boils at 100 degrees.

Time in minutes	Temp Un- known "A"	Temp Un- known "B"	Temp Un- known "C"
1 Minute	3.0°C	3.0°C	3.0°C
2 Minutes	5.2	5.2	5.2
3 Minutes	5.4	5.4	6.5
4 Minutes	5.4	5.4	8.3
5 Minutes	5.5	5.6	11.6
6 Minutes	5.5	5.6	15.8
7 Minutes	5.4	5.6	16.6
8 Minutes	7.8	7.9	16.5
9 Minutes	21.5	21.8	16.6
10 Minutes	33.5	33.5	16.6
11 Minutes	54.6	54.6	34.9
12 Minutes	75.6	75.6	75.6
13 Minutes	80.1	90.7	90.7
14 Minutes	80.2	110.7	110.7
15 Minutes	80.1	146.8	118.1
16 Minutes	80.2	154.2	118.2
17 Minutes	125.5	165.2	118.1
18 Minutes	155.6	177.8	155.6
19 Minutes	182.6	182.6	182.6

7. Based on the data collected:

A. it is impossible to determine approximate melting and boiling points for substance A
B. all three chemicals have approximately the same boiling point
C. solids A and B have approximately the same melting and boiling points
D. solids A and B have approximately the same melting but different boiling points

8. Unknown solid A:

F. has a higher melting point than C
G. has a boiling point lower than water
H. is the same as solid B
J. is probably water

9. The boiling point of unknown B:

    A.   is 5.6 degrees Celsius

    B.   is the same as unknown A

    C.   cannot be determined from these data

    D.   is higher, but similar to the boiling point of unknown C.

10. The approximate boiling point of unknown C is:

    F.   impossible to determine from the data collected

    G.   16.5 degrees Celsius

    H.   90.7 degrees Celsius

    J.   118.2 degrees Celsius.

11. If unknown substance B is collected as a gas, then cooled, at what approximate temperature will the gas condense into a liquid?

    A.   80.1 degrees Celsius

    B.   182.6 degrees Celsius

    C.   118.2 degrees Celsius

    D.   impossible to determine from the data collected

12. Benzene is a chemical that freezes in the 5 to 6 degree range and boils at a temperature lower than the boiling point of water. If one of the unknown chemicals is benzene, then:

    F.   either A or B could be benzene

    G.   either B or C could be benzene

    H.   unknown A could be benzene

    J.   unknown C could be benzene

Passage 3

Several researchers perform an experiment on the electric properties of an unknown substance.

The first researcher connects the substance to an electric circuit, as shown in Figure 1. He measures the current I of the

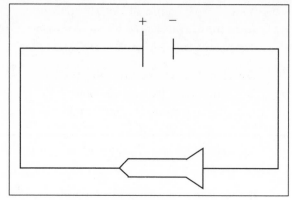

Figure 1.

circuit versus the voltage, keeping the temperature constant.

2. A second researcher hooks up the same substance in the reverse direction and performs another experiment in which he measures the current versus the temperature of the system as shown in Figure 2.

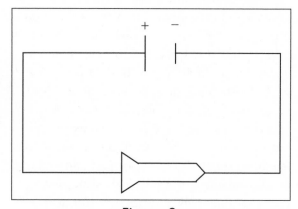

Figure 2.

The results of these experiments are summarized in Tables 1 and 2, respectively.

Table 1.

V (voltage) in volts	I (current) in amps
10.0	2.0
12.0	2.4
14.0	2.8
16.0	3.2

Table 2.

T (Temp) in °C	I (current) in amps
20.0	2.0
30.0	1.9
40.0	1.8
50.0	1.7

13. Based on the information provided, one could safely assume that:

   A. V is directly proportional to I in all circumstances
   B. V is inversely proportional to I provided the temperature remains constant
   C. V is directly proportional to the temperature
   D. none of the above

14. The reason the current decreased in Experiment 2 is that

   F. the temperature increased
   G. the substance was connected in the reverse direction
   H. the voltage was changed
   J. either F, G, or H. There is insufficient information to decide which one

15. Assuming that the substance was connected, as in Figure 1, and the voltage was held constant, then one could say that:

   A. if the temperature increased, the current would also increase
   B. if the temperature increased, the current would stay the same
   C. if the current remained constant, the temperature would not have changed
   D. if the voltage were constant, then the current would also remain constant

16. In order to develop an equation that relates V, I, and T, then one would, in addition to what has already been done:

   F. connect the substance, as in Figure 2, and reperform Experiment 2 at various voltages
   G. connect the substance, as in Figure 1, and reperform Experiment 1 at various temperatures
   H. perform both F and G
   J. do nothing. There already is enough data to relate V < I and T in all circumstances.

17. One could safely say that:

   A. I is directly proportional to T when connected in the reverse position
   B. I is inversely proportional to T when connected in the reverse position
   C. I is directly proportional to V when connected in the forward position
   D. I is inversely proportional to V when connected in the forward position

18. Based on the information provided, one could say that:

   F. the current will drop to zero when the temperature reaches 220°C, provided the voltage remained constant
   G. one would not notice any difference in the experimental results no matter in which direction the substance was connected
   H. if the substance was connected in the forward position, the current would be 4.8 amps if the voltage was 24 volts, provided the temperature did not vary
   J. none of the above

Answers to Data Representation Questions

1. The correct answer is D. The daughter had no fish and no wine. However, the dog also had no wine, but did eat the fish. The husband, wife, and son also ate the fish. All but the daughter got sick, and their common factor was fish consumption.
2. The correct answer is G. The dog and the daughter did not consume wine.
3. The correct answer is D. All consumed the water.
4. The correct answer is G. The pasta and salad would be the likely culprits, but salad is not given as a choice.
5. The correct answer is D. If the husband, wife, daughter, son, and dog have all eaten the same foods and drunk the same liquids and only the dog became ill, it is not likely that any of these items in Table 1 contributed to the dog's illness.
6. The correct answer is G. The fish is still the common item consumed by all who became ill.

The key concept in Passage 2 is understanding how solids behave as they melt and boil (or in reverse: condense and freeze). A substance can essentially "do only one thing at a time"—it can either change temperature, or change phase (changing from a solid to a liquid, or from a liquid to a gas, is considered to be a phase change). Therefore, in the data table, where the temperature does not change over a period of time, the chemical is undergoing a *phase change* (melting or boiling).

7. The correct response is D. Both A and B melt between 5 and 6 degrees Celsius, but they have different boiling points (approximately 80.2 degrees Celsius for A, and the boiling point of B is somewhere above 182.6 degrees Celsius).
8. The correct response is G. Unknown A boils at approximately 80.2 degrees Celsius, which is lower than the boiling point of water (100.0 degrees Celsius).
9. The correct response is C. There is a melting "plateau" of approximately 5.6 degrees Celsius for B, but the temperature continues to climb throughout the remainder of the data presented. The boiling point, therefore, has not been reached.
10. The correct response is J. The boiling "plateau" is approximately 118.2 degrees Celsius for unknown C.
11. The condensation point is the same temperature as the boiling point. Since we do not know the boiling point of B (see answer explanation for question #9), the correct response is D. The condensation point for this unknown cannot be determined from the data presented.
12. The correct response is F. Based on these data, unknown A melts at approximately 5.5 degrees Celsius and boils at approximately 80.2 degrees Celsius (which is lower than the boiling point of water).
13. The correct answer is D. The data shows V is proportional to I, provided the substance is connected in the forward position and at some specific (though unspecified) temperature. V may not be proportional if the connection is reversed or if the temperature changes.

14. The correct answer is J. In Experiment 2, it is not stated that the voltage remained constant. I could change in response to an unmeasured voltage change. In addition, the experiment was performed in only one direction. The results might be different if the experiment were performed again in both directions.

15. The correct answer is D. In Experiment 1, the temperature is held constant. Any change in the current would be as a result of a change in voltage. If the current remained constant, then the voltage must also be constant.

16. The correct answer is H. To develop a relationship between V, I, and T, the experiment must be performed in which everything is held constant except two variables. In this experiment, there were four variables: the way in which the substance was connected, the temperature, the voltage, and the current.

17. The correct answer is C. Two of the variables (position and temperature) are held constant, and the voltage and current are allowed to vary. Clearly, the current and voltage are directly proportional. V/I = constant for all values in graph 1.

18. The correct answer is J. F is incorrect, as the voltage was not specified. G is incorrect, as different experiments were performed on the substance when the connection was changed. H is incorrect, as the temperature was not specified. Graph 1 merely said the experiment was performed at a specific temperature. If the experiment was performed at a different temperature then one might get different values of I.

CONFLICTING VIEWPOINTS PRACTICE

Passage 1

There has been a long-standing dispute among microbiologists, as well as chefs, over whether plastic or wood cutting boards are safer for food preparation.

Scientist 1

Hardwood chopping blocks may contain natural oils and other substances that will kill potentially dangerous bacteria such as *Salmonella, Escherichia coli*, and *Listeria monocytogenes.* Although plastic is a nonporous substance and is less likely to harbor organisms, the rough surface created by repeated cutting may do just that. Thus, the bacteria and debris from food could build up, causing the bacteria to thrive. They would then create a hazard by contaminating food that is prepared at a later time.

Scientist 2

Wood is a porous substance, and repeated cutting of food cause food particles and potentially dangerous bacteria to become trapped. Since wood also holds moisture for hours or even days, this provides an ideal environment for the bacteria to grow in. Plastic, on the other hand, is nonporous and does not hold moisture, which is necessary to support bacterial growth. It is also easy to clean. Consequently, plastic cutting boards are far safer to use for food preparation.

1. Both scientists agree that:

    A. the plastic cutting boards are least suited for food preparation

    B. the wooden chopping blocks are best suited for food preparation

    C. both cutting surfaces are porous and absorbent

    D. bacteria harbored on the cutting board surfaces are potentially dangerous

2. Scientist 2 believes that:

    F. the wooden cutting boards are more likely to permit bacteria to grow

    G. the plastic cutting boards are more likely to permit bacteria to grow

    H. chefs should not use cutting boards at all

    J. any type of surface is suitable for cutting and chopping food

3. Scientist 1, but not Scientist 2, believes that:

    A. moisture retention is the major factor contributing to bacterial growth on cutting boards

    B. plastic is more porous than wood

    C. wood contains substances that will enhance bacterial growth

    D. wood contains inhibitory substances

4. Which of the following would be evidence supporting the position of Scientist 1?

    F. A scraping from the plastic surface produces no growth when cultured.

    G. A scraping from the plastic board, viewed with an electron microscope, shows that bacteria are present.

    H. A scraping from the wood surface produces no growth when cultured.

    J. A scraping from the wood board, viewed with an electron microscope, shows that bacteria are present.

5. Which scientist's position would be supported if cultured scrapings from both wood and plastic surfaces produced growth of bacteria?

    A. Scientist 1
    B. Scientist 2
    C. Scientist 1 and Scientist 2
    D. neither scientist

6. Which of the following would not support the position of Scientist 2?

    F. Bacteria in scrapings taken from plastic boards two days after they were cleaned did not grow when placed in culture.

    G. Bacteria in scrapings taken from plastic boards two days after they were cleaned did grow when placed in culture.

    H. Bacteria in scrapings taken from wooden boards two days after they were cleaned grew when placed in culture.

    J. Bacteria in scrapings taken from wooden boards two hours after they were cleaned grew when placed in culture.

Passage 2

Scientist 1

When a material object having mass travels, it naturally travels in a straight line at a constant speed. If some force acts upon this mass, then it will undergo an acceleration. It will either experience a change in speed or a change in directions. All masses exert forces on all other masses in the universe. This force is called gravity. This gravitational force causes masses to deviate from their natural straight line motion. The reason the moon revolves around the earth is because the gravitational force of the earth bends the straight line motion of the moon into a closed curve. Objects that do not have mass are not affected by the gravitational forces produced by masses. Beams of light, which have no mass, always travel at constant velocity.

Scientist 2

Masses do indeed travel in straight lines when no force is acting upon them. When forces act upon them, they experience accelerations that cause them to change their speed and direction. Masses warp space around them. They cause the curvature of space to change from a flat surface to a curved surface. The reason the moon revolves around the Earth is because the Earth warps space around it. The moon follows its natural straight-line motion, but does so in a curved space. The moon is actually following a straight line, a straight line being the shortest distance between two points. Beams of light will always travel at constant velocity in this curved space.

7. According to Scientist 1, what will happen to a beam of light passing near the Earth's gravitational field?

   A. It will be pulled toward the Earth.
   B. Nothing.
   C. Its direction will change, but its speed will remain constant.
   D. It will orbit the Earth.

8. You are in a rocket ship. You shine a beam of light toward the opposite wall. You see that the beam of light curves downward and hits the wall below the point at which you aimed. Scientist 1 would say that:

   F. the rocket ship must be accelerating
   G. you must be in a powerful gravitational field
   H. you must be dreaming. Such a situation is impossible.
   J. you and the light are both traveling at constant velocity

9. You stand on a scale and notice the scale reads zero. Then:

   A. you must be outside the Earth's gravitational field, according to Scientist 2
   B. there are no gravitational forces present, according to Scientist 1
   C. you must be free falling, according to Scientist 2
   D. it is impossible to tell whether you are free falling or are far from any masses, according to Scientist 2

10. According to Scientist 1, the gravitational force of the Earth will become zero when:

   F. you are exactly halfway between the Earth and the moon
   G. you travel far enough away from the Earth
   H. you are free falling.
   J. it actually never becomes exactly zero

11. According to Scientist 2:

   A. masses do not exert forces on one another
   B. space is curved near the Earth, but flat everywhere else
   C. free-falling objects are not following their natural motion
   D. gravitational fields accelerate beams of light

12. An experiment is performed wherein the position of a star is measured during an eclipse of the sun. Light from this star passes very near the edge of the sun. You notice that the position of the star seems to have shifted from when the position was measured when the light did not pass by the sun. This indicates that:

   F. Scientist 1 is correct. The position of the star was changed by the gravitational field of the sun.
   G. Scientist 2 is correct. The gravitational field of the sun caused light to travel along a curved space.
   H. Scientist 2 is incorrect. Light always travels at constant velocity.
   J. the experiment was irrelevant. The results do not prove or disprove either scientist.

ANSWERS TO CONFLICTING VIEWPOINTS QUESTIONS

1. The correct answer is D. Both scientists have the same general concern. They disagree on the contributing factors and on which type of cutting surface is best.

2. The correct answer is F. Scientist 2 believes that porosity and moisture retention are a major factor in maintaining bacterial growth.

3. The correct answer is D. This question is a simple test of reading comprehension.

4. The correct answer is H. If the wood contains substances that will kill microbes, then even though they may be visible with an electron microscope, the organisms would not grow in culture because they have been killed.

5. The correct answer is D. Each scientist would expect only one type of surface to harbor potentially harmful organisms. If both do so, then both positions would have to be reevaluated, because neither one is correct. Perhaps it would be more appropriate to conduct quantitative studies to compare the number of viable organisms found on each type of surface.

6. The correct answer is G. Scientist 2 maintains that plastic is nonporous and does not retain the moisture required for bacteria to grow. Consequently, one would not expect the bacteria to survive for two days.

7. The correct answer is B. Mass exerts force only on other masses. Light does not have mass; therefore, it should not be affected by gravitational fields, according to Scientist 1.

8. The correct answer is F. Light does not accelerate, according to Scientist 1; therefore, any apparent change in motion must be because the rocket is accelerating.

9. The correct answer is D. Any object free falling is actually following its natural motion, albeit in a curved space. You could be far from masses where the curvature of space approaches flatness or free falling.

10. The correct answer is J. All masses exert forces on all other masses, so the gravitational force never actually reaches zero.

11. The correct answer is A. Masses do not exert forces but warp space. The apparent acceleration of masses is due to the fact that they actually follow a straight-lined path in a curved space, which would appear to be a curved path in a flat space.

12. The correct answer is G. Space would be curved passing near the strong gravitational field of the sun. A beam of light would follow this curved space and the star would appear to shift its position.

Now that you have had a chance to practice the different question types, use the following Science Review section to brush up on your basic knowledge of science. You may use this section to double-check your answers and to try to understand the explanations more fully.

PRACTICE TEST 1

DIRECTIONS: In the five passages that follow, certain words and phrases are underlined and numbered. In the right-hand column, you will find alternatives for each underlined part. You are to choose the one that best expresses the idea, makes the statement appropriate for standard written English, or is worded most consistently with the style and tone of the passage as a whole. If you think the original version is best, choose "NO CHANGE."

You will also find questions about a section of the passage, or about the passage as a whole. These questions do not refer to an underlined portion of the passage, but rather are identified by a number or numbers in a box.

For each question, choose the alternative you consider best and fill in the corresponding oval on your answer document. Read the passage through once before you begin to answer the questions that accompany it. You cannot determine most answers without reading several sentences beyond the question. Be sure that you have read far enough ahead each time you choose an alternative.

Passage I

[1]

A nonjoggers' backlash was not unexpected. Being that there were too many
1
people plodding around the neighborhood or talking about their mileage at cocktail parties or entering marathons and nonjoggers resent the implication
2   3
leaving them out of a new religion. Despite
3
this backlash, jogging or running as it should
4
be called will probably remain popular
4
because they are cheap, healthy, and
5
democratic.

[2]

Running is still cheaper than most other sports. Good racing shoes and good training
6
shoes can still be bought for around twenty smackers. There are expensive shoes with
7
special heel shapes, contours, and colors, but most runners don't need them and may find them painful. Running attire ranges from reasonable to outrageously priced, but
8
most runners can look well dressed for a very modest sum. Clothing seems to matter less than it seems to appear to do for tennis
9
or golf. There is sometimes a holiday atmosphere in the big races—the bus-stop

marathon, for instance — <u>which lead to</u> the
10
sporting of funny shirts and crowd-pleasing
headgear.

[3]
Although there is some pressure to look
good, little value is attached to personal
appearance once the race has started.
Finally, there are no greens fees for runners,
and the reasonable entry fees for the big
races come nowhere near the
<u>level obtained by</u> lift tickets.
11

[4]
Running is generally considered a
healthy pastime, but dissenting voices have
been heard. There is agreement in both the
<u>jogging and running community</u> that
12
moderation is desirable — in beginning to
run and in trying to improve. There is
always the danger of injury, but the body
itself can give off many warnings of exhaustion, of stress, and of <u>impending disease</u>. A
13
runner who has become attuned to his own
body from long training may even be able to
spot a serious problem before a doctor can.

[5]
Race organizers have recognized
running's popularity and <u>will allow</u> as many
14
runners as safety will allow. Can a 10-year-
old ever claim that he has played in the
same golf tournament as Nicklaus or
Watson? He may well have run in a number
of marathons in which Shorter and Rodgers
were only a few feet away — at the start.

1. A. NO CHANGE
   B. In that
   C. However,
   D. OMIT (Start sentence with ''There'')

2. F. NO CHANGE
   G. , and non-joggers resent
   H. , and non-joggers resented
   J. , or non-joggers resenting

3. A. NO CHANGE
   B. being left out
   C. that they had been left out
   D. and were left out

4. F. NO CHANGE
   G. running, as it should be called
   H. running, as it should be called,
   J. running, as it should be handled,

5. A. NO CHANGE
   B. they were
   C. it was
   D. it is

6. F. NO CHANGE
   G. A shoe for racing and training
   H. A good pair of racing or training
   J. Good shoes that are good for racing
      or training

7. A. NO CHANGE
B. bucks
C. treasury notes
D. dollars

8. F. NO CHANGE
G. cheapest
H. reasonably
J. comfortable

9. A. NO CHANGE
B. does
C. counts
D. seem to count

10. F. NO CHANGE
G. that leads to
H. that means
J. that inspires

11. A. NO CHANGE
B. charges of
C. price of
D. scaling of

12. F. NO CHANGE
G. running and medical circles
H. jogging and running communities
J. circle of runners and doctors

13. A. NO CHANGE
B. and impending disease
C. or an impending disease
D. , an impending disease

14. F. NO CHANGE
G. will accept
H. have accepted
J. usually accept

15. Which would be a good introductory sentence for the last paragraph?

A. Running creates medical dangers.
B. Running is a sport geared for the very young.
C. The skills necessary for golf are also necessary for running.
D. The accessibility of running makes it a democratic sport.

Passage II

[1]

To concentrate means to focus on an
16
issue or action at hand; mild worries and

small noises are, for the moment, dismissed;

things are accomplished efficiently. Concen-

tration is equally important in work, sports,

and your schoolwork.
17

[2]

The ability to concentrate develops

with age and self-discipline. From a few
18
minutes in grade school to many hours in

college and business. The more we learn to

concentrate on an assignment or paper, the

better we do them. Unfortunately, there is
19
the possibility of a painful extreme:

stubborn resistance at a task one doesn't
20
understand may lead to despair and stagna-

tion. To avoid this, one must remember that

the mind needs to be relaxed, to start an
21

approach to a subject. If a subject is not understood, <u>the student</u> will not be able to
22
concentrate properly and will quickly become discouraged. <u>The</u> same kind of
23
overconcentration can be detrimental to sports as well. Awareness of other players or spectators can often result in nervous errors <u>which result from paying too little or too</u>
24
<u>much attention to what we are doing.</u>
24
A tennis player, for instance, <u>will have something else on her mind and</u>
25
<u>lose control of a match early and then</u>
25
overcompensate and fail. <u>Some baseball</u>
26
<u>player</u> may try too hard to impress his fans
26
and fail to concentrate on his swing. This will result in a batting slump, which will take him a long time <u>to come out.</u> <u>Athletes</u>
27   28
will begin to improve once they regain the right combination of relaxed confidence and concentration.

[3]
Similarly, a lack of self-consciousness is essential to the ancient discipline of Zen Buddhism, originally developed, in part, to improve the abilities of Japanese swordsmen

and <u>those who used the bow.</u> A neophyte
29
was trained to lose concern or fear for his body; thus, relaxed, his body and mind could be devoted entirely to the use of sword or bow. He would be one with it. Thus, we might conclude that the right concentration is <u>a kind of balance, a kind of</u>
30
<u>well-being,</u> in which we perform a task well
30
without self-consciousness.

16. F. NO CHANGE
    G. making the brain focus
    H. to make the brain focus
    J. the ability to concentrate

17. A. NO CHANGE
    B. school
    C. also in school
    D. while in school

18. F. NO CHANGE
    G. self-discipline, from
    H. self-discipline. It develops from
    J. self-discipline

19. A. NO CHANGE
    B. do the assignment or paper
    C. do it
    D. do

20. F. NO CHANGE
    G. persistence
    H. perseverance
    J. addiction

21. A. NO CHANGE
    B. be relaxed and start a kind of
    C. begin a relaxed
    D. to be in a relaxed state and to

265

22. F. NO CHANGE
   G. one
   H. you
   J. the person

23. A. NO CHANGE
   B. (Begin a new paragraph) The
   C. (Do not begin a new paragraph) But the
   D. (Begin a new paragraph) And the

24. F. NO CHANGE
   G. which result from paying too much or too little attention to the game
   H. of not paying the right kind of attention to what is going on
   J. OMIT

25. A. NO CHANGE
   B. having had something else on her mind and having lost control of a match, will
   C. having lost control of a match early through inattentiveness, may
   D. inattentive and falling behind in a match, may

26. F. NO CHANGE
   G. Or take a baseball player, he
   H. A baseball player
   J. A baseball player, for instance,

27. A. NO CHANGE
   B. to come out from.
   C. to solve.
   D. to come out of.

28. F. NO CHANGE
   G. Some athletes
   H. Both athletes
   J. All athletes

29. A. NO CHANGE
   B. those who pulled the bow string
   C. archers
   D. archery

30. F. NO CHANGE
   G. a kind of balance and well-being,
   H. a kind of balanced well-being
   J. a kind of cool

Passage III

[1]

Every group in society, college, and business <u>want</u> its members to act and speak
31
in acceptable ways. Usually, <u>to succeed,</u>
32
individuals learn to <u>compromise with</u> the
33
larger group in order to be successful. Such conformity, however, does not necessarily fulfill the <u>individual, as many</u> great thinkers
34
have shown, men and women must also learn to develop their spiritual and intellectual potential.

[2]

Socrates's search for knowledge was based on his experience of talking with people who thought they knew the meaning of truth. <u>They did what they knew was the</u>
35
truth of the lawyer or the politician, a truth that did not apply beyond their professions. So Socrates admitted that he himself did not know what truth is, and this admission put him one step ahead of the others. He devoted the rest of his life <u>in</u> thinking
36

according to a method he developed called

"the dialectic." He was led to create the first
                37
useful and moral model of the soul.

[3]

Ralph Waldo Emerson, in the nine-

teenth century, had Socrates example in
                        38
mind when he implored Americans to be

"men" rather than simply farmers or

scholars or factory workers. He felt that the

economic system was grinding people into

ciphers who thought about their jobs but

not about being individuals who think and
                        39
act independently. He wanted Americans to
    39
fulfill the potential within theirselves, their
                            40
feelings, thoughts, their souls. His friend and
        41
fellow philosopher Henry David Thoreau

echoed many of the same thoughts, and
            42
decided to move to secluded Walden Pond

for two years to test his own independence.

He there was able to clarify his thoughts
    43
about life and to exist in nature with a

minimum of tools and expense. The book

that he wrote about his stay is one of the

most striking and provocative examples of

individual thinking in world literature.
                    44

[4]

All of these men have pointed out that,

through disciplined and lengthy thought

about the nature of existence, of justice, of

America, or of a pond, the individual

becomes stronger. A better citizen, in the
                                    45
long run.
    45

31. A. NO CHANGE
    B. wanted
    C. wants
    D. will be wanting

32. F. NO CHANGE
    G. succeeding
    H. in order to succeed,
    J. OMIT

33. A. NO CHANGE
    B. shake hands with
    C. get along with
    D. conform to the standards of

34. F. NO CHANGE
    G. individual. As many
    H. individual. Many
    J. individual, being that

35. A. NO CHANGE
    B. They only knew
    C. They knew no truth except
    D. Their only truth was

36. F. NO CHANGE
    G. around
    H. to
    J. OMIT

37. A. NO CHANGE
B. dialectic." This independence led him
C. dialectic," which led him
D. dialectic," and this led him

38. F. NO CHANGE
G. Socrates's
H. Socrate's
J. Socrateses'

39. A. NO CHANGE
B. as individuals
C. people thinking for themselves
D. about being individuals

40. F. NO CHANGE
G. themselves,
H. themselves —
J. their selves

41. A. NO CHANGE
B. thoughts, and
C. their thoughts, and their
D. thoughts, souls

42. F. NO CHANGE
G. developed similar ideas
H. thought the same way,
J. resembled many of the same thoughts,

43. A. NO CHANGE
B. He could there
C. There, he was able to
D. At Walden pond, he was able to

44. F. NO CHANGE
G. (Place after "is")
H. (Place after "stay")
J. OMIT

45. A. NO CHANGE
B. . He is a better citizen, too, in the long run
C. and a better citizen in the long run
D. and a better citizen

Passage IV

[1]

The largest known planet in our solar system is Jupiter. Since the discovery of its four moons by Galileo in 1610
  46
(12 other moons have been discovered
  46
since that date), it has intrigued scientists. It
  47
is composed mostly of hydrogen and helium, like the Sun. Because the pressure and temperature at its center are nearly high enough to create nuclear fusion. Jupiter
  48
is almost a star.
  48

[2]

In 1977, Congress approved funding for a mission to explore Jupiter. Known as *Galileo*, the spacecraft was to be launched from the space shuttle in 1982. But a series of problems delayed the launch. Rocket design inadequacies, and the *Challenger*
  49
shuttle disaster slowed the project. Finally, in 1989, *Galileo* was launched from the shuttle *Atlantis*. During the voyage, prob-lems arisen. A main antenna for receiving
  50
data did not unfold. Later, a tape recorder failed to rewind, threatening loss of most of

the data that had been collected. Engineers found ways to solve these problems by using alternative and backup systems.

[3]

Scientists planned to send a probe into the atmosphere of Jupiter from the main ship. How could the probe survive the difficult conditions and send back data to the orbiter? It needed to be protected from the intense <u>heat, and it would face</u> pressures
                                                  51
of up to 230 times Earth's gravity. It had to enter the atmosphere at an angle that would <u>neither send it skipping out into space,</u>
                                        52
<u>nor turning it to ashes</u> before entering
                    52
Jupiter's clouds. If the probe survived, it would send approximately 75 minutes of data back to the orbiter before being destroyed. Then heat and pressure would turn it into a gas, which would become part of Jupiter's atmosphere. If that portion of the mission succeeded, the main craft would <u>fire it's engines</u> to position itself to orbit
      53
Jupiter and its moons eleven times over a period of twenty-two months.

[4]

As *Galileo* voyaged toward Jupiter, it provided new and intriguing data about the solar system. It had a close encounter with Asteroid Gastra. When it flew by Asteroid Ida, it saw a moon, later named Dactyl, orbiting the asteroid. This was the first discovery of an asteroid that had a moon. <u>Dramatic pictures and data are sent back</u>
                                55
when a comet crashed into Jupiter in 1994.

[5]

Tension and anxiety were evident at the Jet Propulsion Laboratory in Pasadena, <u>California, on December 7, 1995,</u> as person-
                              56
nel waited to see if the mission would succeed. Some people had been with the laboratory since the project began in 1977. They had been waiting almost twenty years to see <u>if it all paid off.</u> When they received
            57
information that the probe had successfully entered Jupiter's atmosphere, they were jubilant. Several hours later, they learned the main engines had put *Galileo* into orbit around Jupiter. <u>However</u> it would be days
                            58
before data was transmitted back to earth

from the craft, and months or even years

before the data could be analyzed and

interpreted, they now knew that the *Galileo*

mission was a success.

46. F. NO CHANGE
   G. 1610, (12 other moons
   H. 1610, (twelve other moons
   J. 1610 (twelve other moons

47. A. NO CHANGE
   B. since that date,) it
   C. since that date) it
   D. , since that date), it

48. F. NO CHANGE
   G. high enough to create nuclear fusion, Jupiter is almost a star.
   H. high enough to create nuclear fusion; Jupiter is almost a star.
   J. high enough to create nuclear fusion: Jupiter is almost a star.

49. A. NO CHANGE
   B. inadequacies; and
   C. inadequacies and
   D. inadequacies. And

50. F. NO CHANGE
   G. arose
   H. have arisen
   J. were arising

51. A. NO CHANGE
   B. heat and
   C. heat, and,
   D. heat and,

52. F. NO CHANGE
   G. neither send it skipping out into space, nor turns it to ashes
   H. neither send it skipping out into space, nor turn it to ashes
   J. neither send it skipping out into space, nor turned it to ashes

53. A. NO CHANGE
   B. fires it's engines
   C. fire its engines
   D. fires its engines

54. The main subject of paragraph [3] is:
   F. the scientists' plans
   G. the problems that had to be solved for the mission to succeed
   H. how the probe would become part of Jupiter's atmosphere
   J. how many times the main craft would circle Jupiter

55. A. NO CHANGE
   B. Dramatic pictures and data will be sent back
   C. Dramatic pictures and data were sent back
   D. Dramatic pictures and data was sent back

56. F. NO CHANGE
   G. California on December 7, 1995,
   H. California, on December 7 1995,
   J. California, on December 7, 1995

57. A. NO CHANGE
   B. the big picture.
   C. the results of their efforts.
   D. what fruits twenty years of their efforts would bring forth for them.

58. F. NO CHANGE
   G. Since
   H. Nevertheless
   J. Although

59. The writer wants to add the following two sentences to the passage: "But the main goal of the mission had not yet been accomplished. Would the probe survive to send back data from inside Jupiter's atmosphere?" The best place to put those two sentences is:

   A. the first sentence of paragraph 3
   B. the last sentence of paragraph 3
   C. the last sentence of paragraph 4
   D. the first sentence of paragraph 5

Item 60 poses a question about the essay as a whole.

60. The essay's main purpose is best described as:

   F. providing information about Jupiter
   G. narrating the story of *Galileo's* mission
   H. praising the scientists and engineers who worked on the project
   J. arguing for continued exploration of space

Passage V

[1]

This is the story of a sturdy American symbol that has now spread throughout most of the world. The symbol is not the dollar. It is not even Coca-Cola. It was a
          61
simple pair of pants called blue jeans, and what the pants symbolize is what Alexis deTocqueville called "a . . . legitimate
                              62
passion for equality." Blue jeans are favored equally by technicians and cowboys; bankers and deadbeats; fashion models and musicians. They draw no social distinction and recognize no classes; they are merely American. Yet they are sought after almost everywhere in the world.

[2]

Jeans were originated by Levi Strauss, an immigrant from Germany. He went west, taking with him bolts of canvas to sell for tenting. It was the wrong kind of canvas for the purpose, but while talking with a miner,
          63
he learned that pants—sturdy pants that would stand up to the rigors of digging—was
                                        64
almost impossible to find. Strauss measured the man with a piece of string and had the canvas made into a pair of pants. The miner was delighted with the result, word came
                                65
around about "those pants of Levi's," and
                          66
Strauss was in business. When Strauss ran out of canvas, he sent for more. Instead of receiving canvas, he received a tough, brown cotton cloth, called Serge de Nimes, and
                                        67
swiftly shortened to "denim." Almost from the first, Strauss had his cloth dyed the distinctive indigo that gave blue jeans their

271

name. The copper rivets were added in 1870 when, according to a story that may or may not be true, a miner complained to a tailor named Jacob W. Davis that the pockets of his
                                          68
jeans tore when he stuffed them with ore
                                          68
samples. Davis took the pants to a blacksmith
68
and had the pockets riveted; the idea worked
                         69
so well that word got around, and in 1873 Strauss appropriated and patented the gimmick—and hired Davis as a regional manager.

[3]

[1] From their invention until the
          70
1930s, jeans were sold largely to the working people of the West—cowboys, lumberjacks, and railroad workers. [2] Levi's jeans were first introduced to the East, apparently, during the dude-ranch craze of the 1930s when easterners who were on
                                71
their vacations returned and spread the
71
word about the wonderful pants with rivets. [3] Another boost came during World War II, when they were declared an essential commodity and were sold only to people engaged in defense work.

[4]

Blue jeans have become, through
                            73
marketing word of mouth and demonstrable
                                      73
reliability, the common pants of Americans.
73
They can be purchased prewashed, pre-faded, and preshrunk for the suitably proletarian look. They are sold in high-fashion versions with designer labels. They are tailored in regular, slim fit, relaxed, or loose styles. They come with zippers, or five buttons, or three buttons. They adapt themselves to any sort of use; women slit them at the inseams and convert them into long skirts; men chop them off around the knees and turn them into something to be worn while surfing. They can be decorated, by deliberately tearing them, patched,
                              74
beaded, or embroidering them. Their endless
                            74
variety makes them a symbol of American individuality as well as equality.

61. A. NO CHANGE
B. is
C. has
D. had

62. The underlined punctuation is used because:

F. the reader should pause to take a breath
G. the sentence is coming to an end
H. something has been omitted from the quotation
J. commas would not be correct

63. A. NO CHANGE
B. purpose, but,
C. purpose but,
D. purpose but

64. F. NO CHANGE
G. be
H. are
J. were

65. A. NO CHANGE
B. caught
C. got
D. brought

66. F. NO CHANGE
G. Levi's'',
H. Levis,''
J. Levis'',

67. A. NO CHANGE
B. therefore
C. thus, it
D. which was

68. The writer is thinking of changing this clause to read: "when he stuffed them with ore, his jeans pockets tore." The best reason *not* to do so is:

F. it changes the meaning of the sentence
G. it creates ambiguity because it is not clear what "them" refers to
H. it creates clauses that sound like a nursery rhyme
J. it is a clause that is punctuated incorrectly

69. A. NO CHANGE
B. riveted,
C. riveted
D. , riveted;

70. The writer is thinking of omitting this phrase. The best reason *not* to do so is:

F. coherent paragraphs often begin with a prepositional phrase
G. the phrase provides variety in sentence structure in the paragraph
H. the phrase serves as a transition from paragraph 2 to this paragraph
J. to begin the paragraph with the words "until the 1930s" would not make sense

71. A. NO CHANGE
B. vacationing easterners
C. people from the East who vacationed in the Wild West
D. easterners who went west on their vacations

72. The best order for the sentences in paragraph 3 is:

F. NO CHANGE
G. 2, 1, 3
H. 2, 3, 1
J. 3, 1, 2

73. A. NO CHANGE
    B. , through marketing, word of mouth and demonstrable reliability,
    C. , through marketing, word of mouth, and demonstrable reliability,
    D. through marketing word of mouth and demonstrable reliability

74. F. NO CHANGE
    G. deliberately torn, patched, beaded or embroidered.
    H. deliberately tearing them, patching them, beaded or embroidering.
    J. deliberately tearing them, patching them, beading them, or embroidering them.

75. The best title for this essay would be:
    A. Forever in Blue Jeans
    B. The Jeaning of America
    C. How Blue Jeans Were Invented
    D. Why Americans Love Blue Jeans

MATHEMATICS TEST   TIME—60 MINUTES   60 QUESTIONS

DIRECTIONS: Solve each problem, choose the correct answer, and then fill in the corresponding oval on your answer document.

Do not linger over problems that take too much time. Solve as many as you can; then return to the others in the time you have left for this test.

You are permitted to use a calculator.

Note: Unless otherwise stated, all of the following should be assumed:

1. Illustrative figures are NOT necessarily drawn to scale.

2. Geometric figures lie in a plane.

3. The word *line* indicates a straight line.

4. The word *average* indicates arithmetic mean.

1. What is 72 expressed as the product of prime factors?

   A. (2)(3)
   B. (2)(3)(12)
   C. (2)(2)(2)(3)(3)
   D. (8)(9)
   E. (6)(6)(2)

2. The hypotenuse of a right triangle is 10 and one leg is 6. Find the length of the other leg of the triangle.

   F. 16
   G. 10
   H. 8
   J. 12
   K. 4

3. The product of $3x^5$ and $5x^3$ is:

   A. $15x^8$
   B. $8x^{15}$
   C. $15x^{15}$
   D. $8x^8$
   E. $35x^8$

4. Express as a fraction in lowest terms:

   $$\frac{y^2-9}{2y+6} \div \frac{y-3}{y+2}$$

   F. $\dfrac{y+2}{2}$
   G. $\dfrac{y-3}{2y+6}$
   H. $\dfrac{9}{4}$
   J. $\dfrac{y}{-2}$
   K. $y + 2$

5. If each interior angle of a polygon contains 150°, how many sides does the polygon have?

   A. 12
   B. 19
   C. 3
   D. 6
   E. 8

6. Fred invested $4,000 at a simple interest rate of 5.75%. What is the total value of his investment after one year?

   F. $200
   G. $230
   H. $4,200
   J. $4,230
   K. $4,400

7. Express in simplest form the following ratio: 15 hours to 2 days.

A. $7\dfrac{1}{2}$

B. $\dfrac{16}{5}$

C. $\dfrac{5}{8}$

D. $\dfrac{15}{2}$

E. $\dfrac{5}{16}$

8. Find the height of a triangle whose base is 15 inches and whose area is 75 square inches.

F. 5 inches
G. 5 square inches
H. 10 inches
J. 10 square inches
K. 20 inches

9. What is .03 expressed as a percent?

A. .0003%
B. 3%
C. .3%
D. .03%
E. .003%

**Zooko Manufacturing Co.
Closing Price per Share**

10. Leroy bought 25 shares of Zooko stock at the closing price on Tuesday and sold them at the closing price on Friday. How much money did Leroy lose on his investment?

F. $80
G. $200
H. $800
J. $2,000
K. $95

11. .58 · .14 =

A. 812
B. 8.12
C. 81.2
D. 812
E. .0812

12. If $3a - 5 = 7$, then $a =$

F. -4

G. 4

H. $-\dfrac{2}{3}$

J. $\dfrac{2}{3}$

K. $\dfrac{5}{3}$

13. An urn contains five red and three black marbles. If one marble is drawn, what is the probability that it will be red?

A. $\dfrac{5}{3}$

B. $\dfrac{3}{5}$

C. $\dfrac{5}{8}$

D. $\dfrac{3}{8}$

E. $\dfrac{8}{3}$

14. $2^3 + 5^2 =$

F. 16,807

G. 200

H. 33

J. 16

K. 29

15. Evaluate $2a^2 - 3b$, if $a = -3$, $b = -1$.

A. −21

B. 21

C. −15

D. 15

E. 33

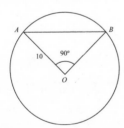

16. How long is chord AB of circle O?

F. $\sqrt{10}$

G. $10\sqrt{2}$

H. 100

J. 10

K. $\sqrt{50}$

17. $(2x^2 - 3x + 5) + (3x - 2) =$

A. $2x^2 + 3$

B. $2x^2 + 6x + 3$

C. $2x^2 + 6x + 7$

D. $2x + 3$

E. $2x^2 - 6x + 3$

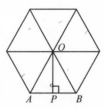

18. Calculate the area of the hexagon. $OP = 4\sqrt{3}$, $AB = 8$

F. $96\sqrt{3}$

G. $32\sqrt{3}$

H. 32

J. $16\sqrt{3}$

K. 16

19. The area of a circle is the same as the area of a square whose side is 5 centimeters. The radius of the circle is closest to:

A. 25 centimeters

B. 3 centimeters

C. 3 square centimeters

D. 8 centimeters

E. 16 centimeters

20. Solve for x: $7x - 3 = 4x + 6$

F. 3

G. −1

H. 4

J. 2

K. −4

21. $2\frac{2}{3} + (-7) =$

   A. $4\frac{1}{3}$

   B. $-4\frac{1}{3}$

   C. $9\frac{2}{3}$

   D. $-9\frac{2}{3}$

   E. $-4\frac{2}{3}$

22. Using the formula $A = p + prt$, find A when $p = 500$, $r = .04$, and $t = 2\frac{1}{2}$

   F. 700

   G. 600

   H. 550

   J. 500

   K. 450

23. If $|3a - 1| = 5$, which of the following is a possible value for a?

   A. −2

   B. −1

   C. 0

   D. 1

   E. 2

24. If x units are added to the length of the radius of a circle, what is the number of units by which the circumference of the circle is increased?

   F. x

   G. 2

   H. 2π

   J. $2\pi x$

   K. x^2

25. What is the y-coordinate of the point on the graph of $y = -x^2$ with x-coordinate 3?

   A. −9

   B. −6

   C. 0

   D. 6

   E. 9

26. If point A has coordinate $(-6, -4)$ and point C has coordinate $(0, 4)$, find the length of $\overline{AC}$.

   F. 24

   G. 22

   H. 15

   J. 10

   K. 8

27. A coat is on sale for $128 after a discount of 20%. Find the original price.

   A. $102.40

   B. $153.60

   C. $160

   D. $180

   E. $148

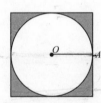

28. Radius $OA = 3$. Calculate the area of the shaded region.

   F. 9

   G. $36 - 36\pi$

   H. 36π

   J. $36 - 9\pi$

   K. 9π

29. In right triangle *ABC*, angle *C* is a right angle and sec *A* = 17/8. What is the value of sin *A*?

   A. 8/17
   B. 15/17
   C. 17/15
   D. 8/15
   E. 15/8

30. If two parallel lines are crossed by a transversal, the alternate interior angles are always:

   F. equal
   G. complementary
   H. supplementary
   J. acute
   K. obtuse

31. Six years ago in a state park the deer outnumbered the foxes by 80. Since then, the number of deer has doubled and the number of foxes has increased by 20. If there are now a total of 240 deer and foxes in the park, how many foxes were there 6 years ago?

   A. 10
   B. 20
   C. 30
   D. 40
   E. 100

32. The length of a side of a square is represented by *x* + 2, and the length of a side of an equilateral triangle by 2*x*. If the square and the equilateral triangle have equal perimeters, find *x*.

   F. 24
   G. 16
   H. 12
   J. 8
   K. 4

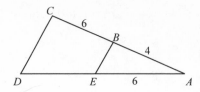

33. Triangles *ABE* and *ACD* are similar. Find the length of *DE*.

   A. 9
   B. 15
   C. 4
   D. 11
   E. 8

34. The expression $(3K^2)^3$ is equivalent to:

   F. $9K^6$
   G. $27K^6$
   H. $27K^5$
   J. $9K^5$
   K. $3K^5$

35. The result of multiplying
$$\frac{x^2-1}{x} \cdot \frac{4x^2}{x+1}$$
is:

   A. $\dfrac{x-1}{4x^3}$

   B. $\dfrac{(x^2-1)(x+1)}{4x^3}$

   C. $4x(x + 1)$

   D. $4x(x - 1)$

   E. $\dfrac{4x}{x+1}$

36. Find the value of *y* in the proportion:
$$\frac{20}{12} = \frac{5}{y}$$

   F. $8\frac{1}{3}$
   G. 3
   H. 15
   J. 8
   K. $8\frac{1}{3}$

37. If $\dfrac{3}{x}$ is subtracted from $\dfrac{4}{x}$, the result is:

   A. 1

   B. $\dfrac{7}{x}$

   C. $\dfrac{-1}{x}$

   D. $\dfrac{1}{x}$

   E. $\dfrac{1}{x^2}$

38. Tom's weekly rent increased from $125 to $143.75. Find the percent of increase.

   F. 1.15%

   G. 1.5%

   H. 8.7%

   J. 87%

   K. 15%

39. Which of the following ordered pairs satisfies the equation $3x - 5y = 17$?

   A. (4, 1)

   B. (3, −2)

   C. (9, 2)

   D. (7, 1)

   E. (12, −5)

40. What is the slope of the line that passes through the points (3, 8) and (7, 2)?

   F. −3

   G. $-\dfrac{3}{2}$

   H. $-\dfrac{2}{3}$

   J. $\dfrac{2}{3}$

   K. $\dfrac{3}{2}$

41. The solution set for $x^2 + 7x + 12 = 0$ is

   A. {1, 6}

   B. {−1, −6}

   C. {3, 4}

   D. {−3, −4}

   E. {0, −2}

42. A girl worked one Saturday from 7:30 a.m. until 3 p.m. at the rate of $4.65 per hour. How much did she receive?

   F. $19.88

   G. $22.53

   H. $19.00

   J. $22.00

   K. $34.88

43. The marked price of a coat was $36.75, which represented 75% of the original selling price. What was the original selling price?

   A. $27.56

   B. $42.35

   C. $45.94

   D. $49.00

   E. $45.35

44. $\left(\dfrac{y^5}{y^8}\right)^3$ is equivalent to:

   F. y^{-9}

   G. y^{-4}

   H. 1

   J. y^4

   K. y^9

45. Two ties and one shirt cost $30. Three ties and two shirts cost $49. Find the cost of one shirt.

   A. $8

   B. $5

   C. $3

   D. $1

   E. $11

46. The expression $\sqrt{162}$ is equivalent to:

   F. $4\sqrt{2}$

   G. $4 + \sqrt{2}$

   H. $9\sqrt{2}$

   J. $3\sqrt{2}$

   K. $9 + \sqrt{2}$

47. Which of the following is equivalent to $\dfrac{\csc\alpha - \sin\alpha}{\cot\alpha}$?

   A. $\sin\alpha$

   B. $\cos\alpha$

   C. $\cot\alpha$

   D. $\csc\alpha$

   E. $\sec\alpha$

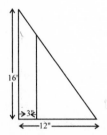

48. In the accompanying figure, the legs of a right triangle are 16 inches and 12 inches. Find the number of inches in the length of the line segment parallel to the 16-inch side and 3 inches from it.

   F. 16

   G. 12

   H. 9

   J. 15

   K. 10

49. The graph shown is the graph of which inequality?

   A. $-2 < x < 3$

   B. $-2 \le x < 3$

   C. $-2 \le x \le 3$

   D. $-2 < x \le 3$

   E. $-2 < x$

50. On a map, 2 inches represents 15 miles. How many miles would 5 inches represent?

   F. 6

   G. 8

   H. 30

   J. $37\dfrac{1}{2}$

   K. 75

51.

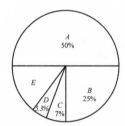

Use this chart to answer question 51.

Fat Freddie's Budget
Weekly net income = $350

A) Food   D) Clothing
B) Rent & Utilities   E) Miscellaneous
C) Entertainment

How much money does Freddie spend on miscellaneous items each week?

   A. $43.05

   B. $19.05

   C. $130.95

   D. $18.55

   E. $44.45

52. What is the *x*-intercept of the line described by the equation $y = 3x + 7$?

F. 7

G. −7

H. $-\dfrac{3}{7}$

J. $-\dfrac{7}{3}$

K. $\dfrac{7}{3}$

53. Line *AB* is parallel to *CD*. Line *EG* bisects *BEF*. How many degrees are in angle *GFD*?

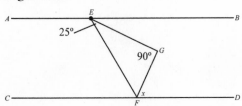

A. 65

B. 105

C. 45

D. 90

E. 25

54. If $4t + 5 \le t - 4$, then

F. $t \le 3$

G. $t \ge 3$

H. $t \le 9$

J. $t \ge 9$

K. $t \le -3$

55. What are the values of *x* that satisfy the equation $(3x + 1)(x - 1) = (5x - 3)(2x - 3)$?

A. $-\dfrac{5}{7}$ and 2

B. $-\dfrac{7}{5}$ and 2

C. −2 and $\dfrac{5}{7}$

D. 2 and $\dfrac{5}{7}$

E. $\dfrac{7}{5}$ and 2

56. Solve for *x* and *y*: $x + 3y = 10$
$\qquad\qquad\qquad 2x - 3y = 2.$

F. $x = 1, y = 3$

G. $x = 7, y = 4$

H. $x = 4, y = 2$

J. $x = 0, y = 0$

K. none of these

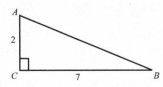

57. In the right triangle *ABC* above, what is the value of sin *B*?

A. $\dfrac{2}{7}$

B. $\dfrac{2\sqrt{53}}{53}$

C. $\dfrac{5\sqrt{53}}{53}$

D. $\dfrac{\sqrt{53}}{2}$

E. $\dfrac{7}{2}$

58. If $f(x) = 2x^3 - 8x$, what are all of the values of *x* where $f(x) = 0$?

F. 0, 4, −4

G. 2, −2

H. 2, 0

J. 2, −2, 0

K. −2, 0

59. A weather balloon is fastened to a cord that makes an angle of 55° with the horizontal. If 450 yards of cord have been let out, how many yards above the ground is the weather balloon?

A. 450 sin 55°
B. 450/sin 55°
C. 450 cos 55°
D. 450/cos 55°
E. 450 tan 55°

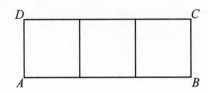

60. Three congruent squares are arranged in a row. If the perimeter of *ABCD* is 80, the area of *ABCD* is:

F. 240
G. 320
H. 640
J. 300
K. 160

READING TEST   TIME—35 MINUTES   40 QUESTIONS

Passage I

Line Although most people go through life
without ever discovering that there is a
subject called "aesthetics," few would find
life bearable without some sort of primitive
5 aesthetic enjoyment—the sight of a loved
face, the taste of a good meal, or the feel of
a comfortable resting place. As civilized
beings, we might find it equally unbearable
to live in a world, such as that described in
10 George Orwell's *1984,* devoid of the
aesthetic pleasures derivable from art.
Fortunately, our world still contains an
almost infinite variety of natural and created
phenomena from which we can derive
15 aesthetic pleasure. Most people usually take
these phenomena and the pleasures
associated with them for granted. Those
who do not take them for granted, but who
seek to understand their nature and value,
20 are engaged in the task (whether they
know it or not) that was initiated by
Socrates and Plato more than two thousand
years ago and that has kept aesthetics ever
since a going concern.
25   But is the task really meaningful? Is it
worth the effort? Can its goal ever be
attained? There are critics of aesthetics who
would without hesitation answer "No!"
Some of these hold that aesthetic experi-
30 ence is ineffable, completely beyond the
reach of rational description and analysis,
and that consequently aesthetics as the
theoretical study of this experience is

impossible. Others claim that aesthetics
35 must be by its very nature such an abstract
form of speculation that it can have little or
nothing to do with real art and with "the
blood and guts" of creative endeavor. . . .
Still others are afraid to study aesthetics for
40 fear that it might "clog up the springs of
creativity" with its obscure ideas about art
and beauty. Among these are some artists
who would as soon have a lobotomy as
take a course in aesthetics, and even a book
45 on the subject is to them, in William
James's phrase, an "abomination of
desolation." Aesthetics has also been
criticized by poets for being too unfeeling
and critical, by art critics for being too
50 general and ill-informed, by psychologists
for being unscientific, by preachers for
being immoral, by economists for being
useless, by politicians for being undemo-
cratic, by philosophers for being dreary,
55 desolate, and dull, and by students for
being "anesthetics in disguise."
        . . . Our purpose here is not to defend
aesthetics against its countless critics, or to
answer all of the objections that have been
60 raised against it. . . . But a few remarks will
be made about some of the criticisms
mentioned earlier. Going back to the
objection that the ineffability of aesthetic
experience makes aesthetics impossible, we
65 would point out that even if the experience
is ineffable this should not prevent us from
being able to discuss intelligibly the
conditions under which it comes about,
some of the components that constitute it,
70 its relations to other aspects of experience,
and the object in which it finds satisfaction.
And if we can do this, aesthetics is possible. As for aesthetics being abstract, like
all theory it cannot avoid being abstract, in
75 that it involves the use of generalizations,
definitions, deductions, etc., but this does
not mean that it cannot be concrete in the
sense that it can refer constantly, consistently, and coherently to experience—to
80 the sensible phenomena, whether natural

or created, which it attempts to explain. Just because some metaphysically biased theories of aesthetics have lacked this coherence of theory with fact does not
85 mean that no aesthetic theory can achieve it.

. . . even when aestheticians do lack the skill to create works of art, as many of them apparently do, this does not mean
90 that they lack the ability to appreciate and evaluate them or to construct theories about them. Socrates is said to have frequented artists' studios, questioning the artists about their works and helping them
95 to get clearer conceptions of their intentions. "You may scold a carpenter who has made you a bad table, though you cannot make a table," said Dr. Samuel Johnson, adding that "it is not your trade to make
100 tables." If it is not the art critics or the aesthetician's "trade" to make works of art, it is their "trade" to deal with these works theoretically, whether it be in order to analyze, interpret, and evaluate them, as the
105 art critic does, or to study them more generally as objects capable of playing a role in bringing about aesthetic experience, as the aesthetician studies them.

1. In the context of the passage, the word *ineffable* most likely means:

   A. indescribable
   B. intellectual
   C. ineffective
   D. inescapable

2. According to the passage, the study of aesthetics was begun by:

   F. psychologists
   G. William James
   H. Socrates and Plato
   J. Dr. Samuel Johnson

3. The primary purpose of the second paragraph is to:

   A. specifically criticize aesthetics
   B. describe the criticisms of aesthetics
   C. argue that aesthetics is unimportant
   D. discuss the value of aesthetics

4. The phrase "anesthetics in disguise" is most likely used to demonstrate the students' attitude that the study of aesthetics:

   F. interests students
   G. puts them to sleep
   H. obscures what it is
   J. makes them hate art

5. According to the passage, poets criticize aesthetics for:

   A. being immoral
   B. being unfeeling
   C. being unscientific
   D. being useless

6. The author suggests that "few would find life bearable without" which of the following?

   I. the feel of a comfortable resting place
   II. the sight of a loved face
   III. the taste of a good meal

   F. I only
   G. II and III only
   H. I and III only
   J. I, II, and III

7. The author most likely uses Samuel Johnson's analogy about scolding a carpenter (lines 96–100) in order to:

   A. justify why lay people criticize art and artists

   B. criticize those who scold trades-people

   C. explain why aestheticians need not be artists

   D. agree that aestheticians must also be artists

8. The opening sentences of the third paragraph suggest a contradiction because the author claims his "purpose . . . is not to defend aesthetics against its . . . critics," yet:

   F. he defends aesthetics against the criticisms mentioned earlier

   G. he begins to offer his own criticisms of the field of aesthetics

   H. he continues to describe all the ways that aesthetics are criticized

   J. he starts to praise the field of aesthetics for all its strengths

9. According to the passage, George Orwell's *1984* would have been an unbearable world because:

   A. it was a repressive totalitarian system

   B. it isolated the individual from society

   C. it contained an infinite variety of pleasures

   D. it was devoid of aesthetic pleasures

10. Lines 100–108 suggest that the role of an art critic is distinct from that of the aesthetician because:

   F. art critics study art more generally than do aestheticians

   G. art critics analyze, interpret, and evaluate works of art

   H. the art critic's "trade" is not to make works of art

   J. the art critic considers how art creates aesthetic pleasure

Passage II

Line We lived in a small town in Monmouths-
hire, at the head of one of the coal valleys.
Unemployment was endemic there, and
enforced leisure gave rise to protracted
5   bouts of philosophy and politics. Most men
leaned toward politics, since it gave an
appearance of energy and deceived some
people into believing they possessed power
and influence. It was, if you like, political
10 theory, imaginative and vituperative. The
hills about our town were full of men
giving their views an airing; eloquence was
commonplace.

    True power lay in the hands of a
15 small group—the aldermen and councillors
of the town. To a man, they sold insurance
and were prosperous. This was because
they ran the municipal transport, the public
parks and gardens, the collection of taxes,
20 the whole organization of local government
in the town and its surrounding villages.
They hired and fired, dispensed and took
away. They were so corrupt that the Mafia
never got a toehold among us. Those Italian
25 boys would have starved.

    In order to get anywhere in our town
you had to buy insurance. When teachers,
for example, got their salaries at the end of
the month, most of them paid heavy
30 insurance. The remainder of the teachers
were the sons and daughters of councillors.

    One day my mother and I were
walking together down Wallhead Road. She
was explaining to me that as I was 18 it
35 was time I found gainful employment and

that no gentleman walked as I walked, his toes turned in, his knees bent, his arms hanging apelike at his sides, his expression vacant, his very being a shame and burden. No family, she continued, had been so vexed. "And, talking of family, there's my cousin."

Her cousin, Harvey Lockwood, was one of the councillors. His insurance business was reputed to be the richest in the county; his daughters, all three, taught in the best schools; his house was full of antiques and carpets. I had seen him smoking a cigar-symbol of incredible wealth. We had never been in his house. We were the poor relations. Seeing us, he thought to avoid us by crossing the street, but the traffic was not kind to him. My mother planted herself in front of him. For a moment, I thought he would knock her down, so steadfastly was he looking at something above her head.

"Good morning," she said to Harvey. It was a nice morning, in fact, but winter was in her eye.

Harvey's start was a pleasant mixture of simulated surprise and delight. "Elsie," he said.

"You remember my name!" said my mother. "That's amazing." She said it cynically and with reproof.

"Now, Elsie," said Harvey, "there's no need for sarcasm. After all, we're family. Our mothers were sisters, after all."

I noticed that he had begun to wriggle and turn red. There was no cure for this, as I knew. My mother examined coldly the growing evidence of Harvey's embarrassment.

"And who is this?" he blustered. "This young man can't be your Selwyn? What a size he's grown!"

"Hullo, Mr. Lockwood," I said nastily.

"Oh, Uncle Harvey," he said. "Call me Uncle Harvey." He turned to my mother. "Now that I look at him," he said, "he has a look of his grandfather about him. What a handsome fellow the old man was! What a big man! Pity he had such expensive habits."

"That's a nice coat you're wearing, Harvey," my mother said. "And where's that lovely new car of yours?" Harvey winced. I could have told him he had no chance. "When are you and Sylvia going to Paris again?" my mother said, turning the steel.

"What are you going to do with this young man of yours?" Harvey said. I had to admit he was game, but this was the opening my mother had been looking for.

"What indeed?" she said. "That is something you might give a little thought to, Harvey. I see your daughters are all nicely settled, your brother Paul is an inspector of local transport. Selwyn must be the only member of the family who hasn't yet enjoyed your generous help." Now that Harvey was on the run, she was almost happy. She smiled: she made small, graceful gestures with her hands. "There's nothing available for him in the town hall, is there?" she said. "He has a good brain, he's industrious. What's more, he can keep his mouth shut." She offered this with a curious nod of the head.

Its effect on Harvey was instant and terrible. He gaped, he turned pale, and, grasping his briefcase firmly under his arm, he shot off into the traffic. "I'll see what I can do," he wailed, running.

"That's all right, then," my mother said.

"Is that why we came out this morning?" I said.

"You're getting sharper, Selwyn," my mother said. "We might make something of you yet. Stand up straight."

11. In the context of the passage, the statement "winter was in her eye" (lines 59-60) probably means that:

    A. she thought it was a nice winter morning
    B. she had an unfriendly expression on her face
    C. she wanted to contradict Harvey
    D. she was expecting an unkind response

12. Selwyn's mother most likely asks Harvey "where's that lovely new car of yours?" (lines 87-88) because:

    F. she believes Harvey bought it with money he obtained illegally
    G. she wants Harvey to buy a new car for Selwyn
    H. she does not approve of Harvey's corrupt activities
    J. she wants Harvey to feel guilty about her poverty

13. According to the passage, Harvey is forced to speak to Elsie because:

    A. he is a town councillor
    B. he does not want to offend her
    C. he is unable to cross the street
    D. he considers her family

14. Harvey is:

    F. Selwyn's uncle
    G. Selwyn's grandfather
    H. Elsie's brother-in-law
    J. Elsie's cousin

15. In the context of the passage, *protracted* (line 4) means:

    A. circular
    B. lengthy
    C. complicated
    D. unintelligible

16. In the context of the passage, the statement "Those Italian boys would have starved" (lines 24-25) means:

    F. the townspeople were prejudiced against other ethnic groups
    G. there was no work in town for the Italians either
    H. the Italians were not corrupt like the town councillors
    J. organized crime would not be able to prosper in the town

17. The discussion of "political theory" in the first paragraph:

    A. serves as a contrast to the "true power" described in the second paragraph
    B. provides the setting for the confrontation that occurs later
    C. prepares the reader for the eloquent political discussion that follows
    D. explains the townspeople's fascination with the town hall

18. According to the passage, the powerful people in town all:

    F. sell insurance
    G. smoke cigars
    H. teach school
    J. own antiques

19. The passage implies that Harvey is frightened by Elsie's comment that Selwyn "can keep his mouth shut" (lines 109-110) because:

    A. he needs to hire someone who is eloquent and energetic
    B. he is afraid that Selwyn will be corrupt
    C. he is afraid Selwyn will learn his trade secrets
    D. he believes Elsie knows about his corrupt activities

20. It can be inferred from the passage that Selwyn's mother decided they should go out for a walk that morning in order:

F. to teach Selwyn to walk like a gentleman

G. to persuade Selwyn to start looking for a job

H. to force Harvey to give Selwyn a job

J. to walk to town hall via Wallhead Road

Passage III

Line North Dakota entered the United States as the thirty-ninth state on November 2, 1989. South Dakota, which is officially recognized as the fortieth state, also became a state the
5 same day. Two other states, Montana and Washington, were added later that same month. Colorado had been named the thirty-eighth state thirteen years before North Dakota's admittance. North Dakota is
10 located at the geographical center of North America in the great plains. North Dakota is bordered on the north by Canada, on the east by Minnesota, south by South Dakota, and west by Montana.
15 North Dakota can be divided into two regions, east and west. The eastern part of the state extends from the Red River Valley. The Red River draws the North Dakota — Minnesota border, and is characterized as
20 the central lowlands. The central lowlands consist of the Red River Valley and the Young Drift Plains. These regions were carved out by glaciers in the last ice age. When these glaciers melted, a prehistoric
25 great lake named Lake Agassiz was formed. With time Lake Agassiz dried up and left very fertile soil in this region. The eastern part of the state also gets an average rainfall of about 30 inches. The combination of
30 rich soil and healthy rainfall during the growing season results in farms that have among the highest yield per acre in the world. Of particular fame is the wheat and barley grown in this region.

35 The drier, western half of the state contains the Missouri Plateau region, which is covered by only a thin, easily eroded layer of soil. The southwestern part of the state is the home of the Badlands, an area
40 of chiseled buttes. Because the farmland is not as good in the western half of North Dakota, there are more ranches than farms. Livestock ranches in western North Dakota generate one-third of the state's farm
45 income.
Sioux Indians were the primary inhabitants of what is now North Dakota prior to the immigration of the European settlers. The Sioux nation was split into
50 many separate, independent tribes. The Sioux were a nomadic people whose life centered on the once monstrous herds of buffalo. The Sioux relied on the buffalo for food, shelter, and clothing. The settling of
55 North Dakota was initiated by Lewis and Clark's expedition through the northwestern United Sates in 1804. Their expedition was, remarkable as they made the long journey alone. Lewis and Clark, unprepared
60 for the harsh North Dakota winter, spent the winter as guests of the Mandan-Sioux near North Dakota's present capital of Bismarck. The way to settling was cleared when the Sioux were pushed west of North
65 Dakota during the Indian wars of the mid-1800s. Although the Sioux were driven from their homeland in the war, their way of life was already in danger due to the destruction of the buffalo herds by poach-
70 ers after the buffalo hides and the impingement of settlers on the eastern border of Sioux lands.

21. South Dakota:

A. is east of North Dakota

B. entered the United States after North Dakota

C. is the geographical center of North America

D. entered the United States before Colorado

22. The Young Drift Plains and the Red River Valley were formed by:

F. continental drift
G. flooding of the Red River
H. an earthquake
J. glaciers from the last ice age

23. Factors contributing to the high per-acreage yield in eastern North Dakota include:

I. fertile soil
II. healthy rainfall during the growing season
III. a long growing season

A. I and II
B. II and III
C. I and III
D. I, II, and III

24. It is stated that the lands in western North Dakota are used for ranching rather than farming because:

F. livestock prices are higher in western North Dakota
G. the climate is more suitable for raising healthy livestock
H. the soil is not good enough so that farming will be more profitable than ranching
J. livestock grow faster in the western part of North Dakota

25. The land in southwestern North Dakota is probably:

A. covered with water
B. used for farming
C. densely populated
D. neither farmed nor ranched

26. The Mandan-Sioux probably hosted Lewis and Clark because:

F. they thought they would be paid
G. they were afraid of Lewis and Clark
H. they were unaware of the danger that Lewis and Clark's expedition posed
J. they planned to sabotage Lewis and Clark's trip

27. The word *impingement* as used in the last paragraph (lines 70–71) can be defined as all of the following *except*:

A. striking
B. effect
C. encroachment
D. increase in numbers

28. North Dakota is bordered on the east by:

F. settlers
G. Colorado
H. Canada
J. the Red River

29. The statement that their way of life was already in danger (lines 67–68) implies:

A. even without the Indian wars it is likely they would be driven from their land
B. the Indians should have won the war
C. the Indians should not have fought
D. the Indians should have moved west on their own

30. From the reading one could infer:

F. North Dakota is highly industrialized
G. North Dakota has many forests
H. North Dakota has many lakes
J. North Dakota is sparsely populated

Passage IV

Line A colloid is larger than a molecule but small enough to be "suspended" in a solvent. It is a particle having dimensions between 1 micron and 1 millimicron. A micron is
5 one-millionth of a meter. A millimicron, or nanometer, is one-billionth of a meter. Such a particle cannot be seen with a micro-scope, but when carried in a solution, it will not diffuse through a membrane made
10 from parchment paper. In contrast, salt molecules or sugar molecules will diffuse. A colloid may consist of grains of a solid, bubbles of a gas, or droplets of a liquid dispersed in three kinds of mediums:
15   1) sols: solid colloids in a liquid or a gas in a liquid.
    2) gels: oblong shaped colloids forming a branched structure in a liquid.
    3) emulsions: minute droplets of a
20 liquid dispersed in a second liquid.
    Colloids have a random motion (they zigzag) because of collisions with other molecules. They are stable while carrying the same electrical charge, which causes
25 them to repel each other and literally disperse themselves in a solvent or gaseous medium. (This phenomenon is known as Brownian motion.) Colloids will provide a path for a sharp beam of light, but may
30 otherwise reflect normal light as a color. (This is known as the Tyndell effect.) They are capable of adsorbing themselves on solid surfaces.
    Solid colloids are prepared by very
35 fine grinding or by controlled condensa-tions, analogous to the way nature makes snow. A very small amount of an electrolyte or a surface wetting agent may be used to make colloids compatible with a specific
40 solvent. For example, clay is a naturally occurring colloid. If water is treated with less than 1 percent of an electrolyte and clay is added in, the clay will disperse to a pourable fluid consistency, which can then
45 be charged into plaster of Paris molds. The latter absorb the water but not the clay particles, which form into thin-walled clay parts. After removal from the molds, these parts are baked and fired into ceramic
50 wares having thin walls.

Similarly, trace amounts of a surface active agent may be added to finely ground plastic powders, which then become compatible with water so that they can be
55 transformed into paints or caulks. Because colloids carry an electrical charge, they may be sprayed onto an oppositely charged surface, where they become electrically bonded. The plate is then heated to smooth
60 out the coating.
    In a similar manner, colloidal particles being exhausted from industrial smoke-stacks can be conveyed between the particles from entering the atmosphere.
65 Solids, which would be impossible to react, could be ground to fine colloids, dispersed in solvent, and reacted.

31. A nanometer is:

    A. larger than a millimicron
    B. smaller than a millimicron
    C. larger than a micron
    D. smaller than a micron

32. A salt molecule is:

    F. larger than a colloid
    G. smaller than a colloid
    H. heavier than a colloid
    J. lighter than a colloid

33. Colloids are stable when:

    A. they have the same electrical charge
    B. they are sols
    C. they are gels
    D. they zigzag

34. The Tyndell effect deals with colloid:

    F. size
    G. reflection of light
    H. motion
    J. shape

35. The example of clay in water is an example of a(n):

A. sol
B. gel
C. emulsion
D. solvent

36. *Disperse* as used in paragraph 3 (line 43) means:

F. absorb water
G. harden
H. disintegrate
J. distribute evenly

37. Surface agents are used to:

A. make colloids compatible with a liquid
B. convert molecules into colloids
C. convert sols into gels
D. solidify sols

38. *Adsorbing* as used in paragraph 2 (line 32) is best described as:

F. spreading
G. wetting
H. adhering
J. solidifying

39. The example in the last paragraph is an example of a(n):

A. sol
B. gel
C. emulsion
D. solvent

40. Tiny bubbles of oil in water is an example of a(n):

F. sol
G. gel
H. emulsion
J. solvent

SCIENCE REASONING TEST   TIME—35 MINUTES   40 QUESTIONS

Passage I

Different strains of the free-living bacterium *Microbiologicus studenticus* showed differences in degree of motility (movement) due to differing numbers of flagella present when each strain of bacterium was grown at 21% oxygen, the concentration present in the normal atmosphere. Studies were conducted to determine whether the number of flagella varied depending on the amount of oxygen in the growth medium.

Experiment 1:

Twelve cultures of the same strain of bacteria were grown with constant temperature, light, and 21% oxygen. The bacteria, upon examination, averaged two polar flagella each, with one at each end of the cells.

Experiment 2:

Twelve cultures of the same strain of bacteria were grown with constant temperature and light, but with 18% oxygen. The bacteria produced an average of four polar flagella each, with two at each end of the cells.

Experiment 3:

Twelve cultures of the same strain of bacteria were grown with constant temperature and light, but with 16% oxygen. The bacteria produced an average of six polar flagella each, with three at each end of the cells.

Experiment 4:

Twelve cultures of the same strain of bacteria were grown with constant temperature and light, but with 12% oxygen. No flagella were produced.

1. Which experiment served as a control?

   A. Experiment 1
   B. Experiment 2
   C. Experiment 3
   D. Experiment 4

2. Which is a valid conclusion based on Experiment 2 alone?

   F. Oxygen levels less than those found in the normal atmosphere make this strain of bacterium produce more flagella.
   G. Oxygen levels less than those found in the normal atmosphere make this strain of bacterium produce fewer flagella than normal.
   H. This strain of bacterium produces flagella only if exposed to oxygen.
   J. This strain of bacterium produces flagella in response to changes to temperature.

3. Which of the following was the experimental variable in this series of experiments?

   A. temperature
   B. nutrients
   C. bacterial strain
   D. oxygen

4. Which of the following is a valid conclusion based on Experiments 2 and 4?

   F. Decreasing oxygen levels eliminate flagella production entirely.
   G. Increasing oxygen levels eliminate flagella production entirely.
   H. Oxygen has no effect on flagella production.
   J. Increasing oxygen levels reduce production of flagella.

5. Which of the following is a method for checking to see if a continued decrease in oxygen levels will increase flagella production?

   A. Grow twelve cultures of different strains of bacteria at the same level of oxygen.
   B. That was checked in Experiment 4.
   C. That was done in Experiments 1 through 4.
   D. This cannot be done.

6. If the investigator wished to study the effects of protein concentration, which of the following would be most helpful?

   F. Experiment 4 should be repeated with several different levels of protein supplement in the growth medium.
   G. All four experiments should be repeated, varying both oxygen levels and protein concentrations.
   H. Protein metabolism occurs only at 21% oxygen, so Experiment 1 should be repeated with varied amounts of protein.
   J. One of the first three experiments should be repeated several times, using different amounts of protein supplement in the growth medium.

Passage II

A 5.0-kg steel ball and a 2.5-kg aluminum ball were carried to heights of 592.9 and 313.6 m respectively. Each of the balls was dropped, and the time to reach the ground was recorded. Air resistance is considered to be negligible. The distance above ground was calculated from the free-fall formula, $d = 1/2\ g\ t^2$. Knowing the distance the object is above the ground allows the calculation of potential energy. Kinetic energy was calculated from the difference in the new potential energy each second and the original potential energy.

Refer to Data Table 1 and Data Table 2 to answer questions 7 through 12.

Data Table 1

Mass = 5.0 kg   Volume = 558.0 cm³   Composition = steel

Time (s)	Distance Above Ground (m)	Velocity (m/s)	Kinetic Energy (J)	Potential Energy (J)
0	592.9	0	0	29052.1
1	588.0	9.8	240.1	28812.0
2	573.3	19.6	960.4	28091.7
3	548.8	29.4	2160.9	26891.2
4	514.5	39.2	3841.6	25210.5
5	470.4	49.0	6002.5	23049.6
6	416.5	58.8	8643.6	20408.5
7	352.8	68.6	11764.9	17287.2
8	279.3	78.4	15366.4	13685.7
9	196.0	88.2	19448.1	9604.0
10	102.9	98.0	24010.0	5042.1
11	0.0	107.8	29052.1	0

Data Table 2

Mass = 2.5 kg   Volume = 926 cm³   Composition = aluminum

Time (s)	Distance Above Ground (m)	Velocity (m/s)	Kinetic Energy (J)	Potential Energy (J)
0	313.6	0	0	7683.2
1	308.7	9.8	120.05	7563.15
2	294.0	19.6	480.2	7203
3	269.5	29.4	1080.45	6602.75
4	235.2	39.2	1920.8	5762.4
5	191.1	49.0	3001.25	4681.95
6	137.2	58.8	4321.8	3361.4
7	73.5	68.6	5882.45	1800.75
8	0	78.4	7683.2	0

7. At what time are the kinetic energy and the potential energy the same in the steel ball?

A. between 3 and 4 seconds
B. between 4 and 5 seconds
C. between 5 and 6 seconds
D. between 7 and 8 seconds

8. The aluminum ball fails to reach the same velocity as the steel ball because:

F. its mass is less
G. its volume is so much greater
H. it is dropped from a lower elevation
J. it has a different density

9. To determine if mass has an effect on velocity:

    A. both balls should have the same mass

    B. both balls should be dropped from the same height

    C. the velocity should be calculated for as many seconds as possible

    D. the densities of the balls should be the same

10. The density of the aluminum ball is approximately:

    F. 9 g/cm^3

    G. 3 g/cm^3

    H. 0.5 g/cm^3

    J. 1.0 g/cm^3

11. At what distance above the ground are the kinetic energy and potential energy the same in the steel ball?

    A. between 279.3 m and 352.8 m

    B. between 470.4 m and 514.5 m

    C. between 102.9 m and 196.0 m

    D. between 416.5 m and 470.4 m

12. Changing the mass in the data tables would affect:

    F. the velocity

    G. the distance above the ground

    H. the densities of the two objects

    J. the potential and kinetic energies

Passage III

In the early part of the eighteenth century, the English scientist John Dalton (1767-1844), proposed an *atomic theory* based on experimentation and chemical laws known at that time. A summary of his proposals is as follows:

Proposal #1: Elements are composed of tiny, discrete, indivisible, and indestructible particles called atoms. These atoms maintain their identity throughout physical and chemical changes.

Proposal #2: Atoms of the same element are identical in mass and have the same chemical and physical properties. Atoms of different elements have different masses, and different chemical and physical properties.

Proposal #3: Chemical combinations of two or more elements always occur in whole-number ratios to form a molecule.

Proposal #4: Atoms of different elements can unite in different ratios to form more than one compound.

Later modifications to Dalton's theory included the discovery of the electron in 1879 by Sir William Crookes; the discovery of the proton in 1886 by Eugen Goldstein and J. J. Thompson; and the discovery of the neutron in 1932 by Sir James Chadwick. The electron was described as a subatomic particle with virtually no mass and a negative (-) electric charge. The proton was described as a subatomic particle with a relative mass of 1 and a positive (+) electric charge. The neutron was described as a subatomic particle also with a relative mass of 1 and no electric (neutral) charge. The number of protons in an element's atom was also defined as that element's *atomic number*.

13. If all of the scientists mentioned in the preceding passage could meet today and discuss atomic theory, they would *all* agree that:

 A. the atom is solid and indivisible
 B. the atom is indestructible
 C. carbon and oxygen can combine in more than one method
 D. more than one form of an element is possible

14. Which of the four major proposals of Dalton's atomic theory described in the preceding passage was essentially disproved when the first nuclear weapon was exploded?

 F. Proposal #1
 G. Proposal #2
 H. Proposal #3
 J. Proposal #4

15. During the development of the atomic theory, *isotopes* were discovered. Atoms having different atomic masses, but the same atomic number, are called isotopes. Using the preceding description of the history of the atomic theory, predict when the term "isotope" was correctly defined.

 A. before 1879
 B. after 1879 but prior to 1886
 C. after 1886 but prior to 1932
 D. after 1932

16. Hypothetical element "X" has an atomic number of 81 and an atomic mass of 204. An atom of element "X" will contain how many neutrons?

 F. 81
 G. 204
 H. 123
 J. impossible to calculate since the number of electrons was not specified

17. The term "allotropy" is used to designate the existence of an element in two or more forms in the same physical state. For example, oxygen (O_2) and ozone (O_3) are called *allotropes*. The concept of allotropy most directly extends which of Dalton's four basic proposals?

 A. Proposal #1
 B. Proposal #2
 C. Proposal #3
 D. Proposal #4

18. Atoms of elements are said to be "electrically neutral." Which of the following statements supports that proposal?

 F. In a neutral atom, the number of protons equals the number of neutrons.
 G. In a neutral atom, the number of electrons equals the number of protons.
 H. In a neutral atom, the number of neutrons equals the number of electrons.
 J. In a neutral atom, the atomic number is the same as the atomic mass.

Passage IV

A geologist conducted three studies to determine the rate of groundwater recharge for an aquifer below a watershed so that an estimate of the amount of water available for pumping at a sustainable rate may be determined and to evaluate any impacts on the environment in the area. Water entering the watershed is called inflow, and water leaving is called outflow.

Study 1:

The only inflow of water into the watershed is precipitation over the area. Measurements of precipitation were taken over a three-year period. The geologist determined that the annual average is 95% 10^6 cubic meters of water per year (m^3/yr). The results are in Table 1.

Table 1

Type of inflow	Average inflow (m^3/yr)
Rainfall over watershed	95 % 10^6

Study 2:

Water leaves the watershed naturally by evapotranspiration, outflowing streams, and outflowing groundwater. Evapotranspiration is the combined process of evaporation of water from the surface plus transpiration or the evaporation of water through the leaves of plants. Measurements of these processes were taken regularly over the three-year period.

Table 2

Type of outflow	Average outflow (m^3/yr)
Evapotranspiration	60 % 10^6
Outflowing streams	25 % 10^6
Outflowing groundwater	5 % 10^6

Study 3:

The geologist installed several monitoring wells to monitor the depth to the water table and monthly readings during the study period These readings were averaged each year to account for seasonal fluctuations. The depth to the water table was found to be stable during the time of this study.

19. If pumping exceeds the rate at which the aquifer can recharge itself, what will be the effect on surface waters in the area?

   A. It will have no effect on surface waters since the water is being pumped from the ground.
   B. It could lower them, especially lakes and wetlands, since the water table is continuous with surface waters.
   C. No effect can be determined with the information provided.
   D. More water will flow from groundwater into surface water to maintain equal surface water outflow.

20. What will be the effect of pumping on the rate of groundwater outflow?

   F. Groundwater outflow will probably increase because the water table will lower.
   G. There will be no change in groundwater outflow.
   H. Groundwater outflow will probably decrease because of the removal of groundwater.
   J. Not enough information is known about the area to draw a conclusion about the effects on groundwater outflow.

21. If the area had received higher-than-normal rainfall during the three-year study period, how would this have affected the results?

   A. Total outflow would be higher.
   B. Total inflow would be higher.
   C. Total outflow would be lower.
   D. There would be no effect on the results.

22. If the watershed is developed with housing and shopping centers with all the associated roadways and parking lots, what would be the effect?

    F. Surface water outflow would decrease and groundwater recharge would increase.

    G. Evapotranspiration would increase.

    H. Surface water outflow would increase and groundwater recharge would decrease.

    J. There would be no effect on any inflow or outflow.

23. Would more accurate results have been obtained if the study period was increased from three to five years?

    A. No, because there are no changes from year to year in any of the variables.

    B. No, because groundwater movement is slow.

    C. Yes, because longer studies are always better.

    D. Yes, because there would be less chance of the results to be skewed by abnormally low or high measurements.

24. Which of the following generalizations can be made about the aquifer's water balance based on the results of these studies?

    F. Pumping groundwater will always have negative consequences.

    G. The water table will change if the rates of inflow are not equal to outflow.

    H. Pumping groundwater will lower surface water levels.

    J. No generalization can be made.

Passage V

    An experiment is performed on a system consisting of a mass m resting on a horizontal surface attached to a free-hanging mass M as shown in the figure below. The system is originally at rest. When released, the mass m is free to move through some displacement, x. The time, t, it takes to move through this distance, x, is measured. The purpose of this experiment is to determine how various physical variables affect the motion of m.

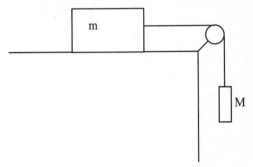

Experiment 1:

    In this experiment the system is released from rest and allowed to move through various distances. The masses m and M are held constant. The distances and the times are summarized in Table 1.

Table 1

x	t
20.0 cm	0.404 s
40.0 cm	0.571 s
60.0 cm	0.700 s

Experiment 2:

    In this experiment mass is transferred from mass m on the horizontal surface to the hanging mass M. The total mass of the system $m + M$ remains constant throughout the experiment. The system is allowed to move through a fixed distance of 60.0 cm. The results are summarized in Table 2.

Table 2

M	t
50.0 g	0.700 s
100.0 g	0.495 s
150.0 g	0.404 s

Experiment 3:

In this experiment the hanging mass M is kept constant, but additional mass is added to mass m on the horizontal surface. The system is released from rest and allowed to move through a distance of 60.0 cm. The results are summarized in Table 3.

Table 3

m	t
100.0 g	0.606 s
150.0 g	0.700 s
200.0 g	0.782 s

25. A suspended 50-g mass M is attached to a 100-g mass m and released from rest. Based on the data, one can conclude that:

A. x will be directly proportional to t
B. x will be directly proportional to t^2
C. x will be inversely proportional to t
D. x will be inversely proportional to t^2

26. In Experiment 2, a student suspends a mass M of 200.0 g. Based on the results given, he would correctly predict the time taken to travel 60.0 cm is:

F. 0.831 s
G. 0.568 s
H. 0.350 s
J. 0.158 s

27. Based on the data presented, one can conclude that:

A. the system is moving at constant velocity
B. the system is accelerating
C. the time of travel is independent of the mass of the system
D. the distance traveled is proportional to the mass M

28. On the basis of all the experiments, the travel time *must* be *increased* by which of the following conditions?
 I. Only the amount that suspended mass M is increased.
 II. The total mass of the system $M + m$ is increased.
 III. Only the mass m resting on the horizontal surface is increased.
F. I only
G. II and III only
H. I and II only
J. III only

29. Which of the following variables (x, t, M, m) is dependent on the other three?
A. x
B. t
C. M
D. m

30. Which of the following conditions would result in the shortest travel time?
F. $M = 200$ g, $m = 50$ g, $x = 100$ cm
G. $M = 200$ g, $m = 50$ g, $x = 60$ cm
H. $M = 50$ g, $m = 200$ g, $x = 60$ cm
J. $M = 50$ g, $m = 200$ g, $x = 100$ cm

Passage VI

The process of *qualitative analysis* often involves mixing aqueous solutions that may produce precipitates (solids). The Alkali Earth Metals exist in compounds as M^{+2} ions (examples, Mg^{+2}, Ca^{+2}, etc.). When solutions containing these ions are mixed with solutions containing X^{-2} ions (examples, SO_4^{-2} [sulfate], CO_3^{-2} [carbonate]), a salt will precipitate if the combination of the positive (M^{+2}) and negative (X^{-2}) ions forms an insoluble (not dissolving in aqueous solution) salt $(MX)_{(s)}$.

The following table summarizes the results of a student experiment that involved combining various alkali earth nitrate solutions with equal volumes and concentrations of solutions containing X^{-2} ions.

	Sulfuric Acid (H_2SO_4)	Sodium Carbonate (Na_2CO_3)	Ammonium Oxalate $[(NH_4)_2C_2O_4]$	Potassium Chromate (K_2CrO_4) – acidic
Barium Nitrate	WHITE PRECIPITATE	WHITE PRECIPITATE	WHITE PRECIPITATE	YELLOW PRECIPITATE
Calcium Nitrate	NO REACTION	WHITE PRECIPITATE	WHITE PRECIPITATE	NO REACTION
Magnesium Nitrate	NO REACTION	WHITE PRECIPITATE	NO REACTION	NO REACTION
Strontium Nitrate	WHITE PRECIPITATE	WHITE PRECIPITATE	WHITE PRECIPITATE	NO REACTION

31. The addition of magnesium nitrate to ammonium oxalate results in "NO REACTION." From your viewpoint as a student, the term "NO REACTION" takes place in qualitative analysis when:

A. a white solid forms
B. a yellow solid forms
C. the resulting solution shows a color change
D. there is no visible solid forming, and no color change in the solution

32. A student is given a beaker with a solution known to contain two of the four alkali earth metal ions [barium, calcium, magnesium, or strontium]. When mixed with a sulfuric acid solution, no visible reaction is the result. Based on the preceding table, the unknown solution probably contains:

F. barium and calcium ions
G. barium and magnesium ions
H. calcium and strontium ions
J. calcium and magnesium ions

33. The student is now given a beaker with a solution that contains *only one* metallic ion, which was *either* Sr^{+2} or Ca^{+2}. The student is then told to choose *only* one reagent to mix with the unknown solution to identify the metallic ion. Using the preceding table, which reagent should the student choose?

A. sulfuric acid
B. sodium carbonate
C. ammonium oxalate
D. potassium chromate

34. Based on the preceding table, which of the experimental sequences and results would confirm that an unknown solution contained magnesium nitrate ions only?

F. no reaction in ammonium oxalate
G. no reaction sulfuric acid, followed by no reaction in potassium chromate
H. no reaction in ammonium oxalate, followed by a white precipitate in sodium carbonate
J. no reaction in ammonium oxalate, followed by no reaction in sulfuric acid

35. A student is given a solution containing a mixture of equal concentrations of barium, calcium, magnesium, and strontium ions. The challenge is to separate the ions sequentially by adding reagents that will precipitate the metal ions so that they then can be removed by filtration. In which *order* should the solutions containing the X^{-2} ions be added?

A. chromate, sulfate, oxalate, carbonate

B. sulfate, chromate, carbonate, oxalate

C. carbonate, sulfate, oxalate, chromate

D. oxalate, sulfate, carbonate, chromate

36. A final unknown alkali metal ionic solution is given to a student. The solution may contain any combination of barium, calcium, magnesium, or strontium ions. The student is told that the solution must contain at least one of the ions listed, but it may contain more than one. When the X^{-2} reagent chromate is added, *no reaction* is observed. Which of the following conclusions may be drawn from this observation?

F. The unknown solution contains only calcium.

G. The unknown solution does not contain barium.

H. The unknown solution does not contain barium, but must contain strontium.

J. The unknown solution contains calcium, magnesium, and strontium.

Passage VII

	Mercury	Venus	Earth	Mars	Jupiter	Saturn	Uranus	Neptune	Pluto
Distance from Sun AU	0.39	0.72	1.00	1.52	5.20	9.54	19.18	30.06	39.44
Millions of Kilometers	58	108	150	228	778	1427	2866	4492	5909
Period of Revolution	88^d	225^d	365.25^d	687^d	12^{yr}	29.5^{yr}	84^{yr}	165^{yr}	248^{yr}
Orbital Velocity (km/s)	47.5	35.0	29.8	24.1	13.1	9.6	6.8	5.3	4.7
Period of Rotation	59^d	243^d	24^h	24.6^h	$\sim10^h$	$\sim10.5^h$	10.75^h	16^h	6.4^d
Diameter	4854	12,112	12.751	6788	143,000	121,000	47,000	46,529	~2400
Relative Mass	0.056	0.82	1.0	0.108	318.00	95.20	14.60	17.30	$\sim0.01(?)$
Average Density (g/cm^3)	5.1	5.3	5.5	3.94	1.34	0.70	1.55	1.64	$\sim1.5(?)$
Number of Known Satellites	0	0	1	2	16	17	15	8	1

37. Which planet is most similar to Earth in size and mass?

A. Mercury

B. Venus

C. Jupiter

D. Neptune

38. What is the ratio of the period of revolution to the period of rotation in days for Mercury?

F. 2/3

G. 180

H. 3/2

J. 1/180

39. Which planet has the greatest mass?

A. Venus
B. Earth
C. Jupiter
D. Saturn

40. What is the relationship between a planet's distance from the Sun and its orbital velocity?

F. The closer a body is to the Sun, the slower the orbital velocity.
G. The greater the distance from the Sun, the greater the orbital velocity.
H. The closer a body is to the Sun, the greater the orbital velocity.
J. There is no relationship between a body's distance from the Sun and its orbital velocity.

QUICK-SCORE ANSWERS

ANSWERS TO PRACTICE TEST 1

English		Mathematics		Reading		Science	
1. D	39. D	1. C	31. B	1. A	21. B	1. A	21. B
2. H	40. H	2. H	32. K	2. H	22. J	2. F	22. H
3. B	41. C	3. A	33. A	3. B	23. A	3. D	23. D
4. H	42. G	4. F	34. G	4. G	24. H	4. F	24. G
5. D	43. C	5. A	35. D	5. B	25. D	5. C	25. B
6. H	44. F	6. J	36. G	6. J	26. H	6. J	26. H
7. D	45. D	7. E	37. D	7. C	27. A	7. D	27. B
8. H	46. J	8. H	38. K	8. F	28. J	8. H	28. J
9. B	47. A	9. B	39. C	9. D	29. A	9. B	29. B
10. G	48. G	10. J	40. G	10. G	30. J	10. G	30. G
11. C	49. C	11. E	41. D	11. B	31. D	11. A	31. D
12. G	50. G	12. G	42. K	12. J	32. G	12. J	32. J
13. A	51. A	13. C	43. D	13. C	33. A	13. C	33. A
14. J	52. H	14. H	44. F	14. J	34. G	14. F	34. H
15. D	53. C	15. B	45. A	15. B	35. A	15. D	35. A
16. F	54. G	16. G	46. H	16. J	36. J	16. H	36. G
17. B	55. C	17. A	47. B	17. A	37. A	17. B	37. B
18. G	56. F	18. F	48. G	18. F	38. H	18. G	38. H
19. D	57. C	19. B	49. B	19. D	39. A	19. B	39. C
20. G	58. J	20. F	50. J	20. H	40. H	20. G	40. H
21. C	59. D	21. B	51. E				
22. G	60. G	22. H	52. J				
23. B	61. B	23. E	53. A				
24. J	62. H	24. J	54. K				
25. C	63. A	25. A	55. D				
26. H	64. J	26. J	56. H				
27. D	65. C	27. C	57. B				
28. H	66. F	28. J	58. J				
29. C	67. D	29. B	59. A				
30. H	68. H	30. F	60. J				
31. C	69. A						
32. J	70. H						
33. D	71. B						
34. G	72. F						
35. B	73. C						
36. H	74. J						
37. C	75. B						
38. G							

EXPLANATORY ANSWERS TO PRACTICE TEST 1

1. The correct answer is D. This corrects the sentence fragment. B perpetuates that error, and there is no justification for the contrary meaning implied by "however."

2. The correct answer is H. The comma comes before a coordinating conjunction that separates two independent clauses. "Resented" is past tense, to be consistent with "were" above.

3. The correct answer is B. Simple past implies, among other things, a state existing in the past: The nonjogger continued to feel left out. The past perfect tense implies a completed action sometime before the particular point in the past and would not work here.

4. The correct answer is H. This expression should be set off on both sides by commas. "Handled" is CB radio slang.

5. The correct answer is D. "Jogging or running" is a singular concept, and it exists in the present tense. The implication of the paragraph is that the backlash will not affect the popularity of jogging.

6. The correct answer is H. It is the most concise answer. G supplies the same "shoe" for both racing and training, and J is unnecessarily wordy, with the repetition of "good."

7. The correct answer is D. This is a matter of correct diction or word choice. "Smackers" and "bucks" are too informal for the tone of the passage; "treasury notes" is too formal.

8. The correct answer is H. "Reasonably" parallels "outrageously" because both are adverbs and together they modify "priced."

9. The correct answer is B. This suffices to carry the meaning and avoids wordiness.

10. The underlined subject and verb are introducing a dependent clause. The antecedent (or word referring to) for "which" is "atmosphere." The clause then needs a singular verb, "leads" and "that" as the subject because it is a restrictive (or essential) clause. Nonrestrictive clauses are usually set off by commas.

11. The correct answer is C. This is precise and accurate. The others have the wrong connotations: "scaling of" implies actual climbing. B is absurd—a lift ticket cannot charge a price.

12. The correct answer is G. "Jogging and running" is absurd repetition. Since the question of health is also a medical one, it seems logical that doctors and runners would be the ones interested here.

13. The correct answer is A. The original retains the parallel series construction. D implies incorrectly that "stress" is an "impending" disease. C is a correct construction, but implies that stress, exhaustion, and disease could not occur simultaneously.

14. The correct answer is J. This avoids the irritating repetition of "will allow," which appears at the end of the sentence.

15. The correct answer is D. This is the only option that makes sense within the context of the paragraph. Running is a sport available to all ages.

16. The correct answer is F. "Making" is nonparallel; "to make the brain focus" is wordy; "ability to concentrate" is nonparallel and redundant.

17. The correct answer is B. "School" parallels the other two nouns. There is no other direct reference to the reader in this essay, so "your schoolwork" is inappropriate. C and D are too wordy for their position in the sentence.

18. The correct answer is G. This incorporates the fragment smoothly into the main sentence. H is redundant, and J is a fused sentence which occurs when two sentences are joined without proper punctuation.

19. The correct answer is D. "Them" refers to both nouns of an "either-or" construction, so the answer should be "it." But "it" sounds wrong because the antecedent is not clear. The idiomatic expression "the better we do" is fine by itself.

20. The correct answer is G. "Perseverance" has good connotations — of successfully sticking to a task. "Persistence" has the necessary connotation of hanging on in an impossible situation. The other two choices make no sense.

21. The correct answer is C. The other two alternatives offer the weak, wordy, and lax word choice of the original. Always be concise.

22. The correct answer is G. "One" has been used throughout the essay and should not be changed to another form of address. Avoid shifting point of view.

23. The correct answer is B. The opening paragraph suggests that sports is a separate category or portion of the main idea and deserves its own paragraph. No further transitional words or phrases are needed with "same" and "as well" working for coherence. Try not to begin sentences with "but" or "and."

24. The correct answer is J. The previous sentence already implies that these errors may occur if the athlete is concentrating too hard and is overly aware of the audience. To add, as the first three alternatives do, further causes of nervousness or inattentiveness confuses the issue.

25. The correct answer is C. Four verbs in the present tense result in a childish writing style. C concisely subordinates less important material and focuses on the important events. The past participle implies action finished before the main verb. D is wrong because its participle is in the present tense, confusing the time sequence.

26. The correct answer is H. G is slang, and J sounds too much like the sentence introducing the tennis player. The transition to baseball from tennis is obvious, and needs no transitional introduction or explanation.

27. The correct answer is D. It is correct according to colloquial usage.

28. The correct answer is H. We are still talking of the two hypothetical examples and "both" refers to them directly.

29. The correct answer is C. "Archers" maintains the parallel structure joining the two nouns.

30. The correct answer is H. Choices F and G are wordy. The ideas go together this way. J is slang.

31. The correct answer is C. "Every group" is singular and requires a singular verb.

32. The correct answer is J. The same idea is included more smoothly at the end of the sentence. Including "to succeed" is needless repetition.

33. The correct answer is D. The exact word needed is "conform;" the rest do not convey the desired meaning.

34. The correct answer is G. This alternative clarifies the relation of the subordinate clause "As . . . shown" to the second sentence. H creates a bad comma splice after "shown" by removing "As."

35. The correct answer is B. This eliminates the redundancy. C and D continue to use the word "truth."

36. The correct answer is H. This is idiomatic usage—one devotes oneself "to" something.

37. The correct answer is C. All of these answers are grammatically correct. But C most succinctly describes the cause-and-effect relationship between Socrates's dialectic and his model of the soul.

38. The correct answer is G. A singular noun takes "s" in the possessive case. If it already ends in "s," you can just add the apostrophe, or, in this case (since all of the other choices are obviously incorrect), add "'s."

39. The correct answer is D. This retains the parallel with "about their jobs."

40. The correct answer is H. This is the correct form and punctuation, which prepares us for the list that follows. A dash indicates a break in the normal syntax, or structure of the sentence, and

emphasizes what follows. "Themselves" is the correct term of the pronoun since it is the object of a preposition.

41. The correct answer is C. In a series like this, which carries emphatic meaning, the possessive pronoun before each noun makes it more emphatic.

42. The correct answer is G. This is the most accurate choice, since the ideas of the two men are not the same — Thoreau, for instance, thought of going to Walden. No comma should separate compound predicates.

43. The correct answer is C. The reference is clear; the full name is merely redundant. B changes the meaning. That he was "able to" clarify his thoughts is made clear later in the paragraph.

44. The correct answer is F. This clarifies the idea that the "examples" come from world literature.

45. The correct answer is D. This eliminates the fragment and avoids the cliché "in the long run."

46. The correct answer is J. Numbers of one or two words should be written out rather than using numerals.

47. The correct answer is A. Because the parenthetical expression is part of an introductory dependent clause, it must be followed by a comma.

48. The correct answer is G. The passage as written has a sentence fragment. The fragment and the complete sentence should be joined to form one sentence.

49. The correct answer is C. Do not separate parts of a compound subject with a comma.

50. The correct answer is G. "Arose" is the correct past form of irregular verb.

51. The correct answer is A. Independent clauses may be joined by using a comma and a coordinating conjunction.

52. The correct answer is H. Correct parallel construction of verbs: "send" and "turn."

53. The correct answer is C. "Its" is the possessive form. "It's is a contraction for "it is."

54. The correct answer is G. The other choices do not include all of the information in the paragraph.

55. The correct answer is C. Verb tense and agreement of subject and verb. The subject is plural: "pictures and data," and the rest of the paragraph is in the past tense.

56. The correct answer is F. Elements in place names and dates, including a year, are followed by commas.

57. The correct answer is C. The other choices are too colloquial, or trite, or wordy.

58. The correct answer is J. This is the only word that supports the logic of the rest of the sentence. Be sure to read a complete sentence before you choose an answer.

59. The correct answer is D. The previous paragraph discussed some successes of the mission. "But" indicates a transition, and the question leads to the "tension and anxiety" that begin paragraph 5.

60. The correct answer is G. Although there is some information in the essay, its tone and form are mostly narrative

61. The correct answer is B. Do not shift tenses within a paragraph unless there is a reason to do so.

62. The correct answer is H. This punctuation mark, known as an ellipsis, indicates that something has been omitted.

63. The correct answer is A. Use a comma to separate clauses joined by a coordinating conjunction. Do not add a comma after the conjunction.

64. The correct answer is J. The verb must agree with its subject in number. "Pants" is the subject of the verb. The verb tense should remain the same throughout the sentence.

65. The correct answer is C. Idiomatic usage.

66. The correct answer is F. The apostrophe indicates possession. Commas are placed inside quotation marks.

67. The correct answer is D. The other answers create illogical sentences.

68. The correct answer is H. The other reasons are not true.

69. The correct answer is A. Join independent clauses with a semicolon.

70. The correct answer is H. It helps to connect the paragraphs smoothly.

71. The correct answer is B. The other choices are wordy.

72. The correct answer is F. The paragraph is arranged in chronological order.

73. The correct answer is C. Items in a series are set off by commas. The entire phrase interrupts the sentence because it comes between the verb and its object. Thus, it is set off by commas.

74. The correct answer is J. Maintain parallelism of coordinate elements.

75. The correct answer is B. A is not descriptive of the essay's content. C and D each name only part of the content of the essay.

PART **2** — **MATHEMATICS**

1. (C) A prime number is a number that is divisible by itself and by 1. Hence, $72 = 8 \cdot 9 = 2 \cdot 2 \cdot 2 \cdot 3 \cdot 3 \rightarrow 2$ and 3 are prime numbers.

2. (H) By the Pythagorean theorem:

$$a^2 + b^2 = c^2$$
$$a^2 + 6^2 = 10^2$$
$$a^2 + 36 = 100$$
$$a^2 = 64$$
$$\sqrt{a^2} = \sqrt{64}$$
$$a = 8$$

3. (A) $(3x^5)(5x^3) = (3)(5)(x^5)(x^3)$

$$= 15x^{5+3} \text{ (multiple numbers; add}$$
$$= 15x^8 \quad \text{exponents)}$$

4. (F) $\dfrac{y^2-9}{2y+6} \div \dfrac{y-3}{y+2}$

$y^2 - 9$ is the difference of two perfect squares

$y^2 - 9 = (y - 3)(y + 3)$

$2y + 6$ has the greatest common factor of 2

$2y + 6 = 2(y + 3)$

$\dfrac{(y-3)(y+3)}{2(y+3)} \cdot \dfrac{y+2}{y-3}$ invert divisor and multiply

$\dfrac{(y-3)(y+3)}{2(y+3)} \cdot \dfrac{y+2}{y-3}$ cancel out common factors of $y + 3$ and $y - 3$

$\dfrac{y+2}{2}$

5. (A) The exterior angle of a regular polygon is the supplement of each interior angle, or the exterior angle = $180 - 150 = 30$.

The formula for an exterior angle is

$\dfrac{360}{N} = $ exterior angle ($N = $ number of sides)

$\dfrac{360}{N} = 30$ cross-multiply

$360 = 30N$

$12 = N$ (number of sides)

6. (J) \$4,230

First find the amount of interest.
$I = P \cdot R \cdot T$
$= \$4,000 \cdot .0575 \cdot 1$
$= \$230$

Then add the amount of interest to the original investment.
$\$4,000 + \$230 = \$4,230$

7. (E) Convert 2 days to 48 hours.

$\dfrac{15 \text{ hours}}{48 \text{ hours}}$ cancel out common factor of $3 = \dfrac{5}{16}$

8. (H) $10''$

Use the formula

$A = \dfrac{1}{2}bh$

$75 = \dfrac{1}{2}(15)h$

$\dfrac{75}{7.5} = \dfrac{7.5h}{7.5}$

$10'' = h$

9. (B) To convert a decimal to a percent, multiply the decimal by 100.

$$.03 \cdot 100 = 3.00 = 3\%$$

10. (J) $2,000

First find the amount Leroy paid for the shares.

$$\$120 \cdot 25 = \$3,000$$

Then find the amount Leroy sold the shares for.

$$\$40 \cdot 25 = \$1,000$$

Then subtract.

$$\$3,000 - \$1,000 = \$2,000$$

11. (E) When multiplying decimals, be sure the final decimal point is in the correct place.

$$
\begin{array}{rl}
.58 & \text{2 places} \\
\times .14 & \text{2 places} \\
\hline
232 & \\
58 & \\
\hline
.0812 & \text{4 places}
\end{array}
$$

12. (G) 4

To solve equations, use inverse operations. First add +5 to both sides.

$$
\begin{array}{rl}
3a - 5 &= 7 \\
+5 &= +5 \\
\hline
3a &= 12
\end{array}
$$

Then divide both sides by 3.

$$\frac{3a}{3} = \frac{12}{3}$$
$$a = 4$$

13. (C) There are eight outcomes, of which five are successes (red).

14. (H) 33

First calculate powers, then add.

$$
\begin{array}{l}
2^3 = 2 \cdot 2 \cdot 2 = 8 \\
5^2 = 5 \cdot 5 = +25 \\
\hline
 33
\end{array}
$$

15. (B) 21

To evaluate, substitute the numerical values and compute.

$$
\begin{aligned}
& 2a^2 - 3b \\
=\ & 2(-3)^2 - 3(-1) \\
=\ & 2(9) - (-3) \\
=\ & 2(9) + (+3) \\
=\ & 18 + 3 \\
=\ & 21
\end{aligned}
$$

16. (G) $OA = OB$ because the radii in the same circle are equal. The triangle AOB is a right triangle. By the Pythagorean theorem:

$$a^2 + b^2 = c^2$$
$$(\text{leg})^2 + (\text{leg})^2 = (\text{hypotenuse})^2$$
$$(10)^2 + (10)^2 = c^2$$
$$100 + 100 = c^2$$
$$200 = c^2$$
$$\sqrt{2 \cdot 100} = \sqrt{c^2}$$
$$10\sqrt{2} = c$$

17. (A) $2x^2 + 3$

To add algebraic expressions, combine like terms.

$$
\begin{array}{rrrr}
2x^2 & -\ 3x & +\ 5 & \\
+ & 3x & -\ 2 & \\
\hline
2x^2 & +\ 0 & +\ 3 & = 2x^2 + 3
\end{array}
$$

18. (F) Area of $\Delta = \dfrac{1}{2}bh$

$$A = \frac{1}{2}(8)\left(4\sqrt{3}\right)$$
$$= 16\sqrt{3}$$

There are six triangles in a hexagon.

$$6(16\sqrt{3}) = 96\sqrt{3}$$

19. (B) 3 centimeters

First find the area of the square.

$A = s^2$

$\quad = (5)^2 = 25$ sq cm

Then, using the formula,

$A = \pi r^2$

$25 \approx (3.14)r^2$

$7.96 \approx r^2$

$\sqrt{7.96} \approx r$

2.8 cm $\approx r$

20. (F) Combine like terms by additive inverse:

$7x - 3 = 4x + 6$

$\underline{-4x + 3 = -4x + 3}$

$3x = 9$

Divide by 3: $x = 3$

21. (B) $-4\dfrac{1}{3}$

To add signed numbers, if the signs are different, subtract and use the sign of the larger.

$2\dfrac{2}{3} + (-7)$

$\begin{array}{r} 7 \\ -2\dfrac{2}{3} \\ \hline 4\dfrac{1}{3} \end{array}$

Since 7 is larger, $-4\dfrac{1}{3}$ is the answer.

22. (H) Substitute values for $p = 500$, $r = .04$, and $t = 2\dfrac{1}{2}$.

$A = 500 + (500)(.04)\, 2\dfrac{1}{2}$

$\quad = 500 + 50$

$\quad = 550$

23. (E) $|3a - 1| = 5$

$3a - 1 = 5$

$3a = 6$

$a = 2$

$-3a + 1 = 5$

$-3a = 4$

$a = \dfrac{-4}{3}$

a can equal 2 or $-\dfrac{4}{3}$

24. (J) Circumference of original circle:

$c = 2\pi r$

Circumference of new circle:

$c = 2\pi(r + x) = 2\pi r + 2\pi x$

Difference between new circle and original circle:

$2\pi r + 2\pi x - 2\pi r = 2\pi x$

25. (A) If $x = 3$, $y = -3^2 = -9$

26. (J) $AC = \sqrt{(x_1 - x_2)^2 + (y_1 - y_2)^2}$

$\quad = \sqrt{(-6 - 0)^2 + (-4 - 4)^2}$

$\quad = \sqrt{(-6)^2 + (-8)^2}$

$\quad = \sqrt{36 + 64}$

$\quad = \sqrt{100}$

$\quad = 10$

27. (C) $160

Since $128 is 80% of the original price, the base price is

$B = \dfrac{P}{R}$

$\quad = \dfrac{128}{.80} = \$160$

28. (J) The area of the square minus the area of the circle equals the shaded area.

$OA = 3$
$2OA = 6 =$ diameter = side of square
area of square = s^2
area of circle = πr^2

$$A = (6)^2 \qquad A = \pi(3)^2$$
$$= 36 \qquad = 9\pi$$

$36 - 9\pi$ equals shaded area

29. (B)

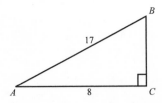

Since $\sec A = \dfrac{17}{8} = \dfrac{Hypotenuse}{Adjacent}$, the hypotenuse of the above triangle is 17, and the side adjacent to angle A is 8.

Use the Pythagorean theorem to compute that the side opposite A is 15.

Then, $\sin A = \dfrac{Opposite}{Hypotenuse} = \dfrac{15}{17}$

30. (F) equal

Angles x and y and a and b are both pairs of alternate interior angles.

31. (B) Let f = number of foxes 6 years ago

(a) $d = f + 80$ = number of deer 6 years ago
(b) $2d + f + 20 = 240$ (present time)

Substitute d = f + 80 in (b):

$$2(f + 80) + f + 20 = 240$$
$$2f + 160 + f + 20 = 240$$
$$3f + 180 = 240$$
$$3f = 60$$

Divide by 3: $f = 20$ foxes 6 years ago.

32. (K) The perimeter of the square = 4s.
$$P = 4s$$
$$= 4(x + 2)$$
$$= 4x + 8$$

The perimeter of the equilateral triangle = 3s.

$$P = 3s$$
$$= 3(2x)$$
$$= 6x$$

$$4x + 8 = 6x$$
$$8 = 2x$$
$$4 = x$$

33. (A) 9

Corresponding parts of similar triangles are in proportion:

$$\frac{AB}{AC} = \frac{AE}{AD}$$

$$\frac{4}{4+6} = \frac{6}{6+x}$$

$$4(6 + x) = 6(4 + 6)$$
$$24 + 4x = 60$$
$$\underline{-24 = -24}$$
$$4x = 36$$
$$x = 9$$

34. (G) $(3K^2)^3 = (3K^2)(3K^2)(3K^2)$
$$= (3)(3)(3)(K^2)(K^2)(K^2)$$
$$= 27K^{2+2+2} \text{ (multiply numbers;}$$
$$= 27K^6 \qquad \text{add exponents)}$$

35. (D) $\dfrac{x^2-1}{x} \cdot \dfrac{4x^2}{x+1}$

$x^2 - 1$ is the sum and difference of a perfect square: $(x + 1)(x - 1)$

$$\frac{(x+1)(x-1)}{x} \cdot \frac{4x^2}{x+1}$$

$$\frac{1}{\cancel{(x+1)}(x-1)} \cdot \frac{\overset{4x}{\cancel{4x^2}}}{\underset{1}{\cancel{x+1}}}$$

cancel out common factors of $x + 1$ and x

$$= \frac{4x(x-1)}{1} = 4x(x - 1)$$

36. (G) The product of the means equals the product of the extremes.

$$\frac{20}{12} = \frac{5}{y}$$

$$20y = (5)(12)$$

Divide by 20: $20y = 60$

$$y = 3$$

37. (D) $\dfrac{4}{x} - \dfrac{3}{x} = \dfrac{1}{x}$

Common denominators; subtract the numerators.

38. (K) 15%

To find the percent of increase, divide the amount of increase by the original amount.

$$\begin{array}{r} \$143.75 \\ -\ 125 \\ \hline 18.75 \end{array}$$

$$\frac{18.75}{125} = .15 = 15\%$$

39. (C) If $x = 9$ and $y = 2$, we obtain

$$3(9) - 5(2) = 17$$
$$27 - 10 = 17$$
$$17 = 17$$

40. (G) Slope $= \dfrac{y_2 - y_1}{x_2 - x_1} = \dfrac{8-2}{3-7} = \dfrac{6}{-4} = -\dfrac{3}{2}$

41. (D) Set $x^2 + 7x + 12 = 0$.

Factor: $(x + 4)(x + 3) = 0$

Set each binomial equal to zero:

$x + 4 = 0$ and $x + 3 = 0$

$\quad x = -4$ and $x = -3$

$\{-3, -4\}$

42. (K) The number of hours from 7:30 a.m. to 3:00 p.m. totals $7\frac{1}{2}$ hours.

Multiply: $7\dfrac{1}{2}$ or $7.5 \cdot 4.65 = 34.875$

$= \$34.88$

43. (D) 75% of $N = 36.75$. Divide the known part by the fractional equivalent of the percent.

$$75\% = \frac{75}{100}$$

$$36.75 \div \frac{75}{100}$$

$$36.75 \cdot \frac{100}{75} \quad \text{invert divisor and}$$

$$\text{multiply; cancel out 25's}$$

$$36.75 \cdot \frac{4}{3} = \frac{36.75 \times 4}{3} = \frac{147}{3} = 49$$

44. (F) $\left(\dfrac{y^5}{y^8}\right)^3 = \dfrac{y^{15}}{y^{24}} = \dfrac{1}{y^9} = y^{-9}$

45. (A) $8

First designate variables.

Let a tie cost $\$t$ and a shirt cost $\$s$.

Then set up two equations.

$$2t + s = 30$$
$$3t + 2s = 49$$

Multiply the first equation by -2 and then add.

$$-2(2t + s = 30) = -4t - 2s = -60$$

$$\begin{array}{l} -4t - 2s = -60 \\ \underline{3t + 2s = 49} \\ -t = -11 \\ t = 11 \end{array}$$

Substitute to find s.

$$\begin{array}{l} 2(11) + s = 30 \\ 22 + s = 30 \\ \underline{-22 = -22} \\ s = \$8 \end{array}$$

46. (H) Find two factors of 162, one of which is a perfect square.

$$\sqrt{162} = \sqrt{81 \cdot 2}$$
$$= \sqrt{81}\sqrt{2} \quad \text{reduce perfect square}$$
$$\sqrt{81} = 9$$
$$= 9\sqrt{2}$$

47. (B)

$$\frac{\csc\alpha - \sin\alpha}{\cot\alpha} = \frac{\dfrac{1}{\sin\alpha} - \sin\alpha}{\dfrac{\cos\alpha}{\sin\alpha}}$$

$$= \frac{\dfrac{1}{\sin\alpha} - \dfrac{\sin^2\alpha}{\sin\alpha}}{\dfrac{\cos\alpha}{\sin\alpha}} = \frac{\dfrac{1 - \sin^2\alpha}{\sin\alpha}}{\dfrac{\cos\alpha}{\sin\alpha}}$$

$$= \frac{\dfrac{\cos^2\alpha}{\sin\alpha}}{\dfrac{\cos\alpha}{\sin\alpha}} = \left(\frac{\cos^2\alpha}{\sin\alpha}\right)\left(\frac{\sin\alpha}{\cos\alpha}\right) = \cos\alpha$$

48. (G) If a line is parallel to one side of a triangle and intersects the other two sides, the line divides those sides proportionately.

$$\frac{16}{12} = \frac{x}{9}$$
$$12x = (16)(9)$$
$$12x = 144$$
$$x = 12$$

49. (B) The line graph with a dark circle on -2 includes -2 and all numbers greater than -2. The open circle on 3 indicates all numbers less than 3. Put together: all numbers greater than or equal to -2 and less than 3:

$$-2 \leq x < 3$$

50. (J) $37\dfrac{1}{2}$

This problem can very easily be solved using a proportion.

$$\frac{2 \text{ inches}}{15 \text{ miles}} = \frac{5 \text{ inches}}{x \text{ miles}}$$

After cross-multiplication, this proportion becomes

$$2x = 75$$
$$x = 37\frac{1}{2}$$

51. (E) $44.45

First find what percent of Freddie's income is spent on miscellaneous items.

$$50\% + 25\% + 7\% + 5.3\% = 87.3\%$$
$$100\% - 87.3\% = 12.7\%$$

Then find 12.7% of $350

$$P = B \cdot R$$
$$= 350 \cdot .127 = \$44.45$$

52. (J) The line described by the equation crosses the x-axis when $y = 0$.

$$0 = 3x + 7$$
$$-7 = 3x$$
$$-\frac{7}{3} = x$$

53. (A) Since acute angles of right Δ are supplementary, $GFE = 90 - 25 = 65$. If $FEG = 25$, $FEB = 2(25) = 50$ because BEF has bisected. $EFC = FEB$ because the measure of alternate interior angles is equal. Since the measure of a straight angle equals 180 degrees,

$$EFC + GFE + GFD = 180$$
$$50 + 65 + x = 180$$
$$115 + x = 180$$
$$x = 65$$

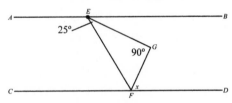

54. (K) $t \le -3$

Solving inequalities is very similar to solving equations.

$$4t + 5 \le t - 4$$
$$\underline{-5 = -5}$$
$$4t \le t - 9$$
$$\underline{-t = -t}$$
$$3t \le -9$$
$$\frac{3t}{3} \le \frac{-9}{9}$$
$$t \le -3$$

55. (D) $(3x + 1)(x - 1) = (5x - 3)(2x - 3)$
$$3x^2 - 2x - 1 = 10x^2 - 21x + 9$$
$$7x^2 - 19x + 10 = 0$$
$$(7x - 5)(x - 2) = 0$$
$$x = 2 \text{ and } \frac{5}{7}$$

56. (H) $x = 4, y = 2$

This system of equations is most easily solved using the addition/subtraction method.

$$x + 3y = 10$$
$$\underline{+2x - 3y = 2}$$
$$3x = 12$$
$$x = 4$$

Substituting in the first equation, we get

$$(4) + 3y = 10$$
$$\underline{-4 = -4}$$
$$3y = 6$$
$$y = 2$$

Again, in this problem it might have been quicker to substitute the given answers.

57. (B) Use the Pythagorean theorem to determine that the hypotenuse of the triangle is $\sqrt{53}$.

Then, $\sin B = \dfrac{\text{Opposite}}{\text{Hypotenuse}}$

$$= \frac{2}{\sqrt{53}} = \frac{2\sqrt{53}}{53}$$

58. (J) If $f(x) = 2x^3 - 8x = 0$, then

$$2x(x^2 - 4) = 0$$
$$2x(x - 2)(x + 2) = 0$$
$$x = 2, -2, 0$$

59. (A)

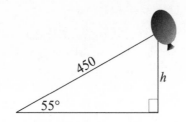

Let h = the height of the weather balloon above the ground.

Then, $\sin 55° = \dfrac{h}{450}$

or, $h = 450 \sin 55°$

60. (J) If the perimeter is 80, count all the exterior sides of *ABCD*; hence, 8 sides = 80, 1 side = 10.

area of rectangle = (length) · (width)
length (*DC*) = 30
width (*AD*) = 10
$A = (30)(10)$
$= 300$

PART 3   READING

1. The correct answer is A. B is an unlikely choice, since the fact that something is intellectual would not make "the theoretical study of [aesthetic pleasure] . . . impossible" (lines 32–34). C and D are unlikely for the same reason. Note that right after the author first uses the word *ineffable*, he includes an explanation of what it means: "completely beyond the reach of rational description and analysis" (lines 30–31); thus, *indescribable* is the best choice.

2. The correct answer is H. Although F, G, and J are all people listed in the passage, lines 20–23 note that those who study aesthetics "are engaged in the task . . . initiated [begun] by Socrates and Plato more than two thousand years ago."

3. The correct answer is B. D is unlikely since the fourth sentence of the second paragraph begins, "There are critics of aesthetics who . . ." and then lists the complaints of critics. Although C is a more likely choice, the author is careful to note that these negative opinions about aesthetics are other people's opinions rather than his own opinion. A, though another likely possibility, is also incorrect—again because the author is not criticizing aesthetics but describing the criticisms of other people, B.

4. The correct answer is G. F is unlikely as an answer since the students, like everyone else in the paragraph, are criticizing aesthetics. H and J are both more likely, since they are both criticisms, but they are less likely interpretations of the phrase "anesthetics in disguise" since "anesthetics" are used to numb a part of the body or make a person unconscious for major surgery—that is, put someone to sleep, G.

5. The correct answer is B. A, C, and D are all listed as criticisms of aesthetics in the passage, but lines 48–49 note that "poets [criticize aesthetics] for being . . . unfeeling," answer B.

6. The correct answer is J. Note that lines 5–7 list all three items (though in a different order). Thus, (I), (II), and (III) are all correct, which eliminates answers F, G, and H, leaving (J), the correct answer.

7. The correct answer is C. B is a poor answer choice for two reasons: Dr. Johnson says it's acceptable to "scold a carpenter" (line 96), and the suggestion that a person may do so should somehow relate to the idea of aesthetics, the subject of the passage. A is a better choice, but lines 100–108 show that the author is comparing "scolding a carpenter" to what art critics and aestheticians do. D is not a good choice; the point of the analogy is that just as a person whose trade is not carpentry may be justified in scolding someone who is a carpenter, so too, an aesthetician who is not an artist may be justified in scolding someone who is an artist, answer C.

8. The correct answer is F. G and J are poor choices since, in the third paragraph, the author says he will make "a few remarks . . . about some of the criticisms mentioned earlier" (lines 60–62). In addition, neither one suggests a contradiction to the author's claim that his "purpose . . . is not to defend aesthetics." H may be a more likely choice; however, the author does not introduce new criticisms, nor does this answer indicate a contradiction. Only answer F suggests a contradiction: the author says his purpose "is not to defend aesthetics," but then he spends the paragraph defending aesthetics against the earlier criticisms that it is ineffable and abstract.

9. The correct answer is D. C is unlikely because it is "our world" that is described as "contain[ing] an almost infinite variety of . . . phenomena from which we can derive aesthetic pleasures" (lines 12–15). A and B are more likely answers, and they are true of 1984, but they are both incorrect for the same reason: they rely on knowledge about the book that is not given in the passage. Lines 10–11 note that the world described in 1984 is "devoid of the aesthetic pleasures derivable from art," answer D. Be sure to choose your answer based solely on information in the paragraph.

10. The correct answer is G. H is unlikely since this is noted as being true of both art critics and aestheticians (lines 100–101). F and J are unlikely choices since they refer to the work of aestheticians. Lines 104 notes that it is the art critic who "analyzes, interprets, and evaluates" works of art, answer G.

11. The correct answer is B. In A, nothing in the passage suggests that Elsie would be feeling happy. B, C, and D are all possible answers; however, both C and D are too specific, going beyond what the passage suggests; thus, B is the best answer.

12. The correct answer is J. G and H are incorrect, because nothing in the passage suggests that Elsie wants Harvey to buy a new car for Selwyn, or that she disapproves of Harvey's corrupt activities. F is incorrect, although Elsie may believe that Harvey bought the car with money he obtained illegally, this answer does not relate to their conversation. Elsie is trying to make Harvey feel obligated to help his poor relatives; therefore, the answer is J.

13. The correct answer is C. Although A, B, and D may be true, none of them is given as a reason why Harvey cannot get away from Elsie. Lines 51–53 note that "he thought to avoid us by crossing the street, but the traffic was not kind to him"— that is, C.

14. The correct answer is J. In paragraph 4, Selwyn's mother says, ". . . talking of family, there's my cousin." H is incorrect because no mention is made of a brother-in-law in the passage. G is incorrect because Harvey mentions Selwyn's grandfather, but Harvey is not the grandfather. F is incorrect also. In lines 79–80 Harvey invites Selwyn to "Call me Uncle Harvey," but lines 41–43 indicate that Harvey is actually Elsie's cousin, answer J.

15. The correct answer is B. Choice A may seem like a possibility because of the word *protractor*; however, it is a less likely answer based on the context. C and D, similarly, are less likely, based on context. Men who are unemployed, with nothing to fill their time, are most likely to engage in lengthy discussions to pass the time, B.

16. The correct answer is J. F is incorrect because there is no suggestion of prejudice in the passage. In H and G, since line 23 mentions the Mafia, the implication is that the Italians being discussed are also corrupt and that they would not be seeking regular employment. The line suggests that since the town councillors are so corrupt, no other corrupt group would be able to operate in the town, J.

17. The correct answer is A. C and D do not relate to the passage: The discussion that follows is not a political discussion,

and the passage does not suggest that the townspeople are fascinated with the town hall. Although B is accurate, it is too general—a description of the usual function of opening paragraphs in fiction. Note that lines 7–9 in the first paragraph states that the discussions of political theory "deceived some people into believing they possessed power and influence"; the second paragraph, in contrast, opens with the words "True power," lines 14.

18. The correct answer is F. Although Harvey smokes cigars and owns antiques (G and J), the passage does not claim this as a characteristic of all the powerful people in town. H is incorrect because the teachers, line 27, are hired by the powerful people; they are not the powerful people themselves. F is incorrect because line 16 states that the powerful people in town "sold insurance."

19. The correct answer is D. A is incorrect. The first paragraph mentions men who are eloquent and energetic; however, there is no indication that Harvey needs to hire someone like this. There is no indication that Harvey is fearful of Selwyn being corrupt or learning his trade secrets (B and C). D is also incorrect because Elsie's comment that Selwyn "can keep his mouth shut" frightens Harvey and suggests that she is aware that Harvey is involved in dishonest activities.

20. The correct answer is H. Although this is the route they take on their walk (J), there is nothing in the passage to suggest that it was the purpose of their walk. Since Elsie mentions both of these as they begin their walk (choices F and G), these are more likely answers; however, just after Harvey promises to "see what [he] can do" for Selwyn in terms of a job (line 115–116), Selwyn asks (lines 119–120), "Is that why we came out this morning?," suggesting that he recognizes his mother's purpose: to make Harvey offer Selwyn a job.

21 The correct answer is B. A, C, and D all contradict statements in the first paragraph. North Dakota was the thirty-ninth state admitted to the United States, South Dakota was the fortieth.

22. The correct answer is J, as stated in the second paragraph. Answers F, G, and H are not mentioned in the reading.

23. The correct answer is A. In the second paragraph, fertile soil and a healthy rainfall during the growing season are listed as the reasons for the high yield; therefore, answer A is the correct answer. No mention is made of the growing season, therefore, choice III is eliminated.

24. The correct answer is H. Livestock prices are not mentioned, so F is not the correct answer. G is not correct either since the only difference in climate mentioned is that the eastern part gets more rain, which would not be less suitable for raising livestock. H is the correct answer; the passage differentiates the western half as having conditions less suitable for productive farming and states that there are more ranches than farms in the west. Thus, the implication is that farmland is commonly used for ranching when the land is not rich enough to yield farms as profitable as ranches. J is incorrect since one would expect livestock to grow just as quickly in the east as in the west.

25. The correct answer is D. Answer A is incorrect; nothing stated suggests this area would be either covered with water or particularly warm. Answers B and C are incorrect; the reading states that the southwestern part of the state is an area of chiseled buttes, a small rocky, mountaineous area. This type of topography or land surface would not be conducive to good farming or ranching.

26. The correct answer is H. F and G are incorrect; two inadequately equipped explorers do not indicate excessive wealth or a force to be feared. The correct answer is H; had the Mandan-Sioux understood the significance of the expedition it is likely they would not have been as hospitable. J is incorrect; they could have easily ended the expedition had they wanted to.

27. The correct answer is A. The other choices all deal with the effect of growing numbers of sellers. "Striking" in choice A implies a more direct attack.

28. J is the correct answer as stated in the second paragraph.

29. Answer A is correct because if the buffalo herds disappeared and settlers started approaching, the Indians probably would have been driven from their lands eventually. Answers B, C, and D are incorrect, as nothing in the reading suggests any of these statements.

30. The correct answer is J. Since the reading did not discuss industrialization, forests, lakes, or the lives today of Native Americans, answers F, G, and H are incorrect. Since the reading extensively discussed farming and ranching, as well as the fact that both farming and ranching use large tracts of land, and therefore there are probably less people, one could infer that North Dakota is sparsely populated.

31. The correct answer is D. A nanometer is equal to a millimicron, which is one-billionth of a meter. A micron is one-millionth of a meter. Therefore, a nanometer is smaller than a micron.

32. The correct answer is G. The reading contrasts the fact that a colloid cannot be seen with a microscope but cannot diffuse through a membrane made from parchment paper. The use of the phrase "but despite its size" following the statement that a colloid is too small to see implies that the colloid is too big to diffuse through the membrane. The salt molecule is small enough to diffuse through the membrane. Therefore, the salt molecule is smaller than the colloid, and G is the correct answer. Nothing was mentioned about weight; therefore, H and J are incorrect.

33. The correct answer is A. Paragraph 2 states "they are stable while carrying the same electrical charge."

34. The correct answer is G. Paragraph 2 states that the Tyndell effect is the property of colloids that provides a path for a sharp beam of light, but may otherwise reflect normal light as a color.

35. The correct answer is A. The clay-in-water mixture is a solid dispersed in a liquid, the definition of a sol.

36. The correct answer is J. If the clay is distributed evenly, the mixture will have the mobility to pour. F is incorrect because if clay only absorbed the water, the mixture would not be pourable. G is incorrect because if the clay was to harden it could not be poured. C is incorrect since the clay is not destroyed; it is suspended.

37. The correct answer is A, as stated in paragraph 3: "A very small amount of an electrolyte or a surface-wetting agent may be used to make colloids compatible with a specific solvent," and paragraph 4, trace amounts of a surface active agent may be added to finely ground plastic powders, which then become compatible with water.

38. The correct answer is H. In order to stick to a solid surface, it is necessary that the colloids adhere to the surface; it is not necessary that the colloid spread on the surface, wet the surface, or solidify on the surface. Therefore, F, G, and J are incorrect.

39. The correct answer is A. The particulate exhaust is an example of a solid suspended in a gas (air), which is the definition of a sol (lines 15–16).

40. The correct answer is H. Oil and water are both liquids. The definition of an emulsion is minute droplets of a liquid dispersed in a second liquid.

PART **4**	**SCIENCE**

1. The correct answer is A. Normal growth conditions were used in this experiment.

2. The correct answer is F. The only variable was a decreased level of oxygen.

3. The correct answer is D. The oxygen levels were the only thing changed from one experiment to the next.

4. The correct answer is F. This is the only possible answer of the choices given.

5. The correct answer is C. The level of oxygen was decreased steadily from experiment 1 to 4.

6. The correct answer is J. Any of the experiments in which flagella actually grew could be used as the experimental design, except that the level of oxygen would then be held constant, and the protein concentration would then be the variable.

7. The correct answer is D. Between 7 and 8 seconds, because when the kinetic energy will be between 11 764.9 and 15 366.4 J, the potential energy will be between 13 685.7 and 17 287.2 J. In this interim the kinetic and potential energies will cross, giving the same value to each. A graph of kinetic vs. potential energy shows an intersection between the 7th and 8th second.

8. The correct answer is H. Velocity is dependent on the product of gravity and time. Since the time is much less when dropped from a lower height, the velocity will be less for the aluminum ball.

9. The correct answer is B. Both balls dropped from the same height would show the same velocity at ground zero. This would prove that mass would have no effect on the velocity, since all objects fall at the same rate.

10. The correct answer is G. Density = mass / volume. 2500 g / 925.9 cm^3 equals approximately 3 g/cm^3.

11. The correct answer is A. The potential and kinetic energy will have the same value when the height is one-half of the original height. Notice that this corresponds to between 7 and 8 seconds, as discussed in question 7.

12. The correct answer is J. The only formulas that rely on mass are the potential and kinetic energies.

13. The correct answer is C. Dalton recognized that the same elements could combine in more than one method (Proposal D) to form different compounds. Carbon monoxide (CO) and carbon dioxide (CO_2) would be an example. The other scientists modified his other proposals. Atoms are not solid; they can be changed (atomic warfare). Finally, allotropes have been discovered.

14. The correct answer is F. Dalton noted in his proposal that atoms are indestructible. Nuclear explosions change atoms and produce energy.

15. The correct answer is D. An isotope is a form of an element with a different atomic mass due to a change in the "neutron count." Neutrons were first described in 1932.

16. The correct answer is H. To calculate the number of neutrons from the information given, subtract the atomic number (the number of protons) from the atomic mass (the number of protons and neutrons): $204 - 81 = 123$.

17. The correct answer is B. The concept of *allotropy* is significant here. For example, ozone is an allotrope of oxygen. They are composed of the *same element*, but have significantly different chemical and physical properties.

18. The correct answer is G. The two subatomic particles that have an electric charge are the proton (+) and the electron (−). Hence, to be electrically neutral, the number of protons must equal the number of electrons in an atom.

19. The correct answer is B. Groundwater and surface water are continuous, and water can flow from groundwater to surface water or vice versa. It is dependent on the hydraulic gradient. Since there is evidence of groundwater-to-surface water flow, pumping could draw down the water table and lower surface water levels.

20. The correct answer is G. Pumping groundwater will change the hydraulic gradient or the potential of the groundwater to flow. This change will have the effect of slowing the rate of groundwater outflow.

21. The correct answer is B. Total inflow would be higher than average due to higher-than-normal rainfall.

22. The correct answer is H. With development of buildings, roads, and parking surfaces, the effect is to reduce the area over which recharge can occur. Water also runs off more quickly when the surface is covered up, so the effect is to increase surface water runoff and reduce recharge.

23. The correct answer is D. Lengthening the time of the study to five years would help eliminate errors if the measurements are abnormally low or high, especially with rainfall, since a better average would be obtained with five years' duration.

24. The correct answer is G. Choice F contains a value judgment that pumping groundwater always has negative results. When talking about a water budget it is always true that if rates of inflow are not equal to rates of outflow that levels will change.

25. The correct answer is B. Since $M + m$ is constant, we can use Table 1 to see that x/t^2 is the same for all three entries.

26. The correct answer is H. M is inversely proportional to t^2. For all values in Experiment 2, $M \times t^2 = 24.5$. If $M = 200$ then $t^2 = 0.1225$ and $t = 0.35$.

27. The correct answer is B. The system is accelerating. In all cases the variables x, M, and m are proportional to t^2. This indicates that the velocity must be changing as time changes.

28. The correct answer is J. From the tables, one can see that as M increases, the travel time decreases. As m increases, the travel time increases. For case II the travel time might increase or decrease as $M+m$ increases, depending on where the increased mass is placed.

29. The correct answer is B. A dependent variable is one that is determined by other variables in the relation. The elapsed time was determined by the distance traveled and the masses added.

30. The correct answer is G. From the tables, the greater the mass M the shorter the travel time. The smaller the mass m, the shorter the travel time. The shorter the distance, the shorter the travel time. Answer G had the greatest M, smallest m, and shortest distance.

31. The correct answer is D. The answer is based on this table only; other criteria for determining if reactions have taken place include the evolution of a gas and/or a change in temperature.

32. The correct answer is J. From the table, only calcium and magnesium produce *no reaction* when mixed with sulfuric acid. The other two metallic ions produce a solid precipitate.

33. The correct answer is A. If the student mixed sulfuric acid with the unknown and there was no reaction, then the solution contained calcium. If a precipitate formed, then the unknown solution contained strontium.

34. The correct answer is H. Of the choices given, only choice H includes mixing with sodium carbonate to give a white precipitate. The other choices do not necessarily establish that any ion is present.

35. The correct answer is A. Adding the reagents in this order will accomplish the following results: Adding the chromate ion will force the precipitation of barium, which is filtered and removed, leaving calcium magnesium and strontium in solution. Then adding sulfate (in the sulfuric acid) precipitates the strontium, leaving calcium and magnesium in solution. Then when oxalate is added, the calcium is precipitated, leaving magnesium in solution, which then can be precipitated by adding the carbonate.

36. The correct answer is G. The other choices are possible, but only choice G is definite. If barium were present, a precipitate would form using chromate.

37. The correct answer is B. Venus has the most similar size and mass to Earth. Earth's diameter is 12, 751, and Venus's is 12,112. Earth's mass is 1.0 and the mass of Venus is 0.82. No other planets are as close to Earth's diameter and mass as Venus.

38. The correct answer is H. Mercury has a period of revolution of 88 days and a period of rotation of 59 days. 88 days/59 days $\approx$ 3/2 (90/60 = 3/2)

39. The correct answer is C. Jupiter has the greatest mass, 318 $\times$ the Earth's mass.

40. The correct answer is H. Mercury, the planet closest to the Sun, has the greatest orbital velocity. Each planet farther from the Sun is progressively slower.

PRACTICE TEST 2

ENGLISH TEST	TIME—45 MINUTES	75 QUESTIONS

DIRECTIONS: In the five passages that follow, certain words and phrases are underlined and numbered. In the right-hand column, you will find alternatives for each underlined part. You are to choose the one that best expresses the idea, makes the statement appropriate for standard written English, or is worded most consistently with the style and tone of the passage as a whole. If you think the original version is best, choose "NO CHANGE."

You will also find questions about a section of the passage, or about the passage as a whole. These questions do not refer to an underlined portion of the passage, but rather are identified by a number or numbers in a box.

For each question, choose the alternative you consider best and fill in the corresponding oval on your answer document. Read the passage through once before you begin to answer the questions that accompany it. You cannot determine most answers without reading several sentences beyond the question. Be sure that you have read far enough ahead each time you choose an alternative.

Passage I

[1]

In recent years, magazine advertisements for expensive cars have included lengthy texts extolling the engineering and safety of the product. Underneath a sleek
                                    1
sportscar or luxury sedan elegantly photo-
                          2
graphed in the spirit of the advertisement:

bright, harsh colors for the "hard sell"; and

soft, muted colors for the "soft sell." The

texts have become literary works of

art themselves subtly using words and
    3
images to appeal to a chosen audience.

A recent advertisement from

Mercedes-Benz illustrates the soft sell, and

a BMW illustrates the hard sell.
    4

[2]

The Mercedes-Benz text takes up three

columns and a full magazine page. It soothes

the reader with assurances of quiet, safety,

and perfection in language that virtually

purrs. The crankshaft provides, for example,
                               5
power that is "nearly liquid," and the engine

is "cradled" in special mountings and shock

absorbers. Every part is coated, padded,
         6
suspended, silent, or simple, in the spirit of

greater "engineering depth." The word

''depth'' evolves suggestions of softness and
<u>evolves suggestions</u>
7

seriousness, from the padding to the expert

engineers. Complete sentences flow

smoothly together, calm <u>and unhurriedly.</u>
8
This advertisement is the perfect soft sell.

<u>The BMW text is</u> the hard sell. It directs its
9

pitch at <u>the younger, more affluent</u>
10

<u>generation</u> <u>and does so</u> by using the honey-
10   11
moon image. Phrase after phrase carries

some <u>sexual innuendo:</u> ''a car must function
12

as one with its driver,'' ''an exhilarating

feeling of control,'' a transmission that ''slips

precisely into each gear.'' This impression is

<u>increased</u> by fragmented sentences and an
13
excited pace. <u>This is</u> the quintessential
14
hard-sell advertisement.

[3]
These are very serious advertisements,

and it's always a tremendous relief to turn to

a Jeep advertisement or <u>a Cadillac blunder-</u>
15
<u>ing its great chassis across a centerfold</u>
15
poking fun at all of the commercialized sex

and overblown dignity prevalent in today's

automobile advertising.

---

1. A. NO CHANGE
   B. These captions are usually placed underneath
   C. It is usually placed underneath
   D. These being placed underneath

2. F. NO CHANGE
   G. sedan, which is
   H. sedan, which are
   J. sedan that is

3. A. NO CHANGE
   B. art, themselves subtly
   C. art, subtly
   D. art itself, subtly

4. F. NO CHANGE
   G. a BMW advertisement illustrates
   H. one from BMW illustrates
   J. a recent BMW advertisement illustrates

5. A. NO CHANGE
   B. The example of the crankshaft provides
   C. The crankshaft, for example, provides
   D. The crankshaft provides

6. F. NO CHANGE
   G. Some other parts are
   H. A few things are
   J. As a last resort, everything else is

7. A. NO CHANGE
   B. connotes suggestions
   C. evokes images
   D. infers meanings

8. F. NO CHANGE
   G. yet unhurried
   H. and unhurried
   J. OMIT

9. A. NO CHANGE
B. (Begin a new paragraph) Just as vigorously, the BMW text embodies
C. (Begin a new paragraph) However, the BMW text is
D. (Do not begin a new paragraph) The BMW text is, however,

10. F. NO CHANGE
G. a younger but equally affluent generation
H. the younger and equally affluent drivers
J. the young and affluent

11. A. NO CHANGE
B. and achieves this
C. and works this
D. OMIT

12. F. NO CHANGE
G. honeymoon overtone, like
H. sexual suggestion; that is,
J. sexual overtones, like in these phrases—

13. A. NO CHANGE
B. enhanced
C. improved
D. enlarged

14. F. NO CHANGE
G. Moreover, this is
H. Thereby, this is
J. Thus, BMW offers

15. A. NO CHANGE
B. to one for Cadillac, which blunders its chassis around
C. to a centerfold Cadillac, shining in its huge complacency,
D. to a centerfold Cadillac with its huge bulk

Passage II

[1]

Annapurna is, at 26,504 feet, the tenth-highest mountain in the world, and <u>its unstable,</u> shifting surfaces of ice and
        16
snow make it very difficult to climb.

<u>The first to reach</u> the top was the French,
        17
led by Maurice Herzog and Louis Lachenal in 1950, and the first successful American expedition was an all-woman group, the American Women's Himalayan Expedition, <u>which made it in 1978.</u> Both expedi-
                    18
tions suffered from the unpredictability of the mountain.

[2]

<u>Having attacked the mountain boldly,</u>
                    19
the insufficient equipment and the mountain's changeable weather proved the undoing of the French expedition's courageous climb. At the last stage of the assault, a number of the climbers noticed the beginnings of frostbite. Not reckless, the sherpa guides returned to the camp below. Herzog, <u>moreover,</u> was faced with a difficult
              20
decision: <u>if he returned</u> to camp to treat the
              21

frostbite, he might not have the energy or supplies for another assault; going ahead meant definite danger. Herzog made the decision to continue, and he and Lachenal reached the summit. On the way down, caught in a blizzard, Herzog, Lachenal, and the two Frenchmen who went to their aid were suffering grievously from frostbite.
                        22
Herzog lost his toes and his fingers to the first joint. Lachenal lost all but two toes. They had, however, climbed higher than any other expedition until Edmund Hillary conquered Everest in 1953.

[3]

The women's expedition of 1978 was as successful as Herzog's—Irene Miller and Vera
                                    23
Komarkova, several other women, and two sherpa guides reached the summit — but even more tragic, since two of their companions
                                    24
died from a fall. The expedition had trouble from the start, with the sherpas grumbling about the equipment and how all the climbers were women.
        25
The mountain also lived up to its reputation,
        26
sending many avalanches valleyward and

offering a tricky surface for crampons. After the two sherpas had to retreat, suffering from altitude sickness, two women slipped and fell 1,500 feet to their deaths. When they were found later, they were still roped together.

In recounting these two climbs, it seems that
                                    27
the sherpas were always retreating at crucial
                28
moments. This accusation was unfair, since their strength (for carrying supplies and messages), their knowledge of the lower mountain, and their basic loyalty made both expeditions possible. There is a picture from the French expedition showing a sherpa actually carrying a blind Frenchman on his
    29
back during the descent. Both expeditions,
                                30
despite initial friction with the Nepalese
                30
sherpas, developed, through the triumph and
30
tragedy of the climbs, a deep fellowship with these people.

16. F. NO CHANGE
    G. it's unstable.
    H. its instability.
    J. Annapurna's

17. A. NO CHANGE
    B. The first reaching
    C. The expedition reaching
    D. The first expedition to reach

18. F. NO CHANGE
    G. of 1978
    H. , which just made it.
    J. that made it in 1978

19. A. NO CHANGE
    B. Attacking the mountain boldly,
    C. Not attacking the mountain boldly.
    D. OMIT (capitalize ''The'')

20. F. NO CHANGE
    G. , however,
    H. finally
    J. then

21. A. NO CHANGE
    B. Whether to go back
    C. Going back
    D. returning

22. F. NO CHANGE
    G. had suffered
    H. suffered
    J. suffer

23. A. NO CHANGE
    B. , since
    C. , because
    D. . (End sentence with Herzog's)

24. F. NO CHANGE
    G. the women
    H. the expedition
    J. the sherpas

25. A. NO CHANGE
    B. that the climbers were women
    C. the gender of female climbers
    D. the women

26. F. NO CHANGE
    G. Moreover, the mountain
    H. However, the mountain
    J. Sometimes, the mountain

27. A. NO CHANGE
    B. (Begin new paragraph) In these two accounts—Herzog's and Miller-Komarkova's—
    C. (Do not begin new paragraph) In these two accounts—Herzog's and Miller-Komarkova's—
    D. (Begin new paragraph) However, in these accounts—Herzog's and Miller-Komarkova's—

28. F. NO CHANGE
    G. retreated
    H. had retreated
    J. wanted to retreat

29. A. NO CHANGE
    B. really
    C. totally
    D. OMIT

30. F. NO CHANGE
    G. Despite initial friction with the Nepalese sherpas, both expeditions
    H. Despite initial friction, the expedition
    J. At first there was friction, but then the expedition

Passage III

[1]

Having written many artistically
<u>　　　　　　　　　　　　　　</u>
                    31
acclaimed plays, *Pygmalion* is certainly
<u>　　　　　　　　　</u>
           31
Shaw's greatest popular success. Not only

was it triumphant in its first stage

production with the renowned Mrs.
<u>　　　　　　　　　　　　　　</u>
                32
Campbell in the role of Eliza Doolittle but it
<u>　　　　　　　　　　　　　　　　　　　</u>
                        32
was also transformed into an Academy
<u>　　　　</u>
  33
Award-winning film in 1938 resurrected after
<u>　　　　　　　</u>
                34
Shaw's death by Alan Jay Lerner and

Frederick Loewe in the enormously popular

musical *My Fair Lady* (1956). Shaw
<u>　　　</u>
                          35
welcomed the success of his play with a
<u>　　　　　　　　　　　　　　　</u>
                35
perverse and irrepressible glee claiming it
<u>　　　　　　　　</u>
                  36
proved that didacticism (even about phonet-
<u>　　　</u>
 36
ics) could be made palatable with an

infusion of wit. That Shaw took the didacti-

cism of the play seriously is demonstrated

not just by the preface but that he took the
<u>　　　　　　　　　　　</u>
                  37
bulk of his estate researching an improved
<u>　　　　　　　</u> <u>　　　　　　</u>
    37   38
phonetic alphabet (though the British courts

subsequently reversed his will in that

regard).

[2]

Although the British magistrates

apparently did not believe in the importance

of correct pronunciation, Shaw felt that

dialectical English was inherent in the fact of
<u>　　　　　　　　　　　</u>
                    39
social prejudice. The premise of *Pygmalion*

is that a woman of the gutter might be
<u>　　</u>
                        40
passed off as a duchess if she can be taught

to speak King's English.

Midway through the play Professor Higgins
<u>　　　　　　　　　　　</u>
            41
comments excitedly on his challenge, "The
<u>　　　　</u>
                          42
hardest job I ever tackled: make no mistake

about that, mother but you have no idea
<u>　　　　　</u>
          43
how frightfully interesting it is to take a

human being and change her into a quite

different human being by creating a new

speech for her. It's filling up the deepest

gulf that separates class from class and

from soul." This premise is still worthy of
<u>　　　　　</u>
  44
sociological investigation, but here, as

elsewhere in the play, Shaw's didacticism is

a good deal muddied by having been
<u>　　　　　</u>
                      45
dramatic and his commitment to the truth.
<u>　　　　　　</u>
    45

31. A. NO CHANGE
B. Although not England's most popular writer,
C. An artistically acclaimed play,
D. While perhaps not Shaw's most artistically acclaimed play,

32. F. NO CHANGE
G. production, with the renowned Mrs. Campbell in the role of Eliza Doolittle,
H. production, with the renowned Mrs. Campbell in the role of Eliza Doolittle.
J. production; with the renowned Mrs. Campbell in the role of Eliza Doolittle,

33. A. NO CHANGE
B. It was
C. the fact is the play was
D. but was

34. F. NO CHANGE
G. and then resurrected
H. resurrected
J. and resurrected then

35. A. NO CHANGE
B. Nonetheless, Shaw welcomed the success of his play
C. (new paragraph) Shaw welcomed the success of his play
D. (new paragraph) Despite this, Shaw welcomed the success of his play

36. F. NO CHANGE
G. glee and claiming it could prove
H. glee, claiming it proved
J. glee, having claimed it proved

37. A. NO CHANGE
B. , but even more dramatically by the fact that he left the bulk of his estate
C. but even more dramatically by the fact that he lost interest in the bulk of his estate
D. OMIT

38. F. NO CHANGE
G. for an
H. to guarantee an
J. for research into an

39. A. NO CHANGE
B. was the inherent cause of much
C. is equivalent to
D. was crucial to

40. F. NO CHANGE
G. could
H. can
J. may

41. A. NO CHANGE
B. Speaking midway through the play,
C. In a speech midway through the play,
D. During the play,

42. F. NO CHANGE
G. challenge
H. challenge:
J. challenge;

43. A. NO CHANGE
B. mother. But
C. mother. (new paragraph) But
D. mother, "but

44. F. NO CHANGE
G. soul."
H. soul to soul."
J. soul from soul."

45. A. NO CHANGE
B. his flair for the dramatic and
C. his being dramatic and
D. OMIT

Passage IV

[1]

I live in the Ozark Mountains in a place so beautiful that it nearly brought tears to
<u>46</u>
<u>my eyes</u> the first time I saw it twelve years
<u>46</u>
ago; I feel the same way today. But the things that make it so beautiful and desirable to me have also convinced others that this is prime land, <u>too,</u> and belongs to them as
<u>47</u>
well. At the moment, for instance, I am feeling a bit of an outsider, having discovered that I live in the middle of an indigo bunting ghetto. As ghettos go, it is a cheerful one in which to live, but it has <u>force</u> me to think about property rights.
<u>48</u>

[2]

Indigo buntings are small but emphatic birds. They believe they own the place, and it is hard to ignore their claim. The male birds perch on the garden posts or on top of the cedar trees. From <u>there they</u> survey their
<u>49</u>
holdings and belt out their songs. The females and juveniles are more interested in eating; they stay <u>more near</u> the ground to
<u>50</u>
search for seeds and an occasional caterpillar.

[3]

Although they act as if it is all theirs, there are other contenders, and perhaps I ought to try to take a census and judge claims before I grant <u>them title.</u> There are
<u>51</u>
other birds who call this place theirs—
<u>buzzards who work the updrafts over the</u>
<u>52</u>
<u>river and creek</u>, goldfinches, wild turkey,
<u>52</u>
phoebes, and whippoorwills.

[4]

And what about the coyote? For a while, she was confident that this was her farm, especially the chicken part of it. She was so sure of herself that once she sauntered by <u>in daylight and picked</u> up the tough
<u>53</u>
old rooster to take back to her pups. <u>Since,</u>
<u>54</u>
the dogs grew wise to her, and the next few times she returned to exercise her rights, they chased her off, explaining that this farm belonged to them and that the chicken flock was their responsibility.

[5]

<u>On the other hand,</u> there are the
<u>55</u>
copperheads, <u>who make</u> it necessary for me
<u>56</u>
to wear boots when walking the fields, and all their snakish kin. How am I to count and

331

judge their claims? There are the turtles who eat the strawberries in the garden, the peepers who own the pond. What about

<u>raccoon's and skunk and deer</u> rights? What
      57

about these bobcat who had a den in the cliff by the river and considered my place to be the merest sliver of her land?

[6]

<u>It begins to make me dizzy even trying</u>
      58

<u>to think of taking a census of everyone who lives here; and all of them seem to have certain claims to the place that are every bit as good as and perhaps better than mine.</u>

46. F. NO CHANGE
    G. made me cry
    H. caused me to weep
    J. dripped tears down my cheeks

47. The least confusing way to word this sentence is:

    A. NO CHANGE
    B. Put the word *too* after the word *others*.
    C. Put the word *too* after the word *well*.
    D. Omit the word *too* from the sentence.

48. F. NO CHANGE
    G. forces
    H. forced
    J. forcing

49. A. NO CHANGE
    B. there, they
    C. their they
    D. they're, they

50. F. NO CHANGE
    G. more nearer
    H. nearest
    J. near

51. A. NO CHANGE
    B. them the title.
    C. the buntings title.
    D. the buntings the title.

52. F. NO CHANGE
    G. buzzards who work the updrafts over the river and creek
    H. buzzards who, work the updrafts over the river and creek,
    J. buzzards, who work the updrafts over the river and creek,

53. A. NO CHANGE
    B. daylight, and picked up
    C. daylight; and picked up
    D. daylight: and picked up

54. F. NO CHANGE
    G. When
    H. Therefore,
    J. However,

55. A. NO CHANGE
    B. For example,
    C. Besides,
    D. Moreover,

56. F. NO CHANGE
    G. who makes
    H. that causes
    J. what cause

57. A. NO CHANGE
    B. raccoon and skunk and deer
    C. raccoon's and skunk's and deer
    D. raccoon's and skunks' and deer's

58. The writer is thinking of changing this sentence to read: "It begins to make me dizzy to think of counting all the creatures to see who own the place; they have as much right to it as I do." The best reason to reject this change is:

F. the new sentence does not show the relation between cause and effect
G. it doesn't say the animals may have a better claim to the place than the writer
H. there is no connection between this sentence and the end of paragraph 5
J. the present sentence unifies the essay by using language from paragraph 3

Items 59 and 60 pose questions about the essay as a whole.

59. The writer wishes to add the following information to the essay: "But it is a pair of cardinals who have ended up with the prize piece of real estate—the spot with the bird feeder." If this sentence is added, the best place to add it is at the end of:

A. paragraph 2.
B. paragraph 3.
C. paragraph 5.
D. paragraph 6.

60. Suppose the writer had been assigned to write a brief essay that uses a series of examples to support the main idea. Would this essay successfully fulfill that assignment?

F. Yes, because the essay describes creatures who share the land with the writer.
G. Yes, because the essay describes the author's feelings about her land.
H. No, because the main idea is not presented until the end of the essay.
J. No, because the essay doesn't use words or phrases like "for example."

Passage V

[1]

[1] Although it may seem odd to think of a building as a communications device, in the fifteenth century a cathedral could serve this purpose. [2] Statues and stone representations of every kind, combined with huge windows of stained glass, <u>tell</u> stories about
$\overline{61}$
religion and referred to the majesty of political power. [3] In addition, by means of bells in bell towers, a cathedral told time for all of <u>its city's residents</u>. [4] The cathedrals
$\overline{62}$
were awesome engines of communication.

[2]

Then the printing press was invented. The new device for mass communications

was portable, could sit on a table, and was easy to duplicate, and yet, in spite of its compact size, it contained more information more systematically presented than even the largest of cathedrals. It was the printed book. And though the book had certain limitations compared with a cathedral (it provided no bells it could not tell time),
65
the superiority overall of the invention was unmistakable. In the next several centuries, humanity produced more books and fewer cathedrals.

[3]
[1] When one thinks about the triumph
67
of the book over the cathedral. It's easy to
67
imagine that progress for civilization was not necessarily progress for every individual. [2] Cathedrals are for bell lovers, statue admirers, and people who gasp at spectacles of height and depth. [3] Books are for people who find silence absorbing who make
68
pictures in their heads, who find nothing boring about parallel lines of black type. To go from cathedrals to books was fine for
69

humanity, but it must have been sheer misery for the cathedral personalities.

[4]
In the last several years, we have been undergoing a similar shift. We are becoming a computer-using population. The gain in
71
portability ease orderliness accuracy
71
reliability and information storage over
71
anything achievable by pen scribbling, typewriting, and cabinet filing is recognizable by all. Yet, just as the book's triumph over the cathedral divided people into two groups, the computer's triumph over writing
72
with a pen or typewriter and cabinet filing
72
has divided the human race.

[5]
Bring a new computer into a room, and some people begin at once to buzz with curiosity and excitement; they sit down to conduct experiments, ooh and ah at the boxes and beeps, and master the use of a new computer or a new program as quickly and happily as athletes playing a delightful
73
new game. But for men whose temperament
73   74

does not naturally respond to computers, the new device is more of a trial than an adventure. Their instincts are all wrong, and no amount of manual-studying and mouse clicking will make them right. These people may be splendidly educated, as measured by book-reading. But computers require a sharply different set of aptitudes, and if the aptitudes are missing, little can be done, and misery is guaranteed.

61. A. NO CHANGE
B. describe
C. pictured
D. told

62. F. NO CHANGE
G. it's citys residents
H. it's city's residents'
J. its cities residents

63. The writer wants to add the following sentence after sentence 3, paragraph 1. "Today we tell time by looking at our watches or clocks." What is the best reason for *not* adding this sentence?

A. We also can find out the time by listening to the radio.
B. The subject of the paragraph is what cathedrals communicated.
C. The paragraph is sufficiently long as it is.
D. Some church bells still ring to tell the hours.

64. Which would be the most appropriate introductory sentence for paragraph 2?

F. NO CHANGE
G. But books became a better device that replaced the cathedral.
H. Then came the transition to something still more awesome.
J. Today we have better devices for mass communications.

65. A. NO CHANGE
B. it provided no bells, it could not tell time
C. it provided no bells; it could not tell time
D. (it provided no bells; it could not tell time)

66. Which sentence best states the main idea of paragraph 3?

F. The book could not do everything the cathedral could do.
G. The invention of the printing press, which made books possible, was an awesome development.
H. As a communications device, the book was superior to the cathedral.
J. It became too difficult for people to continue to build cathedrals.

67. A. NO CHANGE
B. When one thinks about the triumph of the book over the cathedral; it's
C. When one thinks about the triumph of the book over the cathedral, it's
D. When one thinks about the triumph of the book over the cathedral, its

68. F. NO CHANGE
G. they make
H. , who make
J. , who makes

69. A. NO CHANGE
B. were
C. are
D. made

70. The writer wants to add the following sentence to paragraph 3: "The cathedral corresponds to a certain kind of human personality, the book to another kind." Where is the best place in the paragraph to put this sentence to achieve coherence?

F. after sentence 1
G. after sentence 2
H. after sentence 3
J. after sentence 4

71. A. NO CHANGE
B. portability and ease and orderliness and accuracy, and reliability
C. portability and ease, orderliness and accuracy reliability
D. portability, ease, orderliness, accuracy, reliability,

72. F. NO CHANGE
G. pen scribbling, typewriting, and cabinet filing
H. scribbling, writing and filing
J. trying to write with a pen and pencil or typewriter and file in a cabinet

73. Which phrase best expresses the idea of the curiosity and excitement of people who like to use computers?

A. NO CHANGE
B. as figure skaters twirling on ice
C. as ducks taking to water
D. as flowers opening to full bloom

74. F. NO CHANGE
G. they
H. them
J. people

Item 75 poses a question about the essay as a whole.

75. The essay's main purpose is best stated as:

A. describing the differences between cathedrals, books, and computers
B. contrasting the past and the present
C. explaining how technology affects different types of people in different ways
D. arguing that technological progress may be harmful to humanity

MATHEMATICS TEST 60 MINUTES 60 QUESTIONS

DIRECTIONS: Solve each problem, choose the correct answer, and then fill in the corresponding oval on your answer document.

Do not linger over problems that take too much time. Solve as many as you can; then return to the others in the time you have left for this test.

You are permitted to use a calculator.

Note: Unless otherwise stated, all of the following should be assumed.

1. Illustrative figures are NOT necessarily drawn to scale.

2. Geometric figures lie in a plane.

3. The word *line* indicates a straight line.

4. The word *average* indicates arithmetic mean.

1. Which fraction lies between $\frac{2}{3}$ and $\frac{4}{5}$?

   A. $\frac{5}{6}$

   B. $\frac{17}{20}$

   C. $\frac{7}{10}$

   D. $\frac{13}{15}$

   E. $\frac{9}{10}$

2. The circumference of a circle whose diameter is 7 inches is approximately:

   F. 22 inches
   G. 28 inches
   H. 38 inches
   J. 154 inches
   K. 14 inches

3. $(-3)^2 - 4(-3) =$

   A. 3
   B. 151
   C. −15
   D. 108
   E. 21

4. Which of the following is equivalent to .00000072?

   F. $7.2 \cdot 10^{-5}$
   G. $7.2 \cdot 10^{-6}$
   H. $7.2 \cdot 10^{-7}$
   J. $7.2 \cdot 10^{-8}$
   K. $7.2 \cdot 10^{-9}$

5. The three angles of a triangle are in the ratio 8:9:13. Find the number of degrees in the smallest angle.

   A. 36°
   B. 48°
   C. 54°
   D. 78°
   E. 60°

6. $62\frac{1}{2}\% =$

   F. $\dfrac{5}{8}$

   G. $\dfrac{8}{5}$

   H. .62

   J. 62.5

   K. $\dfrac{31}{50}$

---

7. If $\dfrac{2}{c} = \dfrac{6}{9}$, find the value of c.

   A. 3

   B. 2

   C. 24

   D. 9

   E. 18

Zariche Toy Co.
Closing Price per Share

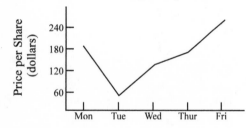

8. Penny bought 16 shares of Zariche stock at the closing price on Monday and sold them at the closing price on Friday. What was Penny's profit on this investment?

   F. $60

   G. $96

   H. $600

   J. $960

   K. none of these

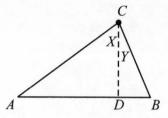

9. In triangle ABC, altitude CD divides angle C into two parts, X and Y. Then:

   A. $X + Y = A + B$

   B. $X - Y = A - B$

   C. $X + A = Y + B$

   D. $X + B = Y + A$

   E. $X + A = Y - B$

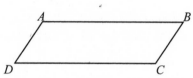

10. The perimeter of $ABCD$ is 100. If $AB > AD$, AB may be equal to:

   F. 25

   G. 35

   H. 50

   J. 75

   K. 55

---

11. 21.49 is closest to:

   A. 22

   B. 21

   C. 21.4

   D. 21.5

   E. 21.45

12. $3\frac{1}{3} + (-6) =$

    F. $2\frac{2}{3}$

    G. $-2\frac{2}{3}$

    H. $9\frac{1}{3}$

    J. $-9\frac{1}{3}$

    K. none of these

---

13. Find the value of $-5ST^2$ when $S = -2$ and $T = -3$.

    A. -90
    B. 90
    C. -60
    D. 60
    E. 30

---

14. If $ab + c = 2$ is solved for a, then a is equal to:

    F. $bc - 2$
    G. $2 - c - b$
    H. $\dfrac{c+2}{b}$
    J. $\dfrac{2-c}{b}$
    K. $b + c + 2$

---

15. Find S using the formula $S = \dfrac{a(1-r^n)}{1-r}$ if $a = -2$, $r = 2$, $n = 3$.

    A. 14
    B. -14
    C. 2
    D. -2
    E. 7

---

16. Find the length of the second leg of a right triangle whose hypotenuse is 30 feet and whose first leg is 18 feet.

    F. 48 feet
    G. 12 feet
    H. 6 feet
    J. 24 feet
    K. 36 feet

---

17. $(3x^2 - 2x + 5) + (2x - 3) =$

    A. $3x^2 + 2$
    B. $3x^2 + 4x + 2$
    C. $3x^2 + 4x + 8$
    D. $3x + 2$
    E. none of these

---

18. If the length and the width of a rectangle are both tripled, the ratio of the area of the original rectangle to the area of the enlarged rectangle is:

    F. $1:3$
    G. $1:6$
    H. $1:9$
    J. $1:18$
    K. $2:9$

---

19. Solve for x: $.02x + .12 = .20$

    A. 3
    B. -1
    C. 4
    D. 2
    E. -4

20. Sally has 3 skirts and 4 blouses ready for wear on a particular day. How many different outfits can Sally choose?

    F. 12
    G. 7
    H. 9
    J. 16
    K. 20

21. $(3a^3 - 6) - (2a^2 + 1) =$

    A. $a - 5$
    B. $3a^3 - 2a^2 - 5$
    C. $3a^3 - 2a^2 - 7$
    D. $-a^2 + a^3 - 1$
    E. none of these

22. $|5x - 3| > 7$ is equivalent to:

    F. $-\dfrac{4}{5} < x < 2$
    G. $-2 < x < \dfrac{4}{5}$
    H. $-2 < x < -\dfrac{4}{5}$
    J. $\dfrac{4}{5} < x < 2$
    K. $x > 2$ or $x < -\dfrac{4}{5}$

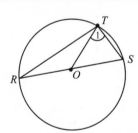

23. *ROS* is a diameter of circle *O*. Radius *OT* and chords *RT* and *RS* are drawn. If TRO = 50, find the measure of 1.

    A. 40
    B. 50
    C. 60
    D. 80
    E. 90

24. What is the center and the radius of the circle described by $(x - 5)^2 + (y - 3)^2 = 16$?

    F. center (5, 3), radius 4
    G. center (−5, −3), radius 4
    H. center (5, 3), radius 16
    J. center (−5, −3), radius 16
    K. center (3, 5), radius 4

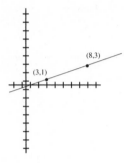

25. What is the slope of the line graphed above?

    A. $\dfrac{2}{5}$
    B. $-\dfrac{2}{5}$
    C. $\dfrac{5}{2}$
    D. $-\dfrac{5}{2}$
    E. $1\dfrac{1}{4}$

26. Triangle *ABC* has vertices *A* (−6, −4), *B* (4, 2), and *C* (0, 4). Find the length of the line segment joining the midpoints of $\overline{BA}$ and $\overline{BC}$.

    F. 24
    G. 22
    H. 15
    J. 10
    K. 5

27. If 35% of a number is 70, find the number.

    A. 24.5

    B. 200

    C. 50

    D. 65

    E. 140

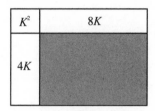

28. The larger rectangle has been divided into a square and three rectangles. The areas of the square and two of the rectangles are indicated. What is the numerical value of the area of the shaded rectangle?

    F. K^2

    G. $12K - K^2$

    H. $K^2 - 12K$

    J. 16

    K. 32

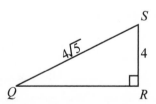

29. In right triangle QRS above, what is the value of $\cos S$?

    A. 1/2

    B. 2

    C. $\dfrac{\sqrt{5}}{5}$

    D. $\sqrt{5}$

    E. $\dfrac{2\sqrt{5}}{5}$

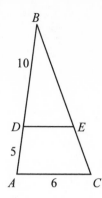

30. In triangle ABC, line DE is parallel to AC. Find the length of DE.

    F. 10

    G. 5

    H. 15

    J. 6

    K. 4

31. An owner of a pizza stand sold small slices of pizza for 15 cents each and large slices for 25 cents each. One night he sold 500 slices for a total of $105. How many small slices were sold?

    A. 300

    B. 200

    C. 400

    D. 250

    E. 350

32. The length of the side of an equilateral triangle is 10. Find the area of the triangle.

    F. 25

    G. 100

    H. $25\sqrt{3}$

    J. $\dfrac{5}{2}\sqrt{3}$

    K. $20\sqrt{3}$

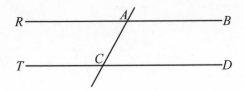

33. (*RB* is parallel to *TD*.)

If *BAC* = (*a* + 30)°, then *ACD* expressed in terms of *a* is:

A. *a* + 30
B. *a* + 120
C. 150 – *a*
D. 60 – *a*
E. 60 + *a*

34. $y^{-2}y^8y^{-6}$ is equivalent to:

F. 0
G. 1
H. –1
J. y^4
K. y^{-4}

35. A father can do a certain job in *x* hours. His son takes twice as long to do the job. Working together, they can do the job in 6 hours. How many hours does it take the father to do the job alone?

A. 9
B. 18
C. 12
D. 20
E. 16

36. How many 12.6'' strips can be cut from a board 189'' long?

F. 1.5
G. 15
H. 150
J. 176.4
K. none of these

37. Find the sum of 2*b* + 5, 4*b*–4, and 3*b* – 6.

A. 9*b* – 5
B. 7*b* – 10
C. $24b^2$ + 120
D. 6*b* – 1
E. 7*b* – 10

38. Factor completely: $3x^2 + 2x - 5$.

F. (3*x* + 5)(*x* – 1)
G. (3*x* – 5)(*x* + 1)
H. (3*x* – 2)(*x* – 5)
J. (*x* + 5)(3*x* – 1)
K. (*x* – 5)(3*x* + 1)

39. What is the point that is exactly midway between (2, 5) and (6, 1)?

A. (8, 6)
B. (4, 3)
C. (4, 6)
D. (8, 3)
E. (5, 5)

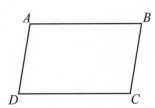

40. Figure *ABCD* is a parallelogram. *A* = 105°. *B* = 75°. Find the measurement of *D*.

F. 105°
G. 75°
H. 160°
J. 150°
K. 190°

41. In right triangle QRS, angle S is a right angle. If $\sin Q = 1/4$, what is the value of $\sin R$?

A. $\dfrac{\sqrt{15}}{5}$

B. $\dfrac{4\sqrt{15}}{15}$

C. 4

D. $\sqrt{15}$

E. $\dfrac{\sqrt{15}}{4}$

42. A salesman earns a commission of 8% of his total sales. How much must he sell to earn a commission of $124?

F. $9,920

G. $1,550

H. $992

J. $9.92

K. $1,148.15

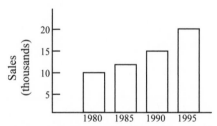

43. What was the percent of increase in sales from 1985 to 1990?

A. 3,000%

B. 30%

C. .25%

D. 25%

E. none of these

44. $\dfrac{9a^2b^2 - 12a^3b + 3ab}{-3ab} =$

F. a^5b^4

G. $-15a^5b^4$

H. $3ab + 4a^2 + 1$

J. $-3ab + 4a^2 - 1$

K. none of these

45. If $5x + 7 \geq x - 1$, then

A. $x \geq 2$

B. $x \leq 2$

C. $x \geq 8$

D. $x \leq 8$

E. $x \geq -2$

46. If a is not equal to 0, then $\left(\dfrac{a^2 a^5}{a^6}\right)^4$ simplifies to:

F. 1

G. a

H. a^2

J. a^3

K. a^4

47. The expression $\dfrac{1}{2}\sqrt{28}$ is equivalent to:

A. $\sqrt{14}$

B. $2\sqrt{7}$

C. $\sqrt{7}$

D. 7

E. $4\sqrt{7}$

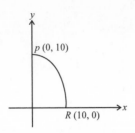

$p\ (0, 10)$

$R\ (10, 0)$

48. Determine the area between the curve and x and y axis.

F. 100π
G. 25π
H. 20π
J. 400π
K. 250π

49. If $x < y$ and $y < z$, which statement about the integers x, y, and z must be true?

A. $x < z$
B. $x = z$
C. $x > z$
D. $y - x = z$
E. $y > z$

50. If $g(x) = 2x^2 - 4x + 5$, what is the value of $g(3)$?

F.   5
G.   11
H.   12
J.   18
K.   29

51. What is the equation of the line passing through the point $(2, 3)$ and parallel to the line $3x - 6y = 12$?

A. $2x + y = -4$
B. $x + 2y = 8$
C. $2x - y = 1$
D. $-x - 2y = 4$
E. $x - 2y = -4$

52. On level ground, a man 6 feet tall casts a shadow 8 feet long at the same time that a tree casts a shadow 20 feet long. Find the number of feet in the height of the tree.

F. $46\frac{2}{3}$
G. $2\frac{4}{5}$
H.   15
J.   8
K.   120

53. Which of the following is equivalent to $\dfrac{\tan^2 \propto \csc^2 \propto -1}{\sec \propto \tan^2 \propto \cos \propto}$?

A.   0
B.   1
C. $\sin \propto$
D. $\cos \propto$
E. $\tan \propto$

54. Solve for x and y:

$x + 4y = 11$
$3x - 4y = 1$

F. $x = 7, y = 1$
G. $x = 7, y = 5$
H. $x = 3, y = 2$
J. $x = 0, y = 0$
K.   none of these

55. If the average of 2 and x is 7, find the value of x.

A.   9
B.   18
C.   12
D.   14
E.   16

56. $\sqrt{16} - \sqrt[3]{27} =$

    F.   1

    G.   7

    H.   −1

    J.   −7

    K.   none of these

57. If $x^2 - 2x = 0$, then $x =$

    A.   −2 and 2

    B.   2

    C.   0 and 2

    D.   −2, 0, and 2

    E.   −2 and 0

58. The price of a 3-pound can of vegetables increased from 80 cents to 93 cents. What percent of increase was this?

    F.   1.6%

    G.   14.0%

    H.   16.25%

    J.   86%

    K.   20%

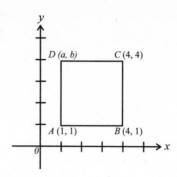

59. Find the coordinates of point D.

    A.   (1, 4)

    B.   (4, 1)

    C.   (4, 4)

    D.   (1, 1)

    E.   (1, 3)

60. A tree casts a shadow of 37 feet when the sun is 33° above the horizon. How many feet high is the tree?

    F. $\dfrac{37}{\cos 33°}$

    G. $\dfrac{37}{\tan 33°}$

    H.   37 tan 33°

    J.   37 sin 33°

    K.   37 cos 33°

READING TEST   TIME—35 MINUTES   40 QUESTIONS

Passage I

Line Shut it off, Steiner told himself, and the
station wagon was silent. He had pulled
into the drive and up to the Chinese elm at
the house without the reality of any of it
5 registering, and now he turned to his
9-year-old, James, in the seat beside him,
and saw the boy's face take on the expression of sly imbalance that Steiner had
noticed in it for the first time this after-
10 noon.

      Steiner got out and James bucked
against his seat belt, holding up a hand, so
Steiner eased back in, shoving his unruly
hair off his forehead, and took hold of the
15 wheel. He was so used to James being out
of the car and headed across the yard the
second after they stopped that he felt
dazed. His white-blond twin daughters, 7,
who were in the rear with his wife, Jen,
20 were whispering, and Steiner turned to
them with a look that meant *Silence!* He
got out again, with a heaviness that made
him feel that his age, 45, was the beginning
of old age, and that the remorse he'd
25 recently been saturated with had a focus: it
was a remorse that he and Jen hadn't had
more children.

      As he was driving home, a twin had
pulled herself forward from the backseat and
30 whispered that James had reached over and
honked the horn while Steiner was in the
department store, where he had gone to look
for a shatterproof, full-length mirror and an

exercise mat of the kind the physical therapist
35 had recommended. And since James hadn't
spoken for two weeks, the incident had set
the twins to whispering about James, in
speculative and hopeful terms (with James
sitting right there!), for most of the long trip
40 home.

      "I'm sorry," Steiner said, seeing that
he was still the only one outside the car, as
if he had to apologize for being on his feet.
He slid back in, brushing aside his hair
45 again, and began to unbuckle James's seat
belt. The boy stared out the windshield
with an intensity Steiner couldn't translate,
and, once free, tried to scoot over to the
passenger door by bending his torso
50 forward and back.

      "Take it easy, honey," Steiner said. Then
he added, for the boy and the others, in the
phrase that he'd used since James was an
infant, "Here we are home." Silence. Steiner
55 turned to Jen, who was leaning close, her
pretty lips set, and said, "Do you have his
other belt?" She gave a nod.

      Steiner got out and looked across the
top of the station wagon, through the
60 leaves of the four-trunked elm, at their
aging farmhouse. He hadn't seen it in two
weeks. He'd spent that time at the hospital
with James, first in intensive care, then in a
private room, where physical therapists
65 came and went. At the sight of the white
siding that he and James and Jen had
scraped and repainted at the beginning of
summer, he had to swallow down the loss
that he'd started to feel when he realized
70 he was grieving for a son he might never
see again. . . .

      The boy's hair was as unruly as his,
and the sandy-colored curls at its edges
needed trimming. James's eyes were nearly
75 covered by it, Steiner saw, and then they
rested on him in a dull love. Steiner
coughed and felt a hand on his shoulder.
Jen was standing above him, smiling—
wisps of hair lifting from her forehead in a
80 wind Steiner hadn't noticed until now—and

the sight of her somehow enabled him to
understand that he could endure handling
James in his helpless condition on home
ground. The boy loved the ranch so much
85 that his usual good health always appeared
to get even better, once they were here; he
seemed to grow an inch his first week
back, each time. Careful of the boy's ribs,
Steiner lifted James from the seat, turning
90 him so his back rested on Steiner's stom-
ach, and the heated weight of James against
him had the effect of blocking the blood to
his brain. His mind went blank.
　　　James started pedaling his feet in a
95 spinning run in place, and Jen laughed and
shook her head. Then she glanced around
the yard and off to a blue-shaded butte, as
if to make the landscape hers again, and
looked buoyant with the breath she took,
100 then wiped at the corner of an eye.
　　　"You're so dear," she said to James, smiling
down at him.

1. According to the passage, James is

   A. Jen's stepson
   B. younger than the twins
   C. Steiner's son
   D. forty-five years old

2. In the context of the passage, the word
   speculative most likely means:

   F. considering possible meanings
   G. unkind
   H. high-spirited
   J. without forethought

3. According to the passage, Steiner has
   spent two weeks:

   A. scraping and repainting siding
   B. looking for an exercise mat
   C. in the hospital with James
   D. not speaking to anyone at all

4. In the context of the passage, the
   statement that Steiner is "grieving for a
   son he might never see again" most
   likely means:

   F. his son, James, has died
   G. he fears James may never recover
   H. he knows he won't have more
      children
   J. his son is still in the hospital

5. Based on the evidence in the passage,
   which of the following best describes
   Steiner's current feelings?

   A. sorrowful
   B. angry
   C. lethargic
   D. uncooperative

6. It can be inferred from the passage that
   Steiner says "Here we are home" in
   order to:

   F. begin a conversation with Jen and
      the twins
   G. suggest that James needs help
      getting out of the car
   H. explain that they have moved to a
      new house
   J. restore a sense of normalcy to the
      situation

7. In the context of the passage, the
   phrase "shut it off" (line 1) most likely
   means:

   A. Steiner wanted to stop thinking
   B. Steiner needed to turn off the car
   C. Steiner wanted the twins to stop
      talking
   D. Steiner was trying to stop grieving

8. According to the passage, James honked the horn while:

    F. Steiner was talking to the physical therapist

    G. the twins were whispering about him

    H. Steiner was looking for an exercise mat

    J. Jen was getting him out of the car

9. The explanation for what has happened to James is presented later in the story. In the context of the story so far, which of the following explanations would be most likely?

    A. James was brain-damaged as a young child

    B. James's chronic illness has suddenly worsened

    C. James ran away from home two weeks ago

    D. James was injured in a terrible accident

10. When in the story does Steiner notice that James's hair needs cutting?

    F. before Steiner helps James out of the car

    G. while the twins are whispering about him

    H. after Jen touches Steiner on the shoulder

    J. while Steiner is lifting James from the seat

Passage II

Line Although it is more than a hundred years since Emile Zola introduced the term "naturalism" to designate the underlying philosophy of his approach to writing
5 novels, critics still struggle to categorize that approach. One school of critics sees it as an appendage to realism, usually a minor appendage. Another school insists that it is worthy of a category of its own. But both
10 groups struggle to define the term.

Realism is most often said to begin with Gustave Flaubert's *Madame Bovary* (1857), although Flaubert vehemently denied he was a realist. Nevertheless, he
15 chose a commonplace heroine and presented her life with realistic details and with a detachment that most critics have come to accept as the basic characteristics of realism. Zola was unquestionably
20 influenced by Flaubert, but he imposed an additional requirement on his own work. It must demonstrate the laws of science, or more accurately, what he was convinced were the laws of science.
25 Zola read a book on heredity as well as one by Hippolyte Taine, who applied what was known of natural science to mankind. Armed with what he gleaned from these and using the scientific method
30 as he understood it, he developed his own science of cause and effect. This was determined by the characters' heredity, the surrounding environment, and the strange notion that, as he said, "A like determina-
35 tion will govern the stones of the roadway and the brain of man."

Unfortunately, one does not become a specialist on heredity by reading a book on the subject, nor does one become a
40 scientist by reading several books. No rational person in the present age could accept Zola's conclusions as valid science. An American critic, William York Tindall, says, "Zola's science was pseudoscience,"
45 and a French history of literature heads its discussion of Zola's ideas with the dismissing phrase "The Scientific Pretensions of Zola."

Those ideas, pseudoscience or mere
50 pretensions, produced twenty volumes, tracing the "natural history" of a single family through five generations. For Zola, the environment determined both what the characters became and their responses to
55 events and to one another, so he roamed the slums of Paris, notebook in hand, recording sights, smells, and events. He pored over police records, medical reports, and books on diseases and addiction. Each

60 item must be as accurately reported as was
humanly possible. It is said that, being
careful of his reputation, he judiciously
took his wife with him as he measured the
room of a prostitute.

65   The responses to his work differ
greatly. Tindall sees his novels as "less
experimental than documentary," and the
French historian surprisingly asserts, "In
spite of his scientific ambitions, Zola is

70 above all a romantic." Whatever one may
think, however, both of his approach and
the resulting works, there can be little
question of the widespread and lasting
influence of his ideas and the pattern of his

75 novels.

The earliest novel in English using
Zola's approach is *A Mummer's Wife*
(1885), by the Irish novelist George Moore.
This is the story of a woman who deserts

80 her husband to follow a traveling actor, the
mummer of the title. During a visit to a
pottery factory with the actor, the woman
is overcome by the heat and noise. The
actor supports her and impulsively kisses

85 her. Assuming he is in love with her, she
goes with him but has no part in his or the
other actors' lives. She takes to drink, and
when she has a baby by the actor, she rolls
onto the infant, in a drunken stupor, and

90 crushes it. She beats the actor, and he at
last is compelled to leave her. She continues drinking until she dies, attended by a
madwoman.

Moore, like Zola, supplies accurate

95 details—of the first husband's asthma, the
pottery works, the lives of the traveling
actors, and the progress of the woman's
alcoholism. He obviously used his notebook
wisely. And, again like Zola, he does not

100 moralize or resort to sentimentalism.

More lasting, however, than the
complete approach, as found in Moore's
work, has been the pattern of a heroine of
mixed heredity, an aristocratic father and a

105 peasant mother, who becomes a servant
and has an illegitimate child. This is the
situation in *Tess of the D'Urbervilles*
(1891), although admittedly the aristocratic
line has been watered down. This novel

110 owes much to Zola, but note that the same

pattern occurs in a later novel that owes
less to Zola, *My Antonia* (1918), by Willa
Cather. Many other weaker novels that have
disappeared also used this pattern. Natural-

115 ism, whatever its relation to realism or how
it is defined, has had an impact of such
import on later writers that perhaps it
deserves more respect than it usually
receives.

11. According to the passage, all of the
following are true of naturalism *except*:

A. critics struggle to define the term
B. Gustave Flaubert used naturalism in
his writing
C. some critics consider it an appendage to realism
D. Zola used the term to describe his
writing philosophy

12. Realism is defined in the second
paragraph in order to:

F. demonstrate its value over the
philosophy of naturalism
G. explain why Flaubert used realistic
details
H. acknowledge that Flaubert was not a
realist
J. explain how naturalism differs from realism

13. The passage suggests that "Zola's
science was pseudoscience" because:

A. his scientific ideas are now
old-fashioned and outdated
B. he did not understand the concepts in the books he read
C. he developed his theory from
reading only a couple of books
D. he believed that characters'
heredity and environment caused
their behavior

14. According to the passage, the influence of naturalism can be found in which of the following novels?

 I. *Madame Bovary*
 II. *A Mummer's Wife*
 III. *Tess of the D'Urbervilles*

 F. II only
 G. I only
 H. II and III
 J. I, II, and III

15. As it is used in the passage, the word *judiciously* (line 62) means:

 A. sensibly
 B. unnecessarily
 C. incautiously
 D. scornfully

16. According to the passage, Zola wrote:

 F. novels tracing a single family through five generations
 G. a novel about a woman who deserts her husband to follow an actor
 H. novels about a heroine of mixed heredity who has an illegitimate child
 J. novels that were weaker and that have disappeared

17. The passage focuses mainly on which of the following?

 A. naturalism as opposed to realism
 B. Emile Zola's methods of collecting information
 C. naturalism as a pseudoscience
 D. naturalism and its widespread influence

18. The final paragraph suggests which of the following contradictions regarding naturalism?

 F. Although Zola's style was documentary, he was also a romantic.
 G. Some critics claim it is realism; others claim it is separate.
 H. Though Zola's science was poor, his observations were careful.
 J. Although difficult to define, its influence makes it important.

19. Which of the following is the best explanation for why Zola "roamed the slums of Paris"?

 A. He was collecting accurate data to use in his novels.
 B. He was trying to trace the influence of events on the people in the slums.
 C. He wanted to learn about the life of prostitutes.
 D. He wanted to prove that naturalism was scientific.

20. According to the passage, *A Mummer's Wife*, *Tess of the D'Urbervilles*, and *My Antonia:*

 F. all described an aristocratic father and a peasant mother
 G. were all influenced to some degree by naturalism
 H. were all written using Zola's naturalistic style
 J. were all weaker novels that have disappeared

Passage III

Line Beneath the surface of [Monterey] Bay lies [a] splendor seen only by a lucky few: Monterey Canyon. Hidden from view by thousands of feet of water, this submarine
5 chasm is as grand as Arizona's famous

tourist attraction, possessing steep, rocky precipices and a series of curving meanders inhabited by strange and elusive marine life. West of the Monterey Peninsula, the

10 canyon walls gradually drop an incredible 7,360 feet (2,300 meters)—a quarter-mile more than the highest cliff of the Grand Canyon.

Monterey Canyon is part of a much

15 larger geologic feature, the Monterey Canyon System, comparable in size to the 278-mile-long Grand Canyon. The 60-mile-long gorge empties into the gently sloping Monterey Sea Valley. The valley continues

20 out into the Pacific Ocean for an additional 180 miles until it reaches the flat abyssal plain of the Pacific Ocean.

Even so, Monterey Canyon is not the world's largest undersea chasm. But to

25 marine researchers, it is surely the most convenient. At the port of Moss Landing, . . . the head of the canyon is within yards of the coast. From here, the floor of the canyon begins its gradual descent to a

30 depth of nearly 8,000 feet.

. . . In the bay's sunless middle depths, otherworldly creatures drift through the darkness, feeding on the blizzard of organic material, or "marine snow," from

35 above. In the canyon itself and its various side branches, dense colonies of clams, tube worms, and bacteria feed on chemical-rich fluids oozing from underwater springs called cold seeps.

40 Monterey Canyon's geology . . . is a focus of intense study. Although its geologic history is understood in its essentials, the details of how it was carved out of the continental shelf are not yet

45 completely known. . . .

Monterey Canyon was carved out of the continental shelf over the past 20 million to 25 million years. . . .

When submarine canyons were first

50 discovered, geologists assumed that they actually started out as canyons on dry land at a time when sea level was lower. Then, the theory went, the canyons were submerged by a rise in sea level. But there

55 was one problem, [Gary] Greene [who has studied the canyon for thirty years] says:

Not all undersea canyons lie near a river old and energetic enough to have carved such chasms. A bigger, older knife was needed.

60 In the 1930s, geologists found a mechanism that could, given enough time, cut even the grandest undersea canyons: turbidity currents. These are enormously powerful underwater debris flows, a dense

65 slurry of sea water, rock debris of various sizes and fine sediments. They cascade down underwater slopes at high speed, scouring away rock and sediment. Over millions of years, most geologists now

70 believe, turbidity currents have carved undersea canyons as surely as the Colorado River has cut the Grand Canyon.

In the 1960s, Greene took on the challenge of explaining Monterey Canyon's

75 history. By then, it was clear that turbidity currents had excavated the world's undersea canyons. Subsequently, Greene discovered evidence that they had carved Monterey Canyon along an ancient fault

80 that once ran east to west across the bay. Turbidity currents eroded the weakened rock along this fracture, cutting a groove that channeled subsequent turbidity currents. With each new debris flow that

85 cascaded down the fault zone, the canyon got slightly deeper. . . .

Today, most geologists agree that turbidity currents played the greatest role in carving the canyon. But there's also

90 circumstantial evidence that another process, called freshwater sapping, has cut some of Monterey's side canyons and may have helped shape parts of the main canyon as well.

95 Greene says there is evidence that at times in the past when the climate was wetter, huge amounts of water from the Santa Cruz Mountains flowed into the canyon through tilted aquifers. The water

100 bubbled out of the canyon walls, which cut across part of the sandstone layer that forms the aquifers. This undermined the slopes of the canyon, triggering landslides.

Greene believes that freshwater

105 sapping may have sculpted the canyon's slopes here and there, playing second fiddle to turbidity currents. But his younger

colleague . . . geologist Dan Orange has
some doubts about that. In fact, in specula-
110 tive moments he wonders if freshwater
sapping could have played a much larger
role. As water seeped up through the bay's
ancient east-west fault zone, could it have
cut the initial groove that, tens of million of
115 years later, evolved into the vast Monterey
Canyon?

    At the moment, too little is known
about Monterey's plumbing system—the
cracks and faults in the bay's founda-
120 tion—to allow Orange to transform his
speculations into a testable scientific idea.

21. According to the passage, Monterey
Canyon is so convenient for marine
researchers because:

  A. it is comparable in size to the
      Grand Canyon
  B. it is close to shore and easily
      accessible
  C. it is the world's largest undersea
      chasm
  D. it is a focus of intense study

22. The main point of the seventh paragraph (lines 49-59) is that the original
theory of how undersea canyons were
formed:

  F. had to be abandoned
  G. wasn't old enough
  H. didn't explain submersion
  J. didn't consider erosion

23. According to the passage, turbidity
currents contain all of the following
except:

  A. fine sediments
  B. rock debris
  C. chemical-rich fluids
  D. sea water

24. According to the passage, current
theories about the origin of the canyon
include which of the following?

  I.   freshwater sapping
  II. turbidity currents
  III. cold seeps

  F. I only
  G. III only
  H. I and II only
  J. I, II, and III

25. According to the passage, "the blizzard
of . . . 'marine snow' " (lines 33-34) is

  A. caused by weather conditions in
      the atmosphere
  B. contains chemical-rich fluids from
      cold seeps
  C. falls from the bay's sunless middle
      depths
  D. organic matter the sea creatures
      feed on

26. It can be inferred from the comment
that Gary Greene believes freshwater
sapping "play[ed] second fiddle to
turbidity currents" (lines 104–107) that
Greene believes freshwater sapping:

  F. has not received the attention it
      rightly deserves
  G. played a less-important role than
      turbidity currents
  H. cut the initial groove that formed
      the Monterey canyon
  J. failed to explain how rivers could
      have cut the canyon

27. It can be inferred from the passage that Dan Orange's speculation that freshwater sapping may have "cut the initial groove" of the canyon:

    A. is not founded on sound geological principles

    B. is scientifically immature and uninteresting

    C. differs from that of the majority of geologists

    D. has been disproven by his colleague Gary Greene

28. It can be inferred from the passage that the theory of turbidity currents differs from the older theory that submarine canyons were formed by the action of rivers in which of the following ways?

    F. Turbidity currents are caused by aquifers.

    G. Turbidity currents rely on cold seeps.

    H. Turbidity currents occur underwater.

    J. Turbidity currents undermine sandstone.

29. According to the passage, the Monterey Canyon is how deep?

    A. 7,360 feet

    B. 60 miles

    C. 278 miles

    D. 180 miles

30. According to the passage, the Monterey Canyon System is "comparable in size to the 278-mile-long Grand Canyon" (lines 16–17) because:

    F. the canyon system extends for a total of 240 miles

    G. Monterey Canyon is 20 to 25 million years old

    H. both canyons were formed by the action of rivers

    J. the canyons are both about the same depth

Passage IV

Line

"Great Carthage made war three times," Bertolt Brecht once wrote, summing up seven centuries of Carthaginian history. "After the first, she was powerful. After the
5 second, she was rich. After the third, no one knew where great Carthage had been."

The last phrase was a slight exaggeration. Everyone had heard about Great Carthage, and about Hannibal and his
10 elephants crossing the Alps in 218 B.C. to start the Second Punic War with Rome ("Punic" comes from the Roman word for "Phoenician"). It was, after all, Roman history. Everyone knew where Great
15 Carthage had been because the Romans built a city of their own on the site, a new Carthage that became a center of industry, learning, and luxury, arguably the second city of the Roman Empire. . . .
20 [In Carthage] there were once great libraries of books in the Punic language. Not a page, not a line, remains. The works of a Carthaginian named Mago, the greatest agronomist of antiquity, were translated and
25 studied by Roman landowners, but now even the translations are lost. What remains of the language, a variety of the Phoenician spoken in Tyre, a near relative of ancient Hebrew, are mostly grave inscriptions
30 (some 6,000 of them) with the names of parents offering children to Ba'al Hammon, or the goddess Tanit, and some lines of comic dialogue put into the mouths of Carthaginian merchants and slaves in the
35 work of a Roman playwright.

One consequence is that practically everything known about the Carthaginians comes from the Greeks and Romans, who made war on Carthage for centuries. Their
40 historians naturally tended to present a biased picture of the enemy as cruel, untrustworthy Orientals. This was the picture touched up with lurid highlights by Gustave Flaubert, whose novel *Salammbo*
45 portrays a Carthage of glittering opulence and unspeakable vice, where rivers of Oriental perfume mingle with rivers of blood from torture chambers and infant holocaust. Flaubert had sometimes the soul
50 of a naughty schoolboy; he was never

happier than when offering such tidbits as the claim that high-born maidens used a paste made of crushed flies' legs to touch up their eyebrows. But there is no reason
55 to think the people of ancient Carthage were any more addicted to cruelty than the Romans, who thought nothing of crucifying prisoners along the public highways and leaving them there till their bones were
60 picked clean by birds. Some scholars challenge the whole idea of Carthaginian infant sacrifice, claiming that the charred bones in the urns, when they are not those of lambs and calves, are of infants who
65 were stillborn or died of natural causes. But excavator Lawrence Stager, director of Harvard's Semitic Museum, thinks there is no doubt that some form of infant sacrifice took place. According to the gloomy
70 prophet Jeremiah, the custom was being practiced in Jerusalem in the sixth century B.C. The early church father Tertullian, who spent most of his life in North Africa, wrote in A.D. 200 that "to this day that
75 holy crime persists."

At one time or another, Rome fought with many of the other peoples of the Mediterranean world, occasionally taking cruel vengeance, but eventually absorbing
80 them into the Roman state or making them allies. Only Carthage was utterly destroyed, because it was the only foe the Romans genuinely feared, the only trade rival that might have supplanted Rome.

85 From 262 B.C. to 146 B.C., these two states, which started out as small towns, groped and then clawed their way toward mastery of the known world. Sometimes the story of those centuries sounds like a
90 dress rehearsal for modern times. Just as the expansion of the Western European world began in the 1400s with Portuguese captains pushing their solid oceangoing ships farther and farther down the coast of
95 West Africa in search of gold, spices, and slaves, so the Phoenicians, 2,400 years earlier, at the beginning of the first millennium B.C., developed sturdier, faster ships than had ever been built before and
100 began sending them on trading or raiding voyages to what was then the wild west

end of the Mediterranean. Homer's *Odyssey* (dated by current scholarship to the latter part of the eighth century B.C.) describes
105 them as "pirates in black boats laden with a thousand *arhythmata*—that is to say, beads and bowls and wine and metalware and all sorts of bric-a-brac. The Phoenicians traded for produce of the iron mines of Elba, the
110 gold mines of Andalusia, and later the tin mines of Cornwall, growing rich on such commerce. They also invented an alphabetic script, which made it easier to keep business records.

31. The passage notes that our knowledge of the Carthaginians is incomplete because:

   I. none of the books written by Carthaginians has survived

   II. the Roman portrayals of the Carthaginians are inaccurate

  III. Mago's book was only about agronomy

   A. I only

   B. II only

   C. I and II

   D. I and III

32. The passage uses all *except* the following evidence to suggest that the Carthaginians did practice infant sacrifice:

   F. Flaubert's description of infant holocaust in his novel

   G. Jeremiah's claim that infant sacrifice was practiced in other parts of the Mediterranean

   H. Tertullian's assertion that it was still practiced in the area in A.D. 200

   J. Stager's conviction from excavations that infant sacrifice took place

33. According to the passage, Rome and Carthage grew and fought for power:

   A. in the sixth century B.C.

   B. from 262 B.C. to 146 B.C.

   C. in the first millennium B.C.

   D. in the 1400s

34. It can be inferred from the passage that the ancestors of the Carthaginians:

   F. traveled along the coast of West Africa

   G. lived in Elba

   H. were Phoenicians from Tyre

   J. moved to Asia

35. In the context of the passage, what is the purpose of the statement that the Romans "thought nothing of crucifying prisoners along the public highways" (lines 57-58)?

   A. The Romans did not practice infant sacrifice.

   B. The Romans were as cruel as the Carthaginians.

   C. The Romans treated the Carthaginians cruelly.

   D. The Romans were even more cruel than the Carthaginians.

36. In the context of the passage, the word *opulence* refers to:

   F. jewelry

   G. the sea

   H. gluttony

   J. great wealth

37. The main idea of the third paragraph (lines 20-35) is that:

   A. the records of the Carthaginians were almost totally destroyed

   B. the city of Carthage was completely destroyed

   C. Punic was a form of the Phoenician language spoken in Tyre

   D. a Roman playwright preserved the Punic language

38. In the context of the passage, the claim that Flaubert "had sometimes the soul of a naughty schoolboy" suggests that Flaubert:

   F. was an immature writer

   G. liked to shock his readers

   H. misbehaved at school

   J. liked practical jokes

39. According to the passage, before the founding of Carthage, the Phoenicians had already:

   A. begun trading in the eastern Mediterranean

   B. searched for gold, spices and slaves

   C. sacked the city of Rome

   D. invented an alphabetic script

40. Although the author calls the claim that "no one knew where Great Carthage had been" (lines 5-6) a "slight exaggeration," (lines 7-8) which of the following statements from the passage reveal(s) how utterly Carthage was destroyed?

   I. The great libraries were completely destroyed.

   II. The Phoenicians began building fast and sturdy ships.

   III. The Romans built a new city on the site of Carthage.

   F. I only

   G. III only

   H. II and III

   J. I and III

SCIENCE REASONING TEST   TIME—35 MINUTES   40 QUESTIONS

DIRECTIONS: There are seven passages in this test. Each passage is followed by several questions. After reading a passage, choose the best answer to each question and fill in the corresponding oval on your answer document. You may refer to the passages as often as necessary.

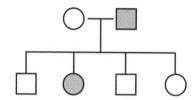

Passage I

Pedigree charts are used to trace inheritance of genetic traits in human families. Information is gathered from family records and histories, examining family members over several generations, in order to determine which family members exhibit the traits (phenotypes) of interest. Development of the pedigree chart makes it possible to analyze which family members carry the gene(s) for certain traits. It may also be possible to determine whether the trait is dominant or recessive and whether the carriers are homozygous or heterozygous for the allele.

Analyze the following pedigree chart, involving the trait of albinism. Albinism is a heritable condition in which individuals lack normal pigmentation in skin and hair, which appear white. They also lack eye pigmentation, and their eyes appear red because one can see the blood vessels. The following symbols can be used to interpret the chart:

Pedigree Chart for Albinism:

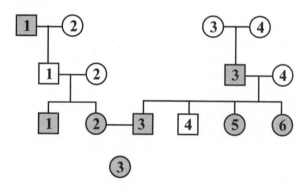

1. Consider the phenotypes of male 3 and female 4 in generation 2. Based on their phenotypes and the phenotypes of their offspring and their parents, it is possible to conclude that:

A. albinism is a dominant trait
B. their parents are both homozygous
C. one of their offspring is albino
D. albinism is a recessive trait

2. Which data in this chart indicate that albinism is a recessive trait?

   F. Male 3 in generation 2 is albino, but his parents are not.

   G. Female 2 and male 3 in generation 3 are albino, and so is their child.

   H. Male 1 and female 2 in generation 2 are normal, but his father and his children are albino.

   J. both F and H

3. What can you conclude about the genotype of female 4 in generation 2?

   A. For any of this female's children to be albino, she must also be albino.

   B. Her children will be albino if they inherit an albino allele from either parent.

   C. This female must have one albino allele.

   D. Since her phenotype is normal, this female must have two normal alleles.

4. What can you conclude about the genotype of male 4 in generation 3?

   F. He is homozygous for the normal allele.

   G. He is homozygous for the recessive allele.

   H. He is heterozygous for the allele and can pass either one on to his offspring.

   J. He inherited both normal alleles from his mother, who is female 4 in generation 2.

5. What can you conclude about the genotype of female 3 in generation 3?

   A. She is heterozygous for the albinism allele.

   B. She is homozygous for the albinism allele.

   C. She is a mutant, carrying faulty alleles not found in either parent.

   D. She could pass either a normal allele or an allele for albinism to each of her offspring.

6. Assuming albinism is controlled by one pair of genes and that albinism is a recessive trait, could two albino individuals ever have children with normal pigmentation?

   F. No. All of their children will die before birth.

   G. No. Neither parent has a normal gene for pigmentation.

   H. Yes, but 75% of the offspring would be albino.

   J. Yes. The allele for pigmentation would always be expressed over the recessive gene for albinism.

357

Passage II

One of the standard laboratory procedures for preparing hydrogen gas is to react solid zinc with a dilute solution of hydrochloric acid. This reaction can be analyzed on an oxidation-reduction basis. In oxidation, an element loses electrons. In reduction, an element gains electrons. According to the equation

$$Zn_{(s)} + 2\ HCl_{(aq)} \rightarrow ZnCl_{2\ (aq)} + H_{2\ (g)}$$

7. The oxidation number of the solid zinc is:

   A. +2
   B. −1
   C. 0
   D. +1

8. The oxidizing agent for the reaction is:

   F. zinc
   G. hydrochloric acid
   H. zinc chloride
   J. hydrogen gas

9. In the reduction phase of the reaction:

   A. chlorine gains 1 electron
   B. hydrogen gains 2 electrons
   C. zinc loses 2 electrons
   D. zinc gains 2 electrons

10. The oxidation number for hydrogen gas in the reaction is:

   F. 0
   G. −2
   H. +1
   J. +2

11. In the oxidation phase of the reaction:

   A. hydrogen gains 2 electrons
   B. chlorine loses 1 electron
   C. zinc loses 2 electrons
   D. zinc gains 1 electron

12. The reducing agent for the reaction is:

   F. zinc
   G. hydrochloric acid
   H. zinc chloride
   J. hydrogen gas

Passage III

Igneous rocks are rocks that form by the crystallization of minerals from molten rock material called magma. The formation of magma occurs mainly in the upper mantle of the Earth, a layer found from 5 km to 70 km below the surface, below the layer called the crust. Partial melting of rocks results in magma rising toward the surface. Once it gets close to the surface, it pools in a magma chamber until conditions may allow an eruption at a volcano. Then the magma comes to the surface, where it is now called lava. Eruptions can be explosive, like the one that occurred at Mount Saint Helens, releasing mainly dust-and-ash-size material; or they can be quiet, like the Hawaiian lava flows.

Geologists studying igneous rocks can learn about how the Earth behaves chemically and how the chemistry of the different parts of the Earth changes with time. The basic principles needed to understand this process are as follows. Table 1 shows a list of the major minerals that comprise the crust and mantle of the Earth and their chemical composition. Table 2 shows major elements and trace elements found in igneous rocks. Table 3 shows the charge and the ionic radius of these elements of concern. A trace element can substitute for a major element in the structure of a mineral, provided that the trace element has the correct charge and is of similar ionic radius. If a mineral is crystallizing from magma, elements that have the same charge and similar radius are compatible and they will go into the solid phase and will decrease in concentration in the liquid. Trace elements that are dissimilar to the major elements are incompatible with the crystallizing solid, and will increase in concentration in the liquid.

Table 1

Mineral	Formula
Olivine	$(Mg, Fe)_2SiO_4$
Pyroxene group	Ca, Mg, Fe, Al silicate
Potassium feldspar	$KA1Si_3O_8$
Plagioclase	$CaAl_2Si_3O_8$ to $NaAlSi_3O_8$
Quartz	SiO_2

Table 2

Major Elements	Trace Elements
Sodium	Rubidium
Titanium	Cesium
Potassium	Strontium
Iron	Barium
Magnesium	Chromium
Calcium	Nickel
Manganese	Cerium

Table 3

Element	Charge	Ionic Radius (A) angstroms
Sodium	+1	1.07
Potassium	+1	1.46
Rubidium	+1	1.57
Cesium	+1	1.78
Magnesium	+2	0.80
Iron	+2	0.69
Calcium	+2	1.08
Strontium	+2	1.21
Barium	+2	1.44
Chromium	+2	0.81
Titanium	+2	0.94
Nickel	+2	0.77
Manganese	+2	0.79
Iron	+3	0.63
Cerium	+3	1.09

13. If crystals of olivine and calcium plagioclase are the first minerals to crystallize in magma, what trace elements would you expect to find increasing in concentration in the remaining liquid?

   A. rubidium and cerium
   B. rubidium and nickel
   C. potassium and strontium
   D. chromium and titanium

14. What trace element would you expect to find substituting for potassium in potassium feldspar?

   F. nickel
   G. titanium
   H. chromium
   J. rubidium

15. What trace element is most similar to iron?

   A. barium
   B. nickel
   C. strontium
   D. titanium

16. Successive lava flows from a volcano on Hawaii are sampled and analyzed chemically. The concentration of the trace element cerium (Ce) is found to be increasing in each younger (higher) flow. What process is probably occurring in the magma chamber below the volcano?

   F. crystallization of minerals that will accept cerium as a substitute
   G. addition of more magma, diluting and replenishing the magma
   H. crystallization of minerals that do not accept cerium as a substitute
   J. addition of more magma to the magma chamber enriching and replenishing the magma

17. What, if any, generalization can be made about the relationship between the charge of an ion and its radius?

A. Ions with a greater positive charge have a larger radius.

B. No relationship exists between charge and ionic radius.

C. Ions with a greater positive charge have a smaller radius.

D. No generalization can be made with the information provided.

18. Learning that the mantle is composed of the minerals olivine and pyroxene, one would expect that continental crust, which can be considered as a fractionation of the mantle, would be enriched in what elements over the mantle?

F. magnesium and iron

G. magnesium and potassium

H. calcium and titanium

J. potassium and sodium

Passage IV

A spring at equilibrium is displaced a distance of 10.0 cm from its equilibrium position. It then undergoes simple harmonic motion. The graph shown in Figure 1 depicts the elastic potential energy U(x) of the spring as a function of its displacement x.

19. According to Figures 1 and 2, what is the total energy of the spring?

A. 10,000

B. 5,000

C. 2,500

D. 0

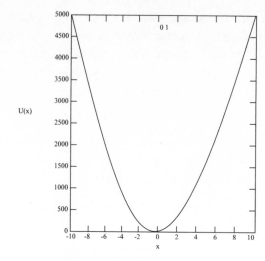

Figure 1

20. At which displacement x would the spring be moving fastest?

F. 10.0 cm

G. −10.0 cm

H. 0 cm

J. 5.0 cm

21. When the spring is at a displacement of 5.0 cm, approximately what is its kinetic energy?

A. 3,250

B. 3,500

C. 3,750

D. 4,000

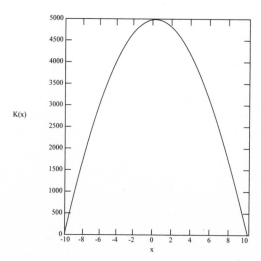

Figure 2

22. If the spring were stretched to a greater displacement of 20.0 cm, what would be its potential energy at this point?

    F. 5,000
    G. 10,000
    H. 20,000
    J. 0

23. Which of the following statements can best be supported by the graphs?

    A. As the spring crosses its equilibrium position x=0, the total energy of the system is zero.
    B. If the spring were stretched to a displacement greater than 10.0 cm., the kinetic energy at the equilibrium position x=0 would also be greater.
    C. The kinetic energy of the spring and its potential energy are directly proportional.
    D. none of the above

24. If the potential energy of the system were 2,000, then:

    F. the kinetic energy is also 2000
    G. the total energy of the system is 3000
    H. the spring is motionless
    J. the spring could be in one of two positions

Passage V

Scientist 1: Living things may arise spontaneously by massing the vital forces from nonliving matter. This is called abiogenesis, or spontaneous generation. Examples include things like: 1. maggots growing on cooked meat or other food left out in the open because the vital forces in the meat provide the energy for maggots to appear spontaneously; and 2. microorganisms growing in broth left out in the open because the vital force of the broth reaches a mass that generates living microorganisms.

Scientist 2: Living things arise only from other living things of their same kind (biogenesis). While variables such as temperature and availability of nutrients and oxygen may affect this process, they cannot by themselves produce living things. Life begets life. Examples include: 1. flies having to come in contact with meat or broth for maggots to appear, and maggots mature into flies; and 2. a broth growing microorganisms only when the broth is directly exposed to air or something else that contains microorganisms, even though we can't see them.

25. A piece of roast beef was thoroughly cooked, then left in a container on the counter. The container was covered with gauze to allow air and room temperature heat to reach the meat. According to the hypothesis of Scientist 1, what will happen to the meat?

    A. The meat will not produce maggots because the meat is out in the open.
    B. The meat cannot give rise to maggots when gauze is present.
    C. The meat left out in the open will give rise to maggots from vital forces within the meat itself.
    D. Cooking the meat destroys all vital forces that give rise to maggots.

26. Based on question 25, what conclusions could Scientist 2 reach that are consistent with his hypothesis?

   F. The meat will produce maggots because it is out in the open and the gauze allows air to contact the meat.
   G. The meat cannot give rise to maggots because the gauze keeps the flies away from it.
   H. The vital forces in the meat will produce maggots with or without gauze present.
   J. The meat was once living; therefore, it can produce other living things such as maggots.

27. Scientist 2 vigorously heated two containers of beef broth to destroy any living microorganisms. Then he kept the containers loosely covered at room temperature. No microorganisms grew in either container. Scientist 1 would support his hypothesis by arguing that:

   A. the broths cannot produce microorganisms when covered
   B. beef broth contains no vital forces and should not be used
   C. microorganisms will not grow in beef broth because they prefer chicken broth
   D. the heat destroyed the vital forces of the beef broth, so microorganisms cannot grow

28. Scientist 2 argued that some invisible organisms in the air were dropping into open containers of broth or food, giving rise to other microorganisms that caused the broths to turn cloudy and spoil. He passed air through chemically treated cotton wool to filter out these "invisible microorganisms." He then showed that broths exposed only to filtered air did not grow microorganisms. Scientist 1 would conclude that:

   F. treatment of the air would be harmful to the process of spontaneous generation
   G. the treated air would support spontaneous generation
   H. the presence or absence of air is irrelevant to spontaneous generation
   J. spontaneous generation requires no air

29. Using the same argument and experimental data as in question 28, Scientist 2 would conclude that:

   A. the treated filter trapped and destroyed microorganisms in the air that would have given rise to microorganisms in the broth
   B. microorganisms would still grow in the broth over time
   C. the treated filter would have no effect on the growth of microorganisms
   D. air is not necessary for microorganisms to grow

30. Scientist 2 heated broth in two flasks to destroy any living microorganisms. One flask neck was left directly open to the air above it. The other flask neck was bent to the side in an S shape so that air could freely enter, but any microorganisms present in the air would be trapped in the neck, unable to reach the broth. His hypothesis would predict that:

   F. nothing could grow in either broth

   G. the broth in the curved-neck flask would grow microorganisms because it got "clean" air

   H. the broth in the straight-neck flask would grow microorganisms because they could fall directly into the broth

   J. both broths would produce growth of microorganisms due to spontaneous generation

Passage VI

Scientists have known for more than 200 years that the Earth's interior is not homogeneous (of one composition). From astronomical data, we know that the overall density of the Earth is 5.5 g/cm^3. The Earth's overall density is much greater than that of surface rocks, which have a density within the range of 2.5 to 3.0 g/cm^3. In order for the overall density to be 5.5 g/m^3, much of the interior must consist of materials with a density greater than the Earth's overall density.

The Earth consists of four layers, each differing in chemical composition and density. Because no direct observations of the interior of the Earth can be made, the structure and composition of the interior are based upon indirect evidence, as from the study of seismic waves from earthquakes. The outermost layer is called the crust, it is the thin skin that covers the Earth. Its thickness averages about 30 km and has a range from 5 to 70 km. The rocks that make up the crust are composed predominately of iron, magnesium, calcium, potassium, sodium, and aluminum silicate (silicon and oxygen). Below the crust and extending about halfway to the center is the mantle, comprising more than 80% of the Earth's volume. Mantle rocks are composed mainly of iron and magnesium silicate minerals. The percentage of iron and magnesium in the mantle rocks is greater than in the rocks of the crust, and the density of mantle rocks ranges from 3.3 to 5.7 g/m^3. The central part of the Earth is the core. Just below the mantle is the outer core with a density of 9.9 to 12.2 g/m^3. It is liquid, with a composition of iron and about 12% sulfur, nickel, silicon and oxygen. The inner core is solid, with a density of 12.6 to 13.0 g/m^3. Its composition is iron, with 10% to 20% nickel.

One of the aspects of the evolution of the Earth deals with the origin of the layered structure of the Earth. There are two models to explain this aspect. The solar system formed from a solar nebula (a cloud of dust and gas in space). This nebula began collapsing to form the sun and planets about 4.6 billion years ago. Most of the mass went into the center to form the sun, and a small part went to form the planets, moons, asteroids, and comets. Accretion is the process by which dust and larger particles collect together from the solar nebula to form a planetary body. There are two models used to explain the origin of the Earth's interior. They involve the accretion of material that formed the Earth.

Homogenous Accretion

This model holds that the material that accreted to form the Earth was all of one composition and that after all the material collected together it later differentiated into the various layers found today. After the material accreted together, it was heated from the energy released by the accretion process and radioactive decay. Eventually the Earth was hot enough that iron separated from the rocky material and sank to the center.

Heterogeneous Accretion

In this model, the material accreting into the Earth changed in composition during accretion. Materials in the hot gas cloud began to condense into solid particles and started to collect together. As cooling continued, the composition of the condensing material changed. The material that first collected formed the core, then the mantle, and finally the crust. This model explains the layering of the Earth with little later differentiation.

31. The two models are alike in that they both assume that:

    I.   the time for accretion to occur was equal in both models
    II. Earth formed from accreted material from the solar nebula
    III. Earth was the third planet to accrete

    A. I only
    B. II only
    C. III only
    D. I and II

32. To accept the heterogeneous accretion model, one must assume that:

    F. all accreted material is of one composition
    G. the Earth became hot enough to melt
    H. rocky silicates accrete first
    J. the order of the elements and compounds that accrete matches the makeup of the Earth today

33. To accept the homogeneous accretion model, one must assume that:

    A. it does not matter in what order different elements and compounds condense and accrete
    B. the layers of the Earth formed one layer at a time
    C. solid iron and nickel accreted first
    D. the accreting material was of one composition

34. Suppose that experimental data predicted that the first materials to condense from the solar nebula were calcium, aluminum, and titanium oxides and silicate minerals. How would this evidence influence the two models?

    F. It would support the homogeneous accretion model and weaken the heterogeneous accretion model.
    G. It would support the heterogeneous accretion model and weaken the homogeneous accretion model.
    H. It would support both models.
    J. It would not support either model.

35. Which of the following discoveries would support the heterogeneous accretion model?

    A. A large amount of light elements were the first elements to accrete.
    B. No iron condenses with magnesium silicates during the accretion of the mantle.
    C. Not enough heat is available to initiate melting of accreted material.
    D. Evidence that the continents are formed from lighter elements and compounds that have separated from the mantle and have grown in size over time.

36. Which of the following discoveries would support the homogeneous accretion model?

   F. Iron and nickel metal would be the first elements to condense from the solar nebula.

   G. Computer models show that accretion would not begin until after all compounds have condensed.

   H. There is not enough radioactive material to heat Earth.

   J. There are meteorites whose composition matches the predicted order of condensation.

Passage VII

An experiment is performed in which two laser beams are shined on interfaces of air and glass (index of refraction n = 1.5) and air and water (index of refraction n = 1.33), respectively. The index of refraction of air is 1.00. Laser 1 has a wavelength λ = 6328 Å, and laser 2 has a wavelength λ = 4468 Å. The angle of incidence (angle x) and the angle of refraction (angle y) are measured. The relationship between the angle of incidence and the angle of refraction is determined by x ÷ y and results in a straight line with positive slope. The experimental setup is shown in Figure 1. The results are shown in Tables 1, 2, and 3.

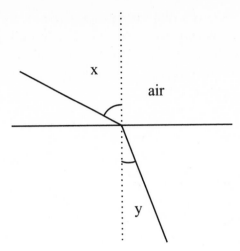

Figure 1.

Table 1. Air to glass—laser 1

angle x	angle y
10°	6.6°
20°	13.1°
30°	19.5°
40°	25.4°

Table 2. Air to glass—laser 2

angle x	angle y
10°	6.3°
20°	12.9°
30°	19.3°
40°	25.1°

Table 3. Air to water—laser 1

angle x	angle y
10°	7.5°
20°	14.9°
30°	22.1°
40°	28.9°

37. According to Tables 1, 2, and 3, the set of conditions that would result in the smallest angle of refraction would be:

   A. laser 1, air—water, angle x = 15°

   B. laser 1, air—glass, angle x = 15°

   C. laser 2, air—water, angle x = 35°

   D. laser 2, air—glass, angle x = 35°

38. Based on the data presented, one could conclude that a bundle of light consisting of several different wavelengths impinging on the air—water interface would:

   F. all be refracted at the same angle
   G. all be refracted at different angles, the shortest wavelength having the smallest angle
   H. all be refracted at different angles, the shortest wavelength having the largest angle
   J. not be refracted at all

39. Light from laser 1 travels from water to glass. Based on the data presented, if the angle of incidence were 30°, then the angle of refraction would be:

   A. 34.3°
   B. 26.3°
   C. 30.0°
   D. impossible to tell

40. Which graph best illustrates the relationship between the angle of incidence and the angle of refraction?

   F.

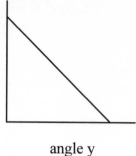

   G.

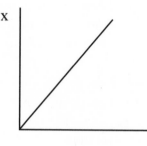

   H.

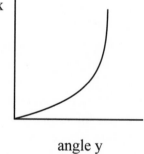

   J.

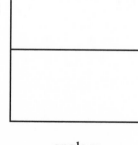

QUICK-SCORE ANSWERS

ANSWERS TO PRACTICE TEST 2

English

1. B	39. B
2. G	40. J
3. C	41. A
4. H	42. H
5. C	43. B
6. F	44. J
7. C	45. B
8. H	46. F
9. B	47. D
10. H	48. H
11. D	49. B
12. F	50. J
13. B	51. D
14. J	52. J
15. C	53. A
16. F	54. J
17. D	55. D
18. G	56. F
19. D	57. B
20. J	58. J
21. C	59. B
22. H	60. F
23. A	61. D
24. G	62. F
25. D	63. B
26. G	64. H
27. B	65. D
28. G	66. H
29. D	67. C
30. G	68. H
31. D	69. A
32. G	70. F
33. A	71. D
34. G	72. G
35. C	73. A
36. H	74. J
37. B	75. C
38. J	

Mathematics

1. C	31. B
2. F	32. H
3. E	33. C
4. H	34. G
5. B	35. A
6. F	36. G
7. A	37. A
8. J	38. F
9. C	39. B
10. G	40. G
11. D	41. E
12. G	42. G
13. B	43. D
14. J	44. J
15. B	45. E
16. J	46. K
17. A	47. C
18. H	48. G
19. C	49. A
20. F	50. G
21. C	51. E
22. K	52. H
23. A	53. B
24. F	54. H
25. A	55. C
26. K	56. F
27. B	57. C
28. K	58. H
29. C	59. A
30. K	60. H

Reading

1. C	21. B
2. F	22. F
3. C	23. C
4. G	24. H
5. A	25. D
6. J	26. G
7. B	27. C
8. H	28. H
9. D	29. A
10. F	30. F
11. B	31. C
12. J	32. F
13. C	33. B
14. H	34. H
15. A	35. B
16. F	36. J
17. D	37. A
18. J	38. G
19. A	39. D
20. G	40. J

Science

1. D	21. C
2. J	22. H
3. C	23. B
4. H	24. J
5. C	25. C
6. G	26. G
7. C	27. D
8. G	28. F
9. B	29. A
10. F	30. H
11. C	31. B
12. F	32. J
13. A	33. D
14. J	34. F
15. B	35. C
16. H	36. G
17. C	37. B
18. J	38. G
19. B	39. B
20. H	40. G

EXPLANATORY ANSWERS TO PRACTICE TEST 2

PART 1 — ENGLISH

1. The correct answer is B. This makes a sentence of the fragment and clarifies what is placed underneath the photograph.

2. The correct answer is G. The original past participle implies that the text is photographed, rather than the car. The clause is nonrestrictive, and therefore should start with "which" and be set off by a comma. "Is" is correct because of the "or" construction of the antecedent.

3. The correct answer is C. The correct form is "themselves," but is unnecessary here. A comma should set off "subtly" to set off the participal phrase.

4. The correct answer is H. This cuts out verbosity and carries the intended meaning without heavy repetition.

5. The correct answer is C. Transitional devices should be placed where they are smoothest and most logical. The original implies that the characteristics listed in the sentence are actually what the parts do. This is not true for the engine—its smoothness in part results from the way it is cradled. Once "for example" is placed after "crankshaft," it is logical to move to "engine" and to the other parts.

6. The correct answer is F. "Every part" is an exaggeration, but catches the spirit of the advertisement. To try to qualify it would create an awkward and heavily pedantic style.

7. The correct answer is C. The other choices are inaccurate or non-idiomatic.

8. The correct answer is H. "Calm" is used here as an adjective, modifying "sentences," so "unhurried," also an adjective, is linked with it.

9. The correct answer is B. A new paragraph should begin here because the first paragraph suggests a natural division between the two advertisements. The transitional phrase indicates the similarity between the two. "However" would be wrong because the comparison between the soft sell and the hard sell does not constitute a relevant conflict or contradiction.

10. The correct answer is H. Both cars are relatively expensive, but there is no indication that the younger people buying the BMW are more affluent than the older people buying the Mercedes; the opposite is probably the case. "Generation" implies too many people; "drivers" is more accurate; "the young and affluent" is ambiguous because it could mean both the young and the affluent as separate groups.

11. The correct answer is D. The phrase is unnecessary.

12. The correct answer is F. The original has the proper phrasing; the colon introduces a list. The alternatives all contain errors. G is top specific with "homeymoon"; H and J are wordy.

13. The correct answer is B. One doesn't "increase" or "improve" or "enlarge" an impression; one can deepen or "enhance" it.

14. The correct answer is J. The original has some ambiguity because "this" echoes "this impression." It is to the whole advertisement that the sentence is addressed. "This" in E, G, and H has no clear antecedent.

15. The correct answer is C. This retains the parallel structure and adds a touch of needed humor.

16. The correct answer is F. The other alternatives create errors or unfortunate repetitions.

17. The correct answer is D. This makes "first" more meaningful and precise.

18. The correct answer is G. This eliminates the verbosity or wordiness.

19. The correct answer is D. This awkward opening is not needed, because "courageous" covers the idea succinctly.

20. The correct answer is J. This indicates the correct time when the decision had to be made.

21. The correct answer is C. This choice is dictated by the balancing of "going ahead." The aim is a balanced, parallel phrase.

22. The correct answer is H. Simple past has been the pervasive tense here; there is no reason for a shift to the past progressive.

23. The correct answer is A. The dash is legitimate here since it emphasizes a complete break in the syntax of the sentence. There is no provision in the other alternatives to eliminate the dash at the other end of the clause.

24. The correct answer is G. "Companions" could be interpreted as sherpas.

25. The correct answer is D. Parallelism calls for a noun; (C) is verbose.

26. The correct answer is G. "Moreover" strikes the right tone here. "Also" would imply that the sherpas had lived up to their questionable reputation. "Moreover" implies that the mountain is a separate, though difficult, problem.

27. The correct answer is B. We have stopped talking about the actual climb and have shifted to some concluding observations—a good place for beginning another paragraph. The original is a dangling modifier because it doesn't logically modify anything.

28. The correct answer is G. "Were always retreating" exaggerates and implies fussily that the sherpas were in the process of retreating when the crisis occurred. Simple past serves the purpose here.

29. The correct answer is D. "Actually" is colloquial and unnecessary–he is either carrying the man or he is not.

30. The correct answer is G. This avoids the original's awkward beginning and retains the reference to both expeditions.

31. The correct answer is D. A and B are incorrect because they deal with dangling modifiers. The meaning of C is incorrect in the context of the sentence and the paragraph as a whole.

32. The correct answer is G. This question specifically tests the use of commas in nonrestrictive modifiers.

33. The correct answer is A. "Not only . . . but also" are coordinating conjunctions; one calls for the other. C is wordy.

34. The correct answer is G. "And then resurrected" denotes the proper meaning and sequence. The other choices do not.

35. The correct answer is C. The idea here shifts to Shaw's delight with the success of his play. A shift of ideas denotes a new paragraph. Answer D denotes a new paragraph, but the meaning is wrong.

36. The correct answer is H. The comma should separate the independent clause from the participial phrase.

37. The correct answer is B. B is the correct answer because it expresses the correct choice of words. "Give up" and "took" do not mean the same thing. Although "the fact that" is wordy, it is necessary here to maintain parallelism.

38. The correct answer is J. This is the only answer that conveys the correct word choice.

39. The correct answer is B. This answer conveys the correct choice of words. C and D are incorrect in meaning and A is too wordy.

40. The correct answer is J. "May" agrees in tense with "can." The other choices indicate tense shifts.

41. The correct answer is A. Choice D changes the meaning of the sentence. B and C are possibilities, but A is more concise.

42. The correct answer is H. Use a colon to precede a long quoted passage. Thus, H is the only possible choice.

43. The correct answer is B. Since there is no punctuation between "mother" and "but," the original is a run-on sentence. D would be a comma splice, and C makes no sense, since it signals a new paragraph in the middle of a quote.

44. The correct answer is J. "Soul from soul" is necessary to balance "class from class." The other choices involve faulty parallelism.

45. The correct answer is B. Choice B comes closest to the correct meaning. It is Shaw's flair for the dramatic that the author refers to, not Shaw's being dramaic. B maintains parallel construction.

46. The correct answer is F. The other choices suggest sadness rather than awe.

47. The correct answer is D. Placement of "too" anywhere in the sentence is either ambiguous, or, confusing and, therefore, unnecessary

48. The correct answer is H. This is the past participle of the verb needed to form the present perfect tense.

49. The correct answer is B. A comma is required after an introductory prepositional phrase. "There" is the correct form of the homonym in this context.

50. The correct answer is J. The other choices are ungrammatical or illogical in context.

51. The correct answer is D. "Them" is a confusing pronoun reference. Does it refer to "they" or to "other contenders"? "The title" is incorrect, because the birds are not being given a name, but title to the land.

52. The correct answer is J. "Who work the updrafts over the river and creek" is a nonrestrictive clause; thus, it must be set off by commas.

53. The correct answer is A. The clause has one subject, ''she,'' and two verbs, ''sauntered'' and ''picked up.'' Thus, no punctuation is needed between the two verbs.

54. The correct answer is J. This is the only logical connective because the sentence contrasts previous content.

55. The correct answer is D. This is the only logical connective because the paragraph provides additional examples.

56. The correct answer is F. A plural verb is required, and ''cause'' is not idiomatic in this construction.

57. The correct answer is B. This is the only choice where the items in the series are parallel.

58. The correct answer is J. It is the only one that is accurate.

59. The correct answer is B. This is the paragraph that lists other birds.

60. The correct answer is F. It presents the best choice.

61. The correct answer is D. A past tense form of the verb is required because ''referred'' is in the past tense, and ''pictured'' does not make sense with ''stories.''

62. The correct answer is F. ''Its'' is a possessive pronoun that does not require an apostrophe; ''city's'' is a possessive noun that requires an apostrophe.

63. The correct answer is B. The other reasons are not relevant to the paragraph's unity and coherence.

64. The correct answer is H. Repeating ''awesome'' from paragraph 1 provides coherence.

65. The correct answer is D. The parentheses are needed because the material interrupts the sentence's main idea. Since each clause in the parentheses is independent, they must be separated by a semicolon.

66. The correct answer is H. This is the only response that summarizes all the material in the paragraph.

67. The correct answer is C. An introductory dependent clause is followed by a comma. ''It's'' is a contraction for ''it is.''

68. The correct answer is H. The ''who'' clauses are a series that must be separated by commas. The verb must be plural because the antecedent of ''who'' is ''people.''

69. The correct answer is A. The subject is the infinitive phrase ''to go from cathedrals to books,'' which is used as a noun and is singular.

70. The correct answer is F. The structure of the paragraph moves from the general to the specific.

71. The correct answer is D. Items in a series must be separated by commas.

72. The correct answer is G. Repeating the phrase from earlier in the paragraph maintains parallelism and provides unity for the paragraph.

73. The correct answer is A. B does not express curiosity; C is a trite phrase; D inappropriately personifies flowers.

74. The correct answer is J. ''Men'' is sexist, and the other responses are ungrammatical.

75. The correct answer is C. This is the only statement that covers all of the essay's content.

PART 2   MATHEMATICS

1. **(C)** Convert all fractions to decimal equivalents:

$$\frac{2}{3} = .666 \qquad \frac{4}{5} = .800$$

$$\frac{5}{6} = .8333 \qquad \frac{17}{20} = .85$$

$$\frac{7}{10} = .7 \qquad \frac{13}{15} = .8666..$$

$$\frac{9}{10} = .9$$

$\frac{7}{10}$ is the only fraction between $\frac{1}{2}$ and $\frac{4}{5}$.

2. **(F)** 22″

Using the formula, C = πd
$$= (3.14)(7)$$
$$= 21.98″$$

3. **(E)** Follow the correct order of operations.

$$(-3)^2 - 4(-3) = 9 - (-12)$$
$$= 9 + (+12)$$
$$= 21$$

4. **(H)** $7.2 \cdot 10^{-7} = .00000072$

5. **(B)** 48°

First find variable expressions to represent the three angles.

Let the three angles be $8x$, $9x$, and $13x$.

Then, since the sum of the angles of any triangle is 180°,

$$8x + 9x + 13x = 180°.$$

Now solve the equation.

$$30x = 180$$

$$x = 6$$

Since the smallest angle was $8x$,

$$8x = 8(6) = 48°.$$

6. **(F)** To change a percent into a fraction, divide by 100.

$$62\frac{1}{2} \div 100$$

$$= \frac{125}{2} \div \frac{100}{1}$$

$$= \frac{125}{2} \times \frac{1}{100} = \frac{125}{200} = \frac{5}{8}$$

7. **(A)** Reduce $\frac{6}{9}$ to the equivalent of $\frac{2}{3}$. Hence, $c = 3$.

8. **(J)** $960

First find the amount Penny bought the shares for.

$$\$180 \cdot 16 = \$2,880$$

Then find the amount Penny sold the shares for.

$$\$240 \cdot 16 = \$3,840$$

Finally, subtract.

$$\$3,840 - \$2,880 = \$960$$

9. **(C)** Altitude *CD* is drawn, forming right angles: *CDA* = *CDB* = 90°. Hence, $X + A + CDA = 180°$. Also, $Y + B + CDB = 180°$. Substitute $X + A = Y + B$.

10. (G) The perimeter of $ABCD = 2L + 2W$ = 100. Divide by 2: $L + W = 50$. If the length (AB) > the width (AD), choice F would make $AB = AD$. Choices H, J, and K are too large. Therefore, choice G is correct.

11. (D) 21.5

To round a number to the tenths place, look at the digit in the hundredths place. If this digit is **5** or larger, raise the tenths digit by one.

21.49

Since 9 is 5 or larger, 21.49 becomes 21.5.

12. (G) $-2\dfrac{2}{3}$

To add signed numbers with different signs, subtract and use the sign of the larger.

$$3\frac{1}{3} + (-6) = 3\frac{1}{3} + (-5\frac{3}{3})$$

$$-5\frac{3}{3}$$
$$+3\frac{1}{3}$$
$$\overline{}$$
$$-2\frac{2}{3}$$

Since 6 is larger, $-2\dfrac{2}{3}$ is the answer.

13. (B) $-5ST^2 = (-5)(-2)(-3)^2$
$= (-5)(-2)(-3)(-3) = 90$

14. (J) $ab + c = 2$

Subtract c: $ab + c = 2$
$$\underline{-c \qquad -c}$$
$$ab = 2 - c$$

Divide by b:

$$\frac{ab}{b} = \frac{2-c}{b}$$

$$a = \frac{2-c}{b}$$

15. (B) -14

Again, substitute and compute.

$$S = \frac{a(1-r^n)}{1-r}$$
$$= \frac{(-2)(1-2^3)}{1-2}$$
$$= \frac{(-2)(1-8)}{-1}$$
$$= \frac{(-2)(-7)}{-1} = \frac{14}{-1} = -14$$

16. (J) $24'$

Using the Pythagorean theorem,

$$a^2 + b^2 = c^2$$
$$a^2 + (18)^2 = (30)^2$$
$$a^2 + 324 = 900$$
$$\underline{-324 = -324}$$
$$a^2 = 576$$
$$a = \sqrt{576}$$
$$a = 24'$$

17. (A) $3x^2 + 2$

To add algebraic expressions, combine like terms.

$(3x^2 - 2x + 5) + (2x - 3) = 3x^2 + 2$

18. (H) Let the original rectangle be expressed as:

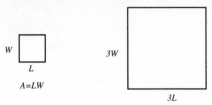

$$A = (3L)(3W)$$
$$= 9LW$$

ratio =

$$\frac{\text{original rectangle}}{\text{enlarged rectangle}} = \frac{1LW}{9LW} = \frac{1}{9} = 1:9$$

19. (C) $.02x + .12 = .20$

Multiply by 100: $2x + 12 = 20$
$$2x = 8$$

Divide by 2: $x = 4$

20. (F) There are 12 different outfits since for every skirt there is a choice of four different blouses.

$$3 \cdot 4 = 12$$

21. (C) $3a^3 - 2a^2 - 7$

To subtract algebraic expressions, change the signs of the subtrahend and use the rules for addition.

$$(3a^3 - 6) - (+ 2a^2 + 1)$$
$$= (3a^3 - 6) + (-2a^2 - 1)$$
$$= 3a^3 - 2a^2 - 7$$

22. (K) $|5x - 3| > 7$

$5x - 3 > 7 \qquad - 5x + 3 < 7$
$5x > 10 \qquad\quad - 5x < 4$

$x > 2 \qquad\qquad x < -\dfrac{4}{5}$

Thus, x must be less than $-\dfrac{4}{5}$ or greater than 2.

23. (A) Diameter *ROS* divides circle *O* into two semicircles. Hence, *RTS* is a right angle because an angle inscribed in a semicircle equals a right angle, or 90°. Also, *OT = OR*: equal radii in same circle. Since ΔRTO is an isosceles triangle, *TRO = RTO*.

$$RTS = RTO + 1$$

Substitute:

$$90 = 50 + 1$$
$$40 = 1$$

24. (F) The general formula for the equation of a circle is $(x - h)^2 + (y - k)^2 = r^2$, where (h, k) is the center of the circle, and r is the radius.

Thus, $(x - 5)^2 + (y - 3)^2 = 16$ has center (5, 3), and radius 4.

25. (A) The line contains the points (3, 1) and (8, 3)

$$\text{Slope} = \frac{y_2 - y_1}{x_2 - x_1} = \frac{3 - 1}{8 - 3} = \frac{2}{5}$$

26. (K) The line segment joining the midpoint of two sides of the triangle is half the length of the third side of the triangle. *GH* is the line segment joining the midpoints of the other two sides. Hence,

$$AC = 10$$
$$GH = \frac{1}{2}(AC)$$
$$= \frac{1}{2}(10)$$
$$= 5$$

27. (B) 35% of $N = 70$. Divide the known part by the fractional equivalent of the percent.

$$35\% = \frac{35}{100}$$

$$70 \div \frac{35}{100}$$

$$70 \times \frac{100}{35} \quad \text{invert divisor and multiply}$$

$$\overset{2}{\cancel{70}} \times \frac{100}{\cancel{35}} = 200 \quad \text{cancel out 35's}$$
$$\underset{1}{}$$

28. (K) Since the area of the square is K^2, each side is K. The area of rectangle I is $8K^2 \rightarrow$ width is K; length is 8. The area of rectangle II is $4K^2 \rightarrow$ width is 4; length is K. The area of rectangle III is $32 \rightarrow$ width is 4; length is 8.

29. (C) $\text{Cos S} = \dfrac{\text{Adjacent}}{\text{Hypotenuse}}$

$$= \frac{4}{4\sqrt{5}} = \frac{1}{\sqrt{5}} = \frac{\sqrt{5}}{5}$$

30. (K) If DE is parallel to AC, similar triangles ABC and DBE are formed. Corresponding sides of similar triangles are in proportion. Hence,

$$\frac{DE}{AC} = \frac{DB}{AB}$$

Substitute and cross-multiply:

$$\frac{x}{6} = \frac{10}{15}$$
$$15x = (6)(10)$$
$$x = 4$$

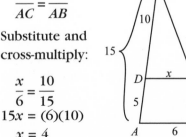

31. (B) Let

x = number of small slices of pizza for $.15 each

$500 - x$ = number of large slices of pizza for $.25 each

$.15(x) + .25(500 - x) = 105.00$

Multiply by 100 $\rightarrow$

$15(x) + 25(500-x) = 10,500$
$15x + 12,500 - 25x = 10,500$
$-10x + 12,500 = 10,500$
$\underline{-12,500 = -12,500} \text{ (additive inverse)}$

Divide by -10: $\dfrac{-10x}{-10} = \dfrac{-2,000}{-10}$

$x = 200$ small slices of pizza
$500 - x = 300$ large slices of pizza

32. (H) $A = \dfrac{1}{2}bh$

$$b = \sqrt{10^2 - 5^2} = \sqrt{100 - 25}$$

$$= \sqrt{75} = 5\sqrt{3}$$

$$\frac{1}{2} \times 10 \times 5\sqrt{3} = 25\sqrt{3}$$

33. (C) BAC and ACD are supplementary angles; hence, $m\,BAC + m\,ACD = 180$.

Substitute $a + 30 + m\,ACD = 180$.

$$m\,ACD = 180 - (a + 30)$$
$$= 180 - a - 30$$
$$= 150 - a$$

34. (G) $y^{-2}y^8y^{-6} = y^{(-2 + 8 - 6)} = y^0 = 1$

35. (A) Let

x = number of hours to complete a job (father)

$\dfrac{1}{x}$ rate of work so that a job can be completed in 1 hour (father)

Let

$2x$ = number of hours to complete a job (son)

$\dfrac{1}{2x}$ rate of work so that a job can be completed in 1 hour (son)

(rate of work) · (time of work) = part of job done

$\dfrac{1}{x}(6) + \dfrac{1}{2x}(6) = 1$ job (completed)

Multiply by 2x: $2x\left(\dfrac{6}{x} + \dfrac{6}{2x} = 1\right)$

$\dfrac{12x}{x} + \dfrac{12x}{2x} = 2x$

Reduce: $12 + 6 = 2x$

$18 = 2x$

$2x = 18$

Divide by 2: $x = 9$ (hours for father to complete the job alone)

$2x = 18$ (hours for son to complete the job alone)

36. (G) 15

This is clearly a problem in division.

$$
\begin{array}{r}
15 \\
12.6\overline{)189.0} \\
126 \\
\hline
630 \\
630 \\
\hline
\end{array}
$$

37. (A) Add like monomials; add coefficients.

$$
\begin{array}{r}
2b + 5 \\
4b - 4 \\
+\ 3b - 6 \\
\hline
9b - 5
\end{array}
$$

38. (F) $3x^2 + 2x - 5$ is a trinomial: The first term is a product of $3x^2 = 3x(x)$. The last term is a product of $-5 = (-1)(+5)$. By trial and error, the trinomial is factored as two binomials.

$(3x + 5)(x - 1)$

39. (B) The midpoint of the line segment with endpoints (x_1, y_1) and (x_2, y_2) is

$$\left(\dfrac{x_1 + x_2}{2}, \dfrac{y_1 + y_2}{2}\right).$$

Thus, for $(2, 5)$ and $(6, 1)$ the midpoint is

$$\left(\dfrac{2 + 6}{2}, \dfrac{5 + 1}{2}\right) = \left(\dfrac{8}{2}, \dfrac{6}{2}\right) = (4, 3).$$

40. (G) In a parallelogram, opposite angles are equal: hence, B = D, D = 75°.

41. (E)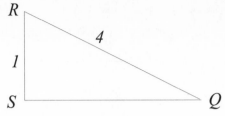

Use the Pythagorean theorem to determine that the side opposite angle R is $\sqrt{15}$.

Then $\sin R = \dfrac{\text{Opposite}}{\text{Hypotenuse}} = \dfrac{\sqrt{15}}{4}$

42. (G) $1,550

Here again, we must find the base.

$$B = \frac{P}{R}$$
$$= \frac{124}{.08} = \$1,550$$

43. (D) 25%

First read the graph to find the sales in 1985 and in 1990. Then find the percent of increase.

$$\begin{array}{r} 1990 - 15,000 \\ 1985 - \underline{12,000} \\ 3,000 \end{array}$$

$$\frac{3,000}{12,000} = \frac{1}{4} = 25\%$$

44. (J) $-3ab + 4a^2 - 1$

To divide a polynomial by a monomial, divide each term of the polynomial by the monomial.

$$\frac{9a^2b^2 - 12a^3b + 3ab}{-3ab}$$

$$= -3ab + 4a^2 - 1$$

45. (E)

Solving inequalities is very similar to solving equations.

$$\begin{array}{r} 5x + 7 \geq x - 1 \\ \underline{-7 \quad = \quad -7} \\ 5x \geq x - 8 \\ \underline{-x = \quad -x} \\ \dfrac{4x}{4} \geq \dfrac{-8}{4} \\ x \geq -2 \end{array}$$

46. (K) $\left(\dfrac{a^2 a^5}{a^6}\right)^4 = \left(\dfrac{a^7}{a^6}\right)^4 = (a^1)^4 = a^4$

47. (C) Find two factors of 28, one of which is a perfect square.

$\dfrac{1}{2}\sqrt{28} = \dfrac{1}{2}\sqrt{4}\sqrt{7}$ reduce perfect

$$\text{square } \sqrt{4} = 2$$

$$= \frac{1}{2}(2)\sqrt{7}$$

$$= 1\sqrt{7} = \sqrt{7}$$

48. (G) A circle has a radius of 10 units. The area of the curve is $\dfrac{1}{4}$ that of the entire circle.

$$A = 2\pi r^2$$

$$A \text{ of } \frac{1}{4} \text{ circle} = \frac{1}{4}(\pi)(10)^2$$

$$A = \frac{1}{4}(\pi)(100)$$

$$= 25\pi$$

49. (A) If $x < y$ and $y < z$, then $x < z$. If one number is less than the second number, and the second number is less than the third number, then the first number is less than the third number.

50. (G) If $g(x) = 2x^2 - 4x + 5$, then $g(3)$ $= 2(3)^2 - 4(3) + 5 = 18 - 12 + 5 = 11$

51. (E) We begin by determining the slope of $3x - 6y = 12$, by writing it in slope-intercept form.

$$3x - 6y = 12$$
$$6y = 3x - 12$$
$$y = \frac{1}{2}x - 2$$

Thus the slope of $3x - 6y = 12$ is $\frac{1}{2}$. The line we are looking for must also have this slope.

Using the point-slope form, the line we are looking for is:

$$m(x - x_1) = (y - y_1), \text{ or}$$
$$\frac{1}{2}(x - 2) = (y - 3)$$
$$(x - 2) = 2(y - 3)$$
$$x - 2 = 2y - 6$$
$$x - 2y = -4$$

52. (H) Let x = height of the tree. The product of the means equals the product of the extremes.

$$\frac{6 \text{ ft}}{x \text{ ft}} = \frac{8 \text{ ft (shadow)}}{20 \text{ ft (shadow)}}$$

$$8x = (6)(20)$$
$$= 120$$

Divide by 8: $x = 15$ ft.

53. (B) $\dfrac{\tan^2 \alpha \csc^2 \alpha - 1}{\sec \alpha \tan^2 \alpha \cos \alpha}$

$$= \frac{\dfrac{\sin^2 \alpha}{\cos^2 \alpha} \cdot \dfrac{1}{\sin^2 \alpha} - 1}{\dfrac{1}{\cos \alpha} \cdot \dfrac{\sin^2 \alpha}{\cos^2 \alpha} \cdot \cos \alpha}$$

$$= \frac{\dfrac{1}{\cos^2 \alpha} - 1}{\dfrac{\sin^2 \alpha}{\cos^2 \alpha}}$$

$$= \frac{\sec \alpha - 1}{\tan^2 \alpha} = \frac{\tan^2 \alpha}{\tan^2 \alpha} = 1$$

54. (H) $x = 3, y = 2$

This system of equations is most easily solved using the addition/subtraction method.

$$\begin{array}{rl} x + 4y = & 11 \\ + 3x - 4y = & 1 \\ \hline 4x \quad\quad = & 12 \end{array}$$

$$\frac{4x}{4} = \frac{12}{4}$$
$$x = 3$$

Substituting in the first equation, we get:

$$\begin{array}{rl} 3 + 4y = & 11 \\ -3 \quad\quad = & -3 \\ \hline 4y = & 8 \end{array}$$

$$\frac{4y}{4} = \frac{8}{4}$$
$$y = 2$$

Again, in this problem it might have been easier to substitute the given answers.

55. (C) To find the average of several numbers, find the sum and divide by the number of items.

$$\frac{2 + x}{2} = 7$$
$$2 + x = 14$$
$$x = 12$$

56. (F) 1

First calculate roots, then subtract.

$$\sqrt{16} = 4$$
$$\sqrt[3]{27} = 3$$
$$4 - 3 = 1$$

57. (C)

$$x^2 - 2x = 0$$
$$x(x - 2) = 0$$
$$x = 0, 2$$

58. (H)

$$\frac{\text{Increase}}{\text{Original Number}} = \text{fraction} \rightarrow \text{converted into } \%$$

$$\frac{93 - 80}{80} = \frac{13}{80}$$

divide 80 into 13:

$$80\overline{)13.0000}^{.1625}$$

Decimals to percent → multiply by 100

$$.1625 \cdot 100 = 16.25$$

59. (A) Point D is vertically aligned with A's x-coordinate, 1, and horizontally aligned with C's y-coordinate, 4.

60. (H)

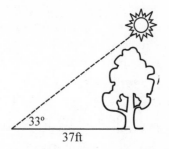

37ft

Let h represent the height of the tree. Then:

$$\tan 33° = \frac{h}{37}$$
$$\text{so, } 37 \tan 33° = h$$

| PART **3** | **READING** |

1. The correct answer is C. A is unlikely, since nothing in the story suggests that Jen is not James's mother. B is unlikely since James is 9 (line 6) and the twins are 7 (line 18). D is unlikely since it is Steiner who is 45 (line 23). C is the correct answer.

2. The correct answer is F. G is a poor choice since the twins are also being "hopeful" (line 38). H and J are both better possibilities, but neither fits with the idea of the sentence that since James hasn't spoken in two weeks, the twins are wondering what his honking the horn may mean, answer F.

3. The correct answer is C. D is unlikely: James hasn't spoken in two weeks, not Steiner. B is also unlikely, since Steiner stops to look for an exercise mat in a department store, apparently leaving the rest of the family in the car. A is a better possibility, but no length of time is given for how long repainting the siding took. Lines 61–62 note that Steiner hadn't seen the farmhouse "in two weeks. He'd spent that time at the hospital with James."

4. The correct answer is G. F is an impossible choice since James is described in the passage as honking the horn, etc. J is unlikely since James is being driven home from the hospital. H is more likely since Steiner is described as feeling bad that he and Jen didn't have more children (lines 25-27); however, the phrase in the question describes Steiner as grieving for a son he already has and "might never see again," so Steiner fears that James may never recover and be the person he once was.

5. The correct answer is A. B and D are unlikely since they are not suggested by the passage. Although it might be assumed that a person in Steiner's circumstances might feel tired or lethargic, C, many words in the passage ("remorse," "swallow down the loss," "grieving") suggest that Steiner feels "sorrowful."

6. The correct answer is J. H is unlikely since it's clear they're returning to a home they have lived in before (lines 65-68). F and G are better possibilities, but lines 52-54 state that Steiner says, "Here we are home" "for the boy and the others, in the phrase that he'd used since James was an infant," so it is unlikely that this is either an invitation to a conversation or that it's a suggestion to help James out of the car. It is more likely that Steiner uses this same phrase to try to make this occasion seem like just another normal ride home.

7. The correct answer is B. Although A, C, and D are all possibilities based on other information in the story, the entire sentence reads, "Shut it off, Steiner said to himself, and the station wagon was silent," suggesting that Steiner is telling himself to turn off the car.

8. The correct answer is H. F is unlikely since any talks with a physical therapist appear to have taken place before this part of the story. J is also unlikely since James honks the horn while he is still in the car. G is a better possibility, but the twins start whispering about him because he honked the horn. Lines 31–34 note that "Steiner was in the department store, where he had gone to look for . . . an exercise mat" when James honked the horn.

9. The correct answer is D. Nothing in the story suggests answer C. A and B are unlikely because James has not been speaking only for two weeks—which would be inconsistent with having been brain-damaged as a child, and he is described having "good health"—which does not fit with a chronic illness. The most likely explanation is that two weeks before, James suffered a terrible accident that has made him unable to speak or walk.

10. The correct answer is F. Steiner notices James's long hair at the beginning of the seventh paragraph, lines 72–74. G is a poor choice since the twins whisper about him in the third paragraph. H and J are better choices since they both occur in the seventh paragraph; however, they occur after Steiner notices James's hair.

11. The correct answer is B. A is true of naturalism: the first paragraph describes critics' problems with defining natural-ism. C is true of naturalism and also described in the first paragraph. D is true of naturalism—described in the first sentence of the opening paragraph. Flaubert is said to have used realism, not naturalism; see the first sentence of the second paragraph. Thus, B is not

true of naturalism, and is, therefore, the correct answer.

12. The correct answer is J. Answer H is an unlikely possibility. First, the verb "argue" here is too strong a word to describe the second paragraph. Also, the first two sentences of the second paragraph note that Flaubert is usually considered a realist. G is an unlikely possibility as well because it is too narrow: only the second sentence of the paragraph relates to Flaubert's use of details. Answer F is a better possibility since it offers a more general and encompassing reason; however, the paragraph does not show how realism is a better philosophy than naturalism. J is the best answer. The first paragraph suggests that some see naturalism "as an appendage to realism," so the second paragraph defines realism in order to explain how naturalism has "an additional requirement," how it differs from realism.

13. The correct answer is C. B is an unlikely answer because it is not suggested in the passage. Although lines 40–42 note that "no rational person in the present age could accept Zola's conclusions as valid science," it is not necessarily a pseudoscience just because his ideas are now outdated. Therefore A is incorrect. Choice D is a theory, not a reason for his theories being considered unscientific.

14. The correct answer is H. J is unlikely because lines 19–20 note that "Zola was unquestionably influenced by Flaubert," who wrote *Madame Bovary*. Therefore, G is not correct. (II) and (III) were both influenced by naturalism. Therefore, F and J are incorrect, leaving H as the correct answer.

15. The correct answer is A. Note that the passage explains that he took his wife with him in order to preserve his reputation. Thus, B, C, and D contradict the sense of the passage. The most likely choice is A, that Zola was being sensible.

16. The correct answer is F. Lines 50-52 note that Zola "produced twenty volumes, tracing . . . a single family through five generations." G is a description of *A Mummer's Wife* by George Moore, not by Zola. H is a description of a pattern for later novels such as *Tess of the D'Urbervilles,* a novel that "owes much to Zola"—not one he wrote himself. The novels described in J are also novels by others who were influenced by Zola.

17. The correct answer is D. B is unlikely because it is too specific, describing only the fifth paragraph. C and A are similarly too specific, relating only to a couple of paragraphs. D encompasses the passage, describing the paragraphs of definition, methods of collections, and the discussion of naturalism's influence on later works.

18. The correct answer is J. F is unlikely since it was the opinion of one critic that Zola's style was documentary, of another that he was a romantic. G and H might be possible answers, but neither of them is discussed in the final paragraph. The final sentence of the passage notes, "Naturalism, . . . [however] it is defined, has had an impact of such import on later writers that perhaps it deserves more respect than it usually receives," and thus the correct answer is J.

19. The correct answer is A. C is unlikely because prostitution was clearly only one of a multitude of interests listed in the paragraph. D is a better possibility; however, the passage suggests that Zola used his ideas of naturalism to write novels—he is not described as being interested in proving the theory. No doubt Zola believed the events he was recording influenced the people in the slums (choice B); however, his concern was to gather the information to use in showing how the characters in his novels were influenced by events in their lives, choice A.

20. The correct answer is G. J is unlikely—the weaker novels are unnamed and unknown. F describes a pattern in novels that occurred after *A Mummer's Wife.* H is a better possibility; however, the author notes that though Moore used "Zola's approach," later novels showed a less complete adherence to naturalism. Thus, they were influenced to some degree by naturalism, answer G.

21. The correct answer is B. C is a poor choice since lines 23-24 note that the canyon "is not the world's largest undersea chasm." Both A and D are likely possibilities, since they are both mentioned in the passage; however, neither explains the convenience of the Canyon. In the third paragraph, the sentence immediately following the claim that the canyon is convenient explains: "At the port of Moss Landing, . . . the head of the canyon is within yards of the coast" (lines 26-28), answer B.

22. The correct answer is F. J is the poorest choice since the subject of erosion is not mentioned in the paragraph. H is also poor since the paragraph explains that "the canyons were submerged by a rise in sea level" (lines 53–54). G is a better possibility since line 59 mentions "A bigger, older knife"; however, the problem is not that the theory wasn't old enough but that the mechanism described wasn't old enough. Therefore, the theory had to be abandoned, answer F.

23. The correct answer is C. Lines 64–66 describe the turbidity currents: "powerful underwater debris flows, a dense slurry of sea water (D), rock debris (B) of various sizes and fine sediments (A)." Since this is a negative question, the only item not in the list is the correct answer, C, chemical-rich fluids.

24. The correct answer is H. III, cold seeps, are mentioned only in the fourth paragraph, which does not discuss the theories about the origin of the canyon. Thus, G and J are incorrect. II is described in detail in the eighth, ninth, and tenth paragraphs as the most widely accepted theory of the origin of the canyon. But I is also described as a theory of the origin of the canyon in the tenth, eleventh, twelfth, and thirteenth paragraphs. Therefore, F is incorrect, and H is the correct answer.

25. The correct answer is D. A is not mentioned in the passage. C is incorrect because the "snow" falls "from above" to the "sunless middle depths" of the canyon (lines 31–32). B is not correct because it describes another substance some of the creatures feed on (lines 37–39). D, the correct answer, is described in lines 33–35, the lines describing the "marine snow."

26. The correct answer is G. J is unlikely since the only paragraph that discusses the theory of river action (the seventh paragraph) does not mention freshwater sapping. H is unlikely since Dan Orange, not Gary Greene, believes that freshwater sapping may have created the initial groove of the canyon (lines 108–116). F is also less likely, since Greene believes the major force in the canyons was the turbidity currents. The very sentence that contains the words "second fiddle" (line 106) notes that "Greene believes that freshwater sapping may have sculpted the canyon's slopes here and there," thus playing a less-important role than the turbidity currents, answer G.

27. The correct answer is C. B and A are unlikely, since nothing relating to either of them is mentioned in the passage. D is more likely, but lines 117–121 note that currently, Orange's speculations cannot be translated "into a testable scientific idea"; therefore, they cannot yet be disproven. Lines 87–89 state that "Today, most geologists agree that turbidity currents played the greatest role in carving the canyon." Thus, Orange's theory is different from what most geologists think, answer C.

28. The correct answer is H. G is unlikely because cold seeps are mentioned only once and in a paragraph that does not relate to the theories of the formation of the canyon (lines 38–39). F and J are more likely choices, but each describes the action of freshwater sapping, not turbidity currents. H is suggested in the eighth paragraph where the currents are described as "underwater debris . . ." that "cascade[s] down underwater slopes" (lines 66–67).

29. The correct answer is A. C is unlikely—it is the length (not the depth) of the Grand Canyon (line 17). B and D are more likely since they do refer to Monterey Canyon; however, they also describe length rather than depth. A is the depth of the canyon as given in line 11.

30. The correct answer is F. Choice H is unlikely because the current theory suggests that Monterey Canyon was formed by the action of turbidity currents rather than a river (lines 81–84). G is unlikely because the age of Monterey Canyon does not relate to the size of either canyon. J is a better choice since the canyons are of similar depth; however, note that the question asks about the Monterey Canyon System and compares it in length to the Grand Canyon. The canyon system is described in the second paragraph: a "60-mile-long gorge" (lines 17–18) and a 180-mile valley (lines 19–21)—a total of 240 miles in length, comparable to the 278-mile length of the Grand Canyon, answer F.

31. The correct answer is C. (III) Since Mago's book has not survived (lines 22–26), the limited subject of his work does not contribute to our lack of knowledge about the Carthaginians; thus, D is not correct. Since (I), lines 20–22, and (II), lines 39–42, are both correct, neither A or B is the right answer. Thus, C is correct.

32. The correct answer is F. G, lines 69–72, H, lines 72–75, and J, lines 65–69, are all used as evidence of infant sacrifice in ancient Carthage. Earlier in the selection, Flaubert's description of infant sacrifice is mentioned (lines 45–49), but it is not discussed as evidence that the practice of infant sacrifice actually existed. The author states, "there is no reason to think [they] were any more addicted to cruelty than the Romans." Therefore, F is the correct answer.

33. The correct answer is B. Although all of the dates listed appear in the passage, A, the sixth century B.C., refers to the practice of infant sacrifice in Jerusalem (lines 70–72). C, the first millennium B.C., refers to the travels of the Phoenicians "2,400 years earlier" (lines 96–97). D refers to the Portuguese explorers of West Africa. Choice B, 262 B.C. to 146 B.C., refers to the time period during which Rome and Carthage "clawed their way toward mastery of the known world" (lines 85–88).

34. The correct answer is H. The answer to this question requires a two-part understanding of the passage: first, the Carthaginians were descendants of the Phoenicians (lines 96–102), and second, that the Punic language is related to the "variety of the Phoenician spoken in Tyre" (lines 27–28). Thus, J is incorrect since Asia is not mentioned in the passage. F is incorrect because it describes the Portuguese captains who traveled along the coast of West Africa (lines 92–96). G is incorrect because the Phoenicians traded with the people of Elba; apparently they did not live there. Since the remnants of the Punic language resemble the Phoenician spoken in Tyre, H is the most likely answer.

35. The correct answer is B. Although it may be true that the Romans did not practice infant sacrifice (A), that is not the purpose of the statement about Roman crucifixion. C is incorrect, since the passage does not suggest that the Romans were cruel to any specific group. D is likewise incorrect—since lines 54–57 read "there is no reason to think the people of ancient Carthage were any more addicted to cruelty than the Romans," the purpose of the description of crucifixion is not to show that the Romans were more cruel, but that they were equally cruel.

36. The correct answer is J. Opulence means wealth or riches. Note that an example of "glittering opulence and unspeakable vice" is described more specifically in the rest of the sentence "Oriental perfume [riches] mingle with rivers of blood [vice]" (lines 47–48). F, G, and H might all be suggested by

other elements of the passage, but are incorrect.

37. The correct answer is A. B, the destruction of the city, is described in the first paragraph (lines 5–6). C and D are both discussed in the third paragraph, but neither is broad enough to be a good description of the entire paragraph. The best, most inclusive description of the main idea is answer A.

38. The correct answer is G. H and J are both unlikely answers since the passage does not discuss Flaubert's personal life at all. It is much more likely that the passage is describing some aspect of Flaubert as a writer, F or G. Of the two, F is not suggested by the passage. G, however, is suggested in the assertion that Flaubert "was never happier than when offering such tidbits as the claim that high-born maidens used a paste made of crushed flies' legs to touch up their eyebrows" (lines 50–54).

39. The correct answer is D. C is not mentioned in the passage. A is incorrect, since the passage states that the Phoenicians had begun trading in the western Mediterranean (lines 96–102). B, again, is incorrect—it was the Portuguese captains who searched for "gold, spices, and slaves" (lines 95–96). Lines 112–113 describe the alphabetic script, therefore D is correct.

40. The correct answer is J. II describes the activities of the Carthaginian ancestors and does not relate to the destruction of Carthage; thus, H is not correct. (I), lines 20–22, and (III), lines 15–16 are both correct. Thus, F and G are not correct. J includes both I and III and is correct.

PART 4   SCIENCE

1. The correct answer is D. The father (male 3) is albino, but the mother expresses a normal phenotype. All offspring inherit an allele from each parent. Since one child has a normal phenotype, albinism must be recessive.

2. The correct answer is J. In F, the parents are both normal, but their son is albino. For this to happen, both parents must have a recessive gene that they passed on to their son. A recessive trait is expressed only if both recessive alleles are inherited. The parents must be heterozygous since their phenotype is normal. In H, the son would inherit a gene from each parent. Since female 2 in generation 1 and her son are normal, but male 1 in generation 1 is not, male 1 in generation 2 is heterozygous, and albinism must be a recessive trait. Answer G, by itself, is not sufficient data to conclude that albinism is a recessive trait without evaluating generation 2, as well.

3. The correct answer is C. In order for any normal parent to have a child who expresses a recessive trait, the parent must be heterozygous for the allele. The child must inherit a recessive gene from both parents in order to express a recessive phenotype. This child would be homozygous for the allele. Thus, female 4 in generation 2 has a heterozygous genotype (one normal allele and one allele for albinism).

4. The correct answer is H. His father is albino. Therefore, male 4 in generation 3 could inherit only a recessive allele for albinism from his father. Since his phenotype is normal, he must be heterozygous. He would have to inherit the normal allele from his mother.

5. The correct answer is C. Albinism is a recessive trait. A person with this phenotype must be homozygous for the allele in order to express it.

6. The correct answer is G. Albinos must have two recessive alleles in order to express the phenotype. Thus, they do *not* have the normal genes for pigmentation. They could pass only the recessive genes to their offspring.

7. The correct answer is C. Any free element has an oxidation number of zero.

8. The correct answer is G. Hydrochloric acid contains the hydrogen that gains 2 electrons. Such substances are called the oxidizing agent.

9. The correct answer is B. Hydrogen in hydrochloric acid gains 2 electrons to become hydrogen gas.

10. The correct answer is F. Any free element has an oxidation number of zero.

11. The correct answer is C. Zinc loses 2 electrons to become the Zn^{+2} ion.

12. The correct answer is F. The reducing agent is the reactant where oxidation occurs. It is the substance that loses electrons.

13. The correct answer is A. Rubidium and cerium do not have the correct charge to substitute in olivine and calcium plagioclase and are incompatible with the solids, and their concentration will increase in the liquid. In choice B, nickel is compatible in olivine substituting for iron. In choice C, potassium is incompatible but strontium is compatible substituting for calcium in calcium plagioclase. In choice D, both chromium and titanium are compatible substituting for iron in olivine.

14. The correct answer is J. Potassium has a charge of +1, and rubidium is the only choice with an equal charge and similar ionic radius. The other choices all have charges of +2.

15. The correct answer is B. Iron can have a charge of +2 or +3. Iron +2 has a radius of 0.69 A, and iron +3 has a radius of 0.63 A. All the choices have charges of +2, and nickel has the closest ionic radius at 0.77 A.

16. The correct answer is H. Magma pools in the magma chamber below the volcano where it sets slowly, cooling and crystallizing. Each successive lava flow is a sample of the magma in the magma chamber at that time. Cerium is increasing in concentration in the magma, and this can only be accounted for by crystallization of minerals that cerium is incompatible with. Choice A cannot be true because cerium would decrease in concentration in the magma. Cerium would also decrease in concentration if choice B was occurring, because when a magma chamber is replenished it is diluted with compatible elements, reducing the concentration of incompatible elements.

17. The correct answer is C. In general, ions with a greater positive charge will have a smaller ionic radius. Looking at Table 3, all the +1 ions are greater than 1.0 A. Only three of the +2 ions are greater than 1.0 A, but are still smaller than all but potassium of the +1 group. Finally, looking at iron, which can be both +2 and +3, its ionic radius decreases with the increase in charge.

18. The correct answer is J. Iron, magnesium, and calcium are the major elements in olivine and pyroxene. Potassium and sodium are incompatible with olivine and pyroxene because of their +1 charges, so over time they will become enriched in the crust over the mantle.

19. The correct answer is B. The total energy is the sum of the potential energy and kinetic energy. At any point the sum is equal to 5,000. When x=0, for example, the kinetic energy = 5,000, and the potential energy = 0. For any other value of x, U(x) + K(x) = 5,000.

20. The correct answer is H. The spring is moving fastest when the kinetic energy is greatest. This occurs when x=0.

21. The correct answer is C. When x=5, draw a vertical line until it intersects with the kinetic energy graph. Draw a horizontal line and read the scale.

22. The correct answer is H. On the potential energy graph, when x=5 the potential energy = 1,250. When x=10, the potential energy = 5,000. When x doubles, U(x) quadruples. This shows U(x) is a function of x^2. If x doubles again to 20, the U(x) would again be quadrupled, to 20,000.

23. The correct answer is B. The greater the displacement, the greater the potential energy, and the greater the total energy of the system. At x=0, the potential energy is zero and the kinetic energy is equal to the total (larger) energy.

24. The correct answer is J. If one draws a horizontal line across the potential energy graph at U(x)=2,000, then it intersects the graph at two different values of x. This shows that at two different positions the spring can have the same positive potential energy.

25. The correct answer is C. Scientist 1 would expect the meat to produce maggots through spontaneous generation if the meat is left out in the open. The gauze and cooking should have no impact on this process, according to his thinking. His hypothesis clearly eliminates answer A.

26. The correct answer is G. Scientist 2 would conclude that the meat could not produce maggots if the gauze kept flies away from the meat. He does not support the hypothesis for spontaneous generation, which rules out F, H, and J.

27. The correct answer is D. Scientist 1 would not choose answers B and C, because those would be inconsistent with his hypothesis. Furthermore, because his hypothesis includes the concept of "out in the open" as a condition for growth (his assumption is that air is needed for growth to occur), then he would also reject answer A—since air could pass in and out of a loosely covered container. Scientist 1 would choose D, which is consistent with the hypothesis of Scientist 2.

28. The correct answer is F. Answer G is not consistent with the outcome. Nothing grew. The hypothesis of Scientist 1 strongly implies that air is required for growth of microorganisms, ruling out H and J as likely answers. Scientist 1 would choose answer F.

29. The correct answer is A. This was the whole point of the experiment.

30. The correct answer is H. Only this choice would be possible, since the experiment allowed free flow of air in both cases, but the S-necked flask would trap contaminants. Scientist 2 would not choose J, as he rejects the hypothesis of spontaneous generation.

31. The correct answer is B. Both models assume a solar nebula collapsing to form the sun and that the planets accreted from material in this nebula.

32. The correct answer is J. In the heterogeneous accretion model, the material that accreted first formed the core, and next the mantle and crust, and then the oceans and atmosphere. The order in which material condenses and accretes must match the makeup of the Earth from center outward.

33. The correct answer is D. The accretion model holds that accretion is of material of one (homogeneous) composition.

34. The correct answer is F. If calcium, aluminum, and titanium oxides were the first to condense, they would also be the first to accrete, and would go into the core. This does not fit with data that have a cohomogeneous recomposition of mostly iron, and would result in a core not dense enough to agree with data on the core.

35. The correct answer is C. If there is not enough heat to initiate melting, then that would help support the heterogeneous accretion model.

36. The correct answer is G. Since homogeneous accretion would not begin until after condensation was through, a computer model predicting this would help support this model. The other choices tend to support the heterogeneous accretion model.

37. The correct answer is B. The smaller the angle of incidence, the smaller the angle of refraction. The air-glass interface produces a greater refraction than the air-water interface. The shorter λ produces a smaller angle, but laser 2 is not a choice for x = 15.

38. The correct answer is G. From Tables 1 and 2, for a given angle of incidence there is a different angle of refraction as the wavelength of the laser light changes. If light consists of a mixture of different wavelengths then they emerge at different angles.

39. The correct answer is B. From Tables 1, 2, and 3, as light travels from a medium with a lower index of refraction to a higher one the angle of refraction is smaller than the angle of incidence. Water has a lower index of refraction than glass. The angle of refraction would be smaller than the angle of incidence.

40. The correct answer is G. According to the passage, the angle of incidence divided by the angle of refraction is a positive constant. This is graphed as a straight line with positive slope.

OFFICIAL ANSWER SHEET FOR PRETEST, pp. 11-53

Name: _____

Date: ____ / ____ / ____

School: _____

Class: _____

Completely darken bubbles with a No. 2 pencil. If you make a mistake, be sure to erase mark completely. Erase all stray marks.

Start with number 1 for each new section. If a section has fewer questions than answer spaces, leave the extra answer spaces blank.

PART 1

1 ⊂A⊃ ⊂B⊃ ⊂C⊃ ⊂D⊃ ⊂E⊃	20 ⊂F⊃ ⊂G⊃ ⊂H⊃ ⊂J⊃ ⊂K⊃	39 ⊂A⊃ ⊂B⊃ ⊂C⊃ ⊂D⊃ ⊂E⊃	58 ⊂F⊃ ⊂G⊃ ⊂H⊃ ⊂J⊃ ⊂K⊃
2 ⊂F⊃ ⊂G⊃ ⊂H⊃ ⊂J⊃ ⊂K⊃	21 ⊂A⊃ ⊂B⊃ ⊂C⊃ ⊂D⊃ ⊂E⊃	40 ⊂F⊃ ⊂G⊃ ⊂H⊃ ⊂J⊃ ⊂K⊃	59 ⊂A⊃ ⊂B⊃ ⊂C⊃ ⊂D⊃ ⊂E⊃
3 ⊂A⊃ ⊂B⊃ ⊂C⊃ ⊂D⊃ ⊂E⊃	22 ⊂F⊃ ⊂G⊃ ⊂H⊃ ⊂J⊃ ⊂K⊃	41 ⊂A⊃ ⊂B⊃ ⊂C⊃ ⊂D⊃ ⊂E⊃	60 ⊂F⊃ ⊂G⊃ ⊂H⊃ ⊂J⊃ ⊂K⊃
4 ⊂F⊃ ⊂G⊃ ⊂H⊃ ⊂J⊃ ⊂K⊃	23 ⊂A⊃ ⊂B⊃ ⊂C⊃ ⊂D⊃ ⊂E⊃	42 ⊂F⊃ ⊂G⊃ ⊂H⊃ ⊂J⊃ ⊂K⊃	61 ⊂A⊃ ⊂B⊃ ⊂C⊃ ⊂D⊃ ⊂E⊃
5 ⊂A⊃ ⊂B⊃ ⊂C⊃ ⊂D⊃ ⊂E⊃	24 ⊂F⊃ ⊂G⊃ ⊂H⊃ ⊂J⊃ ⊂K⊃	43 ⊂A⊃ ⊂B⊃ ⊂C⊃ ⊂D⊃ ⊂E⊃	62 ⊂F⊃ ⊂G⊃ ⊂H⊃ ⊂J⊃ ⊂K⊃
6 ⊂F⊃ ⊂G⊃ ⊂H⊃ ⊂J⊃ ⊂K⊃	25 ⊂A⊃ ⊂B⊃ ⊂C⊃ ⊂D⊃ ⊂E⊃	44 ⊂F⊃ ⊂G⊃ ⊂H⊃ ⊂J⊃ ⊂K⊃	63 ⊂A⊃ ⊂B⊃ ⊂C⊃ ⊂D⊃ ⊂E⊃
7 ⊂A⊃ ⊂B⊃ ⊂C⊃ ⊂D⊃ ⊂E⊃	26 ⊂F⊃ ⊂G⊃ ⊂H⊃ ⊂J⊃ ⊂K⊃	45 ⊂A⊃ ⊂B⊃ ⊂C⊃ ⊂D⊃ ⊂E⊃	64 ⊂F⊃ ⊂G⊃ ⊂H⊃ ⊂J⊃ ⊂K⊃
8 ⊂F⊃ ⊂G⊃ ⊂H⊃ ⊂J⊃ ⊂K⊃	27 ⊂A⊃ ⊂B⊃ ⊂C⊃ ⊂D⊃ ⊂E⊃	46 ⊂F⊃ ⊂G⊃ ⊂H⊃ ⊂J⊃ ⊂K⊃	65 ⊂A⊃ ⊂B⊃ ⊂C⊃ ⊂D⊃ ⊂E⊃
9 ⊂A⊃ ⊂B⊃ ⊂C⊃ ⊂D⊃ ⊂E⊃	28 ⊂F⊃ ⊂G⊃ ⊂H⊃ ⊂J⊃ ⊂K⊃	47 ⊂A⊃ ⊂B⊃ ⊂C⊃ ⊂D⊃ ⊂E⊃	66 ⊂F⊃ ⊂G⊃ ⊂H⊃ ⊂J⊃ ⊂K⊃
10 ⊂F⊃ ⊂G⊃ ⊂H⊃ ⊂J⊃ ⊂K⊃	29 ⊂A⊃ ⊂B⊃ ⊂C⊃ ⊂D⊃ ⊂E⊃	48 ⊂F⊃ ⊂G⊃ ⊂H⊃ ⊂J⊃ ⊂K⊃	67 ⊂A⊃ ⊂B⊃ ⊂C⊃ ⊂D⊃ ⊂E⊃
11 ⊂A⊃ ⊂B⊃ ⊂C⊃ ⊂D⊃ ⊂E⊃	30 ⊂F⊃ ⊂G⊃ ⊂H⊃ ⊂J⊃ ⊂K⊃	49 ⊂A⊃ ⊂B⊃ ⊂C⊃ ⊂D⊃ ⊂E⊃	68 ⊂F⊃ ⊂G⊃ ⊂H⊃ ⊂J⊃ ⊂K⊃
12 ⊂F⊃ ⊂G⊃ ⊂H⊃ ⊂J⊃ ⊂K⊃	31 ⊂A⊃ ⊂B⊃ ⊂C⊃ ⊂D⊃ ⊂E⊃	50 ⊂F⊃ ⊂G⊃ ⊂H⊃ ⊂J⊃ ⊂K⊃	69 ⊂A⊃ ⊂B⊃ ⊂C⊃ ⊂D⊃ ⊂E⊃
13 ⊂A⊃ ⊂B⊃ ⊂C⊃ ⊂D⊃ ⊂E⊃	32 ⊂F⊃ ⊂G⊃ ⊂H⊃ ⊂J⊃ ⊂K⊃	51 ⊂A⊃ ⊂B⊃ ⊂C⊃ ⊂D⊃ ⊂E⊃	70 ⊂F⊃ ⊂G⊃ ⊂H⊃ ⊂J⊃ ⊂K⊃
14 ⊂F⊃ ⊂G⊃ ⊂H⊃ ⊂J⊃ ⊂K⊃	33 ⊂A⊃ ⊂B⊃ ⊂C⊃ ⊂D⊃ ⊂E⊃	52 ⊂F⊃ ⊂G⊃ ⊂H⊃ ⊂J⊃ ⊂K⊃	71 ⊂A⊃ ⊂B⊃ ⊂C⊃ ⊂D⊃ ⊂E⊃
15 ⊂A⊃ ⊂B⊃ ⊂C⊃ ⊂D⊃ ⊂E⊃	34 ⊂F⊃ ⊂G⊃ ⊂H⊃ ⊂J⊃ ⊂K⊃	53 ⊂A⊃ ⊂B⊃ ⊂C⊃ ⊂D⊃ ⊂E⊃	72 ⊂F⊃ ⊂G⊃ ⊂H⊃ ⊂J⊃ ⊂K⊃
16 ⊂F⊃ ⊂G⊃ ⊂H⊃ ⊂J⊃ ⊂K⊃	35 ⊂A⊃ ⊂B⊃ ⊂C⊃ ⊂D⊃ ⊂E⊃	54 ⊂F⊃ ⊂G⊃ ⊂H⊃ ⊂J⊃ ⊂K⊃	73 ⊂A⊃ ⊂B⊃ ⊂C⊃ ⊂D⊃ ⊂E⊃
17 ⊂A⊃ ⊂B⊃ ⊂C⊃ ⊂D⊃ ⊂E⊃	36 ⊂F⊃ ⊂G⊃ ⊂H⊃ ⊂J⊃ ⊂K⊃	55 ⊂A⊃ ⊂B⊃ ⊂C⊃ ⊂D⊃ ⊂E⊃	74 ⊂F⊃ ⊂G⊃ ⊂H⊃ ⊂J⊃ ⊂K⊃
18 ⊂F⊃ ⊂G⊃ ⊂H⊃ ⊂J⊃ ⊂K⊃	37 ⊂A⊃ ⊂B⊃ ⊂C⊃ ⊂D⊃ ⊂E⊃	56 ⊂F⊃ ⊂G⊃ ⊂H⊃ ⊂J⊃ ⊂K⊃	75 ⊂A⊃ ⊂B⊃ ⊂C⊃ ⊂D⊃ ⊂E⊃
19 ⊂A⊃ ⊂B⊃ ⊂C⊃ ⊂D⊃ ⊂E⊃	38 ⊂F⊃ ⊂G⊃ ⊂H⊃ ⊂J⊃ ⊂K⊃	57 ⊂A⊃ ⊂B⊃ ⊂C⊃ ⊂D⊃ ⊂E⊃	76 ⊂F⊃ ⊂G⊃ ⊂H⊃ ⊂J⊃ ⊂K⊃

PART 2

1 ⊂A⊃ ⊂B⊃ ⊂C⊃ ⊂D⊃ ⊂E⊃	16 ⊂F⊃ ⊂G⊃ ⊂H⊃ ⊂J⊃ ⊂K⊃	31 ⊂A⊃ ⊂B⊃ ⊂C⊃ ⊂D⊃ ⊂E⊃	46 ⊂F⊃ ⊂G⊃ ⊂H⊃ ⊂J⊃ ⊂K⊃
2 ⊂F⊃ ⊂G⊃ ⊂H⊃ ⊂J⊃ ⊂K⊃	17 ⊂A⊃ ⊂B⊃ ⊂C⊃ ⊂D⊃ ⊂E⊃	32 ⊂F⊃ ⊂G⊃ ⊂H⊃ ⊂J⊃ ⊂K⊃	47 ⊂A⊃ ⊂B⊃ ⊂C⊃ ⊂D⊃ ⊂E⊃
3 ⊂A⊃ ⊂B⊃ ⊂C⊃ ⊂D⊃ ⊂E⊃	18 ⊂F⊃ ⊂G⊃ ⊂H⊃ ⊂J⊃ ⊂K⊃	33 ⊂A⊃ ⊂B⊃ ⊂C⊃ ⊂D⊃ ⊂E⊃	48 ⊂F⊃ ⊂G⊃ ⊂H⊃ ⊂J⊃ ⊂K⊃
4 ⊂F⊃ ⊂G⊃ ⊂H⊃ ⊂J⊃ ⊂K⊃	19 ⊂A⊃ ⊂B⊃ ⊂C⊃ ⊂D⊃ ⊂E⊃	34 ⊂F⊃ ⊂G⊃ ⊂H⊃ ⊂J⊃ ⊂K⊃	49 ⊂A⊃ ⊂B⊃ ⊂C⊃ ⊂D⊃ ⊂E⊃
5 ⊂A⊃ ⊂B⊃ ⊂C⊃ ⊂D⊃ ⊂E⊃	20 ⊂F⊃ ⊂G⊃ ⊂H⊃ ⊂J⊃ ⊂K⊃	35 ⊂A⊃ ⊂B⊃ ⊂C⊃ ⊂D⊃ ⊂E⊃	50 ⊂F⊃ ⊂G⊃ ⊂H⊃ ⊂J⊃ ⊂K⊃
6 ⊂F⊃ ⊂G⊃ ⊂H⊃ ⊂J⊃ ⊂K⊃	21 ⊂A⊃ ⊂B⊃ ⊂C⊃ ⊂D⊃ ⊂E⊃	36 ⊂F⊃ ⊂G⊃ ⊂H⊃ ⊂J⊃ ⊂K⊃	51 ⊂A⊃ ⊂B⊃ ⊂C⊃ ⊂D⊃ ⊂E⊃
7 ⊂A⊃ ⊂B⊃ ⊂C⊃ ⊂D⊃ ⊂E⊃	22 ⊂F⊃ ⊂G⊃ ⊂H⊃ ⊂J⊃ ⊂K⊃	37 ⊂A⊃ ⊂B⊃ ⊂C⊃ ⊂D⊃ ⊂E⊃	52 ⊂F⊃ ⊂G⊃ ⊂H⊃ ⊂J⊃ ⊂K⊃
8 ⊂F⊃ ⊂G⊃ ⊂H⊃ ⊂J⊃ ⊂K⊃	23 ⊂A⊃ ⊂B⊃ ⊂C⊃ ⊂D⊃ ⊂E⊃	38 ⊂F⊃ ⊂G⊃ ⊂H⊃ ⊂J⊃ ⊂K⊃	53 ⊂A⊃ ⊂B⊃ ⊂C⊃ ⊂D⊃ ⊂E⊃
9 ⊂A⊃ ⊂B⊃ ⊂C⊃ ⊂D⊃ ⊂E⊃	24 ⊂F⊃ ⊂G⊃ ⊂H⊃ ⊂J⊃ ⊂K⊃	39 ⊂A⊃ ⊂B⊃ ⊂C⊃ ⊂D⊃ ⊂E⊃	54 ⊂F⊃ ⊂G⊃ ⊂H⊃ ⊂J⊃ ⊂K⊃
10 ⊂F⊃ ⊂G⊃ ⊂H⊃ ⊂J⊃ ⊂K⊃	25 ⊂A⊃ ⊂B⊃ ⊂C⊃ ⊂D⊃ ⊂E⊃	40 ⊂F⊃ ⊂G⊃ ⊂H⊃ ⊂J⊃ ⊂K⊃	55 ⊂A⊃ ⊂B⊃ ⊂C⊃ ⊂D⊃ ⊂E⊃
11 ⊂A⊃ ⊂B⊃ ⊂C⊃ ⊂D⊃ ⊂E⊃	26 ⊂F⊃ ⊂G⊃ ⊂H⊃ ⊂J⊃ ⊂K⊃	41 ⊂A⊃ ⊂B⊃ ⊂C⊃ ⊂D⊃ ⊂E⊃	56 ⊂F⊃ ⊂G⊃ ⊂H⊃ ⊂J⊃ ⊂K⊃
12 ⊂F⊃ ⊂G⊃ ⊂H⊃ ⊂J⊃ ⊂K⊃	27 ⊂A⊃ ⊂B⊃ ⊂C⊃ ⊂D⊃ ⊂E⊃	42 ⊂F⊃ ⊂G⊃ ⊂H⊃ ⊂J⊃ ⊂K⊃	57 ⊂A⊃ ⊂B⊃ ⊂C⊃ ⊂D⊃ ⊂E⊃
13 ⊂A⊃ ⊂B⊃ ⊂C⊃ ⊂D⊃ ⊂E⊃	28 ⊂F⊃ ⊂G⊃ ⊂H⊃ ⊂J⊃ ⊂K⊃	43 ⊂A⊃ ⊂B⊃ ⊂C⊃ ⊂D⊃ ⊂E⊃	58 ⊂F⊃ ⊂G⊃ ⊂H⊃ ⊂J⊃ ⊂K⊃
14 ⊂F⊃ ⊂G⊃ ⊂H⊃ ⊂J⊃ ⊂K⊃	29 ⊂A⊃ ⊂B⊃ ⊂C⊃ ⊂D⊃ ⊂E⊃	44 ⊂F⊃ ⊂G⊃ ⊂H⊃ ⊂J⊃ ⊂K⊃	59 ⊂A⊃ ⊂B⊃ ⊂C⊃ ⊂D⊃ ⊂E⊃
15 ⊂A⊃ ⊂B⊃ ⊂C⊃ ⊂D⊃ ⊂E⊃	30 ⊂F⊃ ⊂G⊃ ⊂H⊃ ⊂J⊃ ⊂K⊃	45 ⊂A⊃ ⊂B⊃ ⊂C⊃ ⊂D⊃ ⊂E⊃	60 ⊂F⊃ ⊂G⊃ ⊂H⊃ ⊂J⊃ ⊂K⊃

BE SURE TO ERASE ANY ERRORS OR STRAY MARKS COMPLETELY.

DO NOT MARK IN THIS AREA

⊂ ⊃ ⊂ ⊃

Start with number 1 for each new section. If a section has fewer questions than answer spaces, leave the extra answer spaces blank.

PART 3

1 ⊂A⊃ ⊂B⊃ ⊂C⊃ ⊂D⊃ ⊂E⊃	11 ⊂A⊃ ⊂B⊃ ⊂C⊃ ⊂D⊃ ⊂E⊃	21 ⊂A⊃ ⊂B⊃ ⊂C⊃ ⊂D⊃ ⊂E⊃	31 ⊂A⊃ ⊂B⊃ ⊂C⊃ ⊂D⊃ ⊂E⊃
2 ⊂F⊃ ⊂G⊃ ⊂H⊃ ⊂J⊃ ⊂K⊃	12 ⊂F⊃ ⊂G⊃ ⊂H⊃ ⊂J⊃ ⊂K⊃	22 ⊂F⊃ ⊂G⊃ ⊂H⊃ ⊂J⊃ ⊂K⊃	32 ⊂F⊃ ⊂G⊃ ⊂H⊃ ⊂J⊃ ⊂K⊃
3 ⊂A⊃ ⊂B⊃ ⊂C⊃ ⊂D⊃ ⊂E⊃	13 ⊂A⊃ ⊂B⊃ ⊂C⊃ ⊂D⊃ ⊂E⊃	23 ⊂A⊃ ⊂B⊃ ⊂C⊃ ⊂D⊃ ⊂E⊃	33 ⊂A⊃ ⊂B⊃ ⊂C⊃ ⊂D⊃ ⊂E⊃
4 ⊂F⊃ ⊂G⊃ ⊂H⊃ ⊂J⊃ ⊂K⊃	14 ⊂F⊃ ⊂G⊃ ⊂H⊃ ⊂J⊃ ⊂K⊃	24 ⊂F⊃ ⊂G⊃ ⊂H⊃ ⊂J⊃ ⊂K⊃	34 ⊂F⊃ ⊂G⊃ ⊂H⊃ ⊂J⊃ ⊂K⊃
5 ⊂A⊃ ⊂B⊃ ⊂C⊃ ⊂D⊃ ⊂E⊃	15 ⊂A⊃ ⊂B⊃ ⊂C⊃ ⊂D⊃ ⊂E⊃	25 ⊂A⊃ ⊂B⊃ ⊂C⊃ ⊂D⊃ ⊂E⊃	35 ⊂A⊃ ⊂B⊃ ⊂C⊃ ⊂D⊃ ⊂E⊃
6 ⊂F⊃ ⊂G⊃ ⊂H⊃ ⊂J⊃ ⊂K⊃	16 ⊂F⊃ ⊂G⊃ ⊂H⊃ ⊂J⊃ ⊂K⊃	26 ⊂F⊃ ⊂G⊃ ⊂H⊃ ⊂J⊃ ⊂K⊃	36 ⊂F⊃ ⊂G⊃ ⊂H⊃ ⊂J⊃ ⊂K⊃
7 ⊂A⊃ ⊂B⊃ ⊂C⊃ ⊂D⊃ ⊂E⊃	17 ⊂A⊃ ⊂B⊃ ⊂C⊃ ⊂D⊃ ⊂E⊃	27 ⊂A⊃ ⊂B⊃ ⊂C⊃ ⊂D⊃ ⊂E⊃	37 ⊂A⊃ ⊂B⊃ ⊂C⊃ ⊂D⊃ ⊂E⊃
8 ⊂F⊃ ⊂G⊃ ⊂H⊃ ⊂J⊃ ⊂K⊃	18 ⊂F⊃ ⊂G⊃ ⊂H⊃ ⊂J⊃ ⊂K⊃	28 ⊂F⊃ ⊂G⊃ ⊂H⊃ ⊂J⊃ ⊂K⊃	38 ⊂F⊃ ⊂G⊃ ⊂H⊃ ⊂J⊃ ⊂K⊃
9 ⊂A⊃ ⊂B⊃ ⊂C⊃ ⊂D⊃ ⊂E⊃	19 ⊂A⊃ ⊂B⊃ ⊂C⊃ ⊂D⊃ ⊂E⊃	29 ⊂A⊃ ⊂B⊃ ⊂C⊃ ⊂D⊃ ⊂E⊃	39 ⊂A⊃ ⊂B⊃ ⊂C⊃ ⊂D⊃ ⊂E⊃
10 ⊂F⊃ ⊂G⊃ ⊂H⊃ ⊂J⊃ ⊂K⊃	20 ⊂F⊃ ⊂G⊃ ⊂H⊃ ⊂J⊃ ⊂K⊃	30 ⊂F⊃ ⊂G⊃ ⊂H⊃ ⊂J⊃ ⊂K⊃	40 ⊂F⊃ ⊂G⊃ ⊂H⊃ ⊂J⊃ ⊂K⊃

PART 4

1 ⊂A⊃ ⊂B⊃ ⊂C⊃ ⊂D⊃ ⊂E⊃	11 ⊂A⊃ ⊂B⊃ ⊂C⊃ ⊂D⊃ ⊂E⊃	21 ⊂A⊃ ⊂B⊃ ⊂C⊃ ⊂D⊃ ⊂E⊃	31 ⊂A⊃ ⊂B⊃ ⊂C⊃ ⊂D⊃ ⊂E⊃
2 ⊂F⊃ ⊂G⊃ ⊂H⊃ ⊂J⊃ ⊂K⊃	12 ⊂F⊃ ⊂G⊃ ⊂H⊃ ⊂J⊃ ⊂K⊃	22 ⊂F⊃ ⊂G⊃ ⊂H⊃ ⊂J⊃ ⊂K⊃	32 ⊂F⊃ ⊂G⊃ ⊂H⊃ ⊂J⊃ ⊂K⊃
3 ⊂A⊃ ⊂B⊃ ⊂C⊃ ⊂D⊃ ⊂E⊃	13 ⊂A⊃ ⊂B⊃ ⊂C⊃ ⊂D⊃ ⊂E⊃	23 ⊂A⊃ ⊂B⊃ ⊂C⊃ ⊂D⊃ ⊂E⊃	33 ⊂A⊃ ⊂B⊃ ⊂C⊃ ⊂D⊃ ⊂E⊃
4 ⊂F⊃ ⊂G⊃ ⊂H⊃ ⊂J⊃ ⊂K⊃	14 ⊂F⊃ ⊂G⊃ ⊂H⊃ ⊂J⊃ ⊂K⊃	24 ⊂F⊃ ⊂G⊃ ⊂H⊃ ⊂J⊃ ⊂K⊃	34 ⊂F⊃ ⊂G⊃ ⊂H⊃ ⊂J⊃ ⊂K⊃
5 ⊂A⊃ ⊂B⊃ ⊂C⊃ ⊂D⊃ ⊂E⊃	15 ⊂A⊃ ⊂B⊃ ⊂C⊃ ⊂D⊃ ⊂E⊃	25 ⊂A⊃ ⊂B⊃ ⊂C⊃ ⊂D⊃ ⊂E⊃	35 ⊂A⊃ ⊂B⊃ ⊂C⊃ ⊂D⊃ ⊂E⊃
6 ⊂F⊃ ⊂G⊃ ⊂H⊃ ⊂J⊃ ⊂K⊃	16 ⊂F⊃ ⊂G⊃ ⊂H⊃ ⊂J⊃ ⊂K⊃	26 ⊂F⊃ ⊂G⊃ ⊂H⊃ ⊂J⊃ ⊂K⊃	36 ⊂F⊃ ⊂G⊃ ⊂H⊃ ⊂J⊃ ⊂K⊃
7 ⊂A⊃ ⊂B⊃ ⊂C⊃ ⊂D⊃ ⊂E⊃	17 ⊂A⊃ ⊂B⊃ ⊂C⊃ ⊂D⊃ ⊂E⊃	27 ⊂A⊃ ⊂B⊃ ⊂C⊃ ⊂D⊃ ⊂E⊃	37 ⊂A⊃ ⊂B⊃ ⊂C⊃ ⊂D⊃ ⊂E⊃
8 ⊂F⊃ ⊂G⊃ ⊂H⊃ ⊂J⊃ ⊂K⊃	18 ⊂F⊃ ⊂G⊃ ⊂H⊃ ⊂J⊃ ⊂K⊃	28 ⊂F⊃ ⊂G⊃ ⊂H⊃ ⊂J⊃ ⊂K⊃	38 ⊂F⊃ ⊂G⊃ ⊂H⊃ ⊂J⊃ ⊂K⊃
9 ⊂A⊃ ⊂B⊃ ⊂C⊃ ⊂D⊃ ⊂E⊃	19 ⊂A⊃ ⊂B⊃ ⊂C⊃ ⊂D⊃ ⊂E⊃	29 ⊂A⊃ ⊂B⊃ ⊂C⊃ ⊂D⊃ ⊂E⊃	39 ⊂A⊃ ⊂B⊃ ⊂C⊃ ⊂D⊃ ⊂E⊃
10 ⊂F⊃ ⊂G⊃ ⊂H⊃ ⊂J⊃ ⊂K⊃	20 ⊂F⊃ ⊂G⊃ ⊂H⊃ ⊂J⊃ ⊂K⊃	30 ⊂F⊃ ⊂G⊃ ⊂H⊃ ⊂J⊃ ⊂K⊃	40 ⊂F⊃ ⊂G⊃ ⊂H⊃ ⊂J⊃ ⊂K⊃

BE SURE TO ERASE ANY ERRORS OR STRAY MARKS COMPLETELY.

NOTES